WHEN SILK WAS GOLD

Central Asian and Chinese Textiles

When Silk Was Gold:
Central Asian and Chinese Textiles
in The Metropolitan and Cleveland Museums of Art

The Metropolitan Museum of Art
March 3–May 17, 1998

When Silk Was Gold: Central Asian and Chinese Textiles in The Metropolitan and Cleveland Museums of Art is the first exhibition devoted exclusively to the luxury silks and embroideries produced in Central Asia and China between the eighth and early fifteenth century. During this period, textiles were as precious as gold. They were often used as currency, imperial and diplomatic gifts, offerings, and tributes and also were transported as highly coveted commercial goods across vast distances from Asia to ports as far away as Alexandria and Venice. Apart from their intrinsic artistic value, these textiles document the exchange of imagery and techniques that occurred as a result of trade and the movement of people across Central Asia during the period covered by the exhibition. The textiles also provide significant historical evidence about the shifts in the social and economic conditions in Central Asia and China that occurred as dynasties rose and fell and empires expanded and crumbled.

The 65 tapestries, embroideries, drawloom silks, including brocades and cloths of gold, on view represent luxury textiles from Asia in the Middle Ages that have until now received scant attention from scholars in the West. The exhibition studies not only the dazzling appearance, complex patterns, and intricate workmanship of the textiles but also investigates their importance both to their time and to the history of art.

LECTURES

Textiles in the Mongol Empire
James C. Y. Watt, Brooke Russell Astor Senior Curator, Department of Asian Art, The Metropolitan Museum of Art
Sunday, March 15, 3:00
Grace Rainey Rogers Auditorium

Conquerors, Craftsmen, and Cloth: Silk Weaving from Nishapur to Beijng under the Mongols
Anne E. Wardwell, Former Curator of Textiles, The Cleveland Museum of Art
Sunday, March 29, 3:00
Grace Rainey Rogers Auditorium

Cloth and Gold: The Art of the Silk Route
Denise Patry Leidy, Administrator and Associate Curator of Asian Art, The Metropolitan Museum of Art
Sunday, May 10, 3:00
Grace Rainey Rogers Auditorium

GALLERY TALKS	Meet at the Gallery Talk Stanchion in the Great Hall. Friday, March 6, 11:00. Denise Patry Leidy Thursday, March 26, 11:00. Joyce Denney Thursday, April 16, 11:00. Denise Patry Leidy Friday, April 24, 6:00. Joyce Denney Wednesday, May 13, 11:00. Joyce Denney
DOCUMENTARY FILMS	Documentaries will be screened in Uris Auditorium during the weeks of March 3 and April 7. Consult the Calendar or call (212) 570-3710 for times. *The Silk Road: Glories of Ancient Chang-An* *The Silk Road: A Thousand Kilometers beyond the Yellow River* *The Silk Road: The Art Gallery in the Desert* *The Silk Road: Khotan — Oasis of Silk and Jade*
PROGRAMS FOR TEACHERS	**When Silk Was Gold: Connecting East and West** A Teachers' Orientation to the exhibition for elementary and secondary teachers. Friday, March 13, 4:30–6:30 Fee: $15 Preregistration is required. Call (212) 570-3985.
OFFSITE PROGRAMS	We would be pleased to send a Museum lecturer to your library, college, or community organization to present a slide lecture about this exhibition. A fee will be charged. A sign-language interpreter may be requested. Call (212) 570-3930.
CATALOGUE	A catalogue accompanying this exhibition is available in the Museum Bookshop in both hardcover ($60) and soft cover ($45).
URIS LIBRARY AND RESOURCE CENTER	All readers are welcome to explore the Uris Library and Resource Center, open during Museum hours. Visitors may consult catalogues, books, reference materials, teacher resources, and videos.

The exhibition is made possible in part by **MetLife**.
Additional support has been provided by the William Randolph Hearst Foundation.
It is organized by The Metropolitan Museum of Art and The Cleveland Museum of Art.

WHEN SILK WAS GOLD
Central Asian and Chinese Textiles

James C. Y. Watt   Anne E. Wardwell

With an essay by Morris Rossabi

THE METROPOLITAN MUSEUM OF ART

IN COOPERATION WITH THE CLEVELAND MUSEUM OF ART

Distributed by Harry N. Abrams, Inc., New York

This catalogue is published in conjunction with the exhibition "When Silk Was Gold: Central Asian and Chinese Textiles," held at The Cleveland Museum of Art, October 26, 1997–January 4, 1998, and at The Metropolitan Museum of Art, March 3–May 17, 1998.

In New York, the exhibition is made possible, in part, by **MetLife**.

Additional support has been provided by the William Randolph Hearst Foundation.

The exhibition is sponsored at The Cleveland Museum of Art by The Kelvin and Eleanor Smith Foundation, and is supported by a major grant from the National Endowment for the Humanities, a federal agency.

The exhibition is organized by The Metropolitan Museum of Art and The Cleveland Museum of Art.

This publication is made possible, in part, by The Andrew W. Mellon Foundation.

Published by The Metropolitan Museum of Art, New York
John P. O'Neill, Editor in Chief
Emily Walter, Editor
Bruce Campbell, Designer
Gwen Roginsky, Production
Robert Weisberg, Computer Specialist

Photography of textiles in the collection of The Cleveland Museum of Art by Howard Agriesti, Photography Studio, The Cleveland Museum of Art.

Photography of textiles in the collection of The Metropolitan Museum of Art by Oi-cheong Lee, The Photograph Studio, The Metropolitan Museum of Art.

Maps by Wilhelmina Reyinga-Amrhein.
Drawings by Ellen Levine, The Cleveland Museum of Art.

Typeset in Garamond and Diotima
Printed on Mitsubishi Super Matte Art 157 gsm
Color separations by Nissha Printing Co., Ltd.
Printed and bound by Nissha Printing Co., Ltd.

Library of Congress Cataloguing-in-Publication Data

Watt, James C. Y.
When Silk Was Gold: Central Asian and Chinese Textiles /
James C. Y. Watt, Anne E. Wardwell, with an essay by Morris Rossabi.
    p.   cm.
Catalogue accompanying an exhibition at The Cleveland Museum of Art, 10–26–97—1–4–98 and at The Metropolitan Museum of Art, 3–3–98—5–17–98.
Includes bibliographical references and index.
ISBN 0–87099–825–0 (hc.)—ISBN 0–87099–827–7 (pbk.)—
ISBN 0–8109–6513–5 (Abrams)
1. Silk—China—Exhibitions. 2. Silk—Asia, Central—Exhibitions.
3. Textile fabrics—China—Exhibitions. 4. Textile fabrics—Asia, Central—Exhibitions. 5. Embroidery—China—Exhibitions. 6. Embroidery—Asia, Central—Exhibitions.
I. Wardwell, Anne E. II. Cleveland Museum of Art. III. Metropolitan Museum of Art. IV. Title
NK3883.A1W38 1997
746'.0439'095807477132—dc21   97-25856
                                                            CIP

Jacket illustration
Welcoming Spring. Embroidery. Yuan dynasty (1279–1368). The Metropolitan Museum of Art, New York (cat. no. 59, detail)

Frontispiece
Animals, Birds, and Flowers. Embroidery. Eastern Central Asia, late 11th–early 13th century. The Metropolitan Museum of Art, New York (cat. no. 50, detail)

Contents

Directors' Foreword

"When Silk Was Gold" is the first exhibition ever devoted exclusively to the luxury silks and embroideries produced in Central Asia and China between the eighth and the early fifteenth century. These textiles closely mirror the many shifts in the balance of power between Central Asia and China that occurred as dynasties rose and fell and empires expanded and crumbled. It is difficult from our perspective at the end of the twentieth century to comprehend fully the extraordinary importance that luxury silks and embroideries once had. In addition to their timeless uses as clothing and furnishings, they defined imperial, court, and clerical rank. They were given as imperial gifts, and they were always among the offerings bestowed upon and received from diplomatic embassies. As highly coveted commercial goods, richly woven and embroidered silks were transported across vast distances to ports as remote as Alexandria and Venice. Moreover, tribute was frequently paid in the form of silk-and-gold textiles. Not only did silk designs incorporate current decorative motifs and themes, but because they traveled so extensively, silks played a particularly active role in the movement of motifs and styles from one region to another.

"When Silk Was Gold" brings together the collections of Central Asian and Chinese textiles in The Cleveland Museum of Art and The Metropolitan Museum of Art. These are the two most important collections in the West of this material, which dates from the late Tang through the beginning decades of the Ming dynasty but also includes some types of silks and embroideries not preserved in China. These collections are the culmination of many decades of determined effort on the part of each institution to assemble the most important available examples of early Asian textiles, an endeavor greatly accelerated during the mid-1980s to early 1990s, when large numbers of such textiles unexpectedly came to light. Many of these have filled gaps in the history of early Central Asian and Chinese weaving and embroidery, vastly augmenting what had been known only ten years ago. In 1992, the two museums decided to mount a joint exhibition as a way of bringing these textiles to greater scholarly and public attention and of exploring the implications of recent discoveries for the history of Asian textiles.

The legacy of luxury textiles produced in Central Asia and China has yet to be fully explored and published. Despite their importance both to their times and to the history of art, luxury textiles have been woefully overlooked by art historians in the West. In China, important discoveries of textiles dating, in particular, from the tenth to the fourteenth century have been made during the past twenty-five years, though many textiles still await initial examination, photography, and analysis. A comprehensive study of this material has yet to be undertaken.

This publication is an important initiative toward that end. It brings together the scholarly expertise in Chinese art of James C. Y. Watt, the Metropolitan's Brooke Russell Astor Senior Curator of Asian Art, with the extensive knowledge of early textiles of Anne E. Wardwell, Curator of Textiles in Cleveland. In addition, a chapter that provides the historical setting for this complex period has been contributed by Dr. Morris Rossabi, Professor of Chinese and Central Asian History at Columbia University and at Queens College of the City University of New York. The publication serves not only as a catalogue for the exhibition but also as a scholarly work contributing original research on such topics as the evolution of silk tapestry in Central Asia and China, the brocades of the Jin and Mongol periods, and luxury-silk weaving under the Mongols.

In New York, the exhibition is sponsored, in part, by MetLife, with additional support provided by the William Randolph Hearst Foundation. The exhibition is sponsored in Cleveland by The Kelvin and Eleanor Smith Foundation in memory of Miss Gertrude Underhill, the museum's first Curator of Textiles, and is supported by a major grant from the National Endowment for the Humanities. Our gratitude is extended also to The Andrew W. Mellon Foundation for its generous support of this publication.

Robert P. Bergman
*The Cleveland Museum
of Art*

Philippe de Montebello
*The Metropolitan
Museum of Art*

Acknowledgments

This exhibition and catalogue grew out of years of cooperative work between The Cleveland Museum of Art and The Metropolitan Museum of Art. The initial proposal for the exhibition was met with immediate approval and encouragement by Philippe de Montebello, Director of the Metropolitan Museum, and by Evan Turner, former Director of the Cleveland Museum. Unflagging support has continued at Cleveland under Robert P. Bergman, with the help of Diane De Grazia.

Throughout the years of research for this project, we have received generous help and the cooperation of colleagues in other museums: Marianne Yaldiz of the Museum für Indische Kunst, Berlin; Willibald Veit of the Museum für Ostasiatische Kunst, Berlin; Waltraud Berner-Laschinski of the Kunstgewerbemuseum, Berlin; Verity Wilson of the Victoria and Albert Museum, London; Hans Christoph Ackermann, Mechthild Flury-Lemberg, Regula Schorta, and Karel Otavsky of the Abegg-Stiftung, Riggisberg; Margareta Nockert of the Statens Historiska Museet, Stockholm; Evgeny Lubo-Lesnitchenko of the State Hermitage, Saint Petersburg; Valrae Reynolds of the Newark Museum; Patricia Berger of the University of California at Berkeley; Keith Wilson of the Los Angeles County Museum of Art; Stephen Little of The Art Institute of Chicago; and Mihoko Domyo of the Bunka Gakuen Costume Museum, Tokyo. We are additionally grateful to the staff at The British Museum for making the Stein Collection available for study and for providing photographs.

During an extensive research trip to China in 1996, we were met with every courtesy and cooperation in all the institutions we visited. We would like to thank in particular Yang Xin and Chen Juanjuan at the Palace Museum, Beijing; Yang Renkai, Xu Bingkun, and Wang Mianhou at the Liaoning Provincial Museum; Yang Zhijun and Sun Changqing at the Heilongjiang Provincial Museum; Israfel Yusuf and Wu Min at the Xinjiang Uyghur Autonomous Regional Museum, Urumqi; and Wang Binghua at the Xinjiang Institute of Archaeology, Urumqi; Huang Xueyin at the Museum of Inner Mongolian Autonomous Region, Hohhot; Liu Laixue and Qi Xiaoguang at the Inner Mongolia Institute of Archaeology, Hohhot; and Zhao Feng at the China National Silk Museum, Hangzhou. We benefited greatly from discussions with and information provided by many Chinese scholars, particularly Chen Juanjuan and Huang Nengfu in Beijing, Xu Bingkun in Shenyang, Wu Min and Wang Binghua in Urumqi, Zhao Feng in Hangzhou, and Gao Hanyu and Tu Hengxian in Shanghai.

We are indebted also to individuals who graciously allowed us to study material in their collections and, in some cases, provided photographs: Krishna Riboud (Association pour l'Étude et la Documentation des Textiles d'Asie), Chris Hall, Thomas and Margo Pritzker, Jacqueline Simcox, Friedrich Spuhler, Lisbet Holmes, Alan Kennedy, Stephen McGuinness, Arthur Leeper, Fabio and Anna Maria Rossi, David Salmon, Michael Frances, Francesca Galloway, and Diane Hall.

Numerous other persons, too, have served as invaluable resources to the project. We are particularly indebted to Milton Sonday, who generously gave many hours of his time to working out the details of a number of weave structures and who, throughout the preparation of the technical analyses and the glossary of weaving terms for this catalogue, willingly offered assistance. To Daniel De Jonghe for his insight on weaving with twisted versus untwisted warps, to Alan Kennedy for information on early textiles in Japanese collections, and to Frances Pritchard for sources relating to the effects of burial on fibers, we extend our thanks. We are most appreciative of Thomas Allsen for sharing the initial draft of his forthcoming study, *Commodity and Exchange in the Mongol Empire: A Cultural History of Islamic Textiles.* Adam Kessler kindly supplied a copy of an important but inaccessible archaeological report from Inner Mongolia and, with Vuka Roussakis and other members of the staff of the American Museum of Natural History, New York, obtained permission for us to make technical analyses of the textiles in the exhibition "Empires Beyond the Great Wall: The Heritage of Genghis Khan." We greatly appreciate the effort made by Heather Stoddard to examine the backs of tapestry-woven *thangkas* in Lhasa. Amina Malago generously shared her insights on silk-tapestry weaving, and Don Cohn provided information helpful to the planning of our research trip to China. Similarly, Terry Milhaupt while in Japan provided copies of Japanese publications on textiles related to our research, while Hero Granger-Taylor provided a photograph and important technical information on a textile in the church of Sant'Ambrogio, Milan. Robert Linrothe graciously discussed matters pertaining to Tangut Xia material. We are greatly appreciative of Paul Nietupski for his willing assistance and explanation of Tibetan Buddhist rituals and contexts, and of Gennady Leonov for providing the iconographic note on the large mandala with Mongol emperors and empresses (cat. no. 25).

We would like to thank the following people for providing translations: Sheila Blair for her invaluable help with Arabic and Persian inscriptions and with terminology; Hugh Richardson and Heather Stoddard for translating Tibetan inscriptions; Hou-mei Sung and Helen Pao, who translated a number of Chinese archaeological reports and articles; Miki Inagaki and Sayuri Sakarmori for their translations of articles written in Japanese; Yunah Sung for providing translations of both Chinese and Japanese; Mary Rossabi, Eugenia Vainberg, and Dimitry Vessensky for translating material written in Russian; and Ruth Dunnell for her translations of and comments on Tangut texts.

Many people at both museums worked on this project. We wish to acknowledge first and foremost Ellen Levine at the Cleveland Museum and Joyce Denney at the Metropolitan for their indispensable assistance and steadfast attention to countless details relating to the project. In addition, Ellen Levine made the drawings and reconstructions of textile patterns and assisted with the glossary of technical terms, and Joyce Denney worked with cartographer Wilhelmina Reyinga-Amrhein on the maps and with Anita Siu and Shi-yee Fiedler on the glossary of Chinese and Japanese terms. Nina Sweet was responsible for typing James Watt's manuscript.

As expected, considerable conservation work had to be done on the collections in preparation for public display. At the Cleveland Museum, Karen Klingbiel, Hermine Altmann, Katrin Colburn, Bettina Beisenkötter, Bettina Niekamp, and Angelika Sliwka all worked under the general supervision of Bruce Christman, who also provided a number of scientific analyses. At the Metropolitan Museum, conservation and analytical work, as well as micrographic photographs, was done under the direction of Nobuko Kajitani, chiefly with the able assistance of Midori Sato. In addition, we would like to thank Kathrin

Kocher-Lieprecht and Ina von Woyski-Niedermann in Switzerland for assisting with the conservation of the *kashaya* (cat. no. 64).

The library staff at both museums rendered us unfailing support, finding and obtaining publications that are not readily available, processing innumerable inter-library loans, and assisting with the compilation of the bibliography. We would like to thank, in particular, Ann Abid, Louis Adrean, Georgina Toth, and Christine Edmonson at the Cleveland Museum, and Jack Jacoby and Billy Kwan at the Metropolitan Museum.

For effectively raising financial support for the exhibition in Cleveland, we would like to thank Kate Sellers and her staff. The exhibition at Cleveland was coordinated by Katie Solender, and Jeffrey Baxter designed and supervised the installation. At the Metropolitan, Linda Sylling supervised the installation, which was designed by Dennis Kois and Jeffrey L. Daly, with graphics by Barbara Weiss. Howard Agriesti photographed the Cleveland textiles with the assistance of Gary Kirchenbauer, and the Metropolitan textiles were photographed by Oi-cheong Lee with the help of Anna-Marie Kellen. The colorplates in this catalogue testify to their skill and sensitivity.

For public programming relating to the exhibition at Cleveland, we are indebted to Marjorie Williams and Joellen DeOreo. A very special note of thanks goes to The Textile Art Alliance for its donation of several textiles in the exhibition and for the initiation and implementation of the Textile Art Fair in cooperation with the Department of Education and Public Programs of the Cleveland Museum. Kent Lydecker, with the assistance of Elizabeth Hammer and other members of the Department of Education at the Metropolitan Museum, organized the various public and educational programs in New York.

We offer our warmest thanks to Emily Walter, our patient and painstaking editor, to Bruce Campbell for the beautiful design, and to Gwen Roginsky for supervision of the production of this catalogue. We are also grateful for the personal attention paid to this publication by John P. O'Neill.

Finally, we acknowledge Laurence Channing for suggesting the title of the exhibition.

James C. Y. Watt   Anne E. Wardwell

Note to the Reader

In this catalogue, dynasty refers both to the chronological span of a succession of rulers belonging to the same line of descent and to the geographical territory under its control. Eastern Central Asia encompasses the eastern territories of present-day Xinjiang Province (i.e., Kucha to the eastern borders of the province). Eastern Iranian world refers to Khurasan as it existed at the time of the Mongol conquest and to Transoxiana. Iran has been used as a geographical term, while Persian has been used to identify the people and language spoken in that domain. The Mongol period is defined as beginning in 1207, the year that Chinggis acceded to the title Great Khan, and ending with the demise of the Yuan dynasty in 1368.

Both accuracy and a concern for the general reader have governed the transliterations of foreign terms and names in the text. The following standard systems have been adopted for the transliteration of East Asian names and terms: *pin-yin* for Chinese, Hepburn for Japanese, and the Royal Asiatic Society system for Persian. For all West Asian languages, however, diacritical marks have been eliminated, as is currently standard practice. Because the standard for transliterating Tibetan is extraordinarily confusing for the general reader, the modified system used in T. Bartholomew et al., *Mongolia: The Legacy of Chinggis Khan,* has been adopted. Antoine Mostaert's scheme for the transliteration of Mongolian, as modified by Francis Cleaves, has been used except for the following deviations:

č is ch
š is sh
ǒ is gh
q is kh
ǰ is j

The names for cities and towns in Central Asia and China have varied considerably through the centuries. In addition, many Central Asian towns have both Turkic and Chinese names. We have given the historical name followed by the modern name in parentheses.

The textiles were measured in centimeters. Dimensions are given in centimeters followed by inches, which have been rounded off to the nearest eighth of an inch.

WHEN SILK WAS GOLD

Central Asian and Chinese Textiles

Introduction

"When Silk Was Gold" is a joint effort by The Metropolitan Museum of Art and The Cleveland Museum of Art to research and exhibit sixty-four Central Asian and Chinese silks, tapestries, and embroideries dating from the eighth to the early fifteenth century in the collections of the two institutions. These collections are at present the largest body of this material in the West and include some types of woven and embroidered textiles that are not preserved in Chinese museums. Nevertheless, the two collections are not comprehensive, nor do they document fully the history of weaving and embroidery in Central Asia and China through these centuries. The textiles, however, are more or less representative of what survives. While most date from the Mongol period, all the major dynasties from the Tang (618–907) through the Ming (1368–1644) are represented.

Of the many groups of textiles covered by the exhibition, the earliest material—the Tang and Sogdian textiles—has been preserved in surprising numbers and is, to date, the most extensively studied. Conversely, textiles dating from between the tenth and the fourteenth century constitute the least studied chapters in the history of Asian textiles. We have attempted to put these, in particular, into their historical and art-historical contexts. Because the extant material is, at best, only a tiny fraction of one percent of the textiles that were produced, there is very limited available evidence and the ever-present possibility of distortions due to accidents of survival. These circumstances are made even more challenging by the fact that only one textile in the exhibition (the *kesi* mandala with Yamantaka, cat. no. 25) can be dated and attributed on the basis of documentary evidence; by the textiles' having been preserved, in almost every case, far from where they were made; and by their present forms, many of which are totally unrelated to the original purposes for which they were created. References to the production of luxury silks and embroideries in Central Asian texts of the period are too general and scattered to shed any significant light. Chinese sources, including official histories and private writings, provide much more information, but their usefulness is greatly reduced by the lack of clearly defined nomenclature. A particularly exasperating example is the word *jin*. Generally, it refers to any figured silk. It also has a

technical meaning, but that meaning has changed over time, and one is never certain whether a writer in a given historical period is using it in the general or in the specific sense—or, indeed, misusing the term altogether. Thus the term *jinjin* (the first *jin* stands for "gold") can refer to a lampas weave with gold threads or to a gold brocade such as those covered in the third chapter. Conversely, the term *nashishi* (the Chinese transcription of *nasij*) is usually translated into English, via the Chinese term *jinjin*, as "gold brocade"—which it never is. In this regard, we are happy to report that over the past decade this problem has been vigorously tackled by scholars in China who write on textile history and technology. A standard terminology is being established, and much work has been done to elucidate the possible meanings of terms in different historical periods.

The first chapter, "Early Exchanges: Silks from the 8th through the 11th Century," includes drawloom-woven silks and one printed silk that date from between the High Tang and the Liao/Northern Song period. The Tang silks are woven with designs that emerged in the early eighth century, became dominant decorative schemes in the High Tang (roughly the first half of the eighth century), and in some cases continued to evolve in the Liao dynasty (907–1125). The patterns of the Sogdian silks reveal the strategic position on the east-west trade routes of Sogdiana, while related silks woven with Sogdian motifs are testimony to the influence of Sogdian culture throughout the more eastern territories of Central Asia. In contrast to the study of Tang and Sogdian silks, that of Liao silks is still in its infancy. A surprising number of Liao textiles have come to light within the last few decades; nevertheless, many pieces still await initial examination and documentation, and no comprehensive study of the surviving corpus has yet been undertaken. Liao examples in the exhibition document the final evolutionary stages of patterns established during the Tang dynasty and are among the few Liao textiles preserved in the West. The latest textiles in this section date from the eleventh century. Unfortunately, archaeological material has not survived in sufficient quantity to support a comprehensive study of Song—particularly Northern Song—textiles. Nevertheless, the exhibition does include the only Northern Song silk known to have been found in Iran (cat. no. 11) and the only surviving Chinese textile that can be directly associated with the important sea trade in the Song period.

The second chapter includes tapestries made of silk and often gold, known as *kesi*. Dating from approximately the eleventh through the fourteenth century, some belong to the end of a long history of *kesi* weaving among the Uyghur peoples of Central Asia, while others document the transmission of the *kesi* technique from the Uyghurs to the Khitans of the Liao dynasty, the Tanguts of the Xia dynasty (1032–1227), and the Chinese during the Song (960–1279) and Yuan (1279–1368) dynasties. In the hands of the Chinese, the evolution of *kesi* dramatically departed from being strictly a textile tradition and came to emulate painting. Thanks to important examples that have come to light from ancient collections, it is now possible to delineate the migration of the silk tapestry technique from Central Asia to China—a process that has long been debated but without the support of actual examples.

Gold-brocaded silks woven in the Jin territories are the subject of the third chapter. This is another area in which research is new. Textiles from the Jin dynasty (1115–1234) were discovered only less than a decade ago, when the tomb of Prince Qi and his consort was excavated at Acheng, Heilongjiang Province. Concurrent with the study of these archaeological finds, examples from ancient collections were being recognized as Jin for iconographic and technical reasons as well. Whereas the brocades from the tomb were produced for the imperial family, those in the exhibition were woven for the court and thereby provide an additional dimension to the small corpus of Jin brocades known thus far. Of particular interest are the brocades woven following the Mongol conquest, which document the influence of craftsmen from the eastern Iranian world who were resettled in Jin territory, particularly in Hongzhou.

The fourth chapter, "Luxury-Silk Weaving under the Mongols," raises complex art-historical questions, particularly regarding attribution. Several of the textiles discussed in this chapter document the movement of motifs, patterns, and techniques between the eastern Iranian world and northern China, as populations of craftsmen were resettled in distant lands. Others were included in the countless bales of richly woven silks that were transported over trade routes in unprecedented numbers to destinations as remote as European courts and churches. Several of the silk-and-gold textiles in the exhibition appear to have been part of the patronage of Tibetan sects by members of the Mongol imperial family. This patronage was an important step in the solidification of Mongol-Tibetan relations that, in the Yuan and early Ming, gave rise to the so-called Sino-Tibetan style.

In order to place the textiles in the first four chapters—particularly those dating from the tenth to the fourteenth century—in their larger historical and art-historical contexts, each chapter begins with an extensive introduction. With a few exceptions, the catalogue entries that follow are comparatively short. Each provides a description as well as a technical analysis of the textile. Additional discussion, when included, is limited to points specific to the textile that were not discussed in the introduction.

The fifth chapter is dedicated to embroideries. Dating from the Tang to the early Ming dynasty, they include rare examples of Central Asian embroidery of the twelfth and fourteenth centuries, needleloop embroideries, and an important group of Sino-Tibetan embroideries. Unlike the woven material in the first four chapters, they do not fall into clearly defined groups. Rather, as individual examples of their period or type, they contribute a wealth of stylistic, iconographic, and technical information to what has been known thus far of Chinese and Central Asian embroidery. For these reasons, this chapter has been presented differently from those on woven and printed textiles; the information about and discussion concerning each embroidery have been presented in the catalogue entries rather than in the introduction, which is, accordingly, relatively brief.

This is an exhibition that can be studied and enjoyed from many points of view. It is our particular hope, however, that the material will expand what has been known of Asian textiles produced between the Tang and the early Ming period, especially those dating from the tenth to the fourteenth century. It is further hoped that, in the future, there will be greater recognition among art historians of the importance of luxury textiles to the history of Asian art. Costly silks and embroideries were, after all, the primary vehicle in the Tang and particularly the Mongol periods for the migration of motifs and designs from one part of Asia to another. Textiles, moreover, are sometimes the only medium to document the survival and dissemination of a motif over the centuries. This is true, for example, of the Sogdian deer with its mushroom-shaped antler (cat. no. 14). The exhibition also provides examples of the early occurrence on Central Asian textiles of the motif of the lotus plant with trefoil leaf (cat. nos. 13 and 50), which became incorporated in a ubiquitous decorative pattern in fourteenth-century China, not only on textiles but in architectural ornaments and on early blue-and-white porcelain.

The art-historical repercussions of historical events are often clearly evidenced in luxury textiles. Those of the Mongol period, for example, document the movement of both imagery and technique that resulted from the resettlement of artisans so vividly recorded in histories and travel accounts of the period. In addition, textiles often provide material evidence of the cultural and religious ties that linked ethnic peoples, as well as the impetus to artistic creativity spurred by exposure through trade to foreign and exotic goods.

We hope, too, that through this exhibition the importance of luxury textiles in other contexts, such as history, society, economics, and religious expression, will become more apparent. Textiles in the form of costume defined social as well as ecclesiastical position and authority. The finest products of imperial embroidery and weaving workshops were among the gifts presented by emperors and imperial family members to other rulers, emissaries, and distinguished persons. Richly woven textiles formed the backbone of international commerce that extended as far west as Europe. Many textiles were created simply to enhance life by making human surroundings beautiful, while others served to transform secular space into sacred space. And some, representing deities, were central to religious worship and spiritual practices.

In the final analysis, however, luxury silks and embroideries are works of art and, as such, can both move and inspire us. For the Mongols, textiles were a higher form of the plastic arts than painting or sculpture. It is hoped that the exhibition will engender a sense of awe for the magnificence and beauty of textiles created in a period when silk was indeed as precious as gold.

Chronology

The Silk Trade in China and Central Asia

Morris Rossabi

Tea, porcelain, and, in particular, silk evoke images of China. The English words for these valuable commodities reveal their origins. *Tea* derives from the term used for the beverage in Amoy (Xiamen) dialect; *china* preceded *porcelain* as the English designation for that highly prized ware; and *silk* was coined from the Greek name for China (Seres). Silk became so closely identified with China and foreigners craved it so much that the nineteenth-century writer Ferdinand von Richthofen labeled the overland routes radiating from China to Central Asia, West Asia, and Europe the Silk Roads (Seidenstrassen).[1] To foreigners, the silk conveyed along the Silk Roads became as valuable as gold. Similarly, the Chinese prized silk for the astonishing variety of uses it served—as a gift, in rituals, as a demarcation of social status, and as payment of taxes. Like the foreigners, the Chinese virtually converted silk into gold by using it also as currency.

Regular commerce in Chinese silk may be traced to the embassy of Zhang Qian.[2] The Han emperor Wu (r. 141–87 B.C.) had dispatched Zhang to seek allies in Central Asia for a campaign against a bellicose neighbor that was threatening China's northern borders.[3] Zhang failed to attract foreign support, but the mission served to inform China about Central Asia and vice versa, and further, it piqued mutual interest in the goods produced in the other's domain. The Central Asians, and later the Persians and the inhabitants of the Roman Empire, learned of and began to covet Chinese products, particularly silk, which led eventually to the development of the Silk Roads.

The overland Silk Roads, which wound around northwest China, circumvented the Taklamakan Desert, halted at such renowned oases as Shazhou (Dunhuang), Turfan, and Khotan, crossed Central Asia, and headed for Palmyra and the eastern Mediterranean, entailed many hardships—sandstorms, avalanches, banditry, and exorbitant tariffs. Nevertheless, the elites of West Asia and Europe were willing to pay substantial sums for Chinese products, particularly silk, and thus trade was lucrative and persisted. Merchants, aware of the profits to be garnered through the silk trade, gambled on their ability to overcome the many obstacles that awaited them. The fall of the Han in A.D. 220, however, which resulted in political and social disunity, and the proliferation of dynasties that controlled only parts of China led to the virtual cessation of the Silk Roads trade.

THE SILK TRADE UNDER THE TANG

When China was reunified in the late sixth century, commerce in silk increased, partly because the Tang dynasty (618–907) opted for an expansionist foreign policy. By the middle of the seventh century, Chinese troops had consolidated their authority over Central Asia all the way to Kashgar. Safe passage during the seventh and eighth centuries, which allowed merchants and clerics to reach China with new goods, ideas, and technologies, meant that China would be in touch with developments in Iran, India, and Central Asia.[4]

The rapidly accelerating pace of contact with the outside world during the Tang dynasty also resulted in the growth of commerce in silk. Increasing quantities of Chinese silk were taken to Central and West Asia, and Sasanian Iran, too, provided a sizable market. The Sasanians wove their own designs on the silks, and Sasanian motifs achieved renown and popularity, especially in Central Asia. Sogdian merchants from Central Asia purveyed these silks across Asia and served as the most important of the intermediaries in this commerce, introducing throughout Asia "a new gold in the form of silk."[5]

Central and West Asian demand for Chinese silks led not only to the relocation of Chinese silk workers but to their protection. They were also accorded high status. A battle between Arab and Tang armies near the Talas River in Central Asia in 751 resulted in the capture of Chinese artisans whose lives were spared. One of the prisoners,

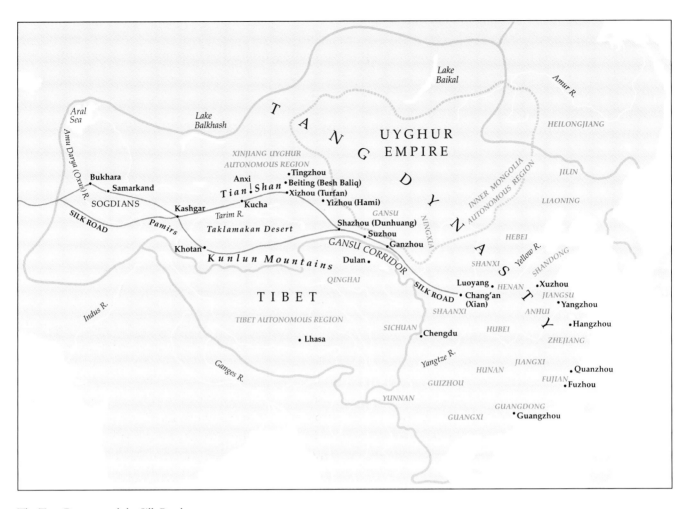

The Tang Dynasty and the Silk Roads, ca. 750

Du Huan, reported that communities of silk weavers, gold and silk workers, and painters had been resettled in Baghdad, the capital of the recently established Arab dynasty, but that some silk weavers had remained in Samarkand. A tenth-century history of the Central Asian town of Bukhara confirms the special position accorded to Chinese merchants and artisans. The author reported that during the Islamic invasion of Bukhara early in the eighth century, the conquerors spared the lives of four hundred captured Chinese merchants and craftsmen, including several textile workers.[6] During this period, Central and West Asian peoples, including craftsmen, also migrated eastward, introducing their techniques to Tang China.

Both Sogdian and Chinese textile artisans lived in many different regions in Asia. Approximately one hundred so-called Sogdian textiles dating from the seventh to the tenth century have been preserved, some found in graves in the northern Caucasus and others in European churches. Of the finds from the northern Caucasus, however, a considerable number have been classified as Byzantine

and Chinese as well as Sogdian, indicating the traffic in the region. Chinese weavers who resided in Central Asia and Sogdian weavers who established communities in or adjacent to China surely intermingled, and their styles were no doubt mutually influential.[7]

Sogdian influence may also readily be observed in the Tang silk trade with the Uyghur Turks then residing in Mongolia. In return for assistance in crushing a rebellion against the Tang imperial family in the 750s, the Uyghurs demanded the establishment of markets along their common borders. The Uyghurs supplied horses, which the Chinese desperately needed, and in return they were given silk. Although most of the Chinese shipments consisted of raw silk, the Uyghurs also obtained silk fabric and, on occasion, silks with designs. The Sogdians, who had established strong commercial links with the Uyghurs, then transported the silk to Central and West Asia. The quantities of silk transmitted to the Uyghurs for their own consumption or for sale to other peoples farther west were staggering and had a decided effect on the Chinese economy.[8]

The Uyghurs would, in fact, turn out to be among the most important of China's northern neighbors. While some were farmers, others were merchants, and they traded throughout Central and East Asia. As increasing numbers of Uyghurs settled, an artisan class developed. Both as traders and as weavers, they would influence the development of silk production and commerce in Central Asia and in China from the mid-eighth to the fifteenth century—the chronological span of this exhibition.

Islam, too, served as a catalyst to the silk trade, Muslim merchants and artisans serving as intermediaries in the transmission of Chinese motifs into Central Asia and Iran. By the middle of the ninth century, Muslims had established autonomous communities in northwest and southeast China. Opposition to trade with these communities from members of the Chinese scholar-official elite failed to impede commerce in silk. Muslim merchants thus persisted in and profited from the transmission of silk to Central and West Asia. Lack of documentation makes it difficult to estimate either the number of Muslim weavers in these settlements or their possible contribution to silk production. It would be surprising, however, if weavers were not integral members of these communities, considering the growing number of fabrics produced in Central and West Asia.

The decline of the Tang dynasty beginning in the middle of the eighth century jeopardized and eventually subverted what had become a lively commerce in silks. Unrest and violence were endemic, and with the Tang military unable to rein in the increasingly unruly bands of outlaws, brigandage and banditry raged in China into the ninth century. At this time as well, the imperial court sanctioned the suppression of Buddhist monasteries. Through lavish gifts from fervent believers and through tax exemptions from court, the monasteries had amassed considerable wealth and had proved generous commissioners of silk banners and sutra covers, among other religious artifacts.[9] In part to obtain badly needed funds, the court in the 840s issued edicts that amounted to a full-scale campaign against the Buddhist establishment, and within a short time 40,000 shrines and 4,600 monasteries had been razed and perhaps more than 260,000 monks and nuns defrocked.[10]

The suppression of the monasteries marked the beginning of a wave of discrimination against all foreigners. China's economic and political ills were attributed to the presence of foreigners and to the influence of foreign trade and culture. Rebel forces were reported to have massacred 120,000 Muslims, Christians, Zoroastrians, and Jews in the city of Guangzhou.[11] Hostility toward foreigners in the mid- to late ninth century reveals a reversal of the tolerance and cosmopolitanism that had marked earlier Tang attitudes and policies, which had fostered not only cultural and artistic interaction but also trade across Asia.

Tang isolationism, abetted by military and political weakness, also resulted in disturbances along the Silk Roads. In the eighth century, Tibetan armies began to force the withdrawal of the Chinese military from the oases of the Tarim River basin. In 766, they moved into Gansu and Suzhou, and in 781, they occupied Hami, one of the critical gateways to Central Asia or the so-called Western Region. Tibet's expansion at the expense of China continued through the middle of the ninth century, when Tibet itself became embroiled with the Abbasid dynasty in a struggle over the control of western Central Asia.[12] Domestic turbulence undermined Tibet's foreign efforts, and about 850 it began to lose its hold on one after another of its Central Asian oases. Although relations with Tibet were hostile, trade between China and its expansionist neighbor nevertheless persisted, eventually contributing to making Tibet "a vast storehouse of medieval textiles."[13]

In 907, the Tang dynasty was finally overthrown. Trade was disrupted, and caravans and merchants had no guarantee of safe passage. Perhaps as significant for silk production and trade in Central Asia and China was the collapse of the Uyghur empire in 840, when the Uyghurs were overtaken by the nomadic Kirghiz peoples, causing mass migration from Mongolia. While the center of Uyghur authority shifted to the Chinese provinces of Gansu and Xinjiang, Uyghurs remained also in Mongolia and found their way to North China, at first accepting Tang jurisdiction and, after the fall of the Tang, living under both Chinese and non-Chinese rule. The political decline of the Uyghurs thus resulted, ironically, in their playing a more important role, that of intermediaries and cultural transmitters in Central and East Asia.

Following the fall of the Tang, foreigners along China's northern and northwestern borders established their own Chinese-style dynasties on Chinese territory. The Khitans, a people from Mongolia, established the Liao dynasty, which from 907 to 1125 controlled the area around modern Beijing and sixteen prefectures in North China. In the early eleventh century the Tanguts, a group influenced by Tibetan culture, founded the Xia dynasty, which dominated much of northwest China until 1227. And in 1115 the Jurchens emerged from Manchuria, overwhelming the Khitans, occupying much of North China, and forcing the Chinese south of the Huai River. Each of these groups—the Khitans, the Tanguts, and the Jurchens—

did not, however, suddenly vanish when their dynasties collapsed. Like the Uyghurs after the fall of their empire in 840, they scattered throughout North China, Manchuria, Mongolia, and Central Asia, transmitting the styles, techniques, and tastes of their respective cultures long after their political power had waned.

The Silk Trade under the Song

The accession to power of Emperor Taizu (r. 960–76) and his successful unification of the country restored confidence in the Confucian system in China. Taizu founded the Song dynasty and moved the capital from Chang'an to the city of Kaifeng. Controlling less territory than had the Tang, the Song court was also confronted by the powerful military of the multistate system, which included the Khitan Liao and the Tangut Xia dynasties, in northeast Asia.[14] By the end of the tenth century, although the uncontested masters of South and much of North China, the Song abandoned attempts to occupy the oases and towns along the old Silk Roads. This had the effect of undermining the trade in silk.

Nevertheless, silk continued to play a role in Song foreign policy. In the late tenth century, the Chinese, recognizing that they did not have the military capability of driving the Khitans from their northern frontier, chose instead to establish commercial and diplomatic relations. The Treaty of Shanyuan, signed in 1004, entailed humiliating concessions for the Song. The court not only promised to make annual payments of 100,000 taels of silver and 200,000 bolts of silk but also agreed that the emperor would henceforth address the Khitan ruler as "imperial younger brother."

This policy of accommodation through the presentation of gifts of silk and silver was so effective that the Song used the same tactic to defuse tensions with the Tanguts, who occupied the lands to the west and northwest. Like the Khitans, the Tanguts established a sedentary Chinese-style dynasty, the Xia, as well as institutions based on Chinese models. A year after the signing of the Treaty of Shanyuan, the Song began to provide annual gifts of 40,000 bolts of silk to the Xia.[15] Border disputes and controversies over proper terms of address, however, erupted into full-scale battles in the mid-eleventh century. Tangut victories culminated in an agreement that increased opportunities for trade and bound the Chinese to make annual gifts of tea and silver and 153,000 bolts of silk.[16]

As in previous dynasties, silk became a valuable instrument in Song foreign relations. Along China's frontiers,

Chinese silk was so highly prized that foreigners refrained from belligerent or provocative acts in order to obtain it, and silk became a weapon in China's foreign relations arsenal. Repeatedly, silk was offered to foreign rulers as a means of averting attack. In 1001, the Song presented the khaghan of the Uyghurs, who now inhabited the regions west of the Tanguts (present-day Xinjiang), with a brocade robe, a gold belt, and 200 bolts of openwork brocade. A decade later, it offered 500 robes and a gold belt to the khaghan, 400 robes to his mother, and 200 robes to his chancellor.[17]

Despite the contraction of Chinese territories on the northwest frontier and the attendant disruptions on the Silk Roads, the silk trade persisted—though on a reduced scale. Merchants, sometimes masquerading as official envoys from oases along the Silk Roads, arrived in China with horses, camels, jade, and carpets to trade for silk, brocade, tea, lacquerware, and gold. The Khitans, in particular, were more ambitious, trading their recently acquired Chinese goods to the Uyghurs and other peoples to the west.[18]

Trade to western Central Asia also declined as a result of warfare among the Turkic peoples. With the rise of the Islamic Karakhanid dynasty (ca. 994–ca. 1211), and its control over such important cities as Bukhara, order was gradually restored in western Central Asia, but more than a century would elapse before silk transport along the Silk Roads reached the same level as in the Tang dynasty.

The Song period was distinguished by an increase in seaborne commerce. By Song times, over half the population of China resided in the southeast and produced much of the country's wealth. The shift of the capital to Lin'an (present-day Hangzhou) in the south following the fall of the Northern Song dynasty in 1127 coincided with an expansion of seaborne trade between China and West Asia. Arab and Persian merchants reached southeast China and began to settle there. Guangzhou was the site of the first of the Islamic communities, but Quanzhou, in the modern province of Fujian, eventually superseded it both as the city with the largest Muslim community and as the center of trade with West Asia. The presence of such a community surely facilitated commerce with the Islamic world, and silk was one of the trade items, though relatively few such silks have survived from this time (see cat. no. 11).

Growing commercialization and urbanization resulted also in an increase in the use of silk, as the nouveau riche, seeking to emulate the elite, provided a sizable market, especially in the south. Eventually, silk became more widely available, as merchants succeeded in distributing it at markets, stalls, and shops.[19]

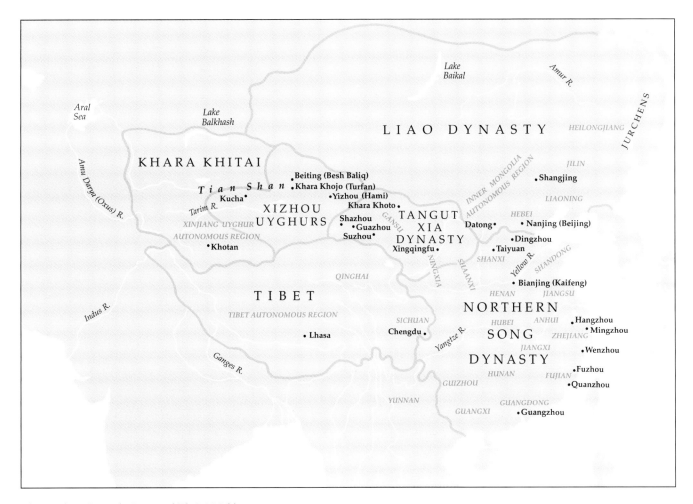

The Northern Song, the Liao, and Their Neighbors

Buddhism, too, provided a market for silk, as *kesi* banners, sutra wrappers, and *kashaya* robes were needed for monastic practice. Despite the repression of Buddhism in the middle of the ninth century, the religion continued to prosper under the Song. Religious leaders and pilgrims traveled extensively to study with Buddhist masters in South and East Asia, which resulted in expanded trade between China and such Buddhist strongholds as Tibet and Amdo (Qinghai). At the collapse of the Tibetan kingdom in the mid-ninth century, Buddhist monasteries vied for power, attempting to bolster their status through commercial as well as religious ties with Northern Song China.

Both Chinese and Central Asian silks were important factors in the Sino-Tibetan connection, and Buddhist monasteries became major repositories of silks and other products. Tibet proved an ideal place for the preservation of textiles, for in the monasteries they were stored in dark, dry rooms that offered protection from light and other potential sources of damage. For their part,

Tibetan traders, determined to maintain the commercial links that offered such valued Chinese products, reciprocated with horses from Amdo, one of the few commodities sought by the Chinese.[20]

The Khitans

The Khitans were the first peoples inhabiting the territory north of China to found a sedentary dynasty, the Liao, using institutions based on Chinese models. Taking advantage of the vacuum created in the north by the decline of the Tang and the fall of the Uyghur empire in the ninth century, the Khitans gradually incorporated lands from Manchuria in the east to the Altai Mountains in the west, and though they never occupied more than sixteen prefectures within China, they dominated what is today Inner Mongolia and regions farther west. At their height, they numbered perhaps only 750,000, yet they controlled a Chinese population of 2,400,000.[21]

The Khitans were the first seminomadic peoples to build cities in the Mongolian steppes. Five of their capitals have been identified, and other urban centers excavated. Most of their Chinese captives they relocated to newly established urban centers to prevent rebellion. Each city had a marketplace and a bazaar, where foreign merchants were encouraged to display their wares. A number of Chinese silk and satin craftsmen settled in the Supreme Capital, which later became the venue for a silk-weaving workshop.[22] The Shizong emperor (r. 947–51) founded a town, Hongzheng xian, specifically for the settlement of captives from Dingzhou, Hebei Province, most of whom were textile workers. A silk-weaving workshop operated by 300 Chinese and other captured textile artisans was established in Zu Prefecture, not far from the Supreme Capital. And from Xian Prefecture, patterned polychrome silks were sent to court, suggesting the existence of a workshop there as well.[23]

Most of the silk craftsmen were Chinese, but the location of the Khitan-dominated lands ensured that they were influenced by North, Central, and West Asian sources, including, most importantly, the Uyghurs. The role of the Uyghurs in the development of *kesi* is well known, and it would appear that the superb quality of Liao *kesi* owes much to Uyghur influence. The silks also reveal the presence of Chinese and non-Chinese motifs, which, when combined, created a style that was uniquely Liao.

By the late twelfth century, dissension among the Khitans and diminished power led to military threats by the Jurchens of present-day Manchuria. In 1115 the Jurchen leader, Aguda, proclaimed himself emperor of a new sedentary dynasty, the Jin. Defeating the Khitans in 1126, he thus brought to an end the Liao dynasty, an era in which the silk industry had been fostered, in which textile decoration had been cross-fertilized by many different cultures, and during which great quantities of silk were sent to Tibet.

THE TANGUT XIA DYNASTY

Northwest China was dominated by the Tanguts. Their capital, Ningxia, was in what is today Gansu Province, and they controlled a line of oases westward along the Silk Roads toward Uyghur territory in present-day Xinjiang. Some Tanguts carefully husbanded the limited water supplies in the region, devised intricate irrigation works, and maintained a self-sufficient agriculture near the oases. Others survived as herders, tending their animals in neighboring grasslands regions.

Establishing an independent state about 982, the Tanguts briefly accepted a tributary position to the Liao, though they rejected vassalage to the Song Chinese, who then imposed restrictions on trade. Tangut involvement in the silk trade belies a reputed disclaimer by the most renowned of the Tangut rulers, the Jingzong emperor (r. 1032–48) that "to dress in skins and furs, to work at herding, such is the nature of the Tangut. Of what use [to us] are brocades and silk."[24]

Like the Khitans, the Tanguts could not themselves make use of all the silk they acquired (mostly from China), so they traded considerable quantities and used it also as tribute and as gifts. Also like the Khitans, they became ardent converts to Buddhism, which put them in contact with the neighboring region of Tibet. A people of Tibetan and Turkic origins, Tanguts were influenced by the Indic-Tibetan, Chinese, and Turko-Mongolian cultures,[25] and the multicultural state they established was noteworthy for its attempt to fuse Tibetan Tantric and Chinese Mahayana Buddhism. Their adherence to Buddhism would prove central to both the silk industry and the silk trade.

The Xia translated Buddhist writings into Tangut, subsidized the printing of religious texts, provided funds for the construction of temples, and organized the collection of Buddhist artifacts and relics. The Tibetan Buddhist preceptors they appointed as teachers to the emperors provided not only religious instruction but counsel on secular matters and legitimacy to the reign.[26] But while they shared a common religion, the Tanguts occasionally clashed with the Tibetans. The hostilities that erupted did not, however, deter trade between the two states. Those Tangut rulers who were devout Buddhists were eager to maintain their relations with monasteries in Tibet, and they sent many gifts of silk.[27] Extant Tangut documentation unfortunately tells us little about the workshops that produced these textiles.

As with the Khitans, internal dissension undermined the Xia, opening the way for the Mongols, who created the greatest steppe confederation in history. In 1209, they attacked the capital, and within a year the Tangut rulers had acquiesced to Mongol demands. In 1219, however, they reneged on a pledge to assist Chinggis Khan in his Central Asian campaigns, and the Mongols exacted a devastating revenge. The Xia dynasty was destroyed by Chinggis Khan in 1227.

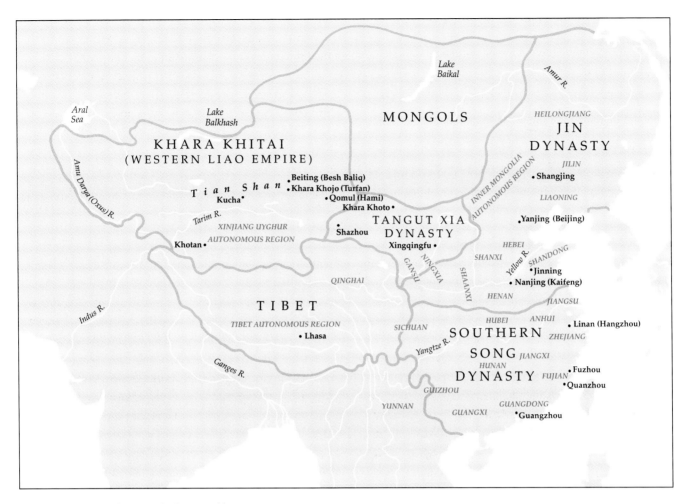

The following locations appear on the map:

Aral Sea

Amu Darya (Oxus) R.

Indus R.

Lake Balkhash

KHARA KHITAI (WESTERN LIAO EMPIRE)

Tian Shan

Kucha•

Tarim R.

•Beiting (Besh Baliq)
•Khara Khojo (Turfan)
•Qomul (Hami)
Khara Khoto •

XINJIANG UYGHUR
AUTONOMOUS REGION

Khotan •

•Shazhou

Ganges R.

Lake Baikal

Amur R.

MONGOLS

TANGUT XIA
DYNASTY
Xingqingfu •

QINGHAI

TIBET
TIBET AUTONOMOUS REGION
• Lhasa

GANSU

NINGXIA

SHAANXI

SHANXI

HEBEI

Yellow R.

SHANDONG

HENAN

SICHUAN

Yangtze R.

HUBEI

ANHUI

JIANGSU

HUNAN

JIANGXI

ZHEJIANG

FUJIAN

GUIZHOU

YUNNAN

GUANGXI

GUANGDONG

HEILONGJIANG
JIN
DYNASTY

JILIN

• Shangjing

LIAONING

INNER MONGOLIA
AUTONOMOUS REGION

•Yanjing (Beijing)

•Jinning
• Nanjing (Kaifeng)

SOUTHERN
SONG
DYNASTY

• Linan (Hangzhou)

•Fuzhou
•Quanzhou

•Guangzhou

The Southern Song, the Jin, and Their Neighbors

THE JIN DYNASTY

The Jurchens of what is today Manchuria were the third group of non-Chinese to establish a dynasty contemporaneous with the Song. Initially inhabiting the forested terrain of eastern Manchuria, they moved around in small groups, eking out their subsistence by hunting and fishing. Toward the end of the ninth century, they had migrated southward to the Liao River area, where over time their mode of life evolved into an agricultural society, though hunting remained a significant element in their economy. By the early tenth century, the Jurchens had become vassals of the Khitans. Two centuries later, under a more centralized leadership, they vanquished the Khitans, establishing the Jin dynasty in 1115.

In 1126 they crossed the Yellow River, entered Chinese territory, and occupied the Song capital, Kaifeng. With the fall of the Northern Song dynasty, the surviving members of the imperial family and court fled south, crossing the Yangtze River and establishing a new capital in Lin'an (present-day Hangzhou). The rulers of the Southern Song lived in fear of Jin incursions, and not until 1142 were hostilities brought to an end. Under the terms of the agreement, the Song abandoned claims to most of North China and pledged to supply 250,000 ounces of silver and 250,000 bolts of silk to the Jin, in effect making them vassals to an overlord.

The Jin adopted many Chinese practices and built their institutions on Chinese models. They enacted a legal code that incorporated many Chinese features. Intermarriage between Jurchens and Chinese increased. Jurchens adopted Chinese surnames. Jurchen farmers became financially dependent on Chinese moneylenders. And in general the two cultures became increasingly interrelated and interdependent. The shift in 1153 of one of the Jurchen capitals from Manchuria to Yanjing, in the area of present-day Beijing, was a true signal of growing sinicization, and this in turn affected many areas of Jurchen life.[28] The decorative arts were supported and the production of fine silks encouraged.[29] Silk workshops, mostly under the supervision of Chinese artisans, were set up. The imperial silk-weaving workshop, which had flourished under the Tang and Song dynasties, was reestablished. Silk was used both as gifts and as currency, in trade and in rituals. As patrons of Buddhism, the Jin rulers provided substantial gifts to Buddhist monasteries. And while grants of land, cash, and silver were common, gifts of silk were also highly prized, used for sutra covers and banners or as backing for paintings. The Jurchens, unlike the Tanguts, followed Chinese, not Tibetan, Buddhism. Indeed, most of their dealings with Tibet, possibly including the dispatch of silks, entailed the use of Tangut intermediaries.

Despite a growing adoption of Chinese institutions, Jurchen attempts to transform their decentralized, tribal society into a Chinese-based, centralized society posed insurmountable difficulties. In addition, the war that had erupted between the Jin and the Southern Song in 1206 led to a general weakening of both sides. In 1215, the Jin capital was attacked, by a new and powerful enemy from the north. The Mongols proved to be the most serious threat to North China. By 1234, the Jin had been destroyed and all of China was forced to contemplate the reality of subjugation under a Mongol khan.

THE MONGOL ERA

The first foreigners to conquer all of China, the Mongols also expanded their domains to include much of Asia. The Mongol Yuan empire eventually encompassed the territories stretching from Korea to western Russia in the north and from Vietnam to Syria in the south. Within half a century, they had overwhelmed the Jin and Song dynasties, the Khwarazmian rulers of Central Asia, and the Abbasid caliphate, which had governed West Asia and North Africa for nearly five hundred years.

The so-called Pax Mongolica they imposed on much of Asia permitted them to foster extensive relations throughout the continent. And though conflicts persisted among the various factions, the Mongol era witnessed the greatest expansion of trade and tribute in Eurasian history. Traders, as well as diplomats and missionaries, traveled with few hindrances across Mongol domains, resulting in the first direct contacts between Europe and China. European missionaries and merchants, the most famous being Marco Polo, voyaged all the way to China, and Asian products—silks and spices—reached Europe, leading Europeans to seek a sea route to the East and its treasures.

First appearing in historical chronicles in the eleventh and twelfth centuries, the Mongols comprised a broad spectrum of nomadic tribes. Under Chinggis Khan (r. 1206–27) they were unified, and with a tightly disciplined army and brilliant political skills Chinggis emerged as supreme ruler in 1206. Within three years he had expanded his rule beyond Mongolia, setting forth on three separate expeditions in two decades. His successful forays against the Tangut Xia of northwest China extended Mongol control over the oases and towns leading to Central Asia. His second campaign, directed against the Jin, continued intermittently for four years until 1215, when he overran Yanjing. His last expedition, in Central Asia, was the largest and most extensive. Chinggis died in 1227.[30]

Although military campaigns had prevented him from turning his attention to the establishment of a regular administration over the territories he had newly subjugated, Chinggis nevertheless developed policies that would aid in governing and in shaping the economies of the conquered lands. Under his rule, Uyghur script was adapted for the writing of Mongolian, previously an unwritten language. A policy of religious tolerance was pursued to win over the newly conquered native populations. And foreigners—most importantly, the Uyghurs—were recruited for skilled administrative positions for which the Mongols lacked experience.

The nomadic lifestyle of the Mongols had precluded the development of an artisan class, but Chinggis, aware of the need for craftsmen, freed them from corvée labor and taxes and moved them to new areas. Chinggis and his son Ögödei eventually established at least three settlements of textile workers in East and Central Asia. Prizing in particular the work of Islamic weavers from Central Asia, they resettled artisans in the northernmost regions of China and the adjacent Uyghur areas across the northwestern borders. Under Ögödei, a certain Ha-san-na was entrusted with transporting 3,000 Muslim households, mostly weavers, from Central Asia to Xunmalin, a site about twenty miles west of what is today Kalgan.

The greatest contribution of the Muslim textile workers was their expertise in weaving cloth of gold (*nasij*).[31] In 1278, an Office of Gold Textiles was established in Xunmalin.[32] By this time, many Chinese had been trained in the techniques and had joined the community. A second community was situated in the Chahar region of Inner Mongolia (present-day Hongzhou, Hebei Province), about thirty miles southeast of Xunmalin. Three hundred weavers and goldsmiths from Central Asia and 300 Chinese weavers from Bianjing were settled at this site, the merging of traditions facilitating a diffusion of techniques. A third community was established in Besh Baliq (the old Uyghur capital), northeast of what is today Urumqi.[33] The native Uyghur craftsmen, who had a long tradition of weaving, were no doubt influenced by and, in turn, influenced the Muslim weavers who had resided in Besh Baliq.[34] In 1275, the weavers from Besh Baliq were moved to the capital Daidu, which became a center for the production of cloth of gold. And the following year a Besh Baliq branch office was established in Daidu.[35]

All three textile communities resided on the outskirts of Chinese territories, mostly in areas near the Mongol homeland, suggesting that the textiles, particularly the cloths of gold, were made on commission to the Mongol elite. And all three communities attracted weavers of diverse backgrounds—Central Asian, Muslim, Uyghur, and Chinese—enabling the intermingling of techniques and designs.

The Mongols also resettled Chinese craftsmen both in Samarkand and in the Upper Yenisei, adjacent to the lands of the Kirghiz peoples.[36] And Chinese textile workers were seen living in the town of Almaliq, in Central Asia.[37]

Unlike the Chinese, who accorded merchants a low social status, the Mongols valued commerce, and under their rule trade across Eurasia was restored, with silk being one of the most valuable products of exchange. Chinggis's successors pursued similar policies. Ögödei (r. 1229–41), like his father, presided over a considerable expansion of Mongol territory. His armies occupied what is today Korea, North China, Georgia, Armenia, and much of Russia; their campaigns extended as far west as Hungary and Poland. Establishing the first Mongol capital at Khara Khorum, Ögödei recruited many foreigners to staff his government and employed foreign artisans to work in his shops.

Ögödei's nephew Möngke (r. 1251–59) sought to consolidate Mongol rule in Tibet, a critical site, as noted earlier, in the history of Chinese and Central Asian textiles. It is not unlikely that some of the textiles in this exhibition which were preserved in Tibet were gifts from Mongol rulers to Buddhist monasteries.

Following the death of Möngke, his younger brother Khubilai emerged to become the most influential of the Mongol rulers. Like his predecessors, Khubilai Khan (r. 1260–94) expanded Mongol territory. By 1279, his troops had overwhelmed Southern Song China, the wealthiest and most populous domain ever to be added to the Mongol empire. Khubilai lifted restrictions on Chinese as well as Uyghur and Muslim merchants, did not impose confiscatory taxes on trade, and granted merchants a higher rank in the social hierarchy. Without government limitations, merchants began to travel more extensively and to trade on a more lavish scale. Other aids to trade were improvements in the transportation system and new roads. Merchants were given access to government postal stations.

Paper money was more widely circulated, which facilitated commercial transactions. The first of Khubilai's notes to be issued, the *sichao* (silk note), was backed by silk, which could in turn be exchanged for a specific amount of silver.[38] Loans and capital, provided by the Mongols to merchant groups known as *ortogh*, offered direct assistance to traders. *Ortogh* were associations of mostly Uyghur and Muslim merchants who joined together to fund long-distance trade—which was a risky venture—and thus to prevent any single merchant from sustaining crippling losses should a caravan be plundered or fall prey to natural disaster. The court loaned funds at low rates of interest to the *ortogh* to subsidize caravans or, occasionally, to enable them to engage in further moneylending.[39] The result, according to Marco Polo, was that "there is not a place in the world to which so many merchants come & that dearer things and of greater value and more strange come into this town [Beijing] . . . than into any city of the world."[40]

Like his predecessors, Khubilai valued artisans and accorded them the status and economic rewards that the Chinese had denied them. He exempted them from corvée labor and provided them with food and other necessities. Court regulations allowed government artisans to sell the wares they produced above the mandated quotas—a policy that no doubt affected textile workers as well.

The astonishing number of government textile offices confirms the value the Mongols accorded to textile production. Of the eighty-odd subdivisions of the Ministry of Works, about half were devoted to the manufacture of textiles. There were, in addition, numerous textile workshops within other official institutions.[41] The court also founded branch offices in the main textile producing centers. Zhending, Jining, and Yongping circuits and the towns of Hongzhou, Datong, Baoding, and Besh Baliq were among the most active. Many of the offices supervised government artisan workshops; others were in charge of private artisans.

Khubilai's other major contribution to the silk industry entailed forging a strong link between the Mongols and Tibet. A Buddhist lama, Phagspa, was recruited from Tibet to serve as Khubilai's mentor. Phagspa later became his adviser on Tibetan affairs.[42] Determined to impose Mongol jurisdiction over Tibet, Khubilai eventually sent him back to his native land in 1264 with the honorary title of ruler of Tibet. Trade between the two countries developed, and judging from the quantity of Chinese textiles preserved in Tibetan monasteries, Chinese silks were especially prized, though the Mongols supported Tibetan monasteries by providing funds, laborers, and artisans as well.

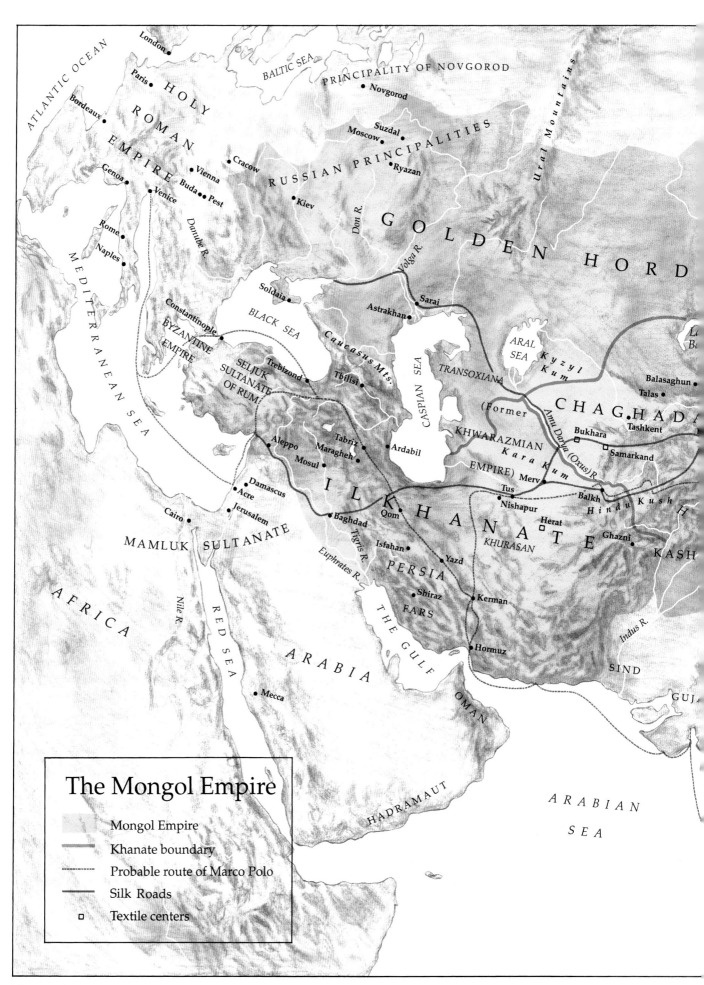

The Mongol Empire

EMPIRE

OF

THE

GREAT

KHAN

SOUTHERN

SONG

EMPIRE

Amur R.

Lake
Baikal

Yenisei R.

Altai Mountains

MINION OF
KHAIDU

Khara Khorum

Shangdu

Liaoyang

Kaesong

KORYO

KAMAKURA SHOGUNATE

SEA OF
JAPAN

Beiting
(Besh Baliq)

Qomul (Hami)

alik
ocheng)

Khara Khojo
(Turfan)

Shazhou (Dunhuang)

Jiayuguan

Kucha

Ningxia

Xunmalin

Hongzhou

Daidu (Beijing)

Taiyuan

YELLOW
SEA

Yellow R.

Kaifeng

Yangzhou

HANATE

*Qinghai
Lake*

Miran

Nanjing

Linan (Hangzhou)

Qingyuan (Ningbo)

EAST
CHINA
SEA

lamakan Desert

Qarqan

Xian

Hanzhong

Xiangyang

Yangtze R.

Kunlun Mountains

Hanyang

Jiangling

Fuzhou

Chengdu

Quanzhou

TIBET

Lhasa

Chaozhou

Huizhou

Wuzhou

Guangzhou

NANZHAO

Dali

Yunnan

SOUTH
CHINA
SEA

ALAYA

ELHI SULTANATE

Ganges R.

Patna

DAI VIET
(ANNAM)

PAGAN
(MIEN)

Thang Long
(Hanoi)

BENGAL

Pagan

CHAMPA

PEGU

Sukhothai

SUKHOTAI

Mekong R.

KHMER
EMPIRE

Angkor

NDU

ATES

ORISSA

BAY OF
BENGAL

SALA

PANDYA

Madurai

Under the Mongols, silk was employed also as it had been traditionally under the Chinese. Nobles received silk as payments from their subjects and as annual grants from the court. A symbol of imperial authority, it was used as currency, as tribute, as gifts for envoys and in the investiture of officials, as rewards for civilian and military officials, and in Confucian rituals and ceremonies. The Mongols prized, in particular, silks woven with gold threads (*nashi*), which they used in robes, headdresses, girdles, and belts, and as linings on *gers* (Mongol tents) and as coverings on wagons. The nomadic heritage of Mongol culture also made silk appealing, as it was light and easy to transport, and thus ideally suited to a nomadic lifestyle.

Under the Yuan, silk textiles were transported farther abroad than they had been previously. By 1257, Chinese silks had arrived in Italy, and Italian—mainly Genoese—merchants traveled to both North and South China to obtain it.[43] In Europe, church treasuries were the repositories of silks obtained in trade or as gifts to envoys, and church treasuries and tombs constitute the main sites of textile preservation. By the fourteenth century, the motifs and patterns of Chinese and especially Central Asian silks were serving as models for those of Italian silks.[44]

The Eurasian trade in Yuan silks and the use of silks in diplomatic missions diminished toward the end of the thirteenth century as Khubilai's last years witnessed catastrophic failures. Abortive and costly naval expeditions against Japan and Java, unprofitable military campaigns in Southeast Asia, and rebellions in Manchuria and Tibet required vast expenditures which added to the staggering costs of the public works projects that Khubilai had initiated. With Khubilai's death in 1294, the Yuan dynasty steadily declined. Fratricidal dynastic struggles weakened whatever imperial power remained. Conditions in society at large mirrored the disarray at court. Inflation increased; efforts at reform faltered; ethnic minorities in South and Southwest China rebelled; tax evasion and revenue shortfalls threatened to bring down the government; and factional struggles led to bloody purges. In the late 1340s the Yellow River overflowed its dikes and changed its course, leading to untold misery for thousands. By the early 1350s, full-scale rebellions were endemic. Zhu Yuanzhang emerged as the most powerful rebel leader and compelled the Yuan court to flee to Mongolia. In 1368, he proclaimed himself Hongwu, the first emperor of the Ming dynasty, and China reverted once again to native rule.

All the Mongol khanates gradually weakened, and with the fragmentation of the Mongol empire, trade was severely curtailed and commerce in silk nearly halted.

MING XENOPHOBIA

Hongwu (r. 1368–98) had more pressing concerns than disruptions in commerce, and indeed his policies contributed to the reduction of the caravan trade across Eurasia. Having endured approximately a century of Mongol rule in South China and nearly a century and a half in the north, the Chinese, fearing further incursions by non-Chinese, adopted policies of restricted trade and curtailed political relations with foreign lands. The court became increasingly xenophobic and the emperor increasingly despotic, claiming he needed additional power to avert Mongol-like invasions.

Hongwu's death brought on another crisis. The emperor bypassed his son Zhu Di and selected his twenty-year-old grandson, Zhu Yunwen (r. 1399–1402), Zhu Di's nephew, as his successor, at which point Zhu Di initiated a civil war that lasted for three years and resulted in his eventual usurpation of the throne. The aura of illegitimacy that clouded Zhu Di's rise to power in many ways shaped government policies, which, not surprisingly, often repudiated those of Hongwu. Adopting the reign title of Yongle, the new emperor (r. 1403–24) moved the capital from Nanjing to Beijing, rebuilding the city on a lavish scale. Expansionism also boosted Yongle's legitimacy, his policies reversing his father's carefully constructed design to limit foreign relations. The embassies he dispatched abroad fostered the most wide-ranging contacts China would have with the lands beyond its borders until the nineteenth century. The Muslim eunuch Zheng He (1371–1433) led seven naval expeditions to Southeast Asia, Iran, and the east coast of Africa, which resulted in the submission of tribute by many states to China.[45] The diplomat Chen Cheng (d. 1457) traveled to Central Asia on three separate occasions and spurred Tamerlane's son Shahrukh (r. 1409–46), a powerful potentate in Herat, to send a mission to Yongle's court. Similarly, a certain Isiha (act. 1409–1451) journeyed to Manchuria and returned with leaders and chieftains who nominally accepted Chinese overlordship. In short, contact with the outside world was encouraged and supported during the reign of Yongle. Trade was revitalized and commerce in silk expanded.[46]

Central Asia became once again the recipient of Chinese textiles. Twenty-three of thirty-five tribute missions from the oasis of Hami were granted silks; twenty-four of thirty-one embassies from neighboring Central Asian towns received raw silk and gauze. And one embassy from Besh Baliq was favored with forty silk garments woven with gold thread.[47]

Yongle also sought to restore the Sino-Tibetan relations that had prevailed during the Yuan dynasty. His father, Hongwu, having been raised in a Buddhist monastery, had been sympathetic to Buddhism and, straying from his policy of restricting foreign contacts, had attempted to reestablish relations with Tibet. He also sought to defuse tensions along the Sino-Tibetan frontier and was eager to trade Chinese tea for Tibetan horses. He initiated relations with the Tibetan Karmapa order, rewarding its envoys handsomely when they came to China in 1372–73 and offering them gifts of elaborate silk robes. In 1403, his son Yongle invited the Fifth Black Hat Karmapa reincarnation, Halima (1384–1415), to visit the Ming court. Arriving in 1407, Halima was showered with gifts.

In 1414, the leader of the Sakya order, which had had strong ties with the Mongol khans, arrived at court, and he, too, was given substantial gifts and many textiles. And while the most renowned Tibetan Buddhist, Tsong-kha-pa, founder of the Gelugs-pa order, declined a similar invitation, eventually he dispatched a disciple in his stead. Greeting him warmly, Yongle presented him with gold and silver vessels and with textiles both for himself and for his mentor. Buddhist emissaries continued to visit from Tibet throughout the Yongle reign, and they continued to be well received.[48]

The death of the Yongle emperor in 1424 brought an end to the expansionist policies of his administration. The missions of Zheng He were brought to a halt, the number of embassies sent abroad curtailed, and restrictions reimposed on tribute and trade missions. And though regulations were sometimes evaded and commercial exchange managed to survive in some frontier regions, in general, economic interchange was discouraged. Contributing also to the demise of the Silk Roads was the discovery of a sea route from Europe to China. Overland, intrepid merchants no longer transported silks throughout Eurasia. But though the oases and towns along the Silk Roads lost much of their color and luster, the products which survive from that wondrous time attest to a glorious era—when silk was resplendent as gold.

1. Toronto 1983, p. 1. I am grateful to my colleagues Anne E. Wardwell and James C. Y. Watt for their incisive comments on the text. Scholars seeking additional references and citations may wish to consult a longer version of this essay presented at the Columbia University Seminar on Traditional China in the fall of 1997 and preserved at the East Asian Library at Columbia.
2. For earlier references to silk and to the silk trade, see Chang Kwang-chih 1986, p. 113, and Hulsewé 1974, pp. 117–35.
3. B. Watson 1961, vol. 2, pp. 264–74.
4. See Schafer 1963 for such exchanges.
5. Narain 1990, p. 176; see also Pulleyblank 1952, pp. 317–56.
6. Frye 1954, p. 113; for confirmation of the status accorded to Chinese artisans in Central Asia, see Barthold 1968, p. 236.
7. On the controversies surrounding the provenance of some of these silks, see Shepherd 1981, pp. 105–22, and Belenitskii and Bentovich 1961, pp. 66–78.
8. On this trade, see Mackerras 1968, p. vii, and Beckwith 1991, pp. 183–98.
9. See Riboud and Vial 1970 and Whitfield 1982–83 for examples of such Buddhist textiles.
10. Ch'en 1964, p. 230.
11. See Levy 1955.
12. Beckwith 1987, pp. 146–47.
13. Gluckman 1995, p. 24.
14. See the essays in Rossabi, China, 1983.
15. Ang 1983, p. 27.
16. Dunnell 1992, pp. 188–89.
17. Pinks 1968, p. 94.
18. Shiba 1983, pp. 97–103.
19. Shiba 1970, p. 112.
20. Smith 1983, pp. 234, 237.
21. The monumental study of the Khitans is Wittfogel and Feng Chia-sheng 1949.
22. In Wittfogel and Feng Chia-sheng 1949, p. 369, Lingjin yuan is translated as Silk Brocade Workshop. However, the words ling and jin at this time served as general terms for figured and polychrome silks.
23. Liaoshi, chap. 39, p. 487.
24. Dunnell 1983, p. 107.
25. Dunnell 1992, p. 156. See also Dunnell 1996 and Kychanov 1989, p. 148.
26. Dunnell 1994, pp. 99–100.
27. Linrothe 1995, p. 2.
28. Tao Jing-shen 1976, p. 19.
29. On Jin culture, see Bush 1995, pp. 183–215, and Jin Qicong 1995, pp. 216–37.
30. The latest study of Chinggis's career is Ratchnevsky 1991.
31. Pelliot 1927, pp. 261–79; Tu Ji [1962], chap. 40, p. 5a; and Boyle 1971, p. 276.
32. Yangyuan xian zhi, chap. 3, p. 4b.
33. The weavers in Besh Baliq may have produced a coat in the tomb of a Yuan general recently discovered in the Salt Lake (Yanhu) region on the road from Urumqi to Turfan. See Wang Binghua 1973, pp. 28–34.
34. Rossabi 1988, pp. 108–9; on the Uyghurs and textiles, see Tikhonov 1966, pp. 82–85.
35. See pp. 130–31, and Farquhar 1990, p. 336.
36. Waley 1931, p. 124.
37. Bretschneider 1967, vol. 1, p. 127.
38. Yang Lien-sheng 1952, p. 63.
39. See Allsen 1989 and Endicott-West 1989.
40. Moule and Pelliot 1938, p. 237.
41. Farquhar 1990 offers brief descriptions of these offices.
42. On Tibetans in Yuan China, see Franke 1981, pp. 296–328.
43. On these merchants, see Petech 1962, pp. 549–74.
44. Cleveland 1968, p. 72, and nos. 301–2.
45. See Mills 1970 about these expeditions.
46. Rossabi 1976, pp. 1–34, and Rossabi, "Translation," 1983, pp. 49–59.
47. On these figures, see Rossabi 1970, pp. 327–37.
48. Goodrich and Fang 1976, pp. 1308–9.

1. Early Exchanges: Silks from the 8th through the 11th Century

Although the five silks in this chapter exhibit a wide range of styles and technical features, they belong to a large class of textiles that has been attributed to Sogdiana.[1] The most complete and best preserved is the outer fabric of a child's coat (cat. no. 5). It is woven with pearl roundels that enclose pairs of confronted ducks standing on split palmettes; four-directional palmettes fill the interstices. The design is strongly influenced by the art of Sasanian Iran (ca. A.D. 224–ca. 640), especially the ribbons (*patif*) worn by the ducks, the necklaces held in their beaks, and the pearl roundels. Other elements, however, are characteristically Sogdian: the symmetrical arrangement of ducks in pairs and their placement on split palmettes; the feet, which are not webbed and which point downward; the ornamental rosettes on the bodies, formed of four small hearts pointing to the center; and the form of the four-directional palmettes.[2] The stiffness and abstraction of the motifs are also typical of Sogdian silks, as is the spacing of the roundels, which are nearly tangent in the weft direction but more widely spaced in the warp direction. The use of five colors and the proportion of the three main warps to every binding warp occur in many silks that have been solidly attributed to Sogdiana. The most important of these is a complete loom piece in Huy, Belgium, on the back of which is a Sogdian inscription giving the name Zandaniji.[3]

Catalogue number 2 is woven with a very different design: roundels that enclose pairs of mounted hunters and palmette trees that fill the interstices.[4] The floral decoration of the roundel frames derives from silks attributed to Alexandria and is closely related to Byzantine silks.[5] The latter served also as models both for the small medallions filled with rosettes, which are superimposed over the roundel frames at their tangent points, and for the palmette trees. Similarly, the prototype for the hunters' faces and curly hair is Byzantine, as is the motif of the

horseman hunting with a lance. The riders' bare feet are a misreading of a type of Late Antique sandal. In spite of the reliance on Byzantine motifs and decorative conventions, the curiously abstracted and somewhat wooden style, together with the detail of the disks on the paws of the lions and dogs, identifies the silk as Sogdian.

The design of catalogue number 1 derives from similar models. This fragment preserves the interstitial motifs between large, aligned roundels: two pairs of mounted hunters shooting backward at two pairs of ibex, and pairs of rabbits above and below the hunters. Small portions of two roundels remain above and below the ibex. Both the mounted hunters shooting backward and the pearl-and-floral decoration of the roundel borders derive from silks of the so-called Alexandrian school. The faces and curly hair of the horsemen are based on Byzantine models but have become highly abstracted.

The diverse origins of the motifs and decorative details in these three silks, which range geographically from Egypt to the Byzantine Empire to Iran, result from the strategic location of Sogdiana along the trade routes linking Iran and Byzantium with China. In the eighth and ninth centuries, Sogdiana was not a political entity but a loose confederation of city-states, the most important of which were Samarkand and Bukhara. One indication of the international diversity of silks transported along these routes is provided by the Byzantine, Syrian, Egyptian, Iranian, and eastern Central Asian or Chinese silks that were found in graves at Moshchevaia Balka, along the northern Caucasian portion of the trade route.[6]

Like the child's coat, catalogue number 3 is woven with a design of paired, confronted ducks standing on a split palmette and enclosed in a roundel. Although the foliate border of the roundel occurs in a number of silks solidly attributed to Sogdiana,[7] the style is notably abstracted. The fineness of both the warps, which have virtually no twist, and the wefts is altogether different from the heavy wefts and strongly twisted warps in the child's coat and the two silks with hunters. Catalogue number 4 is also a light fabric, woven with fine wefts and warps that are virtually untwisted. Its geometric

Figure 1. Micrographic detail, cat. no. 5   Figure 2. Micrographic detail, cat. no. 4

design, including the roundels with triple-pearl borders and the four-directional figures in the interstices, is even more abstract than that of the duck motif.

As mentioned above, these five silks belong to a class of textiles that has been attributed—and extensively published, by Dorothy G. Shepherd and Anna Ierusalimskaia in particular—to Sogdiana.[8] All are woven in a weft-faced compound-twill structure with themes and motifs drawn largely from the art of the Byzantine Empire and Sasanian Iran. Both Shepherd and Ierusalimskaia classify them into three broad groups, known as Zandaniji-I, -II, and -III.[9] Differences, however, exist both between and within these categories. Because Ierusalimskaia bases her groups on style and date, and Shepherd bases hers on technique, the silks assigned by the two scholars to Zandaniji-I and -II do not always correspond, and a different list of silks is designated by each as Zandaniji-III.[10] Neither system, moreover, is without its inconsistencies.[11]

Nevertheless, Shepherd's distinction between the silks with twisted warps (Zandaniji-I and -III) and those with untwisted warps (Zandaniji-II) is well founded. Those with twisted warps (which include cat. nos. 1, 2, and 5) have warp and weft yarns that are substantial and a warp proportion of two or three main warps to each binding warp (fig. 1). Consequently, they are fairly heavy and compact. The weaves of the silks with untwisted warps (including cat. nos. 3 and 4), on the other hand, are woven with warp and weft yarns that are comparatively fine and have a proportion of one or two main warps to each binding warp (fig. 2). Accordingly, they are much lighter fabrics and their weaves are less compact. The two groups are distinguished not only by technique but also by motif.[12] Although animals and birds are common to both groups, human figures occur almost exclusively on the silks with twisted warps, as do geometric designs

on the silks with untwisted warps. Similarly, floral designs are more common on the silks with untwisted warps. Stylistically, the patterns on the silks with the untwisted warps tend to be more abstract and stylized than those on the silks with the twisted warps.

Shepherd explains these differences on the basis of chronology. Proposing an eighth- to ninth-century date for the Zandaniji-II silks, based on datable graves in the Caucasus where some have been found, she assumes a similar date for the Zandaniji-III group and suggests an earlier date (seventh to early eighth century) for the Zandaniji-I group.[13] This reasoning, however, is somewhat perilous, given the absence of any securely dated or datable textiles in her Zandaniji-I and -III groups. Additionally, Sogdian silks with twisted warps that appear to date stylistically to as late as the tenth century have recently come on the market, expanding the time frame originally proposed.

A more compelling explanation for the contrasts between the silks with untwisted warps and those with twisted warps is suggested by the fact that the two groups belong to very different weaving traditions. z-twisted warps are characteristic of weft-faced compound twills produced in Iran and Byzantium, while lighter fabrics woven with untwisted warps occur in silks of the same structure produced in China. Twisted and untwisted warps, moreover, handle differently on the loom. Twisted warps are more cohesive and have greater strength and elasticity, while untwisted warps are more inclined to break as a result of the buildup of static electricity during the weaving process. The very different skills required to weave with twisted, as opposed to untwisted, warps make the likelihood of a single weaver's or workshop's weaving with both types of warp highly improbable.[14]

While the silks with untwisted warps undoubtedly belong to the Chinese tradition of silk weaving, the possibility that they were woven in Sogdiana cannot be excluded. A community of Chinese craftsmen, including a small number of textile workers, is known from historical records to have been residing in Bukhara in the early eighth century. After the Arab defeat of the Tang army near the Talas River in A.D. 751, some of the captured Chinese artisans, including silk workers and weavers, remained in Samarkand. How much the Chinese weavers produced and the extent of their influence, if any, on Sogdian weaving are not known. Also problematic is the fact that at least one of the silks with untwisted warps appears to date from as early as the mid-seventh century, based on the presumed date of the Antinoë silk to which it had been sewn when consigned to a grave in Egypt.[15] Existing historical chronicles do not mention the presence of Chinese craftsmen in Sogdiana before the eighth century.

It seems more likely that the silks with untwisted warps were woven farther east in Central Asia, where sericulture and silk weaving had been learned from the Chinese and where Sogdian influence was strong.[16] Sogdians, the leading merchants of Central Asia, some of whom also served as administrators, colonized strategic points along the principal trade routes.[17] Through their presence and contacts, Sogdian culture was transmitted throughout Central Asia. Not surprisingly, Sogdian silks and silks woven with Sogdian motifs have been found at Dunhuang, Khojo (near Khara Khojo), Turfan, and Dulan.[18] In the Khotan oasis, moreover, some of the textile patterns depicted in late-sixth-century paintings found at Balawaste bear similarities to those in the somewhat later Zandaniji-II group: roundels with pearl borders enclosing concentric circles, rosettes, cross-shaped motifs, volutes, and motifs resembling double axes.[19] Like the silks, the textile patterns in the paintings are predominantly geometric. Sericulture and silk weaving in the Khotan oasis are known to have been introduced from China prior to the Tang period (618–907).[20] At the same time, Khotan had close cultural and economic ties to Sogdiana. Some of the deities that appear in the Buddhist art of Khotan, for example, were adopted from the Sogdian pantheon, while Sogdian texts found in Khotan and in the Upper Indus Valley document Khotan's strategic location on the trade routes connecting Sogdiana with India.[21] Although no Zandaniji silks have survived in the Khotan oasis or in India, material evidence of their transportation along those trade routes is provided by an eighth-century Kashmiri bronze in the Norton Simon Museum, Pasadena, which represents the Buddha seated on a cushion covered with a Zandaniji silk.[22]

TANG, LIAO, AND NORTHERN SONG SILKS

In the sixth century, Chinese weavers began to adopt Persian- and Sogdian-style patterns, while they retained the traditional Chinese technique of warp-faced patterning. The means of transmission, however, is at present far from clear. Persian textiles are mentioned in Chinese literature of the sixth and seventh centuries (see, for example, the story of He Chou below), particularly the type called by the Chinese *jin* (usually translated as "brocade," but much more likely a weft-faced compound weave). While there may well have been Persian textiles traded into China, they were probably carried by Sogdian merchants, and a greater part of *jin* textiles imported into China would have been Sogdian in origin—though greatly influenced by Persian designs and techniques. Besides, from about the third century on, there were various centers of textile manufacture in Central Asia, such as Shule (in the vicinity of Kashgar), Qiuci (present-day Kucha), and Gaochang (Turfan), and terms such as Shule *jin*, Qiuci *jin*, and Gaochang-made Qiuci *jin* appear in documents recovered from tombs in the Turfan area of the fifth to the seventh century.[23] There is no known example of any of these textiles, but we may assume that they were all influenced to various degrees by Persian and Chinese styles. A parallel situation existed with the transmission of Western patterns and working techniques of silver in the sixth and seventh centuries. Many motifs in Chinese silver of this period exhibit Persian, and some Hellenistic, influence; but the greatest influence on Chinese silverwork was Sogdian, and the majority of foreign silver found in early Tang sites is Sogdian—with some exceptions that may be Central Asian.[24]

As noted above, both Sogdian and Chinese silks with Sogdian-style patterns dating from the sixth and seventh centuries have been found at various oases on the Silk Roads. This was a period of cosmopolitan culture in China, and the populations in metropolitan areas like Chang'an and Luoyang included large numbers of traders and settlers from all over Asia, who introduced new skills and artistic styles into China. But it was the Central Asian peoples from such places as Kucha and Sogdiana who made the greatest contribution.[25] Some of the artists and skilled craftsmen were accorded high official positions, and their biographies are found in the histories of the Northern Dynasties (A.D. 386–581) and the Sui (A.D. 581-618) and Tang dynasties.[26]

One of the most prominent of the artistically gifted families from Central Asia was that of He Chou. He was active in the late sixth century and was known for his skills in manufacturing and engineering, including

Figure 3. Coat lining, cat. no. 5

glassmaking and bridge building.[27] One of his achievements was to have made copies of Persian silks that were said to have surpassed the original. If this story is true, it is likely that he was using traditional Chinese weaving methods to re-create Western patterns, as he did not seem to have come from an area with a known tradition in silk weaving, as some scholars suspect. Because his father was skilled in jade carving, it is probable that his family originally came from Khotan, the chief source for nephrite (jade) for all of Asia during this period.[28] In any case, He Chou's family was thoroughly sinicized. He was a third-generation immigrant, and his uncle was head of the Imperial Academy in the Sui dynasty.[29] That he had roots in Central Asia does not necessarily mean that he brought the skills with him, but rather that he was not so totally acculturated to the scholar-official mentality as to have lost interest in practical matters.

Another person who was known for his textile patterns, which from descriptions would seem to have been of Western origin, was Dou Shilun, the duke of Lingyang, who, while he was in charge of public works in Yizhou, Sichuan, created designs that included paired birds and confronted rams.[30] He was said to be the son of Dou Kang, a senior official at the beginning of the Tang dynasty and a good friend of the first emperor of the Tang, Li Yuan (r. 618–26), although his name is not listed as one of the sons of Dou Kang in the emperor's official biography.[31] It is possible that he was one of the many Westerners

who adopted a Chinese name at that time. Unlike He Chou, who was asked by the emperor to copy Persian patterns, Dou himself provided the patterns for the weavers in the official workshops in Yizhou. In any case, He and Dou were active during the time that China was producing silks with Persian and Sogdian patterns.

In the beginning of the eighth century, a new style began to appear in Chinese textile design, and by the middle of the century it had practically replaced the Sogdian-style motifs as the most popular pattern. At the same time, Chinese weavers increasingly employed the Western method of weaving weft-faced compound twills. Two items dating from the eighth century illustrate this change, the brown silk damask that lines the child's coat and pants (cat. no. 5 and fig. 3) and a polychrome compound-twill silk (cat. no. 6). The pattern is dominated by a large floral medallion with four-directional floral devices in the interstices, the latter seen partially in the corners of the silk compound twill. The medallion of a central flower or cluster of flowers circled by rings of flowers is not only one of the most common motifs on Tang textiles of the eighth century; it is seen also on other decorative arts, such as silver and pottery.[32] It is interesting to observe that the motif of the ring of blossoms, which surrounds the central flower, conforms to the ancient convention of alternate open and closed forms seen commonly in the arts of Egypt and the Ancient Near East, thus pointing to an ultimately Western derivation.[33]

The child's pants are made from a white damask silk. Its reverse inverted repeats are formed by large rosettes surrounded by flowers at the cardinal points and, between, by flying birds carrying floral sprigs in their beaks. Historically, this looser pattern structure, with the introduction of naturalistic elements such as the flying birds, comes after the medallions with the four-pointed floral motifs, although the two styles coexisted for some time, as evidenced by the pants and their lining. It is the harbinger of patterns that came later in the Tang period—from the ninth century on—which employed increasingly more naturalistic elements and a less geometric composition. In the reign of Emperor Wenzong (r. 827–40), some of these newer patterns would be sanctioned for official wear by members of the imperial court on formal occasions. A decree issued at the beginning of the reign lists some of the patterns permitted for the robes of senior officials, including "hawks holding auspicious plant in beak" and "geese holding knotted ribbons."[34] This trend was to continue into the Liao period (907–1125; see cat. nos. 8 and 9).

One of the consequences of the adoption of the weft-patterned weave was that the loom width could be greatly increased—from an average of about 56 centimeters for warp-patterned weaves to more than double that.[35] The diameter of the medallion in catalogue number 6 is roughly equal to that in another fragment in the Shōsō-in,

in Nara, Japan, which is estimated to have been originally about 110 centimeters.[36]

The earliest-known datable example of the floral medallion, which was found in a tomb with a document dated 706, is from Astana, just outside the city of Turfan (fig. 4).[37] It is a weft-faced compound twill, with a structure as illustrated in figure 5, which may be taken as a structure typical for early weft-faced compound twills in China. During the eighth century, the weave structure began to change—to that as seen in catalogue number 6. Normally, a compound-twill weave with a weft-faced 1/2 binding on the face has a warp-faced 2/1 binding on the reverse. Here, however, both the face and the reverse are bound in a weft-faced 1/2 twill, the face in the s direction and the reverse in the z direction. We are at present not sure when this change in structure occurred, but we do know that the variation would be commonly used in compound-twill silks of the Liao dynasty. Among the textile fragments collected by Paul Pelliot at Dunhuang in the early years of the twentieth century is one woven with the same structure, but it is difficult to place this fragment as the pattern, a vegetal scroll with trefoil leaves issuing from an undulating split stem, could date from any time in the late Tang to the Liao period.[38] In view of the fact that the floral medallion survived into the late Tang,[39] and that it makes only token appearances in subsidiary roles in Liao designs, we have dated catalogue

Figure 4. Textile with floral medallion, excavated in Astana. Tang dynasty (618–907), ca. 700. Silk, weft-faced compound twill, 8 × 24.6 cm (3⅛ × 9⅝ in.)

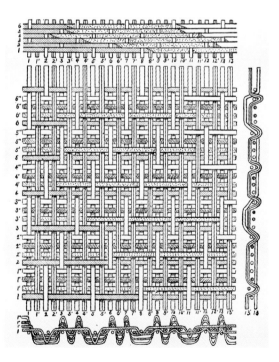

Figure 5. Diagram of weave, fig. 4. Top: external view of surface; center: weave structure; bottom and right: cross sections

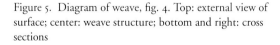

number 6, in spite of its structure, to the eighth to ninth century.

Three Liao silks—a fragment from a garment woven with cranes, clouds, and radiating floral figures (cat. no. 9), a silk from which a small purse was made (cat. no. 8), and the upper portions of a pair of boots (cat. no. 10)—are compound-twill weaves with a weft-faced binding on the reverse as well as on the face. The reverse inverted repeat of the fragment from the garment derives from Tang designs. As mentioned above, in connection with the evolution of Tang designs from the High Tang period onward, the patterns become more loosely structured, with an increase in naturalistic images. This piece may be regarded as an example of the end product of this evolution, where the floral medallion makes a vestigial appearance, the peonies are realistically represented, and the cranes could have come from a contemporary painting. The flying crane had been a popular motif in Chinese textile design since the late eighth century, as can be gathered from the descriptions of textile patterns in mid- to late Tang poetry.[40] The pattern on the purse, while sharing the same quality of a diffused composition, derives its elements from the art of Central Asia. The theme of boys at play is known in paintings found at Astana dating from the eighth century, and the deer is a favorite subject of the arts of Central Asia, as can be seen in several examples in this catalogue.

The design of boys in pomegranates on a painted gauze (cat. no. 7), dating from perhaps the tenth century, is from a different source again. On the surface, it can be taken to be a characteristically Chinese rebus for progeny, as the pomegranate holds many seeds and the character for "seed" is the same as that for "son." For this reason, it may be considered to have a native genesis. However, we may point to other patterns from contemporary textiles, such as one in the Metropolitan Museum, a fragment found in Rayy, Iran (cat. no. 11). It is a cream silk of a type known as *ling* in Chinese nomen-

Figure 6. Buddhist stele, detail. Tang dynasty (618–907), ca. 700. Black limestone. The Metropolitan Museum of Art, New York. Rogers Fund 1930 (30.122)

clature (twill and twill) and patterned with boys sporting in a floral scroll filled with peonies, lotus pods, and pomegranates. This fragment bears a close affinity in structure and design with another piece excavated in a Northern Song tomb in Hengyang, Hunan Province (fig. 11), and can thus be firmly dated to the late eleventh or early twelfth century.[41] The combination of boys and lotus also makes a rebus for progeny. We may compare this motif also with a well-known theme in Buddhist art of the Tang period: the scene of the Paradise of Amitabha Buddha, in which souls who had gained sufficient merit are reborn from lotus pods. Such a scene is depicted at the base of a Buddhist stele in the Metropolitan Museum that dates from about A.D. 700 (fig. 6). Thus, the patterns on the eleventh-century silks may be regarded as a secularized form of the Buddhist iconography. Moreover, the general pattern of boys in a scroll may owe something to the idea of the "inhabited scroll," which derives ultimately from vine scrolls with Bacchic figures that migrated from the eastern Roman Empire into Asia in the Late Antique period.[42] By the late fifth century, it is already in China, as seen on the sides of the stone bases found in the tomb of Sima Jinlong (d. 484), a member of the Chinese aristocracy who served in the Tuoba kingdom of Northern Wei in North China, in Datong, Shanxi Province.[43] By the eighth century, the human figures have become little boys hanging on to lotus plants. The best-known example is the ornament on the side of the stele of the Chan monk Dazhi Chanshi, dated 736, now in the Shanxi Provincial Museum. The boys in lotus scrolls, which one sees so often on Chinese textiles and ceramics of the Song and Jin dynasties—not to mention Korean celadons of the Koryo period (918–1392)—are all in some way faint reflections of a decorative motif from the Greco-Roman world, but utterly transformed. The boys in the pomegranate are perhaps, to coin a phrase, a pregnant symbol of the ultimate absorption of elements of one or two foreign cultures into another. But the possibility must remain that the motif, so expressive of a basic Chinese aspiration, is a purely Chinese invention, without reference to antecedents.

The upper parts of the boots (cat. no. 10) are made from fragments of a compound-twill silk woven with a design featuring paired geese, a motif particularly common among Liao textiles. Although the complete repeat is not preserved, enough remains to see that the geese flank a vase of flowers on a stand and that clouds fill the interstices. The detail of the geese holding in their bills tendrils from the central floral arrangement recalls the large-scale design on a robe found in the tomb of Yelü Yuzhi (d. 941), in which paired geese flank a knotted ribbon that they hold in their bills.[44] The pattern on Yelü

Yuzhi's robe derives directly from a standard late Tang design—see Emperor Wenzong's edict, mentioned above—just as the silver articles in his tomb are closely modeled on late Tang prototypes. In the design on the boots, the shared knotted ribbon has been replaced by a symmetrically ordered flower arrangement issuing from a vase, which may indicate a later date for the boots, since the representation of a flower arrangement in a vase (as opposed to a bowl) seems to have appeared late in the Liao period.

On the whole, one may view the development of textile design in China from the Tang to the Liao period as a progression from rigid structures bound by geometric frames to an increasingly free composition made up of naturalistic elements, with subject matter and stylistic treatment in common with contemporary painting.

CENTRAL ASIA

Although numerous silks from the Liao dynasty have been recovered from tombs, silk weaving in Central Asia at that time is so little represented as to be practically unknown. We know, however, that one textile, with a design of diamonds, was certainly woven there in the eleventh century. The small-scale diaper pattern of this textile (cat. no. 12) was common during the Tang and continued through the Liao. The attribution is based on the combination of silk warps that are virtually without twist and widely spaced, with cotton foundation wefts and silver supplementary wefts made of flat strips of silvered animal substrate (fig. 7). The date is indicated by datable silk fragments with similar designs and structures in Milan and Riggisberg.[45] The fragment in the church of Sant'Ambrogio, Milan, is rectangular and, like catalogue number 12, is woven with a tabby weave with supplementary wefts. It was sewn to one of the dalmatics of Saint Ambrose when they were being wrapped by Aribert of Antimiano, archbishop of Milan from 1018 to 1045.[46] The second fragment, also a tabby weave with supplementary wefts, now in the Abegg-Stiftung, Riggisberg, is one of several found under the collar of the eleventh-century Vitalis chasuble, originally in the Abbey of Saint Peter, Salzburg.[47] The gold wefts in both the Milan and Riggisberg fragments consist of flat strips of gilded animal substrate. The silk warps in the Riggisberg fragment, moreover, have no perceptible twist and are widely spaced, like those in the Cleveland fragment. The selvages of the Riggisberg and Cleveland fragments consist of tabby-woven borders that use mostly paired warps and an outermost bundle of warps, around which the foundation

Figure 7. Micrographic detail, cat. no. 12

wefts turn. While the fragments in Milan and Riggisberg indicate a date for the Cleveland fragment, the latter, in turn, provides evidence of a Central Asian place of production for the small group. All three textiles made their way to Europe, presumably via trade, where they were preserved in church treasuries.

1. Shepherd and Henning 1959; Shepherd 1981; Belenitskii and Bentovich 1961; Ierusalimskaia 1963, 1967, 1972, and 1996.
2. Shepherd and Henning 1959, figs. 3, 14.
3. Ibid., pp. 22–32, 38–39 (the so-called Zandaniji-I textiles); Shepherd 1981, p. 106.
4. Another Sogdian silk woven with this design is in the British Museum, London (Shepherd 1981, fig. 3).
5. Shepherd 1981, pp. 110–14. For a discussion of the so-called Alexandrian silks, see Falke 1922, pp. 6–9.
6. Ierusalimskaia 1996, pp. 233–95.
7. Shepherd and Henning 1959, figs. 3–12.
8. See note 1. In her latest publication, Ierusalimskaia alludes to four groups (which she does not define) into which the Zandaniji silks can be divided but states that the differences between the groups are not altogether clear (Ierusalimskaia 1996, p. 237).
9. Silks attributed to Sogdiana have often been referred to as Zandaniji because one of them, the ram silk in the Church of Notre-Dame in Huy, Belgium, has an early-eighth-century inscription in Sogdian penned on the back identifying it as such (Shepherd and Henning 1959, pp. 16–17, 38–40). This is the earliest written record of a Zandaniji textile and the only textile directly identified as such. The earliest historical reference to Zandaniji textiles occurs in al-Narshakhi's history of Bukhara, which dates from the tenth century (al-Narshakhi 1954, pp. 15–16). Narshakhi's use of the word *kirbās* in reference to Zandaniji textiles has sometimes been translated as "muslin" (e.g., Serjeant 1972, p. 99), leading some scholars to conclude that by the tenth century, at least, Zandaniji was a type of cotton (Belenitskii and Bentovich 1961, p. 77; Shepherd 1981, p. 108). This, however, may be too specific a

translation of the term *kirbās,* which Richard Frye translates more generically as "cloth" (al-Narshakhi 1954, pp. 15, 16). The authors would like to thank Dr. Sheila Blair for her comments on this term (correspondence to Anne E. Wardwell, August 1, 1996). The thirteenth-century historian Juvaini mentions Zandaniji along with gold-embroidered textiles and cottons that were offered to Chinggis Khan by merchants from Khwarazm (Juvaini 1958, p. 77). And he again distinguishes Zandaniji fabrics from cottons in his account of how much Chinggis Khan was willing to pay for the merchants' textiles (ibid., p. 78). Clearly, Zandaniji textiles were valuable and, by implication in Juvaini's text, were not cotton. Zandaniji may eventually have come to designate cotton cloth (Belenitskii and Bentovich 1961, pp. 77–78), but that does not seem to have happened until after the Mongol period.
10. Summarized in Shepherd 1981, p. 106.
11. Ierusalimskaia, for example, includes two silks that are clearly Chinese, and classifies three with apparently untwisted warps as Zandaniji-I, which otherwise comprises silks with z-twisted warps. Some twist was required to obtain a thread (used for the warp) from silk filaments. But the twist could be so occasional that it cannot be detected in a fragmentary silk. In this catalogue, this is described as untwisted warp. Shepherd likewise assigns to her Zandaniji-II category two silks with twisted warps, even though the category is determined primarily on the basis of untwisted, or *grège,* warps. She also places one silk with apparently untwisted warps in her Zandaniji-I group, which is otherwise composed of silks with twisted warps. In addition, Shepherd draws attention to selvages consisting of a fringe of wefts as an identifying feature of her Zandaniji-I group (Shepherd and Henning 1959, pp. 28, 30). Similar selvages have, however, been found to occur among the silks she assigns to Zandaniji-II: in the collection of Sens Cathedral, nos. 39, 42 (Falke 1922, figs. III, 124), and a small fragment, 32.44 (Shepherd 1981, p. 120, no. 42). The fragment is particularly interesting because toward the top of the selvage is preserved a small fragment of white cotton (?), z.
12. Shepherd 1981, pp. 119–22.
13. Ibid., pp. 116–17.
14. Daniel De Jonghe, correspondence to Anne E. Wardwell, April 3, 1996.
15. Shepherd 1981, p. 117.
16. Hero Granger-Taylor has proposed that the silks with untwisted warps may have been woven farther east than Sogdiana, but he did not specify where (1989, pp. 311–12, 313, 316).
17. Mode 1991–92, p. 179; Narain 1990, pp. 175–76; Mackerras 1990, pp. 318, 325.
18. Dunhuang: Whitfield 1985, pls. 6, 39–32, 40, 41–43; Riboud and Vial 1970, EO. 1207, pl. 43, EO. 1199, pl. 39. Khojo: textile in the collection of the Staatliche Museen zu Berlin, Preussischer Kulturbesitz, Museum für Indische Kunst (acc. no. III 6203). Turfan: Huang Nengfu, Arts and Crafts, 1991, pls. 143, 144; Tatsumura 1963, illus. 1, 3. Dulan: Xu Xinguo and Zhao Feng 1991, figs. 7, 8, 10.
19. Gropp 1974, p. 87. For Zandaniji-II silks with similar motifs, see Ierusalimskaia 1972, figs. 4/1, 13/2, 18; and cat. no. 4.
20. Stein 1907, p. 229; Stein 1921, pp. 903, 1277–78; Stein 1928, p. 673; Gropp 1974, pp. 87–88; Santoro 1994, pp. 43–44.
21. Mode 1991–92, esp. p. 183.
22. Pal 1975, pl. 22a.
23. Mu Shunying 1978, p. 8.
24. For Sogdian examples, see Lu Jiugao and Han Wei 1985, black-and-white pls. 2, 3, 9, 11.
25. Xiang Da 1933.
26. Chen Yinke 1944, chap. 2.
27. *Beishi,* Biography of He Chou, vol. 9, chap. 90, pp. 2985–87.
28. Ibid.
29. Ibid., chap. 82, pp. 2753–59; also *Suishu,* vol. 6, chap. 75, pp. 1709–15.
30. Zhang Yanyuan, *Lidai minghua ji,* in *Huashi congshu* 1974, vol. 1, p. 122.
31. *Xin Tangshu,* vol. 12, chap. 95, p. 3848.
32. For examples on silver, see Lu Jiugao and Han Wei 1985, illus. 76–79.

For examples on ceramics and a discussion of the floral medallion, see Willetts 1965, p. 275.

33. Riegl 1992, chap. 3, "The Introduction of Vegetal Ornament and the Development of the Ornamental Tendril."

34. *Xin Tangshu*, vol. 2, chap. 24, p. 531. The word for "hawk" may be a misprint for another bird. For a more detailed discussion of the changes in patterning of Tang silks, see Zhao Feng, *Tang dai*, 1992, chap. 10.

35. Xu Xinguo and Zhao Feng 1991, pp. 78–79.

36. Matsumoto 1984, pl. 1 and detail, entry on p. 222.

37. Xinjiang Museum, "Tulufan," 1973, pp. 7–27, pls. I, II.

38. Riboud and Vial 1970, pp. 135–36, and pl. 28, EO. 1203/H. See also schéma 1 for EO. 1203/H, p. 137.

39. Zhao Feng, *Tang dai*, 1992, p. 167.

40. Ibid., p. 179.

41. Chen Guo'an 1984, p. 80, fig. 2, and pl. VI 5, 6. Reproduced in Gao Hanyu 1992, pl. 43.

42. Rowland 1956.

43. Datong Municipal Museum 1972, p. 25.

44. Hohhot, Museum of Inner Mongolian Autonomous Region (unpublished).

45. A fragmentary silk band from the stocking of Conrad II (d. 1039) in the cathedral treasury at Speyer is of similar date and design, but its lampas structure and z-spun warps indicate a different provenance (Müller-Christensen et al. 1972, pl. 1455 [bottom], p. 934).

46. Church of Sant'Ambrogio, Milan, inv. s.10 (Granger-Taylor 1983, pp. 130–32).

47. Flury-Lemberg 1988, pp. 158–60, figs. 289, 290.

1. Hunters

Weft-faced compound twill
Warp 21 cm (8¼ in.); weft 42.5 cm (16¾ in.)
Sogdiana, 8th–9th century
The Cleveland Museum of Art. Purchase from the J. H. Wade
Fund (1974.98)

This fragment, preserved in the Church of Saint-Omer, retains the interstices between two rows of aligned roundels, of which small parts of the floral borders remain. The motif of a hunter on horseback shooting backward at a fleeing ibex with head turned back toward the hunter is repeated in both the warp and the weft direction to form units of four hunters and four ibex. Above and below the units of hunters are pairs of confronted rabbits, the upper pair oriented upside down.

The design of this silk derives from Byzantine models and from silks belonging to the so-called Alexandrian school. These motifs, however, have been represented in an abstracted style that, together with the character of the weave, indicates a Sogdian provenance.

TECHNICAL ANALYSIS

Warp: Main: tan silk, z. Binding: tan silk, z. Proportion: 2 main warps to 1 binding warp. Step: 4 main warps. Count: 46 main warps and 23 binding warps per centimeter. *Weft:* Polychrome silk, without apparent twist. Colors: purple, yellow, white, green, and tan. Pass: 5 wefts. Step: 2 passes. Count: 32 passes per centimeter. *Weave:* Weft-faced compound twill, 1/2 z; numerous skipped bindings cause lines in the warp direction.

PUBLICATIONS: Shepherd 1981, no. 36 in table on p. 120; Wardwell 1989, fig. 9, p. 182.

2. Hunters in Roundels

Weft-faced compound twill
Warp 28 cm (11 in.); weft 55.5 cm (21⅞ in.), as mounted
Sogdiana, 8th–9th century
The Cleveland Museum of Art. Gift of the Textile Arts Club
(left roundel: 1959.124); Purchase from the J. H. Wade Fund
(right roundel: 1982.284)

This textile consists of two fragments that have been mounted together.[1] These preserve parts of two roundels from an overall design of tangent roundels that enclose confronted horsemen spearing lions; below are dogs that also attack the lions. The roundels are ornamented with an abstracted floral design; superimposed at their points of tangency are small rosette medallions. In the spandrels are palmette trees. As often occurs in Sogdian silks, the two roundels have different diameters, even though the number of warps per repeat is the same. The loom on which the silk was woven was not equipped with a reed, which would have maintained the even spacing of warps during the weaving process.

These fragments, and other silks closely related in design and technique, were found in Egypt, where they were sewn as ornaments (*segmenta*) on tunics.[2] Nevertheless, the stiff, abstract style and the character of the weave indicate its Sogdian origin.

1. Aesthetic considerations determined the present placement of the roundels; they may originally have belonged to different warp repeats.
2. Shepherd 1981, pp. 110, 122, and figs. 2, 3.

TECHNICAL ANALYSIS

Warp: Main: tan silk, z. Binding: tan silk, z. Proportion: 2 main warps to 1 binding warp. Step: 2 main warps. Count: (1959.124) 44 main warps and 22 binding warps per centimeter; (1982.284) 34 main warps and 17 binding warps per centimeter. *Weft:* Polychrome silk, without apparent twist, entered singly. Colors: rose red, dark blue green, and mustard yellow. Pass: 3 wefts. Step: 2 passes. Count: 31–33 passes per centimeter. *Weave:* Weft-faced compound twill, 1/2 s.

PUBLICATIONS: Left roundel: Shepherd 1974, fig. 53 (illus. of reverse), p. 131; Shepherd 1981, no. 98 in table on p. 122, fig. 4, p. 110; Wardwell 1984, no. 16, p. 24; Neils 1985, p. 359; right roundel: unpublished.

3. Ducks in a Roundel

Weft-faced compound twill
Warp 19.2 cm (7¾ in.); weft 20.3 cm (8 in.)
Central Asia, 8th–9th century
The Metropolitan Museum of Art, New York. Rogers Fund, 1941
(41.119)

The fragment preserves one roundel from a large silk that was woven with similar roundels arranged in aligned rows. Within the roundel, defined by an outer foliate border and an inner pearl border, is a pair of confronted ducks standing on a split palmette. Parts of the interstitial motifs are preserved in the corners.

For technical reasons, in particular, this textile is believed to have been woven in Central Asia, east of Sogdiana, where Sogdian culture was strong but where Chinese weaving traditions prevailed.

TECHNICAL ANALYSIS

Warp: Main: tan silk, mostly without apparent twist (very occasionally a slight s twist can be detected); as a result of the lack of twist, the filaments sometimes separate, giving the appearance of two ends per warp. Binding warp: tan silk, without apparent twist. Proportion: 1 main warp to 1 binding warp. Step: 1 main warp. Count: 18 main warps and 18 binding warps per centimeter. *Weft:* Polychrome silk, without apparent twist, entered singly. Colors: reddish brown, cream, and dark blue. Pass: 3 wefts. Step: 1 pass. Count: 32 passes per centimeter. *Weave:* Weft-faced compound twill, 1/2 z.

PUBLICATION: Shepherd 1981, no. 28 in table on p. 119.

4. Textile with Geometric Design

Weft-faced compound twill
Warp 17.6 cm (6⅞ in.); weft 17.6 cm (6⅞ in.)
Central Asia, late 7th–9th century
The Cleveland Museum of Art. John L. Severance Fund (1950.514)

The textile is woven with rows of aligned roundels, each consisting of a cross-and-star motif encircled by three rings of pearls. Filling the interstices are concentric diamonds, the outermost of which have a pendent rectangle at each point.

As noted above, the fine untwisted warps (see fig. 2 on page 22) indicate that this silk was woven in Central Asia east of Sogdiana, where Sogdian influence was strong but where Chinese weaving traditions prevailed. Geometric patterns are particularly common among silks of this class.

TECHNICAL ANALYSIS

Warp: Main: light tan silk, without apparent twist. Binding: light tan silk, without apparent twist. Proportion: 2 main warps to 1 binding warp. Step: 2 main warps. Count: 36 binding and 18 main warps per centimeter. *Weft:* Polychrome silk, without apparent twist, entered singly. Colors: red, green, and tan. Pass: 3 wefts. Step: 2 passes. Count: 35 passes per centimeter. *Weave:* Weft-faced compound twill, 1/2 z.

PUBLICATION: Shepherd 1981, no. 52 in table on p. 120.

5. Child's Coat and Pants

COAT
Weft-faced compound twill
Length (collar to hem), 48 cm (18⅞ in.); width (across sleeves),
82.5 cm (32½ in.)
Sogdiana, 8th century

PANTS
Damask
Length, 50 cm (19¾ in.)
Tang dynasty (618–907), 8th century

LINING
Damask
Tang dynasty (618–907), 8th century

The Cleveland Museum of Art. Purchase from the J. H. Wade
Fund (coat: 1996.2a); (pants: 1996.2b)

This remarkable coat and pants, made to fit a very young child, belong to a rare set of garments dating from the eighth century. The coat is cut in at the waist and flares toward the hem. It has a front opening with facings flared toward the hem, a round collar, and long sleeves, which are only very slightly tapered. The front and back sections were cut separately and seamed at the shoulders so that the pattern would be correctly oriented both front and back. The side seams extend from the underarm only to the waist. The sleeves, collar, and front facings were cut separately and seamed. There are no buttons, loops, or ties, nor is there any evidence of fastening devices that have since been lost. The straight-cut pants are made of three parts: two rectangles folded down their length and joined by an inseam, a center front seam, and a back seam; the third piece is a square folded to form a triangle and inserted into the inseam at the crotch.

The outer fabric of the coat is a Sogdian silk, while the outer silk of the pants and the silk lining of both the pants and the coat are Chinese. The Sogdian silk is a compound twill woven with a design derived from Sasanian Iranian imagery. Aligned pearl roundels enclose paired, confronted ducks that stand on split palmettes; four-directional palmettes fill the interstices. The attributes of the birds—the ribbons (*patif*), the collars, and the necklaces held between each pair—are Sasanian in origin. In contrast to the Sasanian prototypes, however, the stiffness and abstraction of both the motifs and the details are characteristically Sogdian.

Detail, cat. no. 5

5, coat

Figure 8. Coat. Eastern Han dynasty (25–220). Silk, length 133 cm (52⅜ in.). Xinjiang Uyghur Autonomous Regional Museum, Urumqi

Similarly, the decorative elements belong to a particular repertory seen in other Sogdian silks: ducks with unwebbed feet pointing downward, a symmetrical arrangement of ducks placed in pairs on split palmettes, a motif of four small hearts pointing to the center to form rosettes that ornament the ducks, pearl borders, and the form of the four-directional palmettes.[1] Also typical is the spacing of the roundels, which are nearly tangent in the weft direction but more widely spaced in the warp direction. The use of five colors and the proportion of three main warps to each binding warp, moreover, are characteristic of silks that have been solidly attributed to Sogdiana (see fig. 1 on page 22).[2] The fabric is one of the few Sogdian silks that preserves its original colors.

The coat is lined with a Chinese damask silk woven with a large-scale floral pattern composed of a central rosette encircled by two wreaths of flowers. Only portions of the

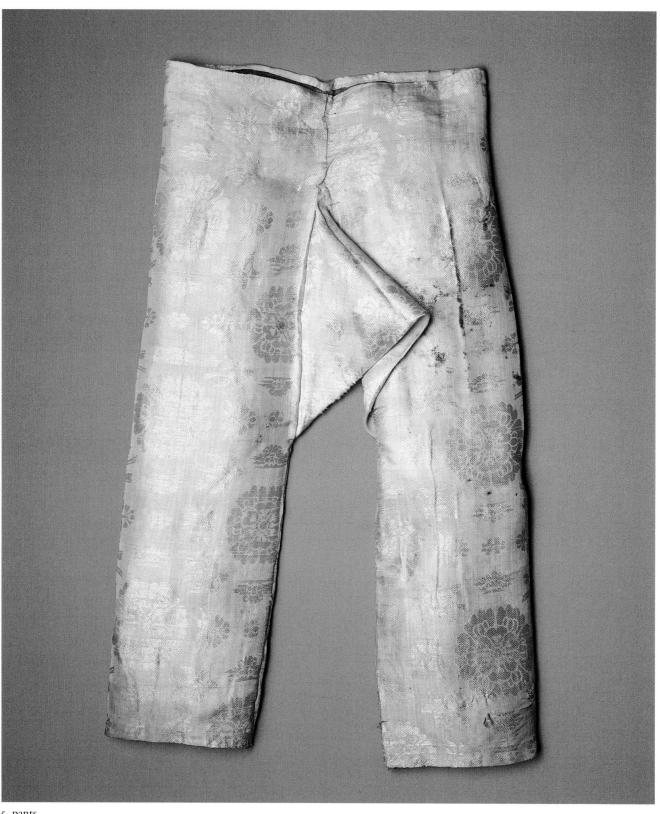

5, pants

large, elaborate quatrefoil that filled the interstices are preserved in the cut of the lining. Originating at the beginning of the eighth century, this pattern became one of the dominant—and most elegant—decorative motifs of the Tang period (see also cat. no. 6). Most of the extant silks with this design have been preserved in the Shōsō-in imperial treasury and the Hōryū-ji in Nara, Japan.[3]

The pants are made from a white twill-patterned silk, also woven in China. The reverse inverted repeats consist of large rosettes surrounded by flowers at the cardinal points and, between, flying birds carrying floral sprigs in their beaks. The apparently loose structure of the pattern and the degree of naturalism of the motifs are characteristic of a trend in patterning that began in the High Tang.

36

This type of pattern evolved shortly after the floral pattern of the lining. That the pants are lined with the same floral silk as the jacket shows, however, that the two patterns coexisted for a time during the eighth century. Other silks woven with this pattern occur among the Tang silks preserved since the eighth century in the Shōsō-in repository and the Hōryū-ji.[4]

Because the study of costume from this period has been based almost entirely on paintings and sculpture, comparative images are limited to outer garments, with only the briefest indications (usually at the neck and wrists) of layers worn beneath. It is therefore not known where the coat and pants fit into the sequence of layers that made up the original costume, nor the number and nature of the additional garments that initially completed it.[5] A small pair of boots, made from the same Sogdian silk as the coat and now in a private collection, most likely belonged to the costume.[6] And, almost certainly, there was an additional pair of pants made from the Sogdian silk that would have been worn over the white silk pants. Because examples of this type of coat are represented neither in paintings nor in sculptures from the period, we can assume that it was probably not the outermost garment of the costume. The closest example to this coat in cut is a coat dating from the Eastern Han period (A.D. 25–220) that was retrieved from a man's grave in Minfeng County, Xinjiang Province (fig. 8). This suggests that the child's coat, and the costume to which it belonged, was a Central Asian type that endured over a long period of time and, further, that the coat and pants were intended for a little boy.

Nothing is known of the history of the coat and pants other than that they are said to have been preserved in Tibet. This would not be surprising, since Tibet's imperialistic initiatives during the seventh and eighth centuries brought it into frequent contact with both China and Sogdiana,[7] and because at the height of its powers during the reign of Khri-stron Lde-brtsan (755–97), Tibet controlled part of Sichuan Province, the Gansu Corridor, Qinghai, and the eastern part of present-day Xinjiang, including Turfan.[8] Considering the cut of the coat and the combination of Sogdian and Chinese silks, this set of garments may very well have been made within Tibet or Tibetan-controlled territories during the eighth century. If so, it is an exceedingly rare set, from the period of the early Tibetan kings (ca. A.D. 600–842), a chapter of Tibet's history from which only traces of material culture have survived.

1. Shepherd and Henning 1959, figs. 3, 14.
2. Ibid., the so-called Zandaniji-I textiles; Shepherd 1981, p. 106.
3. Matsumoto 1984, pls. 1, 8, 10.
4. See, for example, ibid., pls. 92, 93.
5. There is also, in a private collection (unpublished), a garment consisting of two parts joined at the waist and opening down the front: the upper segment has very short sleeves and, like the child's coat, a round collar and facings along the front opening, which flair toward the waist; the lower portion is a very slightly gathered skirt. The garment measures about 30 inches from collar to hem. Whereas the upper part is made from the same Sogdian silk and lined with the same Tang silk as the coat, the skirt consists of a lightweight dark blue silk woven with a lozenge-diaper pattern. Like the coat, the garment has no fastening devices or evidence of ever having had any. It appears to be a type that would have been worn by a small girl. However, because we have virtually no images of small girls from the period, this cannot at present be confirmed. Consequently, it remains uncertain if this type of garment, together with the coat, pants, and boots, would have constituted a single costume, or if they would have belonged to two separate costumes. We are rather inclined to the latter, given the similarity of the coat to a man's coat excavated in Xinjiang Province (fig. 8).
6. Private collection, unpublished.
7. See Beckwith 1987; numerous references to Tibet in Twitchett 1979, pp. 285–86, 430–33; and Hoffman 1994, pp. 376–85.
8. Hoffman 1994, p. 383.

TECHNICAL ANALYSIS

COAT: *Warp:* Main: ecru silk, z. Binding: ecru silk, z. Proportion: 3 main warps to 1 binding warp. Step: 3 main warps. Count: 48 main warps and 16 binding warps per centimeter. *Weft:* Silk, without apparent twist and interrupted. Colors: rose red, deep blue, green, yellow, and white. Pass: 3 wefts, each entered singly. Step: 2 passes. Count: 33 passes per centimeter. *Weave:* Weft-faced compound twill, 1/2 s. There are a number of flaws, in particular, skipped binding warps that leave vertical lines of short weft floats, or wefts on the face passing under instead of over the main warps.

PANTS: *Warp:* White silk, s and z (slight twists), single. Step: 1 warp. Count: 52 warps per centimeter. *Weft:* White silk, without apparent twist. Step: 1 weft. Count: 40 wefts per centimeter. *Weave:* Damask: the ground is a 2/1 s twill, and the pattern a 1/4 s twill. Flaws consist of warps and wefts passing over or under the wrong number of threads, but these do not repeat vertically.

LINING: *Warp:* Brown silk, without apparent twist, single. Step: 1 warp. Count: 48 warps per centimeter. *Weft:* Brown silk, without apparent twist, much denser than warp. Step: 1 weft. Count: 25 wefts per centimeter. *Weave:* Damask, 3/1 twill z for the ground, and the reverse (1/3 twill s) for the pattern. There are occasional flaws in the binding sequence. Selvage: 5 millimeters wide, dense tabby weave; the wefts turn around a single outermost warp, which has a strong z twist.

PUBLICATIONS: "American Museum News," 1996, pp. 51–52; Wardwell, "Clothes," 1996, pp. 4–5; Wardwell, "For Lust of Knowing," 1996, p. 73; Ames et al. 1997, p. 94.

6

6. Floral Medallions

Weft-faced compound twill
Warp 62.7 cm (24⅝ in.); weft 71.5 cm (28⅛ in.)
Tang dynasty (618–907), late 8th–early 9th century
The Metropolitan Museum of Art, New York. Purchase, Joseph Pulitzer Bequest, 1996 (1996.103.1)

The arrangement of floral medallions interspersed with quatrefoil motifs was one of the dominant design patterns in textiles and other decorative arts of the High Tang period (roughly the first half of the eighth century). The floral medallion persisted into the late Tang, and the small floral rosette one sees in Liao textiles may be regarded as a vestige of the larger Tang medallion (see cat. nos. 8 and 9). In a way this motif never disappeared, and different versions of it can be seen in Ming and Qing textiles, especially those in the "antique" style.

The other component of this pattern, the quatrefoil motif, also survived in various forms and can be seen not only in textiles but in other decorative arts in northern Asia until at least the thirteenth century. It appears, in a very much simplified form, both in inlaid porcelain and in lacquer of the Koryo period (918–1392) in Korea.[1] Later revivals of this motif also appear on eighteenth-century Chinese porcelain.[2]

The most remarkable aspect of this textile is the weave structure—one seen commonly in textiles of the tenth century and later (see cat. nos. 8–10)—as both the face and the reverse (fig. 9) are bound in a weft-faced 1/2 twill. It is the only example known to the authors with both this structure and a typical Tang design.

1. For examples in Koryo inlaid celadon, see *Koryo* 1989, nos. 238, 242. The floral sprays seen in many other pieces may be regarded as an adaptation of this pattern. For an example in Koryo inlaid lacquer, see *Oriental Lacquer* 1977, no. 262.
2. Fong and Watt 1996, pp. 522–23, pls. 314, 315.

TECHNICAL ANALYSIS

Warp: Main: tan silk, s, thin, paired. Binding: tan silk, s (the fibers are sometimes split to give the appearance of the warp's being paired). Proportion: 1 paired warp to 1 binding warp. Step: 1 paired warp. Count: 16 pairs of main warps and 16 binding warps per centimeter. *Weft:* Polychrome silk, without apparent twist, entered singly. Colors: brown, dark blue, light blue, yellow, and cream. Pass: 5 wefts. Step: 1 pass. Count: 18 passes per centimeter. *Weave:* Weft-faced compound twill, 1/2 s binding on the face, 1/2 z binding on the reverse. Along one weft edge is a starting (or finishing) edge consisting of three stripes of cream, brown, and yellow wefts, which intersects the design along the weft axis.

PUBLICATION: MMA *Recent Acquisitions* 1995–1996, p. 77, illus.

Figure 9. Reverse, cat. no. 6

7. Boys in Pomegranates

Gauze, painted
Warp 50.6 cm (19⅞ in.); weft 13.5 cm (5⅜ in.)
China, 10th century
The Metropolitan Museum of Art, New York. Purchase, Eileen W.
Bamberger Bequest, in memory of her husband, Max Bamberger,
1995 (1995.143)

This strip is decorated with two repeat patterns, one of pomegranates containing birds and the other of pomegranates containing boys. It is painted in ink, blue and brown pigments, and gold leaf on a complex gauze ground, with the unpatterned area brush-dyed green. The textile is folded in half lengthwise and stitched along one edge, with the patterns repeated on the reverse.

The pattern with birds consists of three pomegranates and three leaves growing from a stalk. All three pomegranates and one of the leaves contain a bird, and each of the four birds is unique. The theme of birds in a floral scroll is common to Tang (618–907) decorative arts and is seen on silver and on the backs of bronze mirrors.

The pattern with boys is incomplete. It consists of two full and one partial pomegranate, each containing a boy adorned with neckband and bracelets in gold leaf. The iconography of this motif is discussed on pages 26–27.

A related theme and what is perhaps a similar type of object can be seen among the Pelliot finds from Dunhuang.[1]

1. See Riboud and Vial 1970, EO. 1204, pl. 64.

TECHNICAL ANALYSIS

Warp: Dark green silk, s (slight twist). Count: 75 per centimeter. *Weft:* Dark green silk, without apparent twist. Count: 21 per centimeter. *Weave:* Gauze, with units of four warps. The design is drawn and painted.

Unpublished.

Detail, cat. no. 7

7

8. Purse

Outer fabric: Weft-faced compound twill
Height 9 cm (3½ in.); width 13.7 cm (5⅜ in.)
Liao dynasty (907–1125)
The Metropolitan Museum of Art, New York. Eileen W.
Bamberger Bequest, in memory of her husband, Max Bamberger,
1996 (1996.39)

The silk from which this purse was made is a compound-twill weave that is weft-faced on both sides and has weft floats on the face, a structure commonly seen on Liao silks and one that provides a secure means of dating the textile. The pattern is a free composition of floral rosettes surrounded by leaping deer, running and tumbling boys, birds, and various floral and leafy motifs. Individual elements, such as the young deer and the boys at play, are favorite themes in the decorative arts of Central Asia, going back to Tang times (618–907).[1] The silk must have been woven expressly for the purpose of making small objects such as this purse, as the scale of the images fits well within the format.

1. The theme of boys playing is seen in paintings from Astana dating from the eighth century. See, for example, *Xinjiang Museum* 1987, pl. 154 and captions for pls. 47 and 154.

TECHNICAL ANALYSIS

OUTER FABRIC: *Warp:* Main: tan silk, usually without apparent twist (although an occasional slight s twist can be detected), thin, paired. Binding: tan silk, without apparent twist (the fibers sometimes separate, giving the appearance of the warp's being paired or triple). Proportion: 1 paired main warp to 1 binding warp. Step: 1 paired main warp. Count: 21 pairs of main warps and 21 binding warps per centimeter. *Weft:* Polychrome silk, without apparent twist, entered singly. Colors: reddish tan, pinkish tan, light blue, dark blue, and white. Pass: 5 wefts. Step: 1 pass. Count: 48 passes per centimeter. *Weave:* Weft-faced compound twill with weft floats. On the face the binding is 1/2 z, on the reverse 1/2 s. In areas of weft floats, the wefts on the face of the textile float, while the wefts of the remaining colors carried on the reverse are bound by the binding warps. The blue wefts, when on the face, always float, while the tan wefts on the face sometimes float and are sometimes bound.

RIBBON: *Warp and weft:* Reddish tan silk, without apparent twist. Warp step: 4; weft step: 2. Count: approximately 64 warps and 44 wefts per centimeter. *Weave:* Tabby, *liseré* (floats of wefts over 5 warps).

8, back of purse

CONSTRUCTION: The purse is composed of a rectangular piece, with one end cut in a bracketed outline, and two oval pieces that form the sides. The rectangular fabric is folded twice to create three sections. The two side pieces are sewn to the bottom and middle sections; the third section (with the bracketed end) overlaps the front of the purse when closed. The purse is secured by a ribbon sewn to the front overlap, which is wrapped around the purse and tied.

Unpublished.

8

9. Flowers, Cranes, and Clouds

Weft-faced compound twill
Warp 37.1 cm (14⅝ in.); weft 46.6 cm (18⅜ in.)
Liao dynasty (907–1125), 10th century
The Cleveland Museum of Art. John L. Severance Fund
(1992.112a)

This fragment preserves part of an overall design of large radiating floral motifs arranged in two staggered horizontal rows; in the interstices are pairs of flying cranes and cloud scrolls, the clouds occurring at the cardinal points of the floral motifs and the cranes between them. In the warp direction, the pattern repeats in mirror reverse.[1]

The fragment comes from a garment that had a thin silk tabby lining with a layer of silk batting between the outer fabric and the lining; seams are preserved in the upper left portion. A larger part of the garment, which preserves incrustation from a metal belt, is also in The Cleveland Museum of Art.[2] The design is difficult to read as a result of extensive discoloration from burial, and the garment cannot be reconstructed. A third fragment was on the London market (fig. 10).

The pattern may be regarded as a highly dissolved version of a late Tang design, with a large floral medallion in the center surrounded by floral sprays, flying birds, and clouds (see pants in cat. no. 5). The relative scale of the medallion and the surrounding elements is the reverse of the late Tang pattern.

1. Technically known as a reverse inverted repeat (Burnham 1980, p. 108).
2. Acc. no. 1992.112; unpublished.

TECHNICAL ANALYSIS

OUTER FABRIC: *Warp:* Main: tan silk, s (very slight twist), thin, paired. Binding: tan silk, mostly without apparent twist, though a slight s twist occasionally occurs, paired (the ends do not always lie side by side; at times one lies over another so that the warp appears single), thin. Proportion: 1 pair (occasionally 3 ends) of main warps to 1 pair of binding warps. Step: 1 pair of main warps. Count: approximately 36 pairs of main warps and 36 pairs of binding warps per centimeter. *Weft:* Polychrome silk, without apparent twist. Colors: dark reddish tan, tan, cream, light blue, and dark blue. Pass: 5 wefts. Step: 1 pass. Count: 17 passes per centimeter. *Weave:* Weft-faced compound twill, 1/2 z binding on face, 1/2 s binding on reverse. Selvage:[1] 4 bundles of unplied warps followed by 8 cords (each composed of 2 silk threads plied z, each thread composed of groups of threads without twist, plied s). The selvage is woven in a simple 1/2 z twill; all wefts turn around the outermost cord.

LINING: *Warp:* Light tan silk, without apparent twist. Count: 68 per centimeter. *Weft:* Light tan silk, without apparent twist. Count: 34 per centimeter. *Weave:* Tabby. Selvage: extends for 8 millimeters, warps are closely spaced, wefts turn around outermost warp.

1. Preserved on the larger fragment, CMA 1992.112.

Unpublished.

Figure 10. Textile with flowers, cranes, and clouds. Liao dynasty (907–1125), 10th century. Silk, weft-faced compound twill. Warp 35.5 cm (14 in.); weft 33 cm (13 in.). Jacqueline Simcox, Ltd.

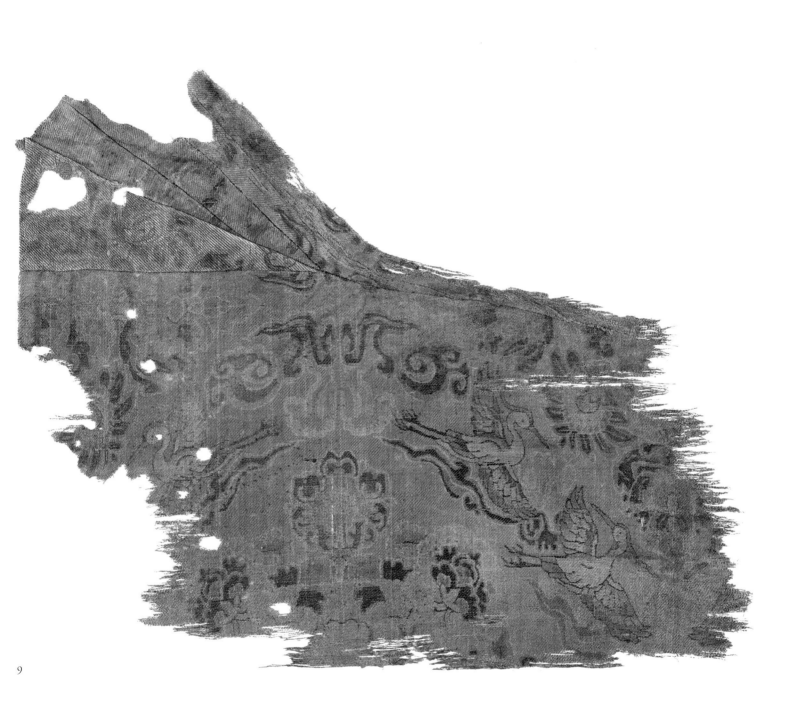

9

10. Pair of Short Boots

Outer fabric: Weft-faced compound twill; silk tapestry (kesi)
1992.350: Top of boot to bottom of heel 32.8 cm (12⅞ in.); toe to
heel, ca. 25 cm (9¾ in.)
1992.349: Top of boot to bottom of heel 34.9 cm (13¾ in.); toe to
heel, ca. 25 cm (9¾ in.)
Liao dynasty (907–1125)
The Cleveland Museum of Art. John L. Severance Fund
(1992.349; 1992.350)

The boots are made of two different outer fabrics: a figured compound-twill silk for the leg portion and silk-and-gold tapestry (*kesi*) for the foot section. At the top of the instep is a lip of three half scallops that was made from the same fabric as the leg portion. The top edge of the lip is finished by blanket stitching, which continues around the upper edge of the sides and the heel of the foot. A vertical line of plaited chain stitches ornaments the back of the heel and the center of the toe. Each boot is lined with a thin tan silk tabby. Silk batting lies between the lining and the outer compound-twill fabric of the leg portions. The foot is reinforced with leather between the lining and the *kesi*. The tops of the boots are incomplete, but both soles (silk tabby and silk gauze with silk batting between) are preserved.

Because the weft-faced compound-twill silk has been pieced, its complete repeat cannot be reconstructed. The pieces, however, preserve parts of two geese flanking a vase of flowers on a stand. In the surrounding space are cloud scrolls.[1]

The motif of paired birds facing one another across a plant or floral arrangement goes back to the Tang period in China (see, for example, cat. no. 49) and to earlier periods in Central Asia and farther west. However, the depiction of a flower arrangement in a vase appears to be a late development in the evolution of this motif. The earliest-known representations in painting of a flower arrangement in a vase are on the walls of the tomb of Zhang Shiqing (d. 1116), a Liao official, in Xuanhua (fig. 77).[2] Among the extant paintings from the Song imperial court is one that depicts a flower arrangement in a slender vase on a stand. It is attributed to the lady painter Yao Yuehua and inscribed by the Song emperor Ningzong (r. 1195–1224).[3] The secular use of flowers in a vase for decoration, as opposed to flowers in a bowl or basket as offerings to Buddhist deities, seems to have become fashionable in the Song period (960–1279).[4] The vases of flowers painted on the walls of the Xuanhua tomb, numbering eighteen in all, are placed in niches and appear to serve a purely decorative function. As Xuanhua is near the border with Song and the date of the tomb is late in the Liao dynasty, and as

Zhang Shiqing was Chinese, we may conjecture that the fashion for flower arrangements in a vase was filtered across the border of the two countries sometime in the eleventh century. These boots would therefore date from the second half of the Liao dynasty.

The *kesi* feet of the boots, also pieced, preserve what appear to be parts of a design of cloud scrolls and possibly also of birds. The substrate of the gold thread has disintegrated in burial, leaving the gold leaf adhering to the warps.[5] Although little can be said about the design, the exceptionally fine tapestry technique is characteristic of *kesi* produced during the Liao dynasty, such as on the knee-high imperial boots (cat. no. 23).

Despite the fact that the boots are incomplete at the top, they are clearly different in style from the imperial boots. Possibly, they were short boots. The costume of a Khitan woman found in a tomb at Wanzishan, Inner Mongolia, included a pair of silk short boots that were worn with a skirt, a vest, three short jackets, and three long outer robes.[6] And silver-gilt replicas of two pairs of short boots were discovered in the tomb of a Khitan princess and her husband.[7] That the Cleveland boots were pieced together, apparently from remnants, is evidence that they were not made for a member of the imperial family. The boots of a military officer found in a thirteenth-century tomb at Salt Lake, between Urumqi and Turfan, Xinjiang, also have external covers made up of *kesi* remnants (see cat. no. 15).

1. Another piece of this fabric (on the market) included, additionally, a bird in flight with two long tail feathers.
2. See *Xuanhua Liao bihua mu* 1975 and Laing 1994.
3. *Songren Huace* 1957, vol. 2, no. 54.
4. For a historical survey of flower arrangements in Japan and China, see *Hanaike* 1982.
5. The substrate was, in all likelihood, proteinaceous (see cat. no. 51) but not tanned leather, which can survive in soil (Crowfoot et al. 1992, p. 2).
6. Inner Mongolia 1985, pp. 72–87.
7. Inner Mongolia 1993, pp. 38–39, and pl. VIII.

TECHNICAL ANALYSIS

COMPOUND TWILL (LEG PORTION): *Warp:* Main: tan silk, virtually untwisted (although occasionally a faint s or z twist can

10

be detected), paired. Binding: tan silk, virtually untwisted (although occasionally a faint s or z twist can be detected), thin, paired. Proportion: 1 pair of main warps to 1 pair of binding warps. Step: 1 pair of main warps. Count: 25 pairs of main warps and 25 pairs of binding warps per centimeter. *Weft:* Polychrome silk, without apparent twist and much denser than the warps. Colors: deep blue, pale blue, light tan, and tan. Pass: 4 wefts. Step: 1 pass. Count: 16 passes per centimeter. *Weave:* Weft-faced compound twill, 1/4 satin binding on both face and reverse. Sewn with tan silk, s, 2-ply z.

KESI (FOOT PORTION): *Warp:* Tan silk, s (very slight twist), 2-ply z. Count: 25 per centimeter. *Weft:* 1) Polychrome silk, s. Colors: purple, pale blue (striated), faded coral(?), and two tans that may originally have been red or pink. Count: approximately 80–200 per centimeter. 2) Gold thread: the substrate of the gold thread has entirely disintegrated, leaving the gold leaf adhering to the warps. The original passage of the wefts over and under the warps can occasionally be detected in the disposition of the

gold leaf. *Weave:* Tapestry (*kesi*) with slit joins and occasional toothed joins (very rare). Vertical diagonals are accomplished mostly with warp steps, sometimes with soumak, and occasionally with toothed joins. In spite of the curvilinear design, there is no eccentric weaving nor are the warps bent; the wefts are all at right angles to the warp. The center seams of the heel and the toe are covered with plaited chain stitches using faded green and tan silks, z, plied s. The boots were lined and the soles (made separately) were attached.

LINING: *Warp and weft:* Cream silk, without apparent twist; 60 per centimeter (warp), and 60 per centimeter (weft). *Weave:* Tabby. Selvage: warps are more closely spaced; wefts turn around the outermost warp.

CONSTRUCTION (LEG AND FOOT): The upper part of each boot has been pieced together. The heel and toe portions of the foot section are sewn together with tan silk, z, plied s, and tan silk, s, plied z. The top edges of the lip and the heel portion of the foot

47

are finished with blanket stitches using doubled threads of tan silk, s, plied z, or faded green silk, z, plied s. The boots are lined with silk. Between the outer fabric and the lining is a layer of silk batting in the leg portions and leather in the silk portions.

SOLES: 1) OUTER FABRIC: *Warp:* Golden brown silk, occasionally s or z, but generally without apparent twist. Count: approximately 56 per centimeter. *Weft:* Golden brown silk, occasionally s, but generally without apparent twist, about three times the density of the warps. Count: 17 per centimeter. *Weave:* Gauze, based on unit of 4 warps.[1] 2) LINING: *Warp:* Tan silk, occasionally s (slight twist). Count: approximately 46 per centimeter. *Weft:* Tan silk, without apparent twist. Count: 30–32 per centimeter. *Weave:*

Tabby (fairly loose weave). 3) SILK BATTING: Between the outer fabric and the lining is a layer of silk batting.

CONSTRUCTION: The outer fabric is covered with running stitches in parallel rows about 3 millimeters apart using silk thread, z, and 2-ply s. The stitching probably secures the inner layer of batting to the outer fabric. The lining and outer fabric are sewn together around the periphery of the sole.

1. For this type, see Riboud and Vial 1970, EO. 1205 bis, p. 385.

Unpublished.

11. *Boys in a Floral Scroll*

Twill damask (ling)
Warp 33 cm (13 in.); weft 29.2 cm (11½ in.)
Northern Song dynasty (960–1127), 11th–12th century
The Metropolitan Museum of Art, New York. Rogers Fund,
1952 (52.8)

This textile is of a type known as *ling* (twill and twill), which began to appear in the Tang period (618–907) and was one of the most popular weaves in the silks of the Song (960–1279) and Yuan (1279–1368) dynasties.[1] The pattern is very similar to that on another fragment found in a Northern Song tomb in Hengyang, Hunan Province (fig. 11).[2] Technically, the two pieces are identical, including the weave structure and the s twist of the warp; the weft is untwisted. As noted earlier (see pp. 8–9), the theme of boys and pomegranates or lotus pods is a rebus for progeny. What adds particular interest to this piece is that it was found in Rayy, Iran, where quantities of ceramics of the twelfth and thirteenth centuries have been excavated, including Chinese trade pottery of this period.[3] Because the Chinese ceramics found at this site, all from southern Chinese kilns, were exported through sea trade, it is almost certain that this silk arrived in Iran by the same route.

1. Zhao Feng, *Sichou,* 1992, pp. 40–43.
2. Chen Guo'an 1984, p. 80, fig. 2, and pl. VI 5, 6.
3. Mikami Tsugio 1969, p. 149.

TECHNICAL ANALYSIS

Warp: Cream silk, s (single). Count: approximately 50 per centimeter. *Weft:* Cream silk, without twist. Count: 30 per centimeter. *Weave:* Twill damask. Ground: 1/5 s twill. Pattern: 5/1 s twill. Selvage: The pattern ends about 1 centimeter from the outermost

Figure 11. Textile with boys in a floral scroll, detail. Northern Song dynasty (960–1127). Twill damask (*ling*). Hunan Provincial Museum, Changsha

edge; the border is a 2/1 s twill binding of the wefts by bundles of warps (3–4 warps per bundle); at the outside edge, the wefts turn around the outermost bundle of warps. The design is oriented at right angles to the warp.

PUBLICATION: Jenyns 1981, no. 27, illus., p. 67.

11

12. Textile with Diamonds

Tabby with supplementary weft
Warp 51.5 cm (20¼ in.); weft 30.3 cm (11⅞ in.)
Central Asia, 11th century
The Cleveland Museum of Art. John L. Severance Fund (1993.139)

The textile, in very fragmentary condition, is woven with an overall design of tiny diamonds within a diamond grid (repeat: 7 mm × 1.2 cm); a complete selvage is preserved along one side. In China at this time, small-scale patterns of diamonds were generally reserved for silks intended as undergarments or linings. The use of silver thread for the tiny diamonds in this example may indicate the greater importance of the design in Central Asia.

This is one of the very few Central Asian textiles that have survived from the eleventh century. The wide spacing of virtually untwisted silk warps combined with cotton foundation wefts and silver supplementary wefts consisting of flat strips of silvered animal substrate confirm a Central Asian attribution (see fig. 7). The textile is closely related stylistically and technically to two fragments preserved in Milan and Riggisberg, for which compelling evidence of an eleventh-century date exists.

TECHNICAL ANALYSIS

Warp: Ecru silk, without apparent twist, very thin, single. Step: 2 warps. Count: 24 per centimeter. *Weft:* Foundation: white cotton, z (unevenly twisted). Lancé: silver thread, flat strips of animal substrate, coated with a dark reddish brown adhesive and a layer of silver (on one side only);[1] the silver wefts are coated with translucent varnish, now yellowed. Pass: 1 foundation weft and 1 supplementary weft. Step: 1 pass. Count: 12 passes per centimeter. *Weave:* Tabby weave with supplementary weft. The warps are grouped in twos with spaces between (fig. 7); the cotton foundation wefts lie beside the silver supplementary wefts. The silver wefts float where needed for the pattern and are otherwise bound with the cotton foundation wefts. A complete selvage is preserved on one side. Eight millimeters from the outermost edge, the silver wefts on the reverse turn back, passing under the adjacent cotton weft. In the selvage border, paired (though occasionally single) warps and foundation wefts form a tabby binding. Toward the outermost edge, the warps are closely spaced. The foundation wefts turn around the outermost warp, which is tripled.

1. Determined by X-ray fluorescence spectrometry by Bruce Christman, chief conservator, The Cleveland Museum of Art.

Unpublished.

12

2. Kesi: Silk Tapestry

Of all the major categories of luxury textiles in China, *kesi* poses the most problems with regard to its origin and early development. Recent archaeological finds in northern and western China and the appearance on the market of material from centuries-old collections have provided many clues toward solving these problems, but we are at present far from being able to write a definitive account of the early history of tapestry weaving in China.

What has come to light in the past two decades are several distinct groups which can be defined technically and stylistically. In one or two cases, it is possible to associate a particular group thus identified with archaeological finds. Another group can be compared with old *kesi* preserved in the National Palace Museum, Taipei, and in the Liaoning Provincial Museum, Shenyang. By means of comparative studies, we can attempt to place the various groups in broad historical and geographical contexts, even if the details remain to be filled in later. The *kesi* in this exhibition are divided into groups according to this line of inquiry. The nomenclature is tentative and is intended to facilitate discussion.

THE CENTRAL ASIAN GROUP

There are a number of *kesi* that in their patterning display distinct characteristics of the arts of Central Asia. Two of these, catalogue numbers 13 and 14, form one group. The most conspicuous aspect of their patterns is the depiction of real or mythical animals and birds on a floral ground. The animal and bird images, as well as the border decorations, seem to derive from the eclectic art of eastern Central Asia (the eastern half of Xinjiang), which developed during the Tang period (618–907), displaying influences from various sources, particularly Sogdiana and interior Tang China.

The combination of flora and fauna in decorative patterns is not unique to Central Asia. What is so distinctive about the patterns on the *kesi* of the type that we have tentatively identified as of eastern Central Asian origin is the way the floral ground is treated. Unlike most flora and fauna patterns, in which the entire design is "homogenized" into a pattern of repeating elements of uniform size and even distribution (see, for example, cat. no. 19), the floral ground of the type of *kesi* in question is a complex composition of floral sprays of varying scale and "species," creating an unevenness both in spatial distribution and in the size of the pictorial elements. The result is a liveliness in the design that is not often seen in most background patterns. The liveliness of the floral ground is matched by that of the animals, especially the dragon in catalogue number 13. Another aspect of the general exuberance of these patterns is the brilliant use of color. The colors, we note, are used both naturalistically and in a purely decorative manner. Thus, whereas most of the leaves are shades of green and yellow in catalogue number 13, some are shades of blue. A parallel phenomenon is seen in the floral pattern, where blossoms and leaves of different plants are represented as issuing from the same stem. This combination of naturalistic representation and creative patternmaking is one of the hallmarks of the decorative art style of Central Asia in the medieval period and was to influence to no small extent Chinese decorative arts when it was introduced to interior China during the Yuan dynasty (1279–1368).

Catalogue number 15 seems to be closely related to these *kesi*. As in catalogue number 14, the bottom part of the design consists of two horizontal bands bound by borders of rosettes and other floral elements that contain similar designs which do not relate to the main pattern above. The main pattern is also composed of bands, but without a graphic border. There are discontinuous stripes that indicate the ground and also serve to demarcate the bands. Again, however, the design is composed of animals and birds on a floral ground. This pattern is strikingly similar to that of some *kesi* fragments found at Salt Lake (Yanhu), between Urumqi and Turfan, Xinjiang (see fig. 23), dating probably from the thirteenth century. There is also considerable animation in the treatment of both the birds in flight in the lower bands and the striding peacocks in the main pattern. Compared with catalogue numbers 13 and 14, however, these designs are somewhat less exuberant and inventive.

Catalogue number 16 has an even more placid design, but nevertheless must also belong to the eastern Central Asian type. The "floral" ground is reduced to a uniform pattern of leaves but endowed with different colors in blocks without borders. Floating on this ground are aquatic fowl and animals (the only animal seen on this fragment is upside down). There is another *kesi* with a similar pattern that includes part of a medallion (about which more will be said later).[1]

Other Central Asian *kesi* are distinguished by a pattern that exhibits a style distinctly different from those discussed above. It is characterized by a compact composition of repeats of similar, if not identical, elements (see, for example, cat. nos. 17, 18, and 19). Again, the motifs are of various origins. On one piece in this group, catalogue number 19, the lions are based on Persian models while the palmettes have antecedents both in the Iranian world and in Central Asia. The two other *kesi*, catalogue numbers 17 and 18, include dragons with clouds and flaming pearls, all basically Chinese motifs but treated in an un-Chinese manner. Apart from the somewhat eccentric form of the dragons, the way they are tightly packed together is highly unusual in a Chinese context. The Persian influence on the patterns, together with the drawloom design of the lions and the absence of frames or borders, suggests that this type of Central Asian *kesi* may have originated in the early Mongol period in the thirteenth century, when there were massive movements of artisans, including weavers, from the eastern Iranian world into eastern Central Asia.[2] It is also possible, though less likely, that these *kesi* were woven farther west by Uyghurs living in the Khotan area. The transmission of eastern Iranian culture to western Central Asia by the Karakhanids, following their conquest of the region in the early eleventh century, opens the possibility that the Uyghurs in the region adopted eastern Iranian patterns and motifs. In connection with this hypothesis, it should be noted that the Karakhanids were in control of Bukhara for a short period in the tenth century. This hypothesis is also based on the assumption that the weaving of *kesi* was already practiced in the Khotan area by the eleventh century.

All these *kesi*, and related specimens known in the West, are fragments of relatively small size. They are rectangular in shape and were preserved for many centuries outside Central Asia. Judging from the way they

have been cut relative to their designs, the purposes to which they were ultimately put were very different from those originally intended. Their fragmentary nature, and the absence of contemporary paintings in which *kesi* are depicted, leaves us with few clues about their original purpose and their overall design. Nevertheless, several observations can be made. Double bands of flora and fauna, for example, are seen only on such pieces as catalogue numbers 14 and 15, where the starting edge is preserved. Thus it would appear that such bands were woven at the base of the total pattern. Considering the age-old tradition in Central Asia of ornamenting garments with bands, particularly at the cuffs, hems, collars, and openings, it would seem likely that one of the double borders at the end of a *kesi* was used for the cuffs of a garment, while the other ornamented the hem. Moreover, the thin stripe that intersects the plain border between the decorative bands in catalogue number 14 may well have marked where the bands were to be separated. The possibility that these *kesi* were originally intended to serve as garments corroborates the records of the Southern Song official Hong Hao concerning the Uyghur custom of weaving robes of *kesi* that were resplendently beautiful—as indeed they are. Some of the *kesi* fragments preserve a medallion with scalloped edges that resembles a cloud collar. With one exception (cat. no. 17), the main flora and fauna pattern inside the medallion is different from that outside. Where selvages are present, they bisect the medallion down the median (see figs. 12, 26, and 28). Thus, two loom widths were required to complete the overall design (see cat. no. 19 and fig. 29).

Catalogue number 16, a fragment with both selvages intact, measures 62 centimeters in width. Other loom widths of approximately 66.5 centimeters have also been recorded.[3] If these represent the more or less standard loom width of *kesi* of this type, then the width of the complete design would measure between 124 and 133 centimeters. The typical contrast of coloring and patterning within and outside the cloud-collar medallions imitates the effect of a separate cloud collar worn over a garment and supports the likelihood that these *kesi* were originally intended to be made up into garments. However, since none of the known *kesi* with cloud-collar medallions includes bands at the starting edge, the possibility that they were used for other purposes cannot be rejected. The cloud-collar motif, after all, had been freely used as a general decorative motif as well as a (perhaps symbolic) pattern at the base of knobs on vessels and the tops of tents following its introduction into Central Asia from Han China.[4]

Technically, these Central Asian *kesi* share common characteristics. With one exception, the *kesi* with a feline and birds on a floral ground (cat. no. 15), their warps

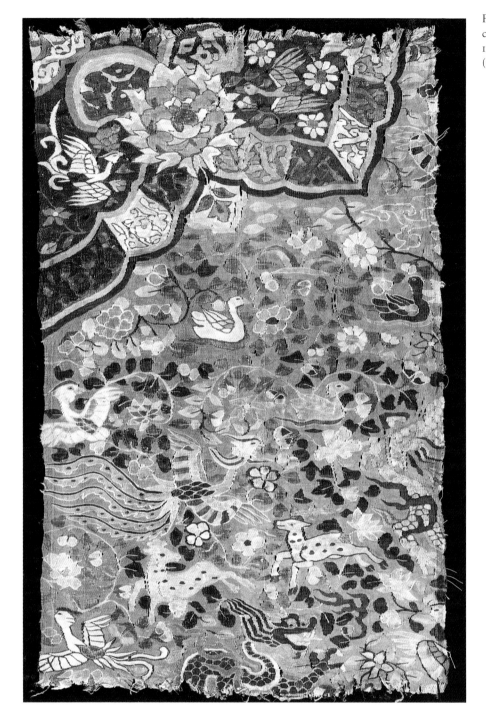

Figure 12. Textile showing partial cloud-collar medallion. Eastern Central Asia, 11th–12th century. Silk tapestry (*kesi*), 56 × 28 cm (22 × 11 in.). Private collection

are silk, s, 2-ply z. The densities of the polychrome silk wefts within a given textile vary greatly, producing thread counts ranging from as few as about 36 wefts per centimeter to as many as about 150. Gold wefts are composed of gilded strips of animal substrate wrapped z around a silk core, z. The tapestry weaves all have slit joins and tabby bindings. There is much eccentric weaving, and some use of soumak and flying shuttle; warps are wrapped along the vertical contours of the design. In all cases, there is an uneven texture to the surface. The reverse sides reveal few broken warps. The ends of broken warps and of those replacing them as well as the ends of introduced wefts are short. With the exception of catalogue

number 16, the warp ends are on the reverse. Similarly, wefts float for only short distances from one area of a given color to another.

Apart from the study of the threads and weave structures, an analytical study of the dyes would add greatly to our understanding of this group of *kesi*, especially if we could trace the sources for the dyes.[5] The importance of textile dyes for the Uyghurs from the tenth to the thirteenth century (the great period for the production of *kesi*) can be gleaned in one of the Uyghur documents collected by Pelliot in Dunhuang.[6] It is a letter from someone in Suzhou (Jiuquan, Gansu Province) to a friend in Shazhou (Dunhuang, also in Gansu) beseeching him to

Figure 13. Detail of textile with birds on a floral ground. Northern Song dynasty (960–1127). Silk tapestry (*kesi*), 131.6 × 55.6 cm (51⅞ × 21⅞ in.). Liaoning Provincial Museum, Shenyang

Kesi that can be attributed with certainty to the Song dynasty fall into two groups. They are conveniently designated Northern Song (960–1127) and Southern Song (1127–1279) according to style and technique, but it is possible that the production of the Northern Song type may have continued into the early Southern Song.

The Northern Song group is represented by catalogue numbers 20 and 21, both removed from the wrapper (external mounting) of handscroll paintings of the Northern Song period. Catalogue number 20 is of the same type as the best-known example of Northern Song *kesi* extant, an uncut piece in the collection of the Liaoning Provincial Museum (fig. 13).

The most remarkable aspect of *kesi* of the Northern Song is its affinity with *kesi* of eastern Central Asia. In both, the most common pattern is composed of animals and birds on a floral ground, the formal treatment of which is strikingly similar. Compare, for example, the general form of the spotted deer in catalogue number 14 and that of the running animals in catalogue number 20 and the ground pattern of leaves and "lotus" blossoms in catalogue numbers 16 and 21. Similarly, the technical features of the Central Asian *kesi* are also characteristic of the Northern Song group, although catalogue number 21 is woven with the typically Chinese gold thread made of wide, flat strips of paper that have been gilded on one side.

On the other hand, the Northern Song and Central Asian *kesi* exhibit marked stylistic differences in the treatment of the total pattern. In the Central Asian group, the animals and plants are not of uniform size, nor is the distribution of the various pictorial elements particularly even. (This is especially true in cat. nos. 13 and 14.) The writhing dragons in catalogue number 13 are portrayed with great expressive power, and the assemblage of floral sprays, while not evenly spaced, is dynamically balanced. In the Northern Song group, the animals, birds, and floral elements are more uniform in size and more evenly distributed in a homogeneous pattern, thereby losing some of the accented liveliness and vigor of the Central Asian patterns. Given that the pattern of dragons on a floral ground did not appear in Chinese art until the late Northern Song and that the Central Asian patterns are likely to have had an earlier beginning, it would seem reasonable to postulate that some of the Northern Song *kesi* derive from Central Asian prototypes.

In addition to the *kesi* woven with animals, birds, and floral elements, there is another class of pattern among

send dyes for textiles. This letter was probably written before 1036, when both Suzhou and Shazhou were overrun by the Tanguts. It is interesting to note that in this particular case the dyes, if they were eventually sent, went eastward toward interior China.

For the reasons stated above, we date the *kesi* with dragons and with lions (cat. nos. 17, 18, and 19) to the thirteenth century or earlier. The type represented by the *kesi* with birds, flowers, and bands (cat. no. 15) certainly survived into the thirteenth century, as evidenced by the example excavated in Urumqi. The panel with aquatic birds and recumbent animal (cat. no. 16) can be dated to the early thirteenth century by comparison with a similar piece from the pagoda of the monk Haiyun (1203–1257), in Beijing. We believe, however, that the dragon *kesi* (cat. no. 13) and the tiger and deer *kesi* (cat. no. 14), given their motifs, which stem from a much earlier period, may well be assigned an earlier date—any time after the tenth century, when the Uyghurs had settled in Turfan. The earlier date for these pieces is corroborated by their similarity to a type of *kesi* in the Northern Song group, which is discussed below.

Figure 14. *Immortals in a Mountain Pavilion*, leaf 5 from the album *Louhui jijin ce*. Northern Song dynasty (960–1127), early 12th century. Silk tapestry (*kesi*), 28.2 × 35.8 cm (11⅛ × 14⅛ in.). National Palace Museum, Taipei

Northern Song *kesi* that is certainly of Chinese origin and inspired by contemporary paintings. One example is the *kesi* of cranes flying over a mountain pavilion, in the National Palace Museum, Taipei (fig. 14), which has been discussed elsewhere.[7]

In the Southern Song, both classes of *kesi* (i.e., those that follow the Central Asian tradition and those patterned after Chinese painting) continued and underwent a further stage of refinement and adaptation to Chinese taste. The square with the dragon on a floral ground woven with colored silk and gold threads (cat. no. 22) is a perfect example of the survival of a Central Asian pattern into the Southern Song period. Although in many respects the tapestry weave of this *kesi* is similar to that of the Central Asian and Northern Song groups, it is distinctly more refined. There are more warps per centimeter, and the silk wefts are so much finer that the degree to which their densities vary can be fully apprehended only under magnification (weft thread counts range from approximately 90 to 210 per centimeter). In this *kesi*, moreover, long slits are secured by occasional dovetail joins, and the surface is smoother than that of Central Asian and Northern Song examples.

A much better known class of Southern Song *kesi* is that which faithfully reproduces court paintings of the period, some bearing the signatures or seals of weavers who had achieved fame for their *kesi* work. One of the best-known *kesi* artists was Zhu Kerou, whose seal is woven into a number of *kesi* paintings, now mostly in the collection of the National Palace Museum, Taipei (fig. 15). In spite of their fame, however, little is known of the lives of these *kesi* weavers. The *kesi* paintings of the

Southern Song are distinguished by the fineness of their threads, by the subtlety of shading achieved by graduating colors and the occasional use of tongues of color extending from one color field into the adjacent color field, by the virtual absence of eccentric weaving, and by the smoothness

Figure 15. Zhu Kerou, *Pied Wagtail on a Blooming Polygonum*, leaf 6 from the album *Louhui jijin ce*. Southern Song dynasty (1127–1279). Silk tapestry (*kesi*), 29.8 × 25 cm (11¾ × 9⅞ in.). National Palace Museum, Taipei

Figure 16. *Dragon amid Flowers*, leaf 1 from the album *Louhui jijin ce*. Northern Song dynasty (960–1127), early 12th century. Silk tapestry (*kesi*), 22.5 × 31.3 cm (8⅞ × 12⅜ in.). National Palace Museum, Taipei

of their surfaces. The end result is that the *kesi* so closely approximates an actual painting that it could at first glance be taken by an unsuspecting viewer as a painting on silk. The art of *kesi* tapestry was thus transformed into an art of reproduction. Nevertheless, it is this very quality of verisimilitude to the painted picture, the supreme art form of the Southern Song, that has been admired and valued by Chinese collectors. Very few *kesi* paintings of the Southern Song are known outside China, although the *kesi* fan (cat. no. 27), which dates from the Yuan period, is quite close in technique.

The transformation of *kesi* in the Southern Song can be viewed as an instance of a process often seen in cultural transmission in which an artistic medium is gradually modified to suit the taste and sensibilities of the country of adoption. If for no other reason, the history of the evolution of *kesi* weaving techniques in Song China would in itself raise the question of its foreign origins—foreign, that is, to the part of China ruled by the native Song dynasty. In contrast to its evolution in the Song empire, the technique of *kesi* weaving in Central Asia seems to have

retained its basic character until at least the Mongol period (and incidentally making the task of dating much more difficult).

A remaining question concerns the moment that Song *kesi* changed in its style of weaving to that of the Southern Song. There is no doubt that the development of *kesi* in the Southern Song was spurred on early in the dynasty by the necessity of producing *kesi* wrappers for hand-scroll paintings in the imperial collection, which was at that time being rapidly reconstituted after the devastating loss at the sack of the Northern Song capital, Bianjing (present-day Kaifeng), by the Jurchen army in 1126–27. Soon after the Song court had settled in the new capital, Hangzhou, in the reign of Gaozong (1127–62), the first emperor of the Southern Song, a great effort was made to reestablish all the institutions of the old capital. The newly acquired paintings had to be mounted in the style of the old collection. The *kesi* for this purpose had to be woven locally in Hangzhou, where there was no shortage of skilled weavers. The patterns for the wrappers were recorded by Zhou Mi (1232–1298) and by

Tao Zongyi (ca. 1316–1402).[8] Some of the patterns mentioned by these writers can be identified on *kesi* wrappers on Song paintings that survive to this day. One of the patterns, "dragon on a floral ground," is seen on *kesi* of the distinctly Southern Song type, such as the canopy (cat. no. 22), as well as on *kesi* in the Northern Song style, such as the *Dragon amid Flowers* in the National Palace Museum, Taipei (fig. 16). However, *kesi* of the size suitable for use as wrappers for handscrolls all seem to be of the Northern Song type—which leads us to believe that the development of the Southern Song style was not an instantaneous occurrence at the very beginning of the Southern Song dynasty, but rather a process that evolved over a period of time in the twelfth century.

If the place of manufacture of *kesi* in the Southern Song is not in doubt, the place of its early production in the Northern Song has been the subject of some discussion. According to Zhuang Chuo (1090–1150), one of the earliest writers to describe *kesi*, the place of manufacture was Dingzhou,[9] and it has been assumed by most writers that the Dingzhou mentioned by Zhuang is the Dingzhou in Hebei Province, which was an important center for all kinds of manufacturing, including textiles, during (and before) the Song period. (It produced, for example, the famous white porcelain known as Ding ware.) Other scholars, suspecting that *kesi* did not originate within the Song empire, have speculated that the Dingzhou in which *kesi* was produced may have been located in the western part of China.[10] However, there is a nearly contemporaneous record of events during the ravaging of Bianjing by the Jurchen army at the very end of the Northern Song, in which the Jurchens are said to have carried off 1,800 pieces of Hebei *kesi*.[11] This would seem to confirm that *kesi* was produced in the Dingzhou in Hebei, within the Song territory, during the Northern Song period.

Kesi of the Liao Dynasty (907–1125)

One of the most gratifying results of recent archaeological work is that it has enabled us to identify Liao *kesi*. The silk wefts of *kesi* produced during the Liao dynasty are extraordinarily fine, ranging from about 60 to 240 per centimeter. Gold thread was used, sometimes extravagantly, although its composition is unknown because the substrates have disintegrated, leaving the gold leaf

Figure 17. Detail, reverse of cat. no. 24

Figure 18. Detail, reverse of the *thangka* of Green Tara (figure 36)

on the warps. Eccentric weaving is used sparingly, usually along the contours of motifs. This and the fineness of the wefts result in a smoother surface than is found among the Central Asian and Northern Song *kesi*.

That Liao *kesi* was woven within the domains of the empire is proved by its distinctive quality and also by the motifs, which are closely related to those seen on Liao gold and silver (see cat. no. 23). That it had an early beginning is substantiated by the finds of *kesi* from a Liao tomb at Yemaotai, Liaoning Province, which has been dated to about the third quarter of the tenth century.[12] *Kesi* seems to have been more extensively used in the Liao than in the Song state. While in Song China *kesi* was used mostly for covering scrolls, Liao *kesi* was used also for furnishings and items of clothing. Among the finds at Yemaotai are a bedcover of several widths of *kesi* sewn together, a pair of *kesi* boots, and headgear trimmed with *kesi* strips.

In contrast to the lack of documentation in the Northern Song, *kesi* is mentioned specifically in records of the Liao court, in regulations regarding official robes. In the chapter on ceremonial paraphernalia in the *Liaoshi* (History of the Liao Dynasty), in the section titled "National Dress" (i.e., Khitan-style dress), it is stated that for minor sacrificial ceremonies, the emperor wore a red *kesi* robe with "tortoise" pattern.[13] It is noteworthy in this connection that the gifts sent by the Liao emperor to the Song emperor on the latter's birthday include *kesi* robes and articles of clothing with patterns of "goose neck" and "duck's head."[14] These patterns are also designated as decorations for the "national style" hunting dress of the Liao emperor.[15] As the Liao emperor seemed to make a point of presenting the Song emperor with Khitan-style dresses (while he himself would don Han-style regalia for state occasions), and as all other gifts seem to have been special products of the Liao state, one may presume that *kesi* was considered a Liao specialty.

Kesi of the Tangut Xia Dynasty (1032–1227)

The production of *kesi* in the Tangut Xia (also known as the Xixia) dynasty in northwest China has been inferred from a passage in a Tangut document relating to official workshops in the Tiansheng reign (1149–69) of Emperor Renzong.[16] This passage, however, is concerned with both silk weaving and wool weaving and is not explicit in its reference to *kesi*.[17] Far more compelling evidence for the production of *kesi* seems to be provided by actual

examples, some woven with pearls, that are of great technical expertise and are closely related stylistically and iconographically to Tangut art.

The most famous of these is the Green Tara *kesi thangka* from Khara Khoto, now in the State Hermitage, Saint Petersburg (fig. 36).[18] The *thangka* with Vighnantaka, in The Cleveland Museum of Art (cat. no. 24), bears a close relationship to the Green Tara and to three *kesi thangkas* in Lhasa that are woven in the Tibetan Kadampa style. Technically, it is distinguished from Central Asian, Song, and Liao *kesi* by the tangle of long weft threads and by the lengthy ends of numerous broken and replaced warps that cover the reverse side (fig. 17). Not all *kesi* that appear to have been woven in the Tangut Xia period, however, exhibit this technical peculiarity. The reverse side of the Green Tara, for example (fig. 18), has much the same appearance as the reverse sides of the Central Asian, Liao, and Song *kesi*. On the other hand, the *kesi* mandala of the Yuan period (cat. no. 25) also has long weft threads tangled on the back. The reasons for these different treatments of the tapestry technique cannot at present be fully elucidated. The most likely explanation lies in the ethnic diversity of the populations in both the Tangut Xia and the Yuan territories.

Kesi of the Yuan Dynasty (1279–1368)

Kesi in the Yuan period served a special purpose. As expounded in the preface to the chapter on painting and sculpture in the *Jingshi dadian* (Record of Yuan Institutions), compiled by order of Emperor Wenzong (Tugh Temür) in 1329:

> In antiquity the making of the likeness of things was by applying colors to patterns, known as drawing and embroidery. Later came sculpture in clay and metal. In recent times, there was the method of making images by silk weaving, and today this work is even more highly skilled.[19]

An earlier version of the preface makes an even more emphatic claim:

> To weave an image so that it seems to come alive is not something that can be equaled by the application of colors [in painting]. To make an image of clay is even more inferior. Thus human skill can match the wonder of nature.[20]

Beginning in the reign of Emperor Chengzong (Temür; r. 1294–1307), numerous orders were given that portraits be painted of the emperors and empresses and that they be converted to woven silk. (*Kesi* is usually meant, but a few records seem to imply that other patterned silks were also used for images.) The earliest recorded order for such activity was given by Temür upon his accession, succeeding his grandfather Khubilai Khan in 1294. The minister of works, a Uyghur by the sinicized name of Tang Renzu, was charged with supervising the weaving of the portrait of Khubilai.[21] The *kesi* took three years to complete. Given the length of time for the task to be accomplished, the *kesi* must have been of great size and complexity. A number of such orders for the painting and weaving of imperial portraits are recorded in the *Jingshi dadian*. Some orders are given for the painting (and weaving) of "imperial portraits with mandalas."[22] Detailed information is given on the date of the order, sometimes the date of commencement of the work, the supervising officials and the government offices responsible for carrying out the order, the size of the paintings and of the *kesi*, the exact quantities of the materials used and their procurement, the master craftsmen involved, and the officer responsible for the board and keep of the workers. The orders are usually given out by officials of the highest rank—a senior chief councillor or privy councillor—to the Directorate General of All Classes of Artisans (Zhuse Zongguan Fu), who would pass it on to the Superintendency for Buddhist Icons (Foxiang Tijusi), which was the office chiefly responsible for all painting and sculptures of imperial portraits and Buddhist icons, and where the finest craftsmen were employed.

As to the workshop responsible for the actual weaving of the portraits and mandalas, the orders do not specify. The *Yuanshi* (History of the Yuan Dynasty), in the section on sacrifices, states that the imperial portraits displayed in the portrait hall (*yingtang*, an independent building within a temple complex that housed portraits of an emperor and his consort and where Buddhist and sacrificial rites to the deceased emperor and empress were performed) were all woven by the Office of Patterned Textiles (Wenqi Ju).[23] The Wenqi Ju is not listed in the *Yuanshi* under any of the state administrations. It is recorded in the *Yongle dadian* (Grand Compilation of Yongle) as having been founded in 1245 by order of Khubilai by rounding up unregistered artisans for training as weavers and given over to the crown prince in 1275.[24] The *Yuanshi* does list a Wenjin Ju that was "founded in the early days of the dynasty and given to the Donggong [the heir apparent's establishment] in 1275."[25] Presumably this was the same workshop with the name changed sometime after 1275.

In spite of the specific reference to the Wenqi Ju, there seems to be no reason why some of the many official textile workshops should not have been assigned the task of weaving imperial portraits. Tang Renzu, the official who supervised the weaving of the portrait of Khubilai, was the minister of works, and there must have been workshops in his ministry capable of carrying out the commission. Another agency that could have taken on this work would have been the Superintendency for Weaving Buddhist Icons (Zhi Foxiang Tijusi), a unit of the administration for the Imperial Household (Xuanhui Yuan).

The information given above provides the background to the large *kesi* of the Yamantaka mandala with imperial portraits in the Metropolitan Museum (cat. no. 25), which will be further discussed in the entry.

Another *kesi* in this exhibition, catalogue number 26, is a cosmological diagram (also a mandala) which, judging from its workmanship and subject matter, was produced in the Yuan dynasty, perhaps also at one of the official workshops—but not necessarily a workshop in the capital, Daidu (present-day Beijing).

THE UYGHUR CONNECTION

In our study of the complex subject of *kesi*, one factor appears common to all the territories connected with the production of this fabric in the several centuries before they were all subsumed under the Mongol empire in the thirteenth century. It is the Uyghur people.

One of the earliest descriptions of *kesi* is in the *Songmo jiwen* (Records of the Pine Forests in the Plains), by Hong Hao (1088–1155), who, as an emissary of the Southern Song to the Jin court, was detained in Jin territory for fifteen years, mostly in the capital at Yanjing (present-day Beijing). The *Songmo jiwen* includes records of his experiences and what he learned during his long involuntary stay in the north. Unfortunately, only fragments of the original manuscript survived, and these were posthumously edited and published by his son.[26] In its present form, the book retains a valuable account of the Uyghurs and their production of *kesi*. There are several interesting points for us to note in Hong Hao's account. The first is that after the collapse of the Uyghur empire (centered in the Orkhon Valley in present-day Mongolia) about the mid-ninth century, a colony of Uyghurs settled in Qinzhou,[27] in Northern Song territory, and became "naturalized." When the Jin Jurchens took over this area (now Tianshui, in Gansu Province) from the Northern Song, the Uyghurs were moved to the vicinity of Yan (or Yanjing, the Middle Capital of the Jin), where Hong Hao came to know about them and witnessed the robes of *kesi* which the Uyghurs wove and wore. These he described as "resplendently beautiful." Hong Hao also recorded that the Uyghurs who settled along the Gansu Corridor remained there after their conquest by the Tanguts of Xia in the early eleventh century, and that those who went farther afield, "beyond the four commanderies" (i.e., present-day Xinjiang), built their own states.

Recent writing on the history of the Uyghurs tends to concentrate on the independent states they established in Xinjiang, with their capitals at Gaochang (in the Turfan Basin) and Besh Baliq, in the second half of the ninth century. The value of Hong Hao's account is to remind us of the Uyghur tribes that stayed on in previous areas of settlement. From this account one can see that the areas of the dispersal of the Uyghur people coincided with the territories that produced *kesi*, beginning, at the latest, in the tenth century. That the Liao state seems to have had an early start can be explained by the fact that the area of the original Uyghur empire in Mongolia became part of the Liao state early in its expansion. The Uyghur connection also explains the close similarity between Northern Song *kesi* and *kesi* we consider to be from eastern Central Asia (the area of the Gaochang Uyghur state). Generally speaking, it would seem that the Uyghurs were the carriers of the technique of tapestry weaving and that the patterns and uses of *kesi* in the various territories were very much determined by the local cultures. Over time, the subsequent development of the technique in different areas also followed distinctly different paths—as may have been gathered from this brief account.

The origin of the technique of silk tapestry weaving in East Asia remains unknown. Here again we return to the Turfan region, where *kesi* dating from as early as the seventh century have been found archaeologically.[28] Some historians believe that Uyghurs had always constituted a minority among the ethnic population in this region—long before they became the dominant inhabitants and rulers of this area.[29] If this is indeed the case, we would have the basic framework to construct a history of *kesi* in East Asia.

1. Plum Blossoms 1988, no. 3.
2. For related examples of Central Asian drawloom silks, see catalogue number 39 and figure 55.
3. Spink & Son 1989, p. 4.

4. In earlier Uyghur frescoes in the Turfan oasis, the cloud-collar design also occurs on the fabric used to wrap a camel's load (Le Coq 1913, pl. 28). For a discussion of the origin and widespread propagation of this motif and its possible symbolic function, see Cammann 1951, pp. 3–10.
5. The dyes of two *kesi,* catalogue number 15 and one similar to catalogue number 19, have been analyzed. See Taylor 1991, pp. 81–83.
6. Li Jingwei 1990, pp. 333–58. The same letter is published in Hamilton 1986, pp. 153–55.
7. Fong and Watt 1996, pp. 248–49.
8. Zhou Mi, *Qidong Yeyu* (Rustic tales told by a native of Shandong; preface dated 1291), and Tao Zongyi, *Chuogeng lu* (Written after setting aside the plow; ca. 1366), chap. 23. Extracts of the relevant passages in these books are found in Zhu Qiqian's *Sixiu biji* (Notes on silks and embroidery), chap. 2, in *Xiupu* (Manuals of embroideries), in *Yishu congbian* 1962, vol. 1, no. 32, pp. 295–305. See also Cammann 1948.
9. Zhuang Chuo, *Jile bian* ("Chicken ribs"), in *Congshu jicheng jianbian*, vol. 727. The relevant passage is translated in Cammann 1948, pp. 90–91.
10. Yang Renkai, introduction to Tapestry Section, in Yang Renkai et al. 1983, p. 230.
11. Xu Mengxin (1126–1207), in *Sanchao beimeng huibian* (Compilation of documents on the treaties with the North during three reigns), chap. 78, p. 588. The Shanghai Guji Chubanshe edition, referred to here, is based on the 1908 Xu Handu edition and contains a few typographical errors. The quantity of *kesi* quoted here is taken from the 1878 Yuan Zu'an edition in the C. V. Starr Library of Columbia University.
12. Liaoning Provincial Museum 1975, p. 33.
13. *Liaoshi*, chap. 56, p. 906.
14. *Qidan guo zhi*, chap. 21, leaf 1.
15. *Liaoshi*, chap. 56, p. 907.
16. The passage most often referred to comes from vol. 4 of I. Kychanov's translation of the Tiansheng code, art. 1256, chap. 17, which deals with allowable quotas of waste and loss in the preparation or transportation of precious resources. The authors gratefully acknowledge Mary Rossabi for the translation of pp. 147–49 of Kychanov 1989.
17. In commenting on this passage (correspondence to Anne E. Wardwell, March 25, 1997), Dr. Ruth Dunnell of Kenyon College writes:
    "The Chinese translation of this sentence reads: 'In the making of *kou si*, the allowable margin of waste is five *liang* out of one hundred *liang* of thread' (or yarn). A *liang* is a Chinese unit of weight. The thread or yarn referred to could certainly be silk.
    "The Tangut graphs here rendered as *kou si* represent a transliteration, or phonetic rendering, of a presumably Chinese compound. The Chinese graph chosen by these translators to render the second sound is the same graph that means silk in Chinese. The *kou* could possibly have the same or similar phonetic value as *ke* in the eleventh- to twelfth-century northwest Chinese dialect. Nevertheless, the transliteration is suggestive of *kesi*, regardless of its placement in the article (i.e., amid passages dealing with wool). The order of matters discussed within individual articles or among articles is not always consistent and logical to our way of thinking. Sometimes the code backtracks, for example. Thus, this may or may not be a reference to *kesi*. . . ."
18. Milan 1993, no. 19.
19. The original text of the *Jingshi dadian* is lost. The chapter on painting and sculpture has been copied from the *Yongle dadian*, commissioned by the Ming emperor Chengzu (r. 1402–24), completed in 1408, and published by Wang Guowei (1877–1927) in the collectanea *Guangcang xuequn congshu*, second collection, vol. 26, under the title *Yuandai huasu ji* (Painting and sculpture of the Yuan period), from which the present quotation is taken.
20. This version of the preface is taken from *Yuan wenlei*, vol. 6, p. 618. The *Yuan wenlei* is a collection of writings compiled by Su Tianjue in the late Yuan period.
21. *Yuanshi*, Biography of Tang Renzu, vol. 11, chap. 134, p. 3254.
22. The term for mandala in the *Jingshi dadian* is *fotan* (Buddhist altarplace). The modern term is *tancheng*.
23. *Yuanshi*, vol. 6, chap. 75, p. 1875. The character *qi* in this context is to

be interpreted as meaning "patterned textile" in general and not taken to be a technical term, the definition of which is in dispute.

24. *Yongle dadian*, chap. 29781, leaf 18. This passage, which records the founding of the Wenqi Ju in some detail and provides the names of the supervising officers, was presumably copied from the *Jingshi dadian* and not from the *Yuanshi*, as the compilers of the *Yongle dadian* claim.

25. *Yuanshi*, vol. 8, chap. 89, p. 2263.

26. Collected in the *Liaohai congshu*, vol. 1.

27. In modern editions there is a misprint for the character *zhou*, but there is no question that Qinzhou was meant in the original text, as other parts of the passage make clear.

28. See a tapestry belt excavated from Astana, reported in Xinjiang Museum 1975, pp. 8–18. Similar fragments of belts are in the Stein Collection, British Museum, London; see London, *Caves,* 1990, nos. 111, 112. See also Riboud and Vial 1970, EO. 1203/A, pl. 23; EO. 1199, pl. 39; and EO. 1207, pl. 43.

29. Cheng Suluo, "Gaochang Huihu wangguo shi zhong ruogan jiben wenti lunzheng" (A discussion of certain basic questions in the history of the Gaochang Uyghur kingdom), in Cheng Suluo 1994, p. 271.

13. *Dragons amid Flowers*

Silk tapestry (kesi)
Warp 53.5 cm (21⅛ in.); weft 33 cm (13 in.)
Eastern Central Asia, 11th–12th century
The Metropolitan Museum of Art, New York. Fletcher Fund, 1987
(1987.275)

The design preserved on this fragment is composed of one complete dragon and the upper half of another; both dragons are in a rampant posture on a field of flowers on a purple ground. On the right edge, which has been cut, are halves of flaming pearls directly in front of the dragons' mouths. The dragons' heads are similar to that of the dragon in catalogue number 14. The style of the dragons' heads (with an extended snout shaped like an elephant's trunk or a crocodile's upper jaw) and the treatment of the tails, which hook under one of the hind legs, are typical features of dragons in the art of eastern Central Asia and in the decorative arts produced in metropolitan areas of interior China during the Tang period (618–907). After the tenth century, the dragon in interior China was gradually modified to a more "native" form, except in textiles (see, for example, fig. 16), while in Central Asia its form persisted unchanged until at least the Yuan period (1279–1368).

The vivacity of the design is enhanced by the brilliant use of colors, both naturalistically and in a decorative manner. The other characteristic of the style exemplified by this piece is the use of naturalistic forms in creative patternmaking. One of the floral sprays deserves our special attention: the plant with the stem that originates from the tip of the mane of the lower dragon and spreads toward the tail of the upper dragon. Growing out of this treelike stem are a white lotus blossom, a green lotus leaf with pale green and white edges, and a trefoil leaf which belongs to another aquatic plant, perhaps a taro. The same stem also supports two-toned, pointed leaves and a yellow "clover." The combination of the lotus blossom, the side-view lotus leaf, and the trefoil leaf constitutes a basic motif in the decorative arts of eastern Central Asia, beginning perhaps in the eleventh century and continuing until at least the fourteenth century. During the Yuan dynasty, this motif was to become ubiquitous in interior China. It is to be found, for example, on the molded decoration on roof tiles excavated from the site of Daidu, the Yuan capital (fig. 19). Its appearance on fourteenth-century blue-and-white porcelain is familiar to all students of Chinese ceramics. The motif also occurs on an embroidery in this exhibition (cat. no. 50) and will be further discussed in that entry.

TECHNICAL ANALYSIS

Warp: White silk, s, 2-ply z. Count: 18 per centimeter. *Weft:* 1) Polychrome silk, s (twists very slight). Count: approximately 28–100 wefts per centimeter. Colors: purple, deep pink, pale pink, medium pink, yellow, light blue, tan, green, pale green, forest green, white, and very dark brown (appears black). 2) Gold thread: strips of animal substrate wrapped z around yellow silk core, z. The gold leaf no longer remains, but the yellow color of the silk core indicates that the weft was gold and not silver. The substrate is coated with a reddish brown substance. Count: approximately 40–50 per centimeter (depending on how tightly beaten in the wefts are). *Weave:* The panel is woven in the tapestry technique with slit joins. Steeply vertical diagonals are achieved by warp steps and, for the gold wefts, the occasional use of a flying shuttle; single warps are only rarely wrapped. Eccentric weaving is used for less steep curves (e.g., the stems of leaves or the outlines and contours of the dragons). The warps form ridges on the surface. The direction in which the wefts overlap indicates that the *kesi* was woven from top to bottom.

On the reverse, only one broken warp was found. The broken warp had been tied into a knot 1.2 centimeters from the point at which it emerged from the wefts and was then tied to a purple weft float about 4.3 centimeters away; the remaining 1.6 centimeters of the end was left loose. Because of damage in the adjacent area, it is not known if the warp was replaced. The reverse side is fairly clear of weft ends and floats. The ends of the wefts are cut short (approximately 1–2.3 centimeters), and wefts float up to 4.2 centimeters from one color area to the next.

On the left side is preserved a selvage, the wefts simply turning around the outermost single warp.

PUBLICATIONS: MMA *Recent Acquisitions* 1987–1988, p. 83, illus.; Simcox, "Tracing the Dragon," 1994, p. 37, and fig. 1, p. 34.

Figure 19. Roof tile with molded decoration, from Daidu. Yuan dynasty (1279–1368). Capital Museum, Beijing

14. Tigers Chasing Deer, with Dragon

Silk tapestry (kesi)
Warp 58 cm (22⅞ in.); weft 27.2 cm (10¾ in.)
Eastern Central Asia, 11th–12th century
The Cleveland Museum of Art. Leonard C. Hanna Jr., Fund
(1988.100)

The design is composed of two horizontal bands and an upper, incomplete field. The designs of the two bands are identical: a tiger chasing a spotted deer with a mushroom-shaped antler amid leaves and flowers that include tree peony, plum, and lotus. The design is woven with polychrome silks and gold against a deep purple ground. The incomplete field preserves part of a four-clawed dragon with flaming mane, horns, and a prominent snout against a ground of flowers and leaves. The design is woven with polychrome silks against a deep pink ground. Each of the two bands is flanked by a border of half rosettes and an outer row of pearls. A chartreuse field articulated across the middle by a thin cream line separates the two bands. At the bottom of the panel is another band of plain chartreuse followed by a fringe of warps. The bottom, top, and right edges are cut; the left edge is a complete selvage. What now appears to be the face is actually the reverse side.

As is characteristic of much of the art of Central Asia, the motifs and patterning scheme on this *kesi* owe something to every major culture that was transmitted along the great trade routes between eastern and western Asia. The patterns on the two bands are composed of elements that originated in the art of Sasanian Iran and Sogdiana. Not only can the pearl borders and split palmettes be traced back, ultimately, to Sasanian art, but the contrast of patterns in the main field and borders was an aesthetic that was known during the Sasanian period (A.D. 211–651). A fragmentary tapestry in The Cleveland Museum of Art dating from the end of the Sasanian period incorporates all these elements (fig. 20). Preserved in the lower portion, against a deep blue ground, is a boar's head within a pearl roundel, parts of two adjacent roundels, and split palmettes in the interstices. Above this, on a red ground, is a thin guard line followed by a double row of pearls and the hooves of a horse. The aesthetic of juxtaposed, contrasting designs probably evolved from the use of silk remnants as borders on costumes and furnishing fabrics. One of the many examples of this practice represented in Sogdian frescoes is a garment patterned with winged horses in pearl roundels and, at the hem, a border of boars' heads in pearl roundels.[1]

The mode of transmission of artistic styles and motifs across Central Asia is far from clear at present. By, at the latest, the early Tang period, some Western motifs had been absorbed into the decorative arts of metropolitan China. The deer with the mushroom-shaped antler, a common motif on Sogdian silver,[2] is seen on a mid- to

Figure 20. Textile with boar's head. Iran or Sogdiana, late 6th–early 8th century. Wool and linen, tapestry weave, 20.7 × 25 cm (8⅛ × 9⅞ in.). The Cleveland Museum of Art. John L. Severance Fund (1950.509)

Figure 21. Bowl. Tang dynasty (618–907), late 8th–9th century. Silver with parcel gilt, diameter 18 cm (7⅛ in.). The Metropolitan Museum of Art, New York. Purchase, Arthur M. Sackler Gift, 1974 (1974.267)

late Tang silver dish with a border of split palmettes (fig. 21). The Sogdian deer disappeared from Chinese art by the end of the tenth century, but is very much in evidence on this *kesi*, which in all likelihood was woven in the Uyghur state of Gaochang, north and south of the Tianshan range.[3] Similarly, the split palmette ceased to be a popular border decoration after the Tang period in interior China, but continued to be used in various forms in paintings on the walls of cave temples in Dunhuang well into the Yuan dynasty (1279–1368). It is possible that the Uyghurs encountered these motifs when they arrived in the metropolitan areas of Tang China in the middle of the eighth century, or that these motifs were already part of the established local tradition in Gaochang when the Uyghurs arrived there in the late ninth century.

The dragon in the main field is, of course, ultimately of Chinese origin. But its particular form, with a snout shaped like an elephant's trunk, betrays the influence of the *makara*, an Indian sea monster, and it is therefore a Central Asian hybrid creature. The placement of a dragon in a flower meadow, however, appears to be a Central Asian innovation.

Often in the process of the transference of artistic motifs, the reinterpreted image takes on a naive quality. This may account for a certain folk element in the scene of the tiger chasing the deer in the Cleveland tapestry, which is rather charming. The same quality is seen in another *kesi* of very similar design (fig. 22). A dragon among flowers that is virtually identical to the dragon in the Cleveland tapestry dominates the upper main field, while the borders are woven with lions chasing a brocaded ball against a floral ground. The two borders are flanked by rows of pearls and by bands of the classic scroll, a motif that commonly occurs in late Uyghur tapestries. Unlike the Cleveland tapestry, the identical designs of the bands are oriented in directions opposite to one another.

The motif of lions chasing a brocaded ball is occasionally seen on Liao (907–1125) and Northern Song (960–1127) textiles.[4] Because the motifs both on the Cleveland *kesi* and in figure 22 originated in an earlier period and because there is no sign of later Persian influence, the two *kesi* almost certainly date from before the beginning of Mongol expansion in the early thirteenth century.

1. Al'baum 1975, fig. 8; for other examples, see figs. 4, 11, 12, 14.
2. See, for example, Marshak 1986, figs. 42, 43.
3. This *kesi* is a rare document of the survival of the Sogdian deer in Central Asia after the Tang period. In the Mongol period, the motif again migrated both east and west: to northern China, undoubtedly with the resettlement of artisans from Central Asia, and west to Iran via trade. It occurs, for example, in a silk and gold (flat strips of gilded paper) brocade from northern China with a design of Sogdian deer standing amid floral and foliate motifs and looking back (art market; unpublished); and in a metal casket made in western Iran in the thirteenth century after 1220 (London 1982, p. 183, fig. 82A).
4. For a published Northern Song example, see Chen Guo'an 1984, pp. 79–80, pl. IV, 3.

Figure 22. Textile with dragon and lions. Eastern Central Asia, 11th–12th century. Silk tapestry (*kesi*), 55.5 × 34 cm (21⅞ × 13⅜ in.)

TECHNICAL ANALYSIS

Warp: White silk, s, 2-ply z. Count: 17–20 per centimeter (the range results from the manipulation and bending of the warps in weaving). *Weft:* 1) Polychrome silk, slight z twist. Colors: coral red, pink, purple, forest green, chartreuse, pale green, deep blue, light blue, yellow, mustard yellow, olive, ivory, light gray, and brown; densities of threads (within and between colors) vary greatly. Count: 36–120 per centimeter. 2) Gold: strips of parchment with metallic surface consisting of gold and silver, wrapped z around a deep yellow silk core, z.[1] From the remaining flecks of gold and the black surface beneath, the metals appear to have been layered. Count: 36–56 per centimeter (some gold wefts are tightly beaten in, while others are loosely beaten in). *Weave:* The panel is woven in the tapestry technique with slit joins and much eccentric weaving. The uneven texture of the surface is largely due to variations in the densities of the weft yarns and the bending of warps. Diagonals are achieved by occasional soumak weaving, by flying shuttle, and by much use of warp steps for steep diagonals. A selvage is preserved on the left side; all wefts turn around the single outermost warp.

Occasionally, wefts were spliced by being tightly twisted. Broken warps, which are very infrequent, were knotted to replacement warps close to the weave. The ends were either cut close to the knot or they were woven together with the replaced section of warp for about 3–4 weft passes before exiting from the weave and being cut. Based on the direction of the broken warp ends, the weaving progressed from bottom to top.

The few remaining weft floats, the knots of broken and replaced warps, and the direction in which the kesi was folded leave no doubt that what appears to be the face of the kesi is actually the reverse. The weft floats have been cut and the loose weft ends pulled to the other side. Similarly, the ends of broken and replacement warps have been cut very close to the weave.

1. Identified by Norman Indictor and Denyse Montegut (correspondence to Anne E. Wardwell, May 10, 1991).

PUBLICATIONS: Simcox 1989, fig. 7, p. 23; J. Wilson 1990, no. 13, p. 316; CMA Handbook 1991, p. 30; CMA 1992, p. 52; Nunome 1992, pl. 30, p. 117; Wardwell 1992–93, p. 246.

15. Feline and Birds on a Floral Ground

Silk tapestry (kesi)
Warp 55.5 cm (21⅞ in.); weft 26 cm (10¼ in.)
Eastern Central Asia, 13th century
The Metropolitan Museum of Art, New York. Purchase, Joseph E. Hotung Gift, 1987 (1987.276)

This *kesi* bears a striking resemblance to several fragments excavated in tombs of the Mongol period at Salt Lake (Yanhu), between Urumqi and Turfan in Xinjiang[1] (fig. 23). The main field is divided into bands by discontinuous lines, some sections of which serve as the ground for the feline and the striding peacocks, others of which seem to be long stems of grass with curling leaf shoots that issue alternately on either side. Stretching between these lines are diagonal stems with pairs of fernlike leaves (the report on the Salt Lake finds describes this motif as willow branches). In between the diagonals are the animals, peacocks, and blossoms. As in the tiger and deer *kesi* (cat. no. 14), the lower part consists of two broad bands, with birds in flight among flowers bound by borders of open blossoms, flower buds, and comma-shaped leaves.

The Salt Lake fragments were originally the external cover of a pair of high leather boots worn by the deceased, a military officer. All have the same pattern, although the color schemes are different. The similarity to the Metropolitan *kesi* goes beyond the pattern of diagonal foliated stems, as the weaving techniques are remarkably alike.[2] The only difference is that the silk warps in the Salt Lake fragments are s, 2-ply z, whereas those of the Metropolitan piece are silk, z, 3-ply z.

The Salt Lake finds are among the few examples of *kesi* of the Mongol period reported to date and provide an important clue for the identification of this *kesi* and other pieces of similar style and technique as originating from eastern Central Asia. One other *kesi* panel with a similar pattern is known.[3]

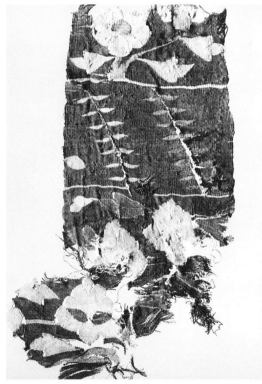

Figure 23. Panel with flowers and diagonal foliated stems, excavated at Salt Lake. Eastern Central Asia, 13th century. Silk tapestry (*kesi*). Xinjiang Institute of Archaeology, Urumqi

1. Wang Binghua 1973, pp. 28–36. The tomb in question has been dated to the Yuan period by the excavators. Analysis of the patterns of other textiles found in the same tomb, however, has led the authors of this catalogue to conclude that the tomb may well predate the official founding of the Yuan dynasty in 1279 (see p. 137).
2. The authors were privileged to examine the Salt Lake fragments at the Xinjiang Institute of Archaeology, Urumqi, in 1996.
3. Simcox 1989, no. 43. The same piece is also published in Spink & Son 1989, no. 4, with a technical analysis of the weave and dyes.

Detail, cat. no. 15

TECHNICAL ANALYSIS

Warp: White silk, z, 3-ply z (i.e., 3 strands, each z twist, that are plied z). Count: 15–22 per centimeter (the warps near the edges—especially the left selvage edge—are closer together than the warps in the center. *Weft:* 1) Polychrome silk, z, plied s. Count: approximately 40–150 per centimeter. Colors: very dark brown (appears black), purple, red, medium and pale pink, orange, light green, medium green, light blue, medium blue (sometimes light and medium blues are combined to produce a striated effect), deep blue green, yellow, white, and tan. The dyeing of reds, blues, and greens is uneven. 2) Gold thread: strips of gilded animal substrate wrapped z around yellow silk core, z. The substrate is very dark red brown or black and is loosely wrapped so that the core is clearly visible. Count: approximately 24–60 per centimeter (the range is caused by how tightly the gold wefts were beaten in). *Weave:* The panel is woven in the tapestry technique with slit joins. The weave is very eccentric in places. Diagonals were achieved by warp steps, flying shuttle, and, for steep diagonals, the wrapping of single warps. Only a few broken warps can be seen on the reverse side. A broken warp was either woven as a separate warp up to its end, at which point a new warp was intro-

duced to replace it, or was woven together with one of the adjacent warps until it ended, at which point the new warp was introduced; only one warp was tied and not replaced. In two instances, the unwoven portion of the new warp was knotted to a weft float about 5.5 to 7.8 centimeters from where the warp was introduced into the weave, and the end (in one case approximately 8.3 centimeters long and in the other 18.3 centimeters long) was left dangling. The broken warp that was not replaced reveals that the panel was woven from bottom to top. The reverse is covered with floats and the cut ends of wefts, both of which are short. The cut ends are 1.3–6.7 centimeters long; and the floats extend 0.5–4.5 centimeters. The floating wefts cross over and under one another; sometimes a group of floats is tied by another floating weft. Broken wefts are knotted. The left side of the panel is a selvage: all wefts turn around the outermost warp. The starting edge consists of a band of yellow followed by a band of blue; the warps are cut and form a short fringe. The guard lines delineating the subdivisions of the bands are each composed of 3 gold wefts treated as a single weft.

Unpublished.

70

15

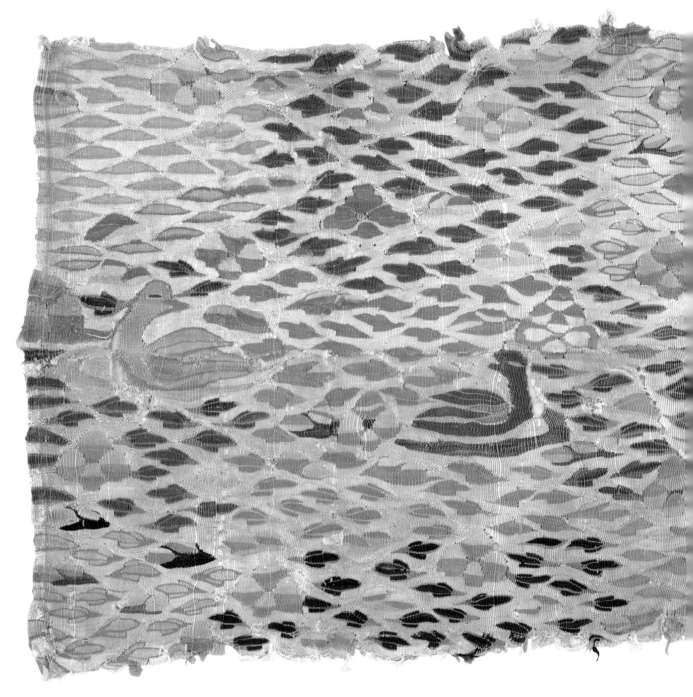

16. Aquatic Birds and Recumbent Animal

Silk tapestry (kesi)
Warp 28.5 cm (11¼ in.); weft 62 cm (24⅜ in.)
Eastern Central Asia, 12th–13th century
The Metropolitan Museum of Art, New York. Purchase, Gifts in
memory of Christopher C. Y. Chen, Gifts from various donors in
honor of Douglas Dillon, Barbara and William Karatz Gift, and
Eileen W. Bamberger Bequest, in memory of her husband, Max
Bamberger, 1997 (1997.7)

Both selvages of this fragment are preserved, providing valuable information on the loom width of *kesi* of this type.

An almost identical piece on purple ground, measuring 65 centimeters in width (presumably selvage to selvage),

was found in 1955 in the twin pagodas for the Buddhist monk Haiyun (1203–1257) and his disciple Ke'an in the Qingshou Temple in Beijing.[1] Another piece with a similar pattern forms part of a legging found at a Mongol-period site in Inner Mongolia.[2]

The design is composed of a ground of two kinds of leaves of different colors, which occupy rectangular areas without boundaries. Occasionally, the leaves from one area intrude into another, creating variation in the basic pattern. Another means of creating visual interest is provided by the tripartite leaves that point in opposite directions in different parts of the pattern. Superimposed on this ground scheme are lotus buds and ducks on water and an upside-down animal (on other known examples of *kesi* with similar

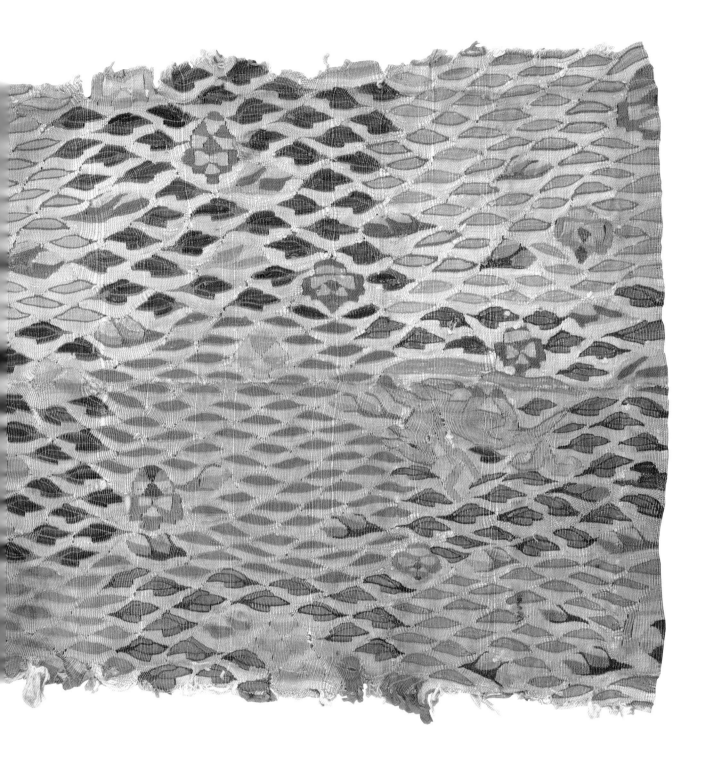

patterns, the animals and birds are always upright and in the same orientation).

The treatment of the waterfowl in this and other *kesi* with similar patterns—in groups of two or more, with one or two heads turned toward each other, such as is seen also in figure 12—is in the Chinese manner, but the subject matter seems to have been popularized initially in northern China. An early example of the theme of waterfowl is seen on a mural in one of the chambers of Qingling, Inner Mongolia Autonomous Region, the tomb of a Liao emperor, either Shengzong (r. 982–1031) or Xingzong (r. 1031–55; fig. 24).[3] This painting vividly illustrates a spring scene by a river—no doubt one of the rivers by which the Khitan emperor conducted his spring hunt. Another

Figure 24. Mural with river scene. Liao dynasty (907–1125). 260 × 177 cm (102⅜ × 69⅝ in.)

Figure 25. Mural with tree peony, detail. Liao dynasty (907–1125)

mural in the same chamber of Qingling is a summer scene in which a tree peony dominates the composition (fig. 25). Some of the smaller leaves of the peony tree take a form very-similar to the tripartite leaves in the Metropolitan *kesi*. Both the motifs of the birds on water and the tripartite leaves that make up the *kesi* pattern may ultimately derive from Liao painting. Waterfowl with heads looking forward and back are also seen on embroidered headpieces dated to the Liao dynasty (see cat. no. 52). (For the farther transmission of the motif of ducks and tripartite leaves, see pp. 129–30 and cat. no. 38.)

This *kesi* is woven in the same technique as other pieces in the eastern Central Asian group. The slight unevenness

in the surface is the result of binding two warps as one where broken warps are not replaced.

1. Beijing City Cultural Bureau 1958, p. 29. Haiyun, a monk of the Linji sect of Chan Buddhism, was an important figure in the early days of the Mongol empire. Moving between Khara Khorum and Yan (present-day Beijing), he was patronized by successive great khans (and empresses and princes), from Chinggis to Möngke and was granted the title of state preceptor (*guoshi*). Khubilai gave him a "seamless robe of gold cloth [*jin*] with pearls," as did Möngke toward the end of the monk's life. Neither of these was found in his pagoda at the Qingshou Temple in Beijing (demolished in 1955). Of the several items of luxury textiles from his pagoda, only the hat has been published with a good illustration (Huang Nengfu, Arts and Crafts, 1985, pl. 10). There is a biography of Haiyun in the *Fozu lidai tongzai*, chap. 21, pp. 702–4.
2. See Los Angeles 1993, p. 161, fig. 106.
3. For the archaeological report on Qingling, see Tamura and Kobayashi 1953. For good color reproductions of some details, see Su Bai 1989, vol. 12, pls. 143–151.

TECHNICAL ANALYSIS

Warp: Tan silk, s, 2-ply z. Count: 18 per centimeter. *Weft:* Polychrome silk, s. Colors: cream, pink, medium deep rose, light plum; light, medium, and dark blue; light, medium, and dark green; blue green, orange, and dark brown. Count: approximately 40–140 per centimeter (with a wide range of densities). *Weave:* The tapestry is woven with slit joins and extensive use of eccentric weaving. Steep diagonals are handled with warp steps. On the reverse are numerous short ends of wefts. There are many broken warps that were not replaced. Instead, the two warps originally on either side of the broken warp were thereafter bound as one, leaving a vertical line in the warp direction. The ends of the broken warps were cut very close to the weave, often on the face.

Unpublished.

17. Dragons Chasing Flaming Pearls

Silk tapestry (kesi)
Warp 60 cm (23⅝ in.); weft 32 cm (12⅝ in.)
Central Asia, 13th century or earlier
The Cleveland Museum of Art. Andrew R. and Martha Holden
Jennings Fund (1988.33)

This panel is woven with a design of dragons plunging, leaping, and turning as they chase flaming pearls amid clouds. The dragons have long, scaly bodies, flaming manes, horns, and snouts that are curled or extended. The design is woven in gold and polychrome silks against a deep purple ground. The left edge, the only side not cut, is a complete selvage.

Several *kesi* with this pattern against a purple ground are known, including another piece in the Metropolitan

Museum (cat. no. 18).[1] And in two panels recently on the art market the dragons chasing flaming pearls surround cloud-collar frames that enclose the same motif on an orange-red ground (figs. 26, 27). One of the panels preserves part of the left portion of the cloud-collar medallion and the other part of the right lobe. As seems to have been characteristic of all *kesi* with cloud-collar medallions, there is a selvage down the center of the medallion, requiring that two panels be sewn together to complete

Figure 26. Textile with dragons and partial cloud-collar medallion. Central Asia, 13th century or earlier. Silk tapestry (*kesi*), 59.7 × 31.1 cm (23½ × 12¼ in.). Dennis R. Dodds, Philadelphia

Figure 27. Textile with dragons and partial cloud-collar medallion. Central Asia, 13th century or earlier. Silk tapestry (*kesi*), 57 × 23 cm (22½ × 9 in.). Private collection

17

the design. In all likelihood, the tapestries woven solely with dragons chasing pearls were originally parts of panels that each included half of a cloud-collar medallion.

The design of dragons chasing flaming pearls in both the Cleveland and the Metropolitan pieces is a total departure from the pattern of animals and birds among flowers, one of the patterns that occurs most frequently in the decorative art of eastern Central Asia that long predated the Mongol conquest. This deviation is indicative of a powerful new influence that overtook the native style, though the cloud collar is still preserved. But even this motif shows evidence of the changes that were in progress in that the medallion differs only in color, not in design, from the rest of the *kesi*. The dragons, while they retain the vigor of movement of earlier Central Asian dragons, have metamorphosed further away from the image of the dragon during the Tang. In comparing the way the dragons are packed together with the dense patterning of the *kesi* with lions (cat. no. 19), which exhibits strong Persian elements, we are led to the conclusion that *kesi* of this type have more in common with that *kesi* than with the group that can more firmly be attributed to the eastern Central Asian tradition.

1. For other examples, see Spink & Son 1994, no. 1; and Plum Blossoms 1988, no. 2.

TECHNICAL ANALYSIS

Warp: White silk, s, 2-ply z. Count: 17–18 warps per centimeter. *Weft:* 1) Polychrome silk, s. Colors: deep purple, pink, orange, white, turquoise, royal blue, pale blue, green, yellow, and brown. Count: 56–128 per centimeter (the yarns vary in density). 2) Gold thread: strips of parchment, with metallic surface consisting of gold and silver, wrapped z around a yellow silk core, z. It is not clear if the metals are layered or alloyed.[1] Count: 64–68 per centimeter. *Weave:* The panel is woven in tapestry technique with slit joins. Eccentric weaving occurs in gradual curves, while steep contours are handled by flying shuttle and warp steps. In vertical parts of the design, the warps are wrapped. The beginning of a weft of one color is hidden under the adjacent weft of a different color.

On the reverse, the wefts float across short spaces (less than 1.5 centimeters) and are cut to 2 centimeters or less. Sometimes wefts of different colors are knotted together. Broken wefts occasionally occur and are knotted. Broken warps occur only occasionally. Either they were not replaced, or a new warp was knotted to the broken warp with the ends of the two warps exposed on the reverse side (the replacement end is longer than the end of the broken warp). Judging by the direction of broken warps that were not replaced, the panel was woven from bottom to top. The selvage on the left side is composed of all the wefts turning around the outermost warp, which is single.

1. Identified by Norman Indictor and Denyse Montegut (correspondence to Anne E. Wardwell, May 10, 1991).

PUBLICATIONS: Simcox 1989, fig. 5, p. 21; J. Wilson 1990, fig. 14, p. 296; *CMA Handbook* 1991, p. 30.

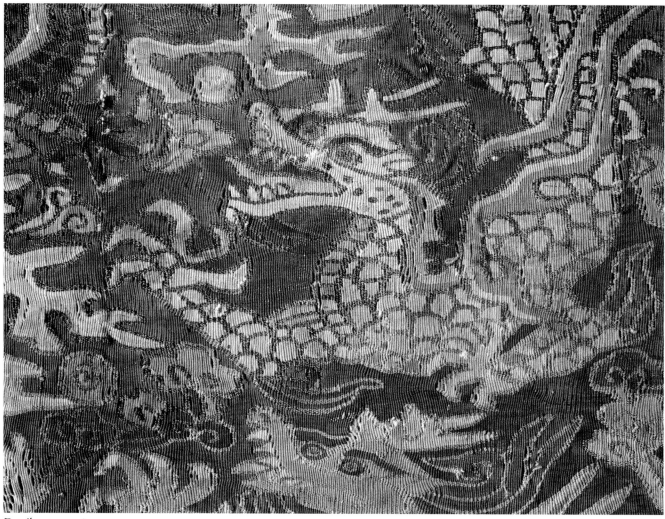

Detail, cat. no. 18

18. Dragons Chasing Flaming Pearls

Silk tapestry (kesi)
Warp 46.5 cm (18¼ in.); weft 32.6 cm (12⅞ in.)
Central Asia, 13th century or earlier
The Metropolitan Museum of Art, New York. Cecile E.
Mactaggart Gift and Rogers Fund, 1987 (1987.8)

Stylistically and technically, this *kesi* in the Metropolitan Museum is very close to one in the Cleveland Museum (cat. no. 17), indicating that the two textiles were woven at related workshops. The gold thread in the Cleveland piece is relatively well preserved, however, while the silver on the metallic thread of the Metropolitan piece is almost completely lost.[1]

As mentioned in the entry for catalogue number 17, a number of *kesi* fragments are known with patterns very similar to this one, providing other instances of the repeated use of the same basic patterns with minor variations in design and color scheme.

1. Analysis by Norman Indictor, February 26, 1987.

TECHNICAL ANALYSIS

Warp: White silk, s, 2-ply z. Count: 17–18 warps per centimeter.
Weft: 1) Polychrome silk, s. Colors: deep purple, tan, white, pink, orange, turquoise, royal blue, pale blue, green, yellow, and brown. Count: 70–170 per centimeter (the yarns vary widely in density).
2) Formerly metallic thread: strips of parchment(?) wrapped z on a yellow silk core, z. No gold was found remaining above the black, corroded surface of the parchment. Count: 50–70 per centimeter.
Weave: The panel is woven in the tapestry technique with slit joins. Eccentric weaving occurs in the gradual curves, while steep contours are handled by flying shuttle and warp steps. In vertical parts of the design, warps are wrapped. No unreplaced broken warps were found. The selvage, on the right side, is composed of all wefts turning around the outermost warp, which is single.

The reverse of this textile could not be viewed.

Unpublished.

18

19. Lions with Palmettes

Silk tapestry (kesi)
Warp 63.5 cm (25 in.); weft 34.7 cm (13⅝ in.)
Central Asia, Mongol period, 13th century or earlier
The Cleveland Museum of Art. Purchase from the J. H. Wade
Fund (1991.3)

Gold lions, delineated in coral and with polychrome manes, are here repeated in horizontal rows that are alternately oriented right and left. The interstices are filled with green leaves and polychrome flowers growing from coral stems. Between the rows of lions are large gold-and-polychrome foliate palmettes; like the lions, their orientation alternates right and left. The gold-and-polychrome design is offset by the very dark brown (almost black) ground. A fringe of warps and a striped starting edge are preserved at the bottom, as is, along the left edge, a selvage.

This *kesi* is distinguished from other Central Asian tapestries by the fact that the repetition of lions and foliate palmettes in staggered horizontal rows is based on drawloom patterns.[1] The lions, with parted manes and tilted heads, derive from Persian models dating to as early as the Sasanian period (A.D. 211–651), while the form of the foliate palmettes has antecedents in both West and Central Asian art.[2] In one of the pink flowers is a debased Arabic letter of the type known as Kufesque.[3] The decorative use of such letters made its way into the repertory of Central Asia long before the Mongol period and, in some *kesi*, plays a more prominent decorative role, particularly in the borders of cloud-collar medallions (see fig. 12).[4]

The degree of Persian influence in the design of this *kesi*, the derivation of the design from drawloom patterns, and the absence of frames and borders suggest that it may date to about or shortly after the Mongol conquest of Transoxiana and Khurasan in 1220–22, when artisans—including weavers—were relocated to eastern Central Asia. It is also possible that it was woven by Uyghurs living in western Central Asia following its conquest in the eleventh century by the Karakhanids, who transmitted Persian culture to the region.

Another *kesi* with virtually the same design (fig. 28) preserves part of a central cloud-collar frame enclosing flowers and a phoenix.[5] In contrast to the surrounding rows of lions and palmettes in the Cleveland *kesi*, the phoenix and flowers on that *kesi* are Chinese. The selvage

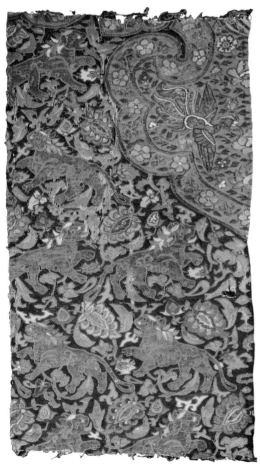

Figure 28. Textile with lions and partial cloud-collar medallion. Central Asia, 13th century or earlier. Silk tapestry (*kesi*), 56 × 23.5 cm (22 × 12¾ in.). Private collection

Figure 29. Diagram of two panels sewn together. Shaded portion shows placement of figure 28

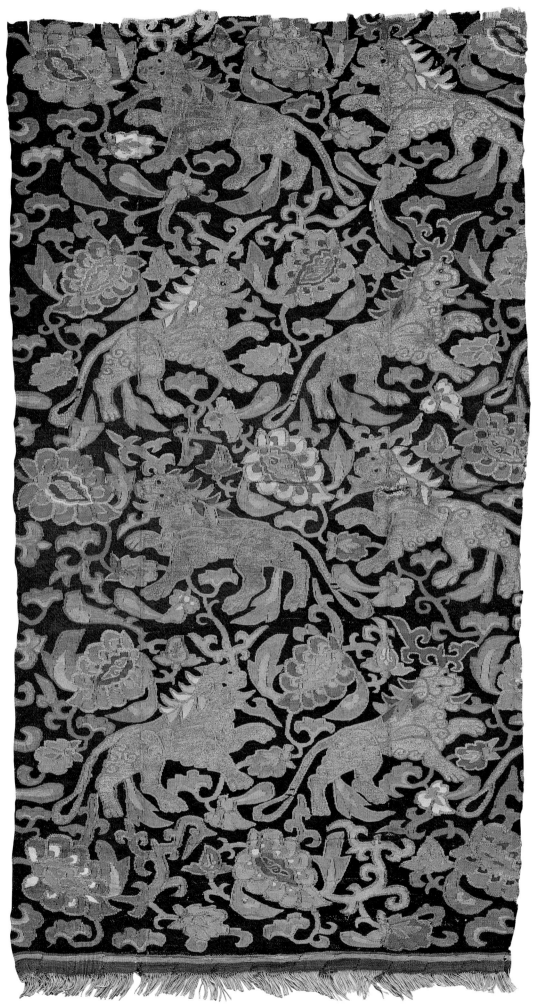

on the right side intersects the cloud collar along its central axis. Because of the narrow width of the loom, two panels with patterns in mirror reverse had to be sewn together along their selvage edges to complete the design of the cloud collar surrounded by rows of gold lions (fig. 29). Close examination of this and the Cleveland *kesi* reveals that they are not from the same loom piece, which is evidence that *kesi* designs were woven repeatedly.

1. See, for example, catalogue numbers 41 and 47.
2. Washington, D.C., 1985, p. 63, fig. 24; Marshak 1986, fig. 29; Soustiel 1985, pl. 20; Wilkinson 1973, p. 151, fig. 22, and p. 364, fig. 1; Le Coq 1913, pls. 20, 23.
3. Ettinghausen 1984.
4. Grünwedel 1920, p. I.82, fig. 79; Plum Blossoms 1988, no. 3.
5. For another *kesi* woven with lions but without the cloud-collar medallion, see Hong Kong 1995, cat. no. 1.

TECHNICAL ANALYSIS

Warp: White silk, s, 2-ply z. Count: 15–16 per centimeter. *Weft:* 1) Polychrome silk, slightly s. Colors: very dark brown (appears black), green, chartreuse, deep blue, light blue, purple, red, ivory, pink, tan, light gray, orange, and yellow. Count: approximately 48–112 wefts per centimeter. The range within the thread count is due to differences in the densities of the yarns. Usually, but not always, the wefts of a given color within one area of the pattern are the same density; however, the wefts of a given color in one area are often of a different density from wefts of the same color in another area. 2) Gold thread: strips of parchment with a metal surface consisting of gold and silver wrapped z around a deep yellow silk core, z. It is not known if the metals are layered or alloyed.[1] The substrate has a very pale translucent yellow adhesive coating. The gold threads are quite thick. *Weave:* The tapestry is woven with slit joins. Steep diagonals are achieved with stepped warps, limited soumak weaving, and some use of the flying shuttle (especially the gold wefts). There is a certain amount of eccentric weaving. A selvage is preserved on the left side: all the wefts turn around the outermost warp, which is single.

On the reverse, the wefts are cut close to the weave (the loose ends are 1.5 centimeters or less). The start or termination of a weft is often invisible; when it is visible, the cut end is always on the reverse side. Wefts are occasionally knotted together and frequently float across short distances (up to 1.6 centimeters). Three treatments for occasionally broken warps can be observed on the reverse. 1) In several places, a new warp was knotted to the broken warp close to the weave, with the loose ends of the two warps cut close to the knot. 2) A new warp may be introduced without being knotted to the broken warp and held in place by tightly beaten-in wefts. In that case, the loose ends of both the broken and the new warps emerge from the weave at the same point, lying in opposite directions. In one break, a gold weft is looped around the replaced warp to hold it in place. 3) The broken warp may not be replaced.

Broken warps that are not replaced reveal that the weaving of the panel progressed from the top to the bottom.

1. Identified by Norman Indictor and Denyse Montegut (correspondence to Anne E. Wardwell, May 10, 1991), and by Bruce Christman, chief conservator, The Cleveland Museum of Art, February 1997.

PUBLICATIONS: Simcox 1989, fig. 2; Spink & Son 1989, no. 5; Taylor 1991, p. 83; Wardwell 1992–93, p. 246.

20. *Animals and Birds amid Flowers*

Silk tapestry (kesi)
Warp 36.4 cm (14⅜ in.); weft 31.8 cm (12½ in.)
Song dynasty (960–1279), 11th–12th century
The Metropolitan Museum of Art, New York. Gift of John M. Crawford Jr., 1983 (1983.105)

This *kesi* was originally the wrapper (external mounting) of a handscroll painting in the Metropolitan Museum, *Trees against a Flat Vista*, by the eleventh-century master Guo Xi (ca. 1000–1090). As in the case of most *kesi* wrappers of Song paintings, it was repaired in the course of one of the periodic remountings of the painting. Particularly obvious is the animal on the lower edge, which has been extensively repaired by needle weaving.

The piece is a classic example of Northern Song *kesi*, which share much with *kesi* of eastern Central Asia, which we associate with the Uyghurs. The patterning and the images of birds and animals are strikingly similar, and in both groups eccentric weaving is very much in evidence. As this kind of pattern has no precedent in earlier Chinese history, we must conclude that the Uyghurs had something to do with the introduction of both the technique and the patterning of *kesi* into Song territory.

A number of similar pieces are known. All are woven on a purple ground—an indication, in the Chinese context, of association with the imperial court.[1] All have been taken off mounts for Song paintings, except for a large uncut piece in the Liaoning Provincial Museum, Shenyang (fig. 13).[2] The pattern is among those recorded by Southern Song and Yuan writers on *kesi* used for mounting paintings in the imperial collection at the beginning of the Southern Song dynasty. Because it is not known how far into the Southern Song this northern style persisted, we have assigned this *kesi* broadly to the Song dynasty.

1. According to the Southern Song writer Wang Yong, in the beginning of the Northern Song dynasty, purple robes could be worn only at court and were not permitted for daily wear. He adds that purple in those days referred to a red purple (as in the purple of the *kesi* in this exhibition, e.g., cat. nos. 13, 14, and perhaps also 17 and 18), while in his own time—in the late twelfth to early thirteenth century—purple refers to a black purple. And he expresses puzzlement at the fact that the northerners (the peoples in the Jin area, including the Jurchens and the Uyghurs) were wearing precisely that color forbidden in the early Song period. (See Wang Yong [1981], chap. 1, p. 8.) This passage confirms the use of red-purple fabrics for costumes by people outside the Song empire.
2. Yang Renkai et al. 1983, pls. 1, 2.

TECHNICAL ANALYSIS

Warp: Cream silk, s (very slight twist), 2-ply z. Count: 15 per centimeter. *Weft:* Polychrome silk, s (twists very slight). Colors:

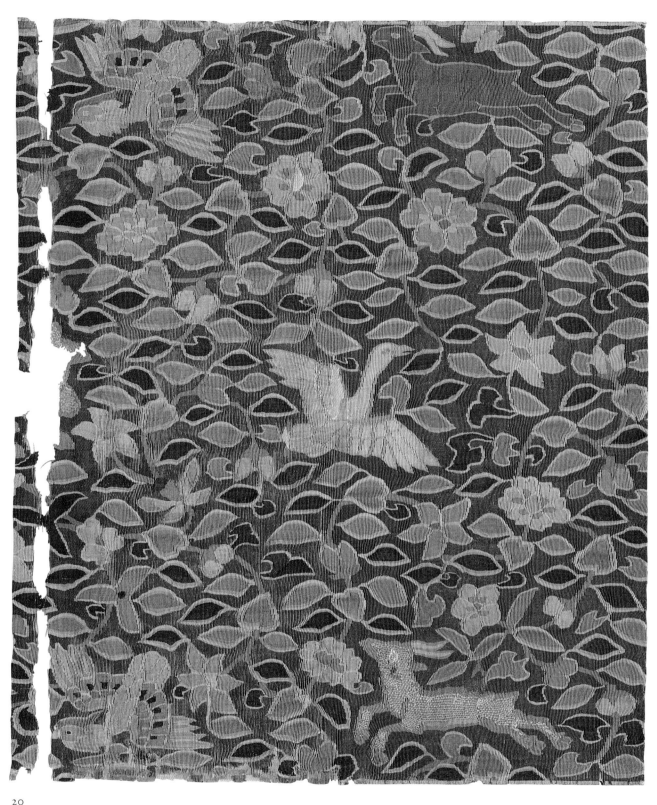

20

purple, forest green, pale green, mustard yellow, sky blue, yellow, white, tan, and brown. The light blue wefts are very uneven in the intensity of the blue, giving an effect of thin bands in the blue leaves; the same is true to a lesser extent of the pale green and the forest green. Count: 54–120 per centimeter. *Weave:* The tapestry is woven with slit joins. The weaving is eccentric, especially along the contours of the leaves and in the details of the birds and animals. Vertically curving stems are achieved by warp steps. The

overlapping of the wefts suggests that weaving progressed from bottom to top. The reverse side is inaccessible, making it impossible to observe the handling of the wefts and broken warps. The animal on the lower edge has been repaired extensively by needle weaving using tan silk, s, 2-ply z, thread.

PUBLICATIONS: New York 1971, no. 6, p. 25; Milhaupt 1992, p. 74, and fig. 2, p. 73; Vainker 1996, p. 173, fig. 18, p. 175.

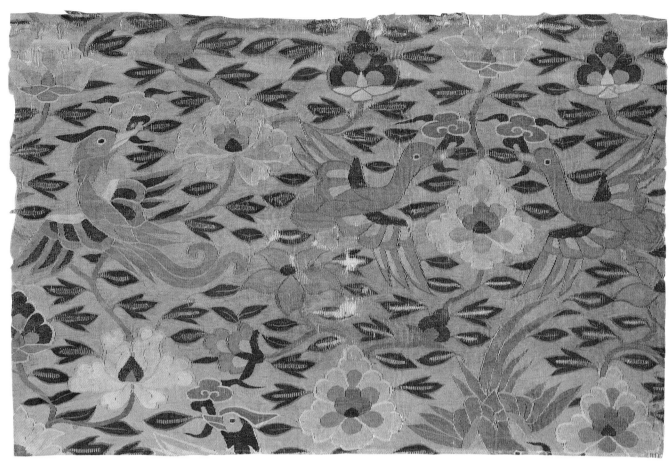

21

21. Birds and Flowers

Silk tapestry (kesi)
Warp 22 cm (8 ⅝ in.); weft 34 cm (13 ⅜ in.)
Song dynasty (960–1279), 11th–12th century
The Metropolitan Museum of Art, New York. Purchase, Bequest of
Dorothy Graham Bennett, 1966 (66.174b)

This piece, like catalogue number 20, was taken from the mounting of an old painting, *Dragon Boat Regatta on Jinming Lake*, after Wang Zhenpeng (ca. 1280–1329). The *kesi* in this case is certainly older than the painting. Again like catalogue number 20, it shares stylistic and technical features with *kesi* of the eastern Central Asian group. The similarity in the pattern is readily seen by comparison with catalogue number 16. However, the aggregate of stylistic and technical elements—the relatively static and balanced design, the paper substrate of the gold wefts (in the center of some of the leaves), and the motif of the *ruyi* or *lingzhi* fungus held in the beaks of the phoenixlike birds—points unmistakably to Chinese manufacture.

It is not at present known how far into the Southern Song period the Northern Song style persisted before giving way to the Southern Song type exemplified by catalogue number 22, or whether the two types coexisted for a period

of time in the Southern Song. The possibility, therefore, that this *kesi* was part of a batch made at the beginning of the Southern Song period for the mounting of paintings in the imperial collection cannot be ruled out.

TECHNICAL ANALYSIS

Warp: Cream silk, s (slight twist), 2-ply z. Count: 19 per centimeter. *Weft:* 1) Polychrome silk, s (slight twist). Colors: pale blue (a combination of white and blue yarns), deep blue, white, light tan, yellow, mustard yellow, pale green, and medium tan. The light blue and green wefts are unevenly dyed, giving a striated effect. Count: 36–120 per centimeter. 2) Gold: gilded strips of paper, approximately 2 millimeters wide (the gold leaf is almost entirely gone). Used for the centers of leaves. *Weave:* The tapestry is woven with slit joins. The weave is very eccentric and employs both soumak and flying shuttle. In the nearly vertical portions of the design, the warps are wrapped. The overlapping of wefts suggests that weaving progressed from bottom to top. The reverse side is inaccessible, and the handling of wefts and broken warps is therefore unknown. There are no finished edges.

PUBLICATIONS: Milhaupt 1992, p. 74, and fig. 1, p. 72; Vainker 1996, p. 173, fig. 1, p. 160, and fig. 19, p. 175.

22. Canopy

Center: Silk tapestry (kesi); borders: lampas
Overall (tabs not included) 80.3 × 78 cm (31⅝ × 30⅞ in.); tapestry
54 × 53 cm (21¼ × 20⅞ in.)
Southern Song dynasty (1127–1279), late 12th century
The Cleveland Museum of Art. John L. Severance Fund (1995.1)

The canopy is composed of a silk-and-gold tapestry sewn to a border of blue silk-and-gold fabric; it is cut on all four edges. The border consists of strips sewn together with the outer edges turned under. At each cor-ner is a yellow tab for handling. The canopy is lined with yellow silk.

The tapestry preserves part of a large, scaly dragon with upturned snout and flames. It is woven in shades of tan, green, blue, and pink, as well as white and very dark brown. Surrounding the dragon are flowers, leaves, a cloud forma-tion, and a flaming pearl. These are woven in white and yellow, as well as in shades of green, blue, pink, and purple. The ground is coral, and the contours and details of the motifs are delineated with gold thread. The border is woven with a delicate overall floral pattern in gold against a deep blue ground. The style of the floral design suggests that the border dates from the fifteenth century.

The theme of the dragon among flowers, unknown in Chinese representations of the dragon prior to the Song dynasty (960–1279), appears to derive from the Uyghur culture of Central Asia. Elements of the form of the dragon, with its upturned snout, horns resembling antlers, and flaming mane, also resemble elements of dragons in Central Asian *kesi* (see cat. nos. 13 and 14). On the other hand, the serpentine treatment of the dragon's body is in the Chinese style. Another Southern Song *kesi* woven with the same theme is preserved in the National Palace Museum, Taipei (see fig. 16 on page 58). The Palace Museum *kesi* is slightly earlier in date, and that dragon more closely resembles the Central Asian prototypes and is likely to have been woven at the beginning of the Southern Song.

The fineness of the silk threads and of the weaving, together with the use of flat gold thread that was gilded on both sides, is evidence that the *kesi* was woven in an imperial workshop. Eventually, it was taken to Tibet, very likely as a gift to a monastery or an important lama. Judging by the condition of the canopy, the *kesi*, the border, and the tabs at the corners were not recently assembled. Creases across the entire canopy have resulted in abraded gold wefts in the border and splits in the tapestry; the corners are worn and the tabs soiled. The condition of the corners and tabs appears to have resulted from the textile's use as a small canopy held over sacred objects or holy persons during Buddhist ceremonies, while the damage along the fold lines is a consequence of the canopy's having been folded when stored.

TECHNICAL ANALYSIS

Warp: Pale yellow silk, spun s, 2-ply z. Count: 24 per centimeter. *Weft:* 1) Polychrome silk, spun s. Colors: coral; light, medium, and dark pink; mauve; purple; light, medium, and dark green; light, medium, and dark blue; light, medium, and dark tan; very dark brown; yellow; charcoal; and white. Count: approximately 90–210 per centimeter. 2) Gold: flat strips of paper, gilded on both sides. *Weave:* The tapestry weave with tabby binding has slit joins. Long slits are joined by occasional dovetails. Steep diagonals are achieved by the progression of the weft from one warp to the next and by wrapped warps; eccentric weaving is kept to a minimum. On the reverse, weft floats are usually 1–1.5 centimeters but sometimes as long as 2.5 centimeters. Cut weft ends are approximately 1 centimeter long. Broken warps occur only occasionally and are variously treated. 1) The broken end is knotted and not replaced. 2) A replacement warp is knotted to the broken warp (the ends of the two warps are about 1 centimeter long). 3) The replacement warp is not knotted but simply secured in place by beaten-in wefts. The two warp ends are cut fairly close to the weave.

BORDER: *Warp:* Foundation: blue silk, s, single. Supplementary: tan (faded from coral) silk, s (occasional twist, usually appears to be without twist). Proportion: 3 foundation warps to one supplementary warp. Step: 2 foundation warps. Count: 58 foundation warps and 20 supplementary warps per centimeter. *Weft:* Foundation: blue silk, s, paired, twice the density of the foundation warps. Supplementary: gold thread formed of flat strips of paper, gilded on one side; orange bole is under the gold leaf. Pass: 1 paired foundation and 1 supplementary weft. Step: 1 pass. Count: 20 passes per centimeter. *Weave:* Lampas variation. Foundation: 1/2 z twill. The supplementary weave is tabby. An incomplete selvage composed of about 7 millimeters of selvage border is preserved on one of the border strips. The foundation warps are blue and single, as in the body of the textile, and the binding is 1/2 z twill. On the reverse, the gold wefts are cut along the inner edge of the border. The outer selvage edge has been cut off.

PUBLICATIONS: Plum Blossoms 1988, no. 6; Shaffer 1989, p. 108.

23. Imperial Boots

Principal fabric: Silk tapestry (kesi)
Height 47.5 cm (18¾ in.); width 30.8 cm (12⅛ in.)
Liao dynasty (907–1125)
The Cleveland Museum of Art. Purchase from the J. H. Wade
Fund (1993.158, 158a)

Of this pair of boots, one is complete and one has been reconstructed with portions of the original outer fabric from the front and back leg sections. The complete boot is composed of layers: silk-and-gold tapestry (*kesi*) on the outside, a layer of silk batting, and a silk lining. The silk sole has a silk lining with a layer of silk floss between the lining and the two outer layers. The boot is seamed down the sides and across the top of the instep to form three sections: one for the front of the leg, another for the back of the leg plus the heel, and the third for the instep (fig. 32). The top opening is faced with a gauze band on which is preserved a faint design, probably originally applied in gold leaf.

The outermost *kesi* is woven with two phoenixes diving in flight on either side of a flaming pearl. The phoenixes have crests, flowing head feathers, and magnificent plumed tails, while the flaming pearl is divided like a *yin-yang* symbol. Other flaming pearls, drawn slightly differently, appear above the phoenixes. Filling the interstices are cloud scrolls. Their form, which resembles a *ruyi* fungus with opposed scrolls and a "tail," is typically Liao.[1] Similarly, the phoenixes chasing the flaming pearls among clouds

23

Figure 30. Detail, cat. no. 23 (warp ↔)

woven with a cloud-and-wave design, and the soles were silk.[5] Pants that tied at the waist were tucked into the boots (which accounts for the wide opening at the top), and over the pants were a skirt and a knee-length jacket. The outer robe was full-length, had wide sleeves, and an opening on the wearer's left, where it was fastened with knotted buttons. Completing the costume were a pair of embroidered gloves and an embroidered hat ornamented with borders of silk-and-gold tapestry.[6]

Women's boots such as these do not appear in Khitan wall paintings because they were almost entirely concealed by the full-length outer robe. Tapestry boots similar to these, however, apparently served as models for bronze and silver-gilt boots that have been found in Liao tombs.[7] One example (fig. 31) is ornamented with dragons chasing pearls, arranged in much the same manner as the phoenixes on the *kesi* boots.

1. Wirgin 1960, p. 32.
2. Tamura and Kobayashi 1953, fig. 118; Jin Fengyi 1980, pl. 3, no. 1; London, *Imperial Gold*, 1990, fig. 28; Inner Mongolia 1993, drawings on pp. 40, 110.
3. *Liaoshi*, vol. 2, chap. 37, p. 442, translated in Wittfogel and Feng Chia-sheng 1949, p. 157.
4. Liaoning Provincial Museum 1975, pp. 28–30.

have many parallels in the art of the Liao.[2] The bright colors of the tapestry have become muted through burial. Gold thread (now disintegrated except for the traces of gold leaf that have adhered to the warps) originally delineated the motifs and filled the wings, necks, and heads of the phoenixes.

The tapestry from which the boots were made is exceedingly finely woven, using silk yarns of subtly varied densities (fig. 30), a level of technical refinement characteristic of silk-tapestry weaving in the Liao empire (see also cat. no. 10). The care and attention to detail that went into the making of the boots are exemplified by the cutting of the tapestry sections so that the flaming pearls occur precisely at the centers of the shin and calf and at the top of the instep. Moreover, in order to accommodate the particular cut and smaller area of the instep, the phoenixes were drawn slightly differently and the design was reduced in scale. These factors, the amount of gold used in the *kesi,* and the theme of the phoenixes chasing a pearl are evidence that the boots were made for a member of the Liao imperial family. Probably they were intended for a woman, given the close association of the phoenix with the empress. The *kesi* may have been woven at Zuzhou (southwest of Shangjing, the Upper Capital of the Liao), where the government operated a silk-weaving workshop for the production of fabrics used by the court.[3]

Similar boots were discovered in the tenth-century tomb of a female member of the Liao aristocracy at Yemaotai, in Liaoning Province.[4] Part of a costume, the boots were knee-high, the outer fabric was a silk-and-gold tapestry

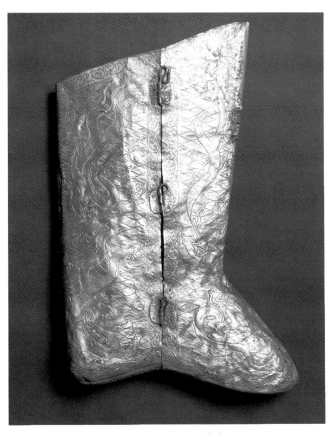

Figure 31. Boot. Liao dynasty (618–1125). Gilt bronze, 43.2 × 29.2 cm (17 × 11½ in.). Private collection

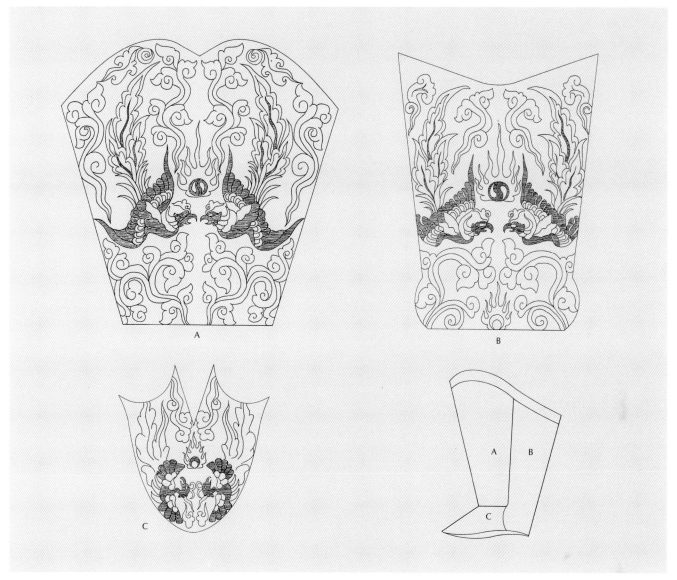

Figure 32. Drawings of *kesi* designs and their placement on cat. no. 23, left

5. The archaeological report (cited in note 4) does not include photographs or drawings of the boots, nor does it provide information regarding the gold thread.

6. For a detail of the hat showing the *kesi* borders, see Gao Hanyu 1987, pl. 59.

7. Two pairs were found in the tomb of a Liao princess and her husband. See Inner Mongolia 1987, colorpl. 1, no. 2; pl. 1.

TECHNICAL ANALYSIS

Warp: Tan silk, s, 2-ply z. Count 20–21 per centimeter. *Weft:* 1) Polychrome silk, s. Colors: tan, light tan, reddish brown (probably originally plum), light and medium blue, and light and medium green. Count: 60–240 per centimeter. 2) Gold thread, now entirely disintegrated except for pieces of gold leaf that adhere to the warps. *Weave:* Tapestry with slit joins. Eccentric weaving occurs along the contours of motifs. Steep diagonals are achieved by warp steps and by wrapped warps that are also often stepped, with some gaps filled with a weft thread in the flying shuttle technique. The design is woven at right angles to the warp.

On the reverse side, weft floats are short (up to 3 centimeters, but usually 1.5 centimeters or less), and the wefts are cut short (1–2 centimeters). In one place, two wefts of the same color are knotted together. Broken warps occur only occasionally. One replaced warp was secured by the weave, without being knotted to the end of the original warp. Usually the replaced warp was knotted to the end of the broken warp very close to the weave. The loose ends of broken and replaced warps are short (approximately 3 centimeters) and are not tied to other ends or to weft floats. Broken warps that were not repaired were not found. In the selvage the wefts simply turn around the outermost warp.

FACING BAND AT OPENING OF BOOT: *Warp:* Tan silk, mostly without apparent twist, but with an occasional slight s or z twist. The density of the warps varies. *Weft:* Tan silk, mostly without apparent twist, though a very slight s twist can occasionally be detected; several strands are thrown z (very slight and occasional twist); the wefts are at least twice the density of the warps. *Weave:* Gauze, based on a unit of 4 warps. Selvage: The gauze weave toward the outer edge becomes tight; the wefts turn around the outermost warp. A faint design of scrolling clouds(?) is preserved on the band. It appears to be the discoloration of an adhesive to which gold leaf was applied.

LINING: *Warp:* Tan silk, mostly without apparent twist, but occasional s or z twists can be detected, single. Count: 46 per centimeter. The densities of the warps are uneven. *Weft:* Tan silk, mostly without apparent twist, but an occasional s twist can be detected; one repaired weft was plied s. Count: 42 per centimeter. *Weave:* Tabby, very uneven (sometimes loose and other times tight). There are flaws, especially short floats of warps and wefts. Selvage: The selvage border, about 7 millimeters wide, is woven with tan warps more closely spaced than in the body of the fabric; all wefts turn around the outermost warp.

SOLE: The sole is constructed of four layers: 1) The outermost fabric is woven with a diaper pattern of tiny diamonds. *Warp and weft:* Tan silk, without apparent twist, single, 42 × 52 per centimeter. *Weave:* 4-end twill damask. 2) Under the outermost fabric is a brown tabby silk with no pattern. *Warp* (?): Brown silk, strongly z, single, 24 per centimeter. *Weft* (?): Brown silk, without apparent twist, 20 per centimeter. *Weave:* Tabby, very loose but even. 3) Between the brown tabby silk and the lining is a layer of silk batting. 4) The lining (very damaged) is an unpatterned silk. *Warp and weft:* Tan silk, without apparent twist. No count was possible. *Weave:* Tabby. The layers of the sole were originally held together by neat rows of running stitches, from which only the holes in the outermost fabric remain.

PUBLICATIONS: Cleveland 1994, no. 37, pp. 325–28, 347; "Fit for an Empress" 1994–95, p. 99; Wardwell 1994, pp. 6–12; Wardwell 1995, p. 7.

24. A Vighnantaka Thangka

Silk tapestry (kesi)
Warp 105 cm (41⅜ in.); weft 74 cm (29⅛ in.)
Tangut Xia dynasty (1032–1227), early 13th century
The Cleveland Museum of Art. Purchase from the J. H. Wade Fund (1992.72)

This *thangka*, or icon, is dominated by the fierce and powerful figure of Vighnantaka, a protective Tantric Buddhist deity who destroys obstacles standing in the way of spiritual enlightenment.[1] He is dark blue in color, holds a noose in his left hand with the forefinger raised in a menacing gesture, and brandishes a sword in his right hand. The sword associates him with the Transcendent Buddha, Amoghasiddhi, who appears in Vighnantaka's crown. Beneath his left foot is the prostrate elephant-headed god, Ganesha, and under his right foot the prone figure of Shiva. Vighnantaka radiates a flaming aureole through which charge miniature figures of his entourage, symbolic of his tremendous powers. The entire scene is supported on a lotus base and surrounded on three sides by a floral vine scroll.

In the register above the central scene are the Five Transcendent Buddhas seated on lotus thrones. Originally, a pearl ornamented the forehead and topknot of each of the Buddhas; only three remain. Five dancing *dakinis* and, at either end, a small image of Vighnantaka are depicted in a frieze in the corresponding register below. Enclosing the central scene and the two registers is a narrow border of angular U-shaped motifs with small dots in the centers; a band similarly ornamented separates the central and

lower registers, while a band of half circles partitions the central and upper registers. The three central registers are surrounded by a floral vine scroll that is narrow along the vertical sides of the *thangka* and wide across the top and bottom. Among the flowers are sixteen lotuses which support symbols that derive from the eight auspicious symbols and seven jewels of Buddhism.[2] The *thangka* is edged by a blue band articulated with pearls, each with a central dot. An additional pearl border occurs along the bottom edge. The top and bottom portions of the *thangka* flare, giving an overall hourglass shape.

Vighnantaka, whose name means "destroyer of obstacles," originated in the Buddhist legends of Nepal.[3] These tell of a certain sage who failed to propitiate Ganesha before performing a Tantric sacrifice. Insulted and furious, Ganesha threw numerous obstacles in the path of the sage which ultimately destroyed the desired effects of his sacrifice. The sage, ascertaining the cause of the disturbance, summoned Vighnantaka to vanquish Ganesha. On the basis of this story, Ganesha, subdued underfoot, is the identifying iconographic feature of Vighnantaka. Shiva, similarly disposed, does not figure in the story; and why this Hindu god, the father of Ganesha, is thus represented here is not clear.

24

Figure 33. *Thangka* of Akala. Tangut Xia dynasty (1032–1227). Silk tapestry (*kesi*). 90 × 56 cm (35⅜ × 22 in.). Potala Palace, Lhasa

The Vighnantaka *thangka* is one of a small group of silk-tapestry icons woven in the Tibetan Kadampa style that, with one exception, have been preserved in Lhasa. One, the Akala *thangka* (fig. 33), is very similar in its iconography and decorative detail to the Vighnantaka *thangka*. The central figure of Akala, radiating a flaming aureole, stands on a lotus support and is framed by a floral vine scroll. The Five Transcendent Buddhas appear in the register above, while deities are depicted in the lower register. The framing bands, moreover, are ornamented with rectangles articulated with dots. This *thangka* bears an inscription stating that it was commissioned for the great Sakya historian Gragpa Gyalmtshan (1147–1216) by his Khampa disciple, can br Tsongrus grags.[4] They are portrayed in the upper left and right corners, respectively, of the central zone. This and the Vighnantaka *thangka* share a technical feature so unique as to suggest a common weaving center for both: the small pearls on the foreheads and topknots of the Five Transcendent Buddhas were threaded down the warps prior to weaving instead of being sewn on the tapestry after the weaving had been completed (fig. 34).[5]

A second, related *thangka* in Lhasa depicts Vighnantaka, again trampling both Ganesha and Shiva (fig. 35). As in the Cleveland *thangka*, Vighnantaka's retinue charge through his flaming aureole brandishing weapons. The central scene is similarly set within a floral vine scroll, the Five Transcendent Buddhas are represented above, and five deities below. Framing the entire *thangka* is the same border of half circles that separates the central and upper registers in the Cleveland piece.

A third *kesi thangka* in the group is the *thangka* of Green Tara in the State Hermitage, Saint Petersburg (fig. 36). It has the same hourglass shape as the Vighnantaka *thangka*, dancing *dakinis*, and a narrow pearl border delineating the outer edges. Closely related to the Green Tara is a fourth *thangka* preserved in Lhasa that portrays the Tibetan lama Zhang Yudrakpa Tsondru Drakpa (1123–1194; fig. 37). It is very similar to the Green Tara, particularly in the stylization of the mountains and in the strings of pearls above the central figure.[6]

Although the *kesi thangkas* follow the Tibetan Kadampa style, certain iconographic details indicate that they were produced in Tangut Xia, which had close ethnic, cultural, and religious ties to Tibet. The hourglass shape of the Vighnantaka and Green Tara *thangkas* occurs, for example, in many of the painted *thangkas* that were discovered in the Tangut garrison city of Khara Khoto.[7] Dancing *dakinis*, in both the Vighnantaka and Green Tara *thangkas*, frequently occur in Tangut art but are thus far unknown in the art of central Tibet.[8] Moreover, the rug on the throne in the *thangka* of Lama Zhang has a red ground with a floral pattern and a blue cloth border that falls in folds. Such throne rugs with this color scheme and floral decoration consistently occur in the painted *thangkas* found at Khara Khoto.[9] That only one of these Tangut *thangkas*—the Green Tara *thangka*—was found in Tangut Xia, in the ruins of Khara Khoto, while the remainder were preserved in Tibet is not surprising given the close ties that existed between the Tangut imperial court and the monasteries of central Tibet.[10] In none is this better exemplified than in the portrait *thangka* of the lama

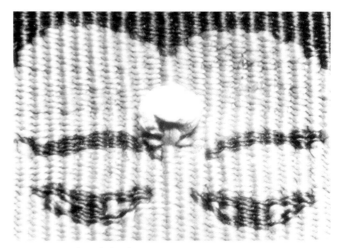

Figure 34. Enlarged detail, cat. no. 24

Figure 35. *Thangka* of Vighnantaka. Tangut Xia dynasty (1032–1227), 13th century. Silk tapestry (*kesi*), 53 × 40 cm (20⅞ × 15¾ in.). Potala Palace, Lhasa

Figure 36. *Thangka* of Green Tara. Tangut Xia dynasty (1032–1227), 13th century. Silk tapestry (*kesi*), 101 × 52.5 cm (39¾ × 20⅝ in.). State Hermitage, Saint Petersburg

Zhang, the founder of the Tsalpa suborder of the Kagyu order of Tibet, which regularly sent monks to the Tangut court.[11]

There is one important technical difference within the *thangkas* of this group. The reverse side of the Vighnantaka *thangka* is covered with a tangle of long weft threads and the lengthy ends of numerous broken and replaced warps (fig. 17). In contrast, the reverse side of the Green Tara *thangka* has few broken warps and relatively closely cut weft ends (fig. 18). The technique of the latter is in keeping with silk tapestries produced in other areas either at this time or in earlier periods, including Central Asia, the Liao and Jin dynasties, and Song China. In fact, the only other *kesi* known thus far to be woven in the manner of the Vighnantaka *thangka* is the Yamantaka mandala (cat. no. 25), which dates from a century or so later. (Whether the related *kesi thangkas* in Lhasa are woven in the same technique is not known, as efforts to examine their reverse sides have regrettably proved impossible.) The contrasting weaving techniques of tapestries attributed to Tangut Xia can best be explained by the diversity of its population: Tanguts, Uyghurs, Chinese, and Tibetans. Again, the technical similarities between the Vighnantaka *thangka* and the Yamantaka mandala, which was woven much later, in the official workshops of the Yuan dynasty (1279–1368) in

Figure 37. *Thangka* of Lama Zhang. Tangut Xia dynasty (1032–1227). Silk tapestry (*kesi*), 84 × 54 cm (33⅛ × 21¼ in.). Potala Palace, Lhasa

Detail, cat. no. 24

interior China, can be seen as a consequence of the movement of artisans within the Mongol empire.

That the Vighnantaka *thangka* was made no later than the thirteenth century is evidenced by the simple juxtaposition of color fields and by the lack of shading. The technical and iconographic similarities of the Vighnantaka *thangka* to the Akala *thangka* in Lhasa indicate a more specific date, shortly before the fall of the Tangut state to the Mongols in 1227.

1. Mallmann 1955, pp. 41–46; Mallmann 1975, pp. 447–49; Dr. Heather Stoddard, unpublished notes.
2. The eight auspicious symbols are the parasol, golden fish, conch, lotus, chakra, banner, vase, and endless knot. The seven jewels are the perfect general, perfect minister, perfect wife, wish-fulfilling gem, perfect horse, perfect elephant, and wheel of Buddhist teaching.
3. Mallmann 1955, pp. 41–43; Alsop 1984, p. 209ff.
4. Dr. Heather Stoddard, unpublished notes and correspondence to Anne E. Wardwell, January 19, 1993; Dr. Hugh Richardson, correspondence to Anne E. Wardwell, February 1993.
5. Berger 1994, p. 121 n. 66.
6. Huang Ti 1985, pl. 62.
7. Milan 1993, nos. 5, 8, 23, 33, 35, 40, 42.
8. Ibid., p. 72, and nos. 22, 24, 27, 30, 32.
9. Ibid., pp. 72, 74.
10. Sperling 1987.
11. Berger 1994, p. 102.

TECHNICAL ANALYSIS

THANGKA: *Warp:* Ecru silk, s, 2-ply z (strong ply). Count: 19 per centimeter. *Weft:* 1) Polychrome silk, s. Colors: white, pale blue, teal blue, deep blue, pale green, medium green, maroon, pale yellow, tan, orange, and pale pink. Count: approximately 52–200 picks per centimeter. 2) Ecru silk, s, 2-ply z (strong ply). *Weave:* Tapestry weave with tabby binding; near the bottom edge is a narrow ornamental tabby border. The tapestry is woven with slit joins; long slits are secured by occasional dovetail joins usually consisting of two wefts, but occasionally of one. The silk weft yarns vary in density; most picks are one weft, but sometimes there are two per pick, loosely plied s. The design is indicated by color changes as well as by the use of slits and by the different thicknesses of the picks. Curves are achieved by the use of eccentric weaving and stepped slits.

The reverse side is covered with long, loose wefts that are tangled, and with the often long ends of broken and replaced warps that are sometimes tied to tangles of wefts (fig. 17). Broken warps occur frequently, particularly in the register with the *dakinis* and in the bottom border. In some cases the new warp was overlapped with the broken warp and secured in place by the wefts; in others, the broken warp was simply not repaired.

Selvages occur along the straight portions of both side edges: wefts turn around the outermost warp, which is single. Along diagonally extended edges, wefts turn around successive warps to form a diagonal; warps are cut about half a centimeter from the tapestry weave. The starting and finishing edges are both completed by a section of tabby weave using 2-ply z silk wefts. At the bottom edge, about 6 passes remain; at the top edge, only 2. The warps at both ends are cut. Interrupting the tapestry about 2.5 centimeters above the beginning of the tapestry weave at the bottom edge is a narrow horizontal band of open tabby weave using 3 picks of the plied ecru silk wefts.

Each of the pearls on the foreheads and topknots of the Five Transcendent Buddhas was threaded down a warp prior to weaving and then surrounded by tapestry weave (fig. 34).

LINING: Fragments of a silk damask lining remain around the edges of the *thangka*. They are sewn with tan silk thread (s, 2-ply z) with running stitches. The lining is patterned with small roundels arranged in staggered rows. The roundels are about 4 millimeters in diameter; the repeat is 8 millimeters (warp) × 1.6 centimeters (weft). The single warps are tan silk, z (twist very slight); 50 per centimeter. The wefts are tan silk, without apparent twist; 34 per centimeter. The damask weave is a 3/1 z twill in the ground and 1/3 s for the pattern.

PATCHES: At some point, the *thangka* was repaired with patches of resist-dyed tan silk with a pattern of light tan roundels (about 2.7 centimeters in diameter) arranged in aligned rows (repeat: 5 × 4.8 centimeters). *Warp and weft:* Tan silk, occasionally slightly s or z, but mostly without twist; 42 × 23 threads per centimeter. *Weave:* Tabby.

PUBLICATIONS: Wardwell 1992–93, p. 245; Wardwell 1993, p. 136; Simcox, "Tracing the Dragon," 1994, fig. 12, p. 45; Barnett 1995, p. 142; Reynolds, "Silk," 1995, no. 9, p. 92.

25. Yamantaka Mandala with Imperial Portraits

Silk tapestry (kesi)
Warp 245.5 cm (96⅝ in.); weft 209 cm (82¼ in.)
Yuan dynasty (1279–1368), ca. 1330–32
The Metropolitan Museum of Art, New York. Purchase,
Lila Acheson Wallace Gift, 1992 (1992.54)

This mandala, in the style of the Sakyapa school (originating from Sakya monastery in Tibet), shows Yamantaka (also known as Vajrabhairava), the wrathful manifestation of the bodhisattva Manjushri, as the central deity.[1] The basic scheme of the mandala follows the convention of this school in the fourteenth century, and the decoration is rich and complex. (For a detailed description of the iconography, see p. 100.) The design is made by color changes and slits in the weave, and by the use of gilded paper in such areas as crowns and jewelry, which gives a three-dimensional effect. Shading is achieved by the interpenetration of wefts of two different colors or two shades of the same color, a technique developed in the Southern Song (1127–1279).

The donors depicted in the lower corners, identified by Tibetan inscriptions in cartouches above their portraits, are, from the left: Tugh Temür, great-great-grandson of Khubilai Khan, who reigned as Emperor Wenzong of the Yuan dynasty in China from 1328 to 1332; Khoshila, elder brother of Tugh Temür, who reigned briefly in 1329 as Emperor Mingzong; and Budashiri and Babusha (fig. 69), their respective spouses. The vertical strips that originally extended from the cartouches, which may have included the names of the emperors and empresses in Chinese, have been cut out.

A mandala is the representation of a magical and sacred realm. It is occupied in the center by a deity, the ultimate subject of an adept's meditation, who is surrounded by a series of worlds (or spiritual stages) that the believer must pass through before he or she can reach the center—and enlightenment. The cult of Yamantaka, the central deity in this mandala, was introduced into China by a disciple of Phagspa, preceptor to Khubilai Khan and the most powerful lama in China in the early Yuan dynasty (1279–1368). The disciple, a monk whose name, transliterated, was Ji-ning Sha-luo-ba-guan-zhao, was sent by Phagspa to study with the great teacher La-wen-bu, who was famed for his knowledge of the esoteric doctrine of Yamantaka.[2] Within the Yuan palace compound there was a temple to Vajrabhairava (Yamantaka) west of Huiqing Pavilion, in which was housed a statue of the deity Mahakala.[3] The deity in the bottom row next to the images of the emperors is tentatively identified as Mahakala.[4]

The chapter on paintings and sculpture in the *Jingshi dadian* (Record of Yuan Institutions) includes detailed

Detail, cat. no. 25

95

information on orders for imperial portraits and mandalas. In some of these, it is specified that woven portraits were to be made immediately upon the completion of the painted portraits; in others, this was not spelled out, but it may be assumed. Some orders were for separate portraits and mandalas, even when they seemed to form a set, and some were for mandalas with portraits, as in the present *kesi*. In all cases, when specified, the dimensions were always 9½ × 8 feet (in Yuan measure), which corresponds to the dimensions of the Metropolitan *kesi*.[5]

This *kesi* is not recorded in the existing version of the paintings and sculpture chapter of the *Jingshi dadian*;[6] nor, for that matter, is the *kesi* portrait of Khubilai, which is mentioned only in the biography of Tang Renzu, a Uyghur who was the supervising officer for the work. Nevertheless, in the order given on January 15, 1321, for the double portrait of Ayurbarwada (Emperor Renzong; r. 1312–20) and his consort, together with mandalas on the left and right, it was specified that the portrait (in triplicate) should conform to the style of Khubilai's portrait, and that each copy should measure 9½ × 8 feet. (The dimensions for Yuan imperial portraits were perhaps those established by the dimensions of the portrait of the first emperor of the dynasty, Khubilai; r. 1260–94.) The image of Tugh Temür in this tapestry appears to be based on a portrait of him in the collection of the National Palace Museum, Taipei (fig. 38). It is also highly likely that the portrait of Khubilai Khan now also in the National Palace Museum served as

the cartoon for his official portrait in woven silk (fig. 39).

The senior official involved in giving the order for the Metropolitan *kesi* is likely to have been Mingli Donga (d. 1340), whose name is mentioned in connection with the orders for the production of all imperial portraits and mandalas—first in the year 1323, when he was the head of the Bureau for Imperial Manufacture (Jiangzuo Yuan, a service agency for the imperial court under which was the Superintendency for Weaving Buddhist Icons), and later as privy councillor, during the reign of Tugh Temür. Mingli Donga seems to have been one of a number of artistically gifted men who achieved high office in the Yuan administration. (Another was the aforementioned Tang Renzu, who was also a talented musician.) In 1321, while he was head of the Bureau for Imperial Manufacture, Mingli Donga was charged, with other senior officials, with the design of imperial carriages used for ceremonial processions, which involved highly elaborate and ornamented construction.[7] Unfortunately, little is known of his background as there is no biography of him in the *Yuanshi* (History of the Yuan Dynasty) or any other historical record of the Yuan dynasty. This is probably because of his close association with Tugh Temür—of which more later.

The artist who directed the production of the mandala would have been Li Xiaoyan, whose name appears on every order issued for imperial portraits and mandalas. Li was a portraitist in the Superintendency for Buddhist Icons during the reign of Ayurbarwada and was named the artist

Figure 38. *Emperor Wenzong*. Yuan dynasty (1279–1368), 14th century. Album leaf, ink and color on silk, 59.4 × 47 cm (23⅜ × 18½ in.). National Palace Museum, Taipei

Figure 39. *Khubilai Khan as the First Yuan Emperor, Shizu*. Yuan dynasty (1279–1368), 13th century. Album leaf, ink and color on silk, 59.4 × 47 cm (23⅜ × 18½ in.). National Palace Museum, Taipei

for the aforementioned portrait of the emperor and empress. In the reign of Tugh Temür he was superintendent for Buddhist icons, receiving his orders for imperial portraits and mandalas from Mingli Donga.

The history behind the Yamantaka mandala is complicated, as is everything having to do with the imperial Mongol house of the Yuan dynasty. Briefly, when Yesün Temür (the Taiding emperor; r. 1323–28) and his son Aragibag (the Tianshun emperor) died in quick succession in 1328, the brothers Khoshila and Tugh Temür, sons of Khaishan (Emperor Wuzong; r. 1308–11), became contenders for the throne. Both were away from Daidu at the time of Aragibag's death, but Tugh Temür, who was in Jiangling, reached Daidu first, having been guided on his way by Mingli Donga, and was proclaimed emperor with the support of the powerful official El-Temür (d. 1333). In May 1329, Tugh Temür abdicated in favor of Khoshila, who was still in Khara Khorum. The two brothers met in August that year halfway between Daidu and Khara Khorum. But after a few days of happy reunion Khoshila died under mysterious circumstances, whereupon Tugh Temür regained the throne and ruled until his death in 1332. Babusha, Khoshila's widowed consort, was at first well treated; shortly after Tugh Temür reascended the throne, she was given a large sum of money for expenses.[8] At her request, a solemn Buddhist mass for the dead was held for Khoshila for seven days in November 1329 and masses were said for him in four Daoist temples and at the sacred mountains of Wudang and Longhu.[9] But on May 9, 1330, Babusha died[10]—said to have been murdered by Budashiri.[11] After the death of Tugh Temür, Budashiri became de facto regent. First, she put the seven-year-old Irinjinbal, son of Khoshila and Babusha, on the throne in preference to her own son. Irinjinbal died within a week of his accession. Then, in 1333, she recalled from exile Khoshila's elder son by his first wife and made him emperor. This was Toghon Temür (Emperor Shundi; r. 1333–68), at that time thirteen years old. When Toghon Temür came of age in 1340, he exiled Budashiri and her son El Tegüs—who was quietly put away en route. Tugh Temür's spirit tablet was removed from the imperial ancestral temple, and Mingli Donga—the only surviving member of the conspiracy to murder Khoshila— was executed.[12] Thus, at least three of the four personages represented on this *kesi* died unnatural deaths. Thirteen forty was also the year that in many parts of China saw the beginnings of uprisings that eventually led to the expulsion of the Mongol rulers in 1368 and the founding of the Chinese Ming dynasty.[13]

It is likely that this *kesi* was commissioned before the death of Babusha, in 1330, and completed after the death of Tugh Temür, in 1332. The subject of the mandala suggests that it may have been produced for an initiation ceremony. We know from his biography in the *Yuanshi* that Tugh Temür underwent two initiations as emperor[14] and

that Yamantaka initiations were practiced by the Yuan imperial family.[15] However, because the paintings and *kesi* of imperial portraits and mandalas were always produced in triplicate or (more rarely) in duplicate, and because no mention of the occasion is ever given in connection with the orders, it is most probable that these portraits and mandalas were meant to be housed or displayed in the imperial ancestral halls and portrait halls (*yingtang*) for emperors and their consorts that were in temples connected with the imperial family. More than one copy of this *kesi* was made, and there is indeed a small fragment of the same mandala that is known to have survived. Nevertheless, up to the present, the Metropolitan mandala with imperial portraits is the only complete example known of this singular class of imperially commissioned works of art from the Mongol empire.

1. For an art-historical account of the *thangkas* of the Sakya school, see Pal 1984, "The Sakya-pa Style," pp. 61–96.

2. *Fozu lidai tongzai*, vol. 49, chap. 22, pp. 729–30.

3. *Xijin zhi jiyi* 1983, p. 111. The *Xijin zhi jiyi* is a reconstituted version of the *Xijin zhi*, a gazetteer of the district of Daidu written at the end of the Yuan dynasty by Xiong Mengxiang. The original text is now lost, and this reconstituted version has been reassembled from extensive quotes from standard works such as the early Ming *Yongle dadian* (Grand compilation of Yongle) and the early Qing *Rixia jiuwen* (Old tales of Rixia). According to the *Rixia jiuwen*, the Mahakala statue was in the Huiqing Pavilion. The *Rixia jiuwen*, another gazetteer of Beijing, was compiled by Zhu Yizun (1629–1709) but was subsequently enlarged and annotated by scholar-officials at the court of the Qianlong emperor (r. 1736–95) and published under the title *Rixia jiuwen kao*. An edition in four volumes was published in Beijing in 1985.

4. Mahakala was the most important deity of the Mongol imperial house, and to Mahakala were attributed some of the most crucial battle victories. The first image of Mahakala in Yuan China was sculpted by Anige (1245–1306), the legendary Nepali artist, at the instruction of Phagspa (see Chen Qingying 1922, pp. 163–65). However, of the hundreds, if not thousands, of Mahakala images produced all over China in the Yuan period, only a very few have survived, of which the best known is a rather damaged stone sculpture, dated 1322, on the grounds of the former Baocheng Temple in Hangzhou (reproduced in Yang Boda 1988, vol. 6, pl. 23). This image of Mahakala is generally in keeping with that of early paintings of the Sakya school, of which Phagspa was the patriarch. The blue deity next to the imperial images in the Yamantaka *kesi*, though he holds in his hands the usual attributes of Mahakala, does not adopt the stance of this protective deity characteristic of early Sakya and Yuan images.

5. Values for weights and measures in historical periods in China are difficult to determine since, in addition to regional differences, there were for different purposes variations in standards (the foot-measure was different, for example, for construction work and textiles). The present conversion is based on the value of the official Song "textile foot," given in diagram 19 in Wu Chengluo 1984. According to Wu, there was little change in standards for weights and measures from the Tang to the Ming period, and there was no change between the Song and the Yuan. Yang Kuan (1957) is also of the opinion that Yuan measures followed those of the Song. However, he arrived at various values, from between 31.1 and 31.4 centimeters, for the Song textile foot-measure (p. 81). Using these larger values, the 9.5 × 8 Yuan feet would not correspond exactly to the 97 × 82 inches of our *kesi*. But the fact remains that the proportions of the Metropolitan *kesi* are exactly the same as those for imperial portraits and mandalas of the Yuan dynasty.

In view of the many uncertainties in the value of this foot-measure in any historical period, the Yamantaka mandala may well be taken as proof that the value for the Song textile foot-measure given by Wu Chengluo was the same one used at the official workshops of the Yuan court.

6. See pp. 60–61 and note 19 in the introduction to this chapter.
7. *Yuanshi*, chap. 79, p. 1946.
8. *Yuanshi*, Biography of Wenzong, chap. 33, pp. 738–39.
9. Ibid., p. 744.
10. Ibid., chap. 34, p. 756.
11. See Feng Chengjun 1962, vol. 1, p. 351. The *Duosang Menggu shi* (1962) is Feng Chengjun's translation of Constantin d'Ohsson, *Histoire des Mongols* (1824). According to contemporary gossip, Babusha was hammered to death in a barbecue pit. See Kong Qi, *Zhizheng zhiji*, chap. 1. Kong Qi wrote at the end of the Yuan dynasty.
12. *Yuanshi*, Biography of Shundi, chap. 40, pp. 856–57.
13. Feng Chengjun 1962, vol. 1, p. 351.
14. *Yuanshi*, chap. 33, p. 744, chap. 34, p. 752.
15. In the first year of Taiding (1324), Yesün Temür, the Taiding emperor, underwent a Yamantaka initiation conducted by the imperial preceptor, and in 1326 his empress underwent the same ceremony. Both ceremonies took place in the Crystal Hall (Shuijing Dian) in the palaces of Shangjing, the Upper Capital (*Yuanshi*, Biography of the Taiding emperor, chap. 29, p. 648, and chap. 30, p. 671). It is quite possible that the same imperial preceptor conducted a Yamantaka initiation for Tugh Temür and Budashiri in 1329. At the beginning of 1330, the imperial preceptor was changed before the imperial family underwent a second initiation (*Yuanshi*, Biography of Wenzong, chap. 33, p. 745).

TECHNICAL ANALYSIS

Warp: White silk, s, 2-ply z. Count: 26–30 per centimeter. *Weft:* 1) Polychrome silk, s. Colors: brick red, light coral, pale pink, maroon, pale orange, dark blue, medium blue, light blue, teal blue, slate blue, blue black, chartreuse, medium green, blue green, white, tan, brown, dark gray brown, and yellow. The blue areas have light and dark streaks. Count: approximately 68–230 wefts per centimeter. 2) Wrapped gold thread: strips of gilded paper wrapped z around a pale yellow silk core, z (no bole visible). Count: 80 per centimeter. 3) Flat gold thread: strips of gilded paper woven flat (most of the gold leaf is missing); pale coral bole under the gold leaf. Count: approximately 36 per centimeter. *Weave:* The mandala is woven entirely in the tapestry technique with slit joins. The binding is the usual weft-faced tabby, except for some areas in which flat gold wefts are bound in an extended tabby (most notably in the horizontal guard bands that separate the top and bottom borders from the central zone). The flat gold wefts were woven in a soumak weave, passing over two warps (A and B), then behind the second (B) and then over the second and third warps (B and C), and so on. This creates a brick pattern on the face. In the portraits, flat gold wefts sometimes wrap single warps. Slit joins are used throughout, except for long slits in vertical portions of the design, where dovetail joins of 2–4 wefts occur at intervals. The design is indicated by color changes and slit joins. The three-dimensional effect of some details (e.g., the crowns and jewelry) is achieved with flat gold wefts. Eccentric weaving is restricted to gradual curves. Diagonals are usually woven using warp steps; for steep diagonals and vertical portions of the design, the warps are wrapped. Shading is achieved by the interpenetration of tongues of color, either different shades of the same color or different colors. Occasionally, the ends of two wefts of the same color that have been knotted together appear on the face of the mandala. The warps are not flat; rather, some protrude slightly and some recede

Figure 40. Detail, reverse of cat. no. 25

slightly, so that the surface has an uneven, "lined" texture.

On the reverse side (fig. 40), most wefts float for only short distances (less than 3.5 centimeters) from one area to another. Tangles of floating wefts or of ends of wefts occur when many different colors are used in a comparatively small area. The starting end of a weft is hidden, and the end is cut short (approximately 3 millimeters). The mandala is replete with broken warps. Rarely were such warps not replaced. In one case, a new warp was seen knotted to the end of the broken warp. Almost always, the end of the new warp was simply added (without being knotted) at the point where the broken end of the original warp emerged from the weave and was held in place by the ensuing wefts. Several centimeters of a new warp and/or a broken warp are exposed, and often one of them has a knot about 4 millimeters from the weaving. The long ends of both the original and introduced warps may be knotted to the long ends of other broken or introduced warps, or the ends of both the original and introduced warps may be fairly short (only a few centimeters long) and unattached to other warp ends. Occasionally, only the end of the introduced warp is visible (presumably the original warp broke close to the weaving), and the wefts float over the break for several (3–14) passes prior to the point at which the end of the new warp was introduced into the weave.

The direction of the ends of the few broken warps that were not replaced indicates that the tapestry was woven from bottom to top.

At the bottom of the mandala is a starting edge consisting of a chartreuse band 2 centimeters wide interrupted by thin blue and white stripes. The outermost edge consists of the cut ends of warps.

The selvages are simple, the wefts turning around an outermost warp, which is single.

PUBLICATIONS: MMA *Recent Acquisitions* 1991–1992, pp. 84–85, illus.; Reynolds, "Silk," 1995, pp. 92–93, fig. 1, p. 86; Stoddard 1995, p. 209, figs. 5a, 5b, and p. 210; Folsach 1996, pp. 86–87, fig. 13.

A Note on Inscriptions and Iconography

Gennady Leonov

The main deity of the mandala is nine-headed, thirty-four-armed, sixteen-legged Vajrabhairava (Yamantaka), who tramples on gods, human beings, demons, animals, and birds, thus symbolizing victory over existence.

The second circle of the mandala is surrounded by a chain of *kapalas* (skulls) and divided into eight sectors, each one of them containing a deity of Vajrabhairava's retinue–Dharmaraja–a form of Yama, Lord of Death. Each of the eight Dharmarajas protects one of the four main and one of the four intermediate points of the compass. They stand on buffalo, holding in the left hand *kapalas* and in the right various Tantric attributes—a *vajra*, severed heads of Brahma, and severed limbs of human bodies. The circle is enclosed within a square formed by thirty-six Dharmarajas, eight on each side and one in each corner. Each of the four T-shaped gates—entrances to the inner sanctum of the mandala—is protected by a Dharmaraja and connected by a *vajra* fence. The four gates are rendered in the style of the early East Indian tradition, with rams standing on elephants' heads that support the upper part of the gate, from which *makaras* spout water fountains. The ground is decorated with characteristic Yuan floral ornament.

The central square is enclosed within a four-level circle comprising a fire- and a *vajra*-mountain where the adept experiences the first purification upon entering the mandala, a circle of eight graveyards where he must cleanse himself of all worldly attachments and sentiments, and a lotus mountain, where he is ultimately purified before entering the abode of Vajrabhairava.

Each of the eight graveyards includes (clockwise from the top) a *siddha* preaching to his disciple, a guardian deity (in this case, Dharmaraja), a *dikpala*, a *naga*, a *stupa*, and a demon from the netherworld (a *preta*?). *Dikpalas* are the guardians of the Ten Directions (the four main and the four intermediate points of the compass plus the zenith and the nadir). Sometimes, as here, the group is composed of nine deities, with the ninth protecting the center. It includes traditional Hindu deities, among them Brahma seated on a goose, Indra on an elephant, Varuna on a *makara*, and Vayu on a deer. Each of the eight graveyards includes one *dikpala*. But, as the intention of the author of the mandala was to present nine

dikpalas, one of the graveyards (above Vajrabhairava's head) contains two *dikpalas*—Brahma and Varuna. It is interesting to note that Brahma is shown as four-armed instead of four-faced. Severed human limbs are scattered in each of the graveyards.

Each corner of the outer square is occupied by a group of four deities. The main deity in each group is Dharmapala, who stands on a buffalo accompanied by two female deities of a lower rank and a small image of a Vajrabhairava-related Dharmapala.

The upper row is occupied by fourteen personages beginning with the primordial Adi-Buddha Vajradhara followed by a *dharmapala* (probably a form of Mahakala) and Mahasiddha Virupa (Birvapa). Then follow eleven images of lamas. None of these bear any specific iconographic characteristics except the first lama, whose red hat suggests that he could be one of three personages: the founder of the Sakya monastery (1073), dKon-mchog rGyal-po (1034–1102); his son Sa-skya-pa Kun-dga sNying-po (1092–1158), who formulated the teachings of the Sakya school; or Phagspa Lama (1235–1280), who successfully propagated the Buddhism of the Sakya school at the court of Khubilai Khan and invented the so-called square script for the Mongols. This would suggest that the lamas represent the Sakya lineage. The presence of Mahasiddha Virupa (active in the eighth century) at the beginning of the row of the Sakya lamas is explained by their importance in the development of the teachings of Mahamudra, which Virupa himself followed. Virupa was also connected with the cult of Vajrabhairava, having been initiated into it by one of his teachers, Nagabodhi.

The lower row includes (left to right) seven guardian deities: a blue Mahakala(?) and various forms of Yama. The guardian deities are flanked by images of the donors of the *kesi*. The names of the donors, cited in Tibetan, are sewn in cartouches above their heads. The inscriptions read as follows (bottom left corner): *rGyal po Thug the mur* and *rGyal bu Ko shi la*; (bottom right corner): *dPon mo Bha bu cha* and *dPon mo bHu dha shri*.

Tugh Temür's title, *rGyal po* (king), is given in the inscription; *rGyal bu* (prince) is the title given for his brother; and *dPon mo* (official's wife) is inscribed as the title of the empresses.

26. Cosmological Mandala

Silk tapestry (kesi)
Warp 83.8 cm (33 in.); weft 83.8 cm (33 in.)
Yuan dynasty (1279–1368)
The Metropolitan Museum of Art, New York. Purchase, Fletcher
Fund and Joseph E. Hotung and Michael and Danielle Rosenberg
Gifts, 1989 (1989.140)

This *kesi* features a Tibetan cosmological diagram with the world mountain, Meru (or Sumeru), the axis of the cosmos, in the center. It is surrounded by seven square ranges of gold mountains interspersed with an equal number of oceans. Outside these mountain ranges, at the four

cardinal directions, in the vast space of a gigantic ocean, are the four great continents, each flanked by two lesser continents. The continents are represented by landscapes in the Chinese style and framed by different shapes according to the location. Videha in the east is in a semicircle, Godaniya in the west in a circle, Uttarakuru in the north in a square, and Jambudvipa (the world of humans) in the south in a trapezoid (originally the shape of the shoulder blade of a sheep). The four directions also have color attributes: the east is silver (white); the west, ruby (red); the south, lapis lazuli (blue); and the north, gold (yellow).

Detail, cat. no. 26

The four colors are reflected on the sides of Mount Meru.[1] The cosmic world is illuminated by the sun and the moon, represented here in purely Chinese iconography, with the three-legged crow in the sun and the rabbit under a cassia tree in the moon pounding the elixir of immortality.

The heavens of various orders of divinities are usually shown above Mount Meru. In the present work, the celestial sphere on top of Mount Meru is, instead of a paradise

scene, an oval form with a scroll pattern, which changes color along a narrowing path leading to the ultimate mystery, symbolized by an eight-petaled lotus flower. In the four corners, outside the double mountain range border of the diagram, are four vases from which issue lotus scrolls and the eight auspicious symbols of Buddhism.[2] The form of the lotus scrolls derives ultimately from the art of Pala India. A visual representation of Tibetan cosmology, the diagram provides a basic scheme for Tibetan religious thought and structures, from abstruse theological systems to the actual layout of Tibetan temples; it can also serve as a mandala.

Densely woven with fine silk threads, the *kesi* falls technically into an intermediate stage between the Southern Song (1127–1279) and the Ming (1368–1644). The slits are not used to delineate pattern, and there is only limited use of eccentric weaving. Shading—most obvious in the two outer mountain ranges—is achieved by the interpenetration of spurs from two color fields. This technique was to become a constant element in Ming *kesi*.

Another means of ascertaining the date and place of manufacture is afforded by the treatment of the landscapes in the continents. The designer of the mandala was no doubt well acquainted with the latest artistic movements in interior China. The landscapes are done in the blue-green style, which was practiced in the Tang period (618–907) and revived by early Yuan artists such as Qian Xuan (ca. 1235–after 1300). A typical example of the blue-green style landscape of the Yuan period is seen in the painting *Wang Xizhi Watching Geese,* in the Metropolitan Museum (fig. 41). This type of painting was obviously the model for the landscapes within the continents that appear in this *kesi*.

1. For the interpretive description of the cosmic mandala, the authors have referred to Lauf 1976, pp. 131–37.
2. For the eight auspicious symbols, see note 2 in catalogue number 24.

Figure 41. Qian Xuan (ca. 1235–after 1300), *Wang Xizhi Watching Geese*, detail. Late Southern Song to early Yuan dynasty. Handscroll, ink, color, and gold on paper, 24.1 × 91.4 cm (9½ × 36 in.). The Metropolitan Museum of Art, New York. Gift of The Dillon Fund, 1973 (1973.120.6)

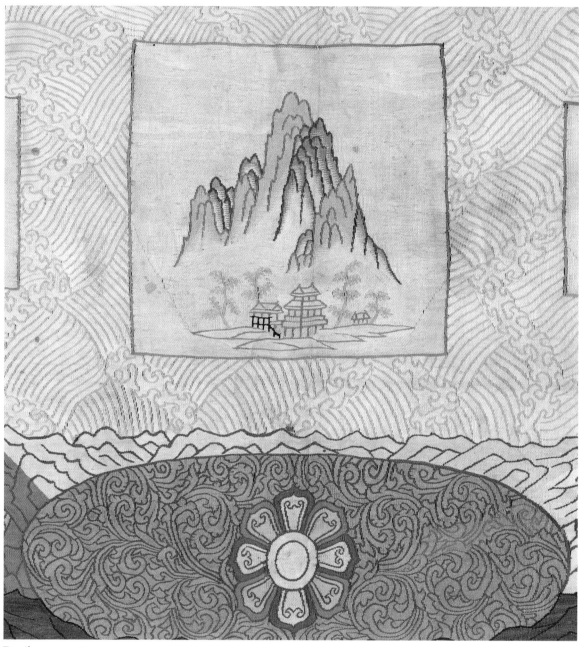

Detail, cat. no. 26

TECHNICAL ANALYSIS

Warp: White silk, spun s, 2-ply z. Count: approximately 31 per centimeter. *Weft:* Polychrome silk, s, some plied s. Colors: light blue, medium blue, and sky blue; light coral, coral, pale pink, dark red; light, medium, and deep green; pale blue green, yellow, white, black, light tan, cream, and taupe. The blue yarns are unevenly dyed from deep blue to white, giving a striated effect. Count: approximately 60–280 per centimeter. *Weave:* The tapestry weave is extremely fine. There are both slit and toothed joins (2–3 wefts along the long vertical slits), but slits are not used to indicate pattern. Diagonals and curves are achieved by warp steps, steep diagonals by soumak weaving, and vertical lines by much wrapping of single warps. Eccentric weaving is used sparingly and only for the gradual curves. Shading is created by thin tongues of color that extend in the weft direction from one color area into the adjacent color area.

On the reverse, broken ends occur throughout. The loose ends of broken and new warps are fairly short, less than 2.5 centimeters long. Sometimes the end of the broken warp was knotted and not replaced. In one instance, the broken end was not knotted but was caught by a weft that was eccentrically woven. In other cases, a new warp was introduced and held in place by tightly packed wefts. The wefts on the reverse float about 2.8 centimeters (occasionally as much as 4.4 centimeters) from one area of color to another. The floats cross over one another, but are not tangled. The loose ends of the wefts are about 2 centimeters long.

Broken warps that were not replaced show that the mandala was woven from bottom to top.

PUBLICATIONS: MMA *Recent Acquisitions* 1989–1990, pp. 86–87, illus.; *Textiles* 1995–96, p. 74, illus.

27. Fan with Dragon

Silk tapestry (kesi)
Warp 26 cm (10¼ in.); weft 25.8 cm (10⅛ in.)
Yuan dynasty (1279–1368)
The Metropolitan Museum of Art, New York.
Fletcher Fund, 1947 (47.18.42)

According to the *Xijin zhi*, a gazetteer of Xijin (present-day Beijing) written at the end of the Yuan dynasty (1279–1368),[1] on the occasion of the Duanwu Festival (the fifth day of the fifth lunar month, now celebrated as the Dragon Boat Festival), the Ministry of Rites would present to the imperial court *kesi* fans with various pictorial subjects, including narratives, human figures, flowers and birds, and landscape and architecture. The author mentions in particular *kesi* fans with dragons in clouds.[2] There is no doubt that the surface of this *kesi* fan, with a dragon breathing out a flaming pearl above waves, is a relic from one of the Duanwu Festivals in the Yuan period. The composition is designed to fit into a round format, and the weaving technique is exactly like that in the *kesi* paintings of the Southern Song (see fig. 15 on page 57). As described in the *Xijin zhi*, "the shading and washes are like real life, surpassing the effect of painting."

Dragon painting was a major genre of Chinese art in the Yuan period, especially among Daoists. In the Metropolitan Museum there is a long handscroll painting of dragons by Zhang Yucai, the thirty-eighth patriarch of the Tianshi (Heavenly Master) sect of Daoism (r. 1295–1316) and an accomplished painter (fig. 42).[3] It can readily be seen that the *kesi* fan and Zhang Yucai's painting share common features, such as the heads of the dragons and the treatment of dark clouds (dragons are associated with rain). The whirlpool, seen on the fan, is a constant element in Yuan dragon paintings (it appears also in Zhang Yucai's painting, but in a section not illustrated in figure 42).

The Daoist association with the Duanwu Festival was an ancient one, and it continued until the end of the Qing dynasty (1644–1911). In the *Xijin zhi*, preceding the description of the customs associated with the festival, there is a poem that mentions the display of "the charms of the Heavenly Master" (to ward off evil spirits). The same custom is described in the *Yanjing suishi ji* (Annual Customs and Festivals in Peking), a work of the late Qing.[4]

This fan provides concrete proof that the Southern Song tradition of weaving *kesi* painting was very much alive in the Yuan dynasty. Although the high degree of technical refinement was not maintained after the Yuan, the pattern persisted through to the Qing. A set of five *kesi* cases in the Metropolitan Museum is woven with the same pattern and dates from the second half of the Qing dynasty, the late eighteenth to the nineteenth century.[5]

1. On the *Xijin zhi*, see catalogue number 25, note 3.
2. *Xijin zhi jiyi* 1983, p. 218.
3. For more on this painting and on Zhang Yucai and the Daoists at the Yuan court, see Fong 1992, pp. 363–67, pls. 81a,b. See also Fong and Watt 1996, p. 54.
4. Dun Lichen 1936.
5. Illustrated in Milhaupt 1992, fig. 9.

TECHNICAL ANALYSIS

Warp: Tan silk s (not plied). Count: 34 per centimeter. *Weft:* Polychrome silk, s. Colors: shades of gray, from light to charcoal, cream, tan, and red. Count: approximately 90–120 per centimeter. *Weave:* The tapestry is woven with slit joins. Eccentric weaving and flying shuttle are limited to delineating details of the design. The dragon's breath is woven with wefts passing over two warps (instead of one).

PUBLICATIONS: Hartford 1951, no. 122, illus.; New York 1971, no. 8, illus.

Figure 42. Zhang Yucai (r. 1295–1316), *Beneficent Rain*, detail. Yuan dynasty (1279–1368). Handscroll, ink on silk, 27 × 271.2 cm (10⅝ × 106¾ in.). The Metropolitan Museum of Art, New York. Gift of Douglas Dillon, 1985 (1985.227.2)

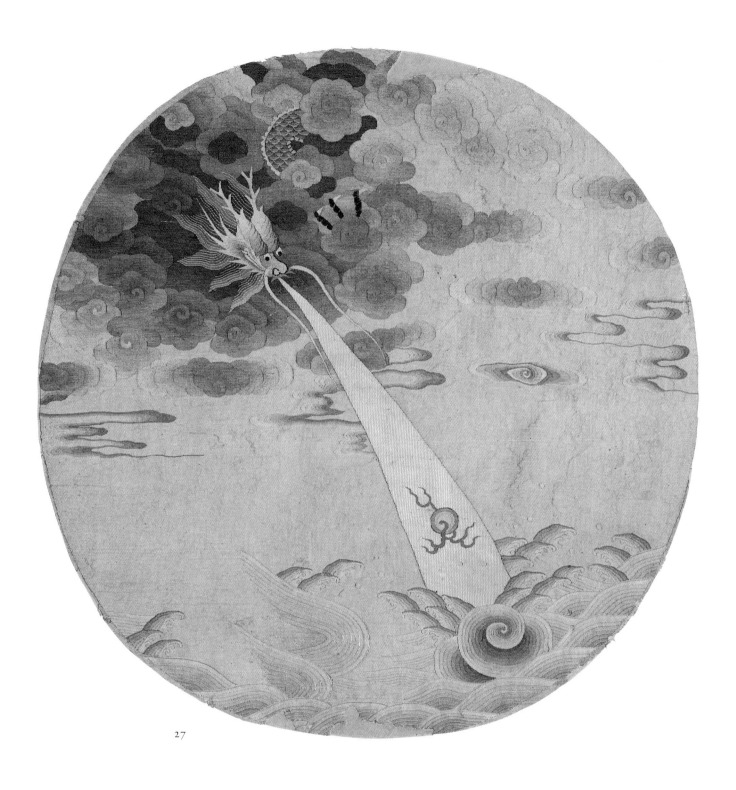

27

3. Brocades of the Jin and Mongol Periods

Brocades produced in the Jin territories from the twelfth to the thirteenth century constitute an important group of textiles. Technically and stylistically, they fall into two categories: those that clearly belong to the weaving and decorative traditions of the Jin dynasty, and those that were influenced by weavers originally from the eastern Iranian world who were relocated by the Mongols into conquered Jin territories.

Central to the attribution of the brocades to the first category are both the theme of the swan hunt, which is seen on a brocade in the Metropolitan Museum (cat. no. 28),[1] and the stylistic similarities that are shared between this and related brocades and those found in a Jin tomb near Acheng, in Heilongjiang Province. The tomb, dated 1162, was that of Prince Qi, a member of the Jurchen imperial family and, for a number of years, resident (i.e., governor) of the old Jin capital of Shangjing, near Acheng.[2] In the swan hunt brocade, a hawk swoops down upon a swan in flight against a floral setting. The image, woven with gold thread against a green ground, closely resembles the same theme carved on jade buckles that were worn by Jin officials during the annual swan hunt. Following the custom of the Khitans of the Liao dynasty (907–1125), the Jurchens of the Jin dynasty (1115–1234) engaged in the spring and autumn hunts.[3] This practice was institutionalized in 1143 by an imperial decree that henceforth the Jin emperor would "follow the custom of the Khitans [in the] hunts of the four seasons: spring-water [spring hunt by the water] and autumn-mountain [autumn hunt in the mountains], the *nabo* [seasonal camps] of winter and summer."[4] According to the *Jinshi* (History of the Jin Dynasty), the officials who attended the emperor on the occasion of the spring hunt wore uniforms "embroidered with gold [threads]" on the chest, shoulders, and sleeves, and the pattern was that of a "hawk attacking a swan, combined with floral motifs."[5] The *Liaoshi* (History of the Liao Dynasty) gives descriptions

of the spring hunt (for swans returning from the south) in much greater detail. The officials on this occasion were said to have worn costumes of a dark green color.[6] This tradition was apparently observed also by the Jurchens, as the fragments of gold brocade with the swan hunt pattern that have surfaced in recent years are all dark green.

In the brocade, the swan hunt motif is in the shape of a teardrop that has no border and appears to have been abstracted from a larger image. The repeated image, oriented to the right or to the left in alternate rows, is asymmetrical and generously spaced one from another. Its distinguishing technical features are: single z-spun warps; paired foundation wefts, one of which is unspun while the other is spun z; gold brocading wefts composed of flat strips of animal substrate gilded on one side;[7] the floating of foundation wefts at fairly regular intervals across the reverse of the brocaded areas (see fig. 45 on page 112) in order to accommodate the much heavier gold brocading wefts; the continuous passage of gold brocading wefts from one shed into the next; the floating of gold wefts on the reverse side of brocaded areas; and the warp-faced tabby binding of the foundation weave and the twill binding of the brocading wefts on the face. A selvage is preserved on a piece of the swan hunt brocade in Paris.[8] Intersecting the brocaded units down their centers, the selvage consists of green warps that are double, triple, or quadruple. The foundation wefts, bound in tabby by these warps, turn back around the outermost bundle of warps, while the gold brocading wefts on the reverse side turn into the next shed at the inner edge of the selvage.

A number of brocades are closely related stylistically and technically to the swan hunt brocade.[9] One, woven with the motif of a *djeiran* (a Central Asian antelope) amid foliage crowned by a sun or a moon supported by clouds (present location unknown), preserves a loom width of 59–62.3 centimeters.[10] Within this group, several technical variations can be observed. In some (for example, cat. no. 29), the foundation wefts are single instead of paired. In most of the brocades of this group, including the swan hunt, the gold wefts are bound in twill by two consecutive warps within a regular sequence of warps. In the Cleveland brocade with soaring phoenixes amid clouds (cat. no. 31), however, the gold wefts are bound in twill by all the warps. That some silks within the swan hunt group are brocaded with the same image but not identical in technique or choice of colors indicates that stock patterns were used and were woven repeatedly.[11]

These brocades share several technical and stylistic elements with brocades from the Jin tomb of Prince Qi: single warps, foundation wefts that are either paired or single, the floating of foundation wefts at intervals across the reverse sides of brocaded areas, and the continuous passage of flat gold brocading wefts from one shed into the next. Many of the brocades from the tomb, moreover, are woven with a warp-faced tabby foundation weave and the twill binding of the gold brocading wefts. In addition to these technical similarities, asymmetrical images also occur among the brocades from the tomb.[12] There are, on the other hand, differences between the brocades of the two groups. The binding of gold brocading wefts by a sequence of adjacent warps observed in the swan hunt, the coiled dragon, and the *djeiran* (cat. nos. 28–30) is not found among the brocades from the tomb. But most important, the gold threads with which the silks from the tomb are brocaded are much finer than those of the swan hunt group. Furthermore, there seems to have been no concern for economizing on the gold threads of the princely brocades, as the brocading wefts were sometimes floated across the back of the fabric from the pattern units in one repeat to those in the next repeat. Gold wefts gilded on both sides, moreover, occur among the brocades from the tomb, whereas the flat gold wefts in the swan hunt group are gilded on one side only.

Available evidence suggests that gold brocade was the most representative luxury textile of the Jin dynasty. Although earlier gold-brocaded textiles have been found in Liao archaeological sites, they are rare.[13] The same is true of textiles from early Song sites. In the entire Northern Song area, only one tomb so far has produced a single example of brocade; unfortunately, it is not specified in the report whether gold thread was used.[14] Nonetheless, the special importance of gold brocades in the Jin dynasty is borne out by the preponderance of such textiles found in the tomb of Prince Qi. The textile finds from this tomb are of a higher quality than those that have come into the collections of museums outside China. This would suggest that the textiles from the prince's tomb are the finest products of the imperial textile workshop, while the fragments such as the brocade with the swan hunt were made for use by officials outside the imperial family.

Although some motifs, such as the coiled dragon and the phoenix, had earlier beginnings in textiles as well as in other decorative arts,[15] others, such as the *djeiran* (cat. no. 29), in spite of its venerable antecedent in seventh-century Sogdiana, seem to have been adopted in China only during the Jin period. A particularly interesting case is that of the swan hunt. In the absence of archaeological evidence for its occurrence in the Liao period, we may seek clues in literature and in the history of related arts. In his study of hunting motifs in jade carving, Yang Boda has concluded that none of the numerous extant examples of spring-water jade carvings predate the Jin period.[16] It is also noteworthy that there is no mention of the swan hunt image as a decorative motif either in the official records of the Liao dynasty or in eyewitness accounts of the spring hunt conducted by the Khitans. There is a detailed description in the *Jinshi*, however, of the swan hunt motif in the robes and jade ornaments worn by the participants in the spring hunt. It is thus quite likely that while the ceremonial hunt was instituted by the Khitans, the swan hunt motif in textile decoration and in jade carving was an innovation of the Jin court.

A distinct group within the category of brocades belonging to the Jin weaving tradition is represented by two brocades: one, in the exhibition, with a design of standing phoenixes against a white ground (cat. no. 32) and the other, in a private collection, with a motif of a *djeiran* against a yellow ground.[17] The exceptional length of the *djeiran* textile (approximately 212 centimeters) preserves three reverses of pattern orientation; the motif of the *djeiran* is nearly identical to that of the brocades in Cleveland and Paris belonging to the swan hunt group; and its loom width of 59.1 centimeters is consistent with that group. Like the swan hunt group, foundation wefts in both brocades are floated at intervals across the reverse side of the brocaded areas.

These brocades, however, have technical peculiarities which distinguish them from the swan hunt group and suggest that they were woven in a different, possibly more southern, region of the Jin territories. First and foremost, their gold wefts are made with a paper substrate instead of an animal substrate.[18] In addition, when foundation wefts are floated across the reverse of the brocaded images, four to six successive wefts float together, causing small puckers to occur along the contours (cat. no. 32). This is curious, considering that the purpose of the floating wefts was to maintain a smooth surface around the brocaded images. The selvages of the *djeiran*, moreover, are not formed with bundles of warps (the foundation wefts simply turn around a single outer warp). The s direction of both the warps and the wefts in the brocade

Figure 43. Textile with framed confronted birds, detail. North China, Mongol period, 13th–mid-14th century. Silk and gold thread; tabby, brocaded, 58 × 63 cm (22⅞ × 24¾ in.). AEDTA, Paris (no. 3262)

with phoenixes, however, may not be as great a point of distinction as the consistency of z-spun warps among the swan hunt group might suggest. The warps in the *djeiran* are spun s and plied z, and both z- and s-spun warps occur among the brocades from the tomb of Prince Qi.

The brocades in the exhibition that belong to the second category—those influenced by the weaving tradition of the eastern Iranian world—fall into two groups. The first is represented by the brocade with lotuses (cat. no. 33).[19] Here, z-spun warps are paired instead of single, and the color of the bundles of warps in the selvage contrasts with that of the rest of the warps. The brocaded units, moreover, are symmetrical. In other brocades of this group, such as one in the collection of the Association pour l'Étude et la Documentation des Textiles d'Asie (AEDTA) in Paris (fig. 43), the brocaded images are not only symmetrical but also framed.[20] Except for the contrasting color of the selvage warps, these technical and stylistic features reveal the influence of weavers from Khurasan and Transoxiana, who had been captured by the Mongols and eventually settled in the former Jin

territories—some in Hongzhou, in western central Hebei Province, before Ögödei became khan in 1229, and others in Xunmalin, west of the modern city of Zhangjiakou, during the reign of Ögödei (1229–41). The center at Hongzhou is of particular interest in connection with the gold brocades, as it was staffed by weavers from both the Western Region (Central Asia) and from Bianjing, the last capital of the Jin state.[21]

The second group of brocades in this category is represented by the brocade with hares (cat. no. 34).[22] As in the brocades of the first group, the warps are paired. Here, however, thick foundation wefts compensate for the density of the gold wefts, obviating the need to float occasional foundation wefts across the reverse. This technique was also used during the Jin dynasty and occurs among some of the brocades found in the tomb of Prince Qi.[23] Among the brocades of this group, the gold wefts, made with an animal substrate, may be bound by a regular sequence of adjacent warps (cat. no. 34) or by all of the warps. Again, the selvages intersect the brocaded units down their centers and sometimes have warps that contrast in color with those

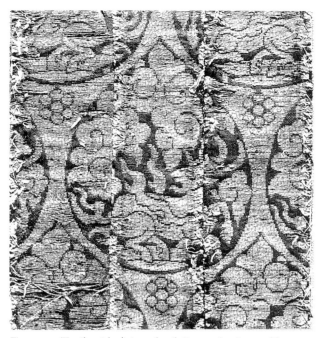

Figure 44. Textile with *djeiran*, detail. Eastern Iranian world, late 13th–14th century. Silk and gold thread, lampas weave. Germanisches Nationalmuseum, Nuremburg (no. 394)

forming the body of the textile. A loom width of about 66.5 centimeters is preserved on a brocade that is identical in design and technique to the brocade with hares, except for the green warps of the selvages. Another, exceptionally long brocade, in which the motif of the *djeiran* is repeated in square units (present location unknown), preserves several reversals in the orientation of the brocaded images.[24] Some images appear to belong to an established decorative tradition. That of the hare, for example, may well be related to hunting activities, as the hare was among the game hunted by the Khitans, the Jurchens, and the Mongols. Not only are occasions for hare hunts recorded in the *Liaoshi*,[25] but envoys from the Song court to the northern states often returned with descriptions of the hunt, including the hunting of hares.[26] Other images, by contrast, are symmetrical and sometimes completed with a border, in the tradition of West Asian silk design.[27]

During the Mongol period, the brocades of the Jin territories were known in West Asia and influenced Persian silk designs. A Persian textile in Nuremberg, for example, is woven with the common Jin motif of the *djeiran* (fig. 44). Both the form of the animal and the teardrop shape of the repeated motif are similar to Jin brocaded images. In this textile, however, the motifs are not isolated in staggered horizontal rows against a plain ground, but are set within a framework. Also, the moon, which is invariably associated with the Jin version of the *djeiran*, is missing, which suggests that the Persian weavers either failed to comprehend the significance of the moon in the Chinese image or chose to ignore it.

1. Other pieces of this brocade are known: one in The Cleveland Museum of Art (1990.80) and another in the collection of the Association pour l'Étude et la Documentation des Textiles d'Asie (AEDTA), Paris (Riboud 1995, fig. 10).
2. Heilongjiang 1989, pp. 1–10; Zhu Qixin 1990. The garments are preserved in the Provincial Museum of Heilongjiang, Harbin.
3. The Khitan emperors, after the conquest of a major part of North China, continued the pastoral traditions of following the grass and the water and engaging in the seasonal activities of hunting and fishing. The Liao court would move four times a year to seasonal camps known as the *nabo*. Specific hunting (and fishing) activities were engaged in at each of the camps, or residences. The spring camp would begin with fishing while participants awaited the return of the *yan* and *tian'e* (wild goose and swan), which were hunted with a small but fearless hawk known as the *haidongqing*. A detailed study of the seasonal camps of the Khitans appears in Fu Lehuan 1984, pp. 36–172. For translations of the relevant passages in the *Liaoshi*, see Wittfogel and Feng Chia-sheng 1949, pp. 131–34.
4. See *Da Jin guo zhi jiaozheng* (annotated by Cui Wenyin), p. 166. The first part of the *Da Jin guo zhi*, including the passage quoted above, can be reliably attributed to Yuwen Mouzhao, who submitted his *History of the Jin State* to the Song court in 1234.
5. *Jinshi*, chap. 43, pt. 24, p. 984.
6. See, in particular, the section on the seasonal camps in chap. 32, pp. 373–74; and, in *Jinshi*, the section on geography, chap. 40, p. 496. For translations of these passages, see Wittfogel and Feng Chia-sheng 1949, pp. 132, 134.
7. Analysis with a scanning electron microscope of substrates from the swan hunt in The Metropolitan Museum of Art and from the *djeiran* in Cleveland has identified them as parchment. The analysis was done by Norman Indictor and Denyse Montegut. The Leather Conservation Centre of Northampton, England, has further identified the substrate of the gold thread in the swan hunt piece as goat hide, which is scraped so thin that all that remains is the surface epidermal layer of the hide (correspondence from Arthur Leeper to James C. Y. Watt, September 27, 1989).
8. Paris, AEDTA; see Riboud 1995, fig. 15.
9. Catalogue numbers 29–31; Riboud 1995, figs. 3, 8, 10, 15, 16; Ogasawara 1989, fig. 12; Spink & Son 1989, no. 13; Spink & Son 1994, no. 10.
10. Simcox 1989, no. 13, p. 21 (the right selvage is turned under).
11. For example, the brocade with a *djeiran* at AEDTA, Paris (Riboud 1995, fig. 15) has paired foundation wefts, while the brocade in Cleveland with the same motif (cat. no. 29) is woven with single foundation wefts. A third brocade, also at AEDTA, with a *djeiran* is woven with a yellow ground (ibid., fig. 16).
12. Zhu Qixin 1990, figs. 5, 7, 11, 12.
13. Fragments of gold-brocaded silks (using flat strips of gilded animal substrate) found in the Tomb of the Husband of the Princess are in the Museum of Inner Mongolian Autonomous Region, Hohhot.
14. Chen Guo'an 1984, pp. 77–81, pl. VI, no. 1.
15. The earliest mention of the coiled dragon is in the *Tang huiyao* (Records of Tang institutions), in which is recorded a list of patterns decreed in A.D. 694 for the official robes of members of the imperial family and senior officials; see *Tang huiyao*, p. 582. For a historical survey and discussion of the dragon and the phoenix in Chinese art, see Rawson 1984, where both the Liao dragon and the phoenix are illustrated in fig. 131. See also cat. no. 30.
16. Yang Boda 1983, no. 2.
17. Present whereabouts unknown (not the same textile as Riboud 1995, fig. 16).
18. It should be noted that while the use of a paper substrate indicates Chinese work, the presence of animal substrates does not negate a Chinese origin. See reference to Yu Ji on page 138 and note 57 to the introduction to chapter 4.
19. For others in Paris, see Riboud 1995, figs. 27, 31, 33.
20. Compare the design of this brocade to that of a Persian ceramic pot, in Paris 1977, pl. 292.

21. In the biography of Chinkhai (Chinese: Zhen Hai) in the *Yuanshi*, it is said that in the reign of Taizong (Ögödei), "over three hundred households of weavers of gold thread and twill patterns from the Western Region and three hundred households of weavers of *maohe* from Bianjing" were gathered at Hongzhou, and that previously (before Taizong's accession) an office was established at Hongzhou with young boys, young girls, and artisans from all over the empire. Chinkhai was given "hereditary charge" of this office (*Yuanshi*, chap. 120, p. 2964). Although the term *maohe* can be interpreted as a woolen or coarse hemp fabric, there is another possible interpretation. It may be the earlier version of *maoge* (the characters for *he* and *ge* differ only in the qualifying radical), which is still in use today. The modern *maoge* is a fabric woven of silk warps and cotton wefts used for jackets (with fur or padded silk lining) and bedcovers.

22. Other examples are in a private collection (unpublished).

23. See, for example, Zhu Qixin 1990, fig. 12.

24. For a textile with the same pattern, see Krahl 1997, fig. 6.

25. For a complete listing of the major hunts of the Khitans in the Liao dynasty, see Fu Lehuan 1984, pp. 106–58.

26. A Song envoy returning from the Liao state in 1013 reported that the Khitans made hammers of stone and bronze and hit hares with them (*Xu Zizhi tongjian changbian*, chap. 54.2, vol. 3, p. 266). The poet-official Su Zhe (1039–1112), as envoy to the Liao state in 1089, wrote a number of poems during his travels in Liao territory, including one that describes the Khitan seasonal camps, in which he mentions the hare hunt. See Jiang Zuyi and Zhang Diyun 1992, p. 313.

27. Private collection (unpublished).

28. Swan Hunt

Tabby, brocaded
Warp 58.5 cm (23 in.); weft 62.2 cm (24½ in.)
Jin dynasty (1115–1234)
The Metropolitan Museum of Art, New York. Purchase, Ann Eden Woodward Foundation Gift and Rogers Fund, 1989 (1989.282)

Against a green ground, teardrop units brocaded in gold are arranged in staggered horizontal rows (the textile preserves two complete and two partial rows), each unit composed of a falcon swooping down upon a swan in flight among floral and foliate branches. The orientation of the units to the right and to the left alternates from one row to the next. A selvage border is preserved along the right edge.

This textile is one of a group of brocades that has been assigned to the Jin territories on the basis of the theme of the swan hunt. The asymmetry of the scene, the absence of borders around the brocaded units, and their arrangement in staggered horizontal rows are all characteristic of the group. The occasional floating of a foundation weft across the reverse sides of the brocaded units to eliminate puckering of the foundation weave due to the introduction of the much thicker gold wefts (fig. 45) also is typical. Similarly, the gold brocading wefts, carried from one shed into the next, are bound on the face by a regular sequence of warps and float unbound on the reverse.

TECHNICAL ANALYSIS

Warp: Green silk, spun z, single. Step: irregular (2 or more). Count: 76 per centimeter. *Weft:* Foundation: green silk, paired (one z and the other without apparent twist). Supplementary: gold thread composed of flat strips of gilded parchment[1] with reddish or yellowish brown adhesive; little gilding remains. Pass: 1 paired foundation weft and 1 supplementary weft, except when wefts are floated. Step: 1 pass. Count: 24 pairs of foundation wefts per centimeter in the ground areas; 16 supplementary gold wefts per centimeter. *Weave:* Tabby, brocaded. Foundation: warp-faced tabby; weaving flaws consist primarily of short warp and weft floats and occur only occasionally. Brocade: 1/3 s twill binding of gold supplementary wefts by the first two warps of each sequence of four. The first warp passes over one foundation weft and one gold supplementary weft, while the second warp passes over the same gold weft and the next foundation weft. The gold wefts are not bound on the reverse side and turn into the next shed along the contours of the brocaded areas. Every sixth to ninth, or occasionally twelfth to thirteenth, foundation weft is floated across the reverse sides of the brocaded areas; floats begin and end along or just inside the contours of the units. A selvage border is preserved

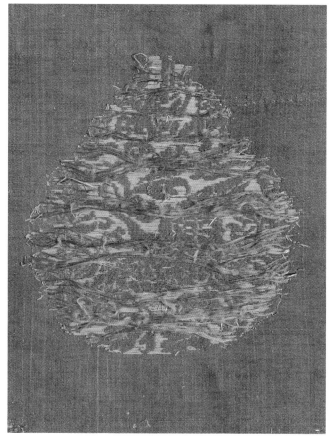

Figure 45. Detail, reverse of cat. no. 28

along the right side (the outer edge is missing). The weave is the same as the foundation weave, also with single warps; on the reverse, the gold wefts turn into the next shed at the beginning of the selvage border. The selvage intersects the brocaded units along their warp axes.

1. The identification of the substrate as parchment was made by Norman Indictor and Denyse Montegut (correspondence to Anne E. Wardwell, May 10, 1991).

PUBLICATION: MMA *Recent Acquisitions* 1989–1990, pp. 85–86, illus.

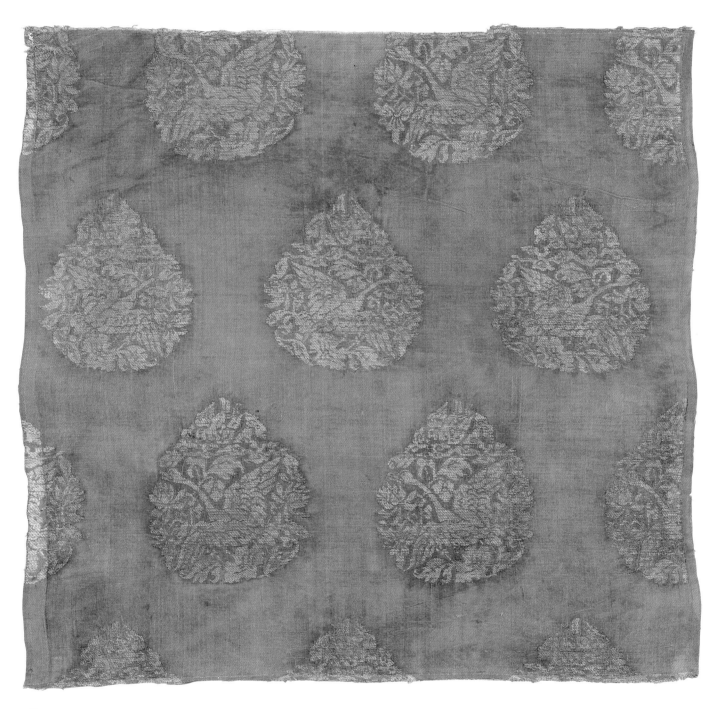

28

29. Djeiran with Floral Branches and Moon

Tabby, brocaded
Warp 109.8 cm (43¼ in.); weft 38.5 cm (15⅛ in.)
Jin dynasty (1115–1234)
The Cleveland Museum of Art. Purchase from the J. H. Wade Fund (1991.4)

This textile, brocaded with gold against a red ground, consists of three fragments joined together, a large upper portion and two smaller pieces at the bottom. The placement of the seams indicates that the fragment was part of a garment. Spaced in staggered horizontal rows are gold-brocaded units, each composed of a recumbent *djeiran* (a Central Asian antelope) gazing back and up at a full moon among clouds; floral branches fill the space between the *djeiran* and the clouds. The orientation of the scenes to the right and to the left alternates from one row to the next. Four complete and eight incomplete brocaded units are present, comprising over two vertical repeats and one complete horizontal repeat. Two selvage borders are preserved, one along the upper right edge of the main portion and the other along the left side of one of the bottom pieces. Both technically and stylistically, the textile belongs to the small corpus of brocades identified as Jin by the motif of the swan hunt.

The motif of the *djeiran* is commonly seen on Chinese art of the Jin dynasty (1115–1234) and survives into the Yuan period (1279–1368). It appears on the backs of Jin mirrors and serves also as a mirror stand. Invariably, it is associated with a sun or a moon supported by clouds, except when it serves as a mirror stand, when the mirror itself represents the sun or the moon (fig. 46). In popular writing in China, this motif is generally referred to as "a *xiniu* gazing at the moon"; the original meaning of *xiniu* was rhinoceros. Some authors, wishing to confer on the image a more classical derivation, have suggested that it is, rather, the cow of Wu panting upon seeing the moon (mistaken for the sun). However, neither a *xiniu* nor a cow fits the image nearly so well as a *djeiran*, which frequently appears on Sogdian silver from the seventh century onward. One example is a bowl in the State Hermitage, Saint Petersburg, dating from the seventh century (fig. 47).

It is somewhat remarkable that the image of the *djeiran* should have taken some five centuries to travel from Sogdiana to Jin China, while other Sogdian motifs made the transfer to Chinese silver already in the Tang dynasty (618–907; see, for example, the recumbent deer with the mushroom-shaped antler on the silver dish in fig. 21, which dates from the late Tang). There is as yet no known instance of the occurrence of this motif on any Chinese object before the Jin period, whether on textiles, metal, or porcelain. Nor is it seen on contemporary objects outside the Jin territo-

Figure 46. Mirror stand with *djeiran*. Song, Jin, or Yuan dynasty. Parcel-gilt bronze, length 27 cm (10⅝ in.). Victoria and Albert Museum, Salting Bequest (M.737-1910)

Figure 47. Bowl with *djeiran*. Sogdiana, second half of the 7th century. Silver, diameter 19 cm (7½ in.). State Hermitage, Saint Petersburg

ries.[1] It is also remarkable that the image should have arrived, after all these years, entirely intact, both in form and in posture. The origin of the association of the sun or the moon with the Jin version of the *djeiran* is unknown, though it is possible that the association was suggested by a stand in the form of a *djeiran* holding up a mirror, which then became a sun (or a moon); but it is the moon that

114

came to be identified with the circle—hence the expression "a *xiniu* gazing at the moon." In some Jin and Yuan porcelain as well as textiles, the full moon is replaced by a crescent. This kind of ad hoc nomenclature has often been applied to imported motifs that arrived without proper identification. Other examples are the *makara* and the *senmurv*, which were given various names in China before they were correctly identified.

1. For a discussion of this image on porcelain, see Wirgin 1979, pp. 197–98.

TECHNICAL ANALYSIS

Warp: Orange-red silk, z, single. Step: irregular (2 or more). Count: approximately 76 per centimeter. *Weft:* Foundation: orange-red silk, z (slight twist). Supplementary: gold thread composed of flat strips of parchment gilded on one side.[1] Pass: 1 foundation and 1 supplementary weft, except when wefts are floated (see below). Step: 1 pass. Count: 28 foundation wefts (in the ground areas) and 18 supplementary wefts per centimeter. *Weave:* Tabby, brocaded. Foundation: warp-faced tabby; flaws are noticeably absent, except for the occasional entering of two warps instead of one. Brocade: 1/3 s twill binding of gold wefts on the face of the textile by the first two warps in each sequence of four warps (the first warp passes over one foundation weft and one gold weft; the second warp passes over the same gold weft and the next foundation weft; the third and fourth warps bind only the foundation wefts). On the reverse, the gold wefts are not bound. They turn into the next shed along the contours of the brocaded motifs, often forming loops, some of which are broken. Every sixth foundation weft was floated across the reverse side of the brocaded areas to prevent the foundation weave from puckering from the introduction of the thick gold wefts. This occurs along or just outside the contours of the brocaded units. Two selvage borders are preserved; the weave is the same foundation weave using single warps, as occurs in the rest of the textile; the gold supplementary wefts turn into the next shed along the inner selvage edge. The outermost selvage edge has been cut.[2] The selvages intersect the design down the centers of the brocaded units.

1. Identified by Norman Indictor and Denyse Montegut (correspondence to Anne E. Wardwell, May 10, 1991).
2. The formation of the outer selvage edge is known from another piece of this textile in which both selvages are preserved (Spink & Son 1989, no. 13, p. 21; the right selvage is turned under in the illustration). At the outer edge are seven bundles of warps (right selvage) or ten bundles of warps (left selvage), around which the foundation wefts turn. The irregular loom width is approximately 59–62.3 centimeters.

PUBLICATION: Wardwell 1992–93, pp. 244–51, and fig. 4, p. 247.

30. Coiled Dragons

Tabby, brocaded
Warp 74.5 cm (29⅜ in.); weft 33.2 cm (13⅛ in.)
Jin dynasty (1115–1234)
The Metropolitan Museum of Art, New York. Gift of Lisbet
Holmes, 1989 (1989.205)

Against a red ground, gold-brocaded coiled dragons chasing pearls are arranged in staggered horizontal rows, the dragons in one row oriented to the right, those in the next row oriented to the left. The dragons, in profile, have forked horns, gaping mouths with extended tongues, five claws, flames, and an expansive tail that curls around the hind leg as it arches over the head. The textile preserves more than three vertical (warp) and two horizontal (weft) repeats, as well as a selvage along the left side.

The dragon as magic serpent (*ling she*) has been associated with the pearl in Chinese literature since the Han period (206 B.C.–A.D. 220). In the plastic arts, the dragon-and-pearl motif began to appear in the Tang dynasty (618–907). The Tang was also the time of the appearance of the coiled dragon, as seen on silver and on the backs of mirrors. As with many decorative motifs of the Tang period, the dragon-and-pearl motif, particularly that with a coiled dragon, may have had its origin in Central Asia, with remote precedents in the late Roman world.[1] By the tenth century, it appears in various media in the decorative arts and also on textiles. It is seen, for example, on the sleeves of an inner robe

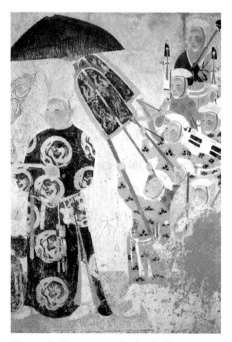

Figure 48. Donor portrait, detail. Cave 409, Dunhuang. Tangut Xia dynasty (1032–1227)

worn by Taizu, the first emperor of the Song dynasty (r. 960–76), in a portrait in the National Palace Museum, Taipei,[2] and in a donor portrait in Cave 409 at Dunhuang, usually identified as that of a king of Tangut Xia, in which the subject is shown wearing a full-length robe with an overall design of coiled dragons arranged in rows (fig. 48). Cave 409 has been dated to the middle period of the Tangut Xia dynasty and would be roughly contemporary with the early Jin dynasty.[3] In spite of the early appearance of the coiled dragon motif on textiles, this piece has been attributed to the Jin period on technical and stylistic grounds.[4] As in the other Jin brocades, the brocaded designs are asymmetrical and have no borders.

1. The designs on several late Roman shields are those of a dragonlike creature, coiled around the boss and chasing a sun or a moon. See Nickel 1991; see also the entry on a Tang mirror in New York 1993, p. 10.
2. See Fong and Watt 1996, pl. 63, and detail facing p. 141. The earliest mention of the coiled dragon in literature is in the *Tang huiyao* (Records of Tang institutions), in which is recorded a list of patterns decreed in A.D. 694 for the official robes of members of the imperial household and senior officials. The coiled dragon is one of the patterns for princes' robes. See *Tang huiyao*, p. 582.
3. Liu Yuquan 1982, pp. 273–318.
4. Another brocade in the collection of AEDTA, Paris, with the same design was carbon-dated. The resulting date ranged between A.D. 720 and 1010 at 95 percent confidence (Riboud 1995, p. 119), which would appear to be too early for the group to which the Metropolitan's brocade belongs.

TECHNICAL ANALYSIS

Warp: Red silk, poil z, single; uneven spacing causes vertical lines in the ground area. Step: irregular. Count: 72 per centimeter. *Weft:* Foundation: red silk, without apparent twist; each is composed of approximately 5 strands; the twists are imperceptible. Supplementary: gold thread composed of flat strips of gilded animal substrate; the substrate has a translucent tan coating under the gold leaf and is dirty white; the gold surface is bright and generally intact. Pass: 1 foundation weft and 1 supplementary weft, except when wefts are floated. Step: 1 pass. Count: 26 foundation wefts per centimeter in the ground areas and 20 supplementary wefts per centimeter. *Weave:* Tabby, brocaded. Foundation: warp-faced tabby; flaws consist of skipped bindings. Brocade: gold supplementary wefts are bound in 1/3 s twill by every first and second warp in each group of four (the first warp binds one foundation weft and one supplementary weft, the second warp binds the same supplementary weft and the following foundation weft, while the third and fourth warps bind only the foundation wefts). On the reverse, every sixth foundation weft is floated across the brocaded area; the supplementary wefts are not bound and turn into the next shed. A selvage is preserved along the left side: on the reverse, gold supplementary wefts turn into the next shed at the inner edge of the selvage border (6–7 millimeters from the outermost edge); the warps in the selvage border are arbitrarily paired, tripled, or quadrupled (fig. 49); the foundation wefts turn around the outermost warp (quadruple).

Unpublished.

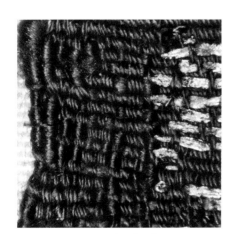

Figure 49. Micrographic detail,
cat. no. 30

31. Phoenixes Soaring amid Clouds

Tabby, brocaded
Warp 56.2 cm (22⅛ in.); weft 62.1 cm (24½ in.)
Jin dynasty (1115–1234)
The Cleveland Museum of Art. John L. Severance Fund
(1994.292)

Teardrop units, each formed by a soaring phoenix amid clouds, are brocaded in gold against a blue ground. Arranged in staggered horizontal rows, the phoenixes are oriented to the right and to the left in alternate rows.

At least three other textiles with this same design, brocaded in gold against a blue ground, are known: one at the Association pour l'Étude et la Documentation des Textiles d'Asie (AEDTA), Paris; a second in the collection of the Uragami Sōkyū-dō Company, Tokyo; and a third that was on the London art market.[1] Although the foundation weaves are tabby, the twill bindings of the gold brocading wefts are different. A Jin date for all four brocades is indicated by details of their structures.

1. Riboud 1995, figs. 2, 8, 9; Ogasawara 1989, p. 42, fig. 12; Spink & Son 1994, no. 10.

TECHNICAL ANALYSIS

Warp: Blue silk, z, single. Step: irregular. Count: 72 per centimeter. *Weft:* Foundation: blue silk, paired (one z and one without apparent twist). Supplementary: gold thread composed of flat strips of gilded animal substrate with a brown adhesive. Pass: 1 paired foundation weft and 1 brocading weft, except when wefts are floated. Step: 1 pass. Count: 26 paired foundation wefts per centimeter (in the ground areas) and 19 brocading wefts per centimeter. *Weave:* Tabby, brocaded. Foundation: warp-faced tabby; flaws consist of skipped bindings. Brocade: on the face, the gold supplementary wefts are bound by the warps in a 1/8 s twill. On the reverse, the gold wefts are unbound and turn into the next shed at the contours of the brocaded areas. (The supplementary wefts that formed loops as they turned into the next shed have broken; those that turned close to the weave remain intact.) Approximately every sixth (occasionally every fourth or seventh) paired foundation weft is floated across the reverse of the brocaded areas with floats beginning and ending along or just inside the contours of the brocaded units. No selvages are preserved.

Unpublished.

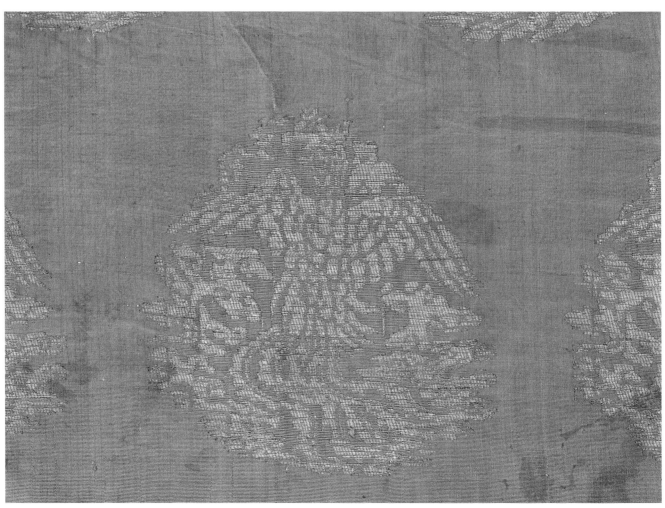

Detail, cat. no. 31

31

32. Brocade with Phoenixes

Tabby, brocaded
Warp 81.8 cm (32¼ in.); weft, without extended weft threads,
25.6 cm (10⅛ in.)
Jin dynasty (1115–1234)
The Cleveland Museum of Art. Gift of the Textile Art Alliance
(1994.27)

Single phoenixes forming teardrop units are here brocaded in gold against a white ground. The body of
each phoenix appears in three-quarter view, with the wings
outstretched and the heads in profile. Because the clouds
and vegetal elements along the contours of the units are
incomplete, the brocaded motifs appear to have been
extracted from a larger decorative program. The units are
arranged in staggered horizontal rows oriented alternately
to the right and to the left. Over four vertical (warp) and
three horizontal (weft) repeats are preserved.

The sides and one end of the textile are turned under
and the other end folded to form a V shape. Preserved in
Tibet, the brocade is stamped in red ink with a seated
Buddha flanked by two standing bodhisattvas just above
the V-shaped end and with Tibetan inscriptions, framed
and unframed, as well as a Tibetan letter.[1]

Two other textiles with the same design brocaded in
gold against a white ground are known. One, a rectangular piece seen on the art market, is similarly stamped in
red ink with a Buddhist inscription (part of which is bordered) and the letter *ka.*[2] The other, consisting of the
pointed end of a textile similar in shape to the Cleveland
piece, is in the collection of the Association pour l'Étude
et la Documentation des Textiles d'Asie (AEDTA), Paris.[3]
It, too, is stamped in red ink with a seated Buddha flanked
by two bodhisattvas. All three brocades belong to a small
group characterized by gold brocading wefts made with a
paper substrate, which would suggest possible production
in the southern Jin territories.

1. The stamped inscriptions and image are oriented in the opposite direction from the brocaded design of the textile. A framed inscription
   translates, "The Bhagavan, the Tathagata, the Arhat, the completely
   perfect Buddha," and an unframed line of inscription, "Salutations to
   Blo gnas." (The inscriptions were translated by Dr. Richard Kohn, Asian
   Art Museum, San Francisco.) A single letter between the inscription and
   the scene of the Buddha and the bodhisattvas is *ka*, the first letter of
   the Tibetan alphabet. Its presence indicates that the textile served as
   the cover for the first volume of a set of books. The point with the stamped
   image of the Buddha and bodhisattvas would have hung over the front
   of the book. (Verbal communication, 1995, from Dr. Paul Nietupski,
   Assistant Professor of Asian Religions, John Carroll University, Cleveland.)
2. Spink & Son 1994, no. 11.
3. Riboud 1995, figs. 36, 37.

TECHNICAL ANALYSIS

Warp: White silk, s, single. Step: irregular. Count: 48 per centimeter. *Weft:* Foundation: white silk, s. Supplementary: gold thread
composed of flat strips of paper gilded on one side. Pass: 1 foundation weft and 1 supplementary weft, except when wefts are floated.
Step: 1 pass. Count: 38 foundation wefts per centimeter in the
ground areas; 23 supplementary wefts per centimeter. *Weave:* Tabby,
brocaded. Foundation: warp-faced tabby; there are occasional
flaws in the form of skipped bindings. Brocade: the gold supplementary wefts are bound in a 1/5 z twill by all the warps. On the
reverse of the brocaded units, after every 11–12 wefts, 6 (occasionally 4 or 5) successive foundation wefts float, causing puckers along
the contours of the units on the face. The gold wefts are unbound
on the reverse side and carried into the next shed; with only a
couple of exceptions, however, the wefts have broken at the turns.
No selvages remain.

Unpublished.

32

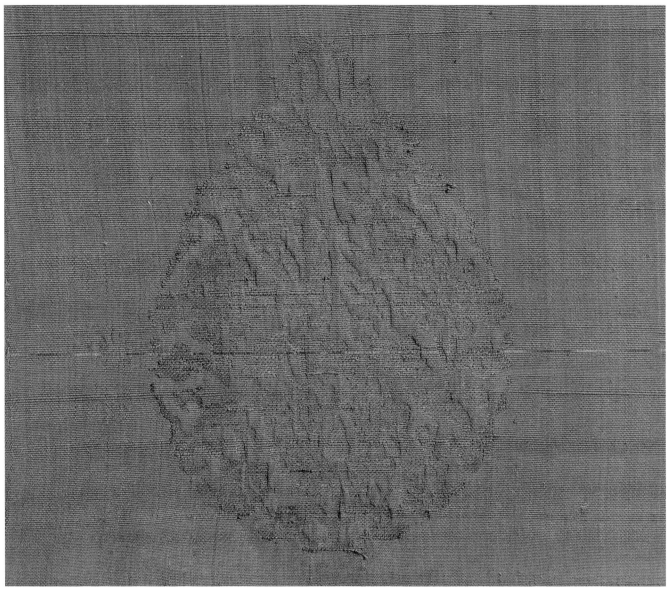

33. Lotus Flowers

Tabby, brocaded
Warp 58.4 cm (23 in.); weft 67 cm (26⅜ in.)
North China, Mongol period, 13th–mid-14th century
The Cleveland Museum of Art. John L. Severance Fund
(1994.293)

Brocaded, symmetrical floral arrangements in the shape of lotus bulbs are here seen in staggered horizontal rows against a brick red ground. From the bottom of each bulb grows a lotus flower and two stems that curve around the flower and then join to form a single stem supporting another lotus flower. Leaves and an additional lotus flower grow from each of the lateral stems. Both selvages are preserved, intersecting the design along the warp axis.

Both the symmetrical composition of each brocaded unit and the use of paired warps are characteristic of the weaving tradition of the eastern Iranian world. The textile may well have been produced at a center such as Hongzhou,

where Chinese from Bianjing (present-day Kaifeng), the former Jin capital, and weavers brought from Central Asia worked together.

TECHNICAL ANALYSIS

Warp: Orange-red silk, z, paired. Step: irregular. Count: 56 pairs (112 warp ends) per centimeter. *Weft:* Foundation: orange-red silk, mostly without apparent twist, although occasionally a slight z twist can be detected. Supplementary: gold thread composed of flat strips of gilded animal substrate coated with a dark reddish brown adhesive; little gilding remains. Pass: 1 foundation and 1

33

supplementary weft, except when wefts are floated. Step: 1 pass. Count: 16 foundation wefts per centimeter in the ground areas and 15 gold supplementary wefts per centimeter. *Weave:* Tabby, brocaded. Foundation: warp-faced tabby. The gold supplementary wefts are bound in tabby by the first and fourth pair of warps within every group of eight pairs of warps (i.e., one paired warp binds, the next two do not; the fourth pair of warps binds, and the following four pairs do not). On the reverse side of each brocaded motif, there are four floats of foundation wefts, each composed of two adjacent wefts. These occur after 31, 36, and 48 wefts. The gold wefts float on the reverse side and turn into the next shed along the contours of the unit. Most of these are now

broken as they did not turn close to the weave but formed loops. The gold wefts that turn into the next shed close to the weave, however, remain intact. Both selvages are composed of several bundles of warps, 8 on the right and 15 on the left, that form a tabby binding with the foundation wefts. These warps are purple silk, z, except for the third and eighth bundles in the right selvage, which are red silk, z. The foundation wefts turn around the outermost bundle of warps. The incomplete units at the selvage edges terminate along the warp axes; on the reverse, the gold wefts turn into the next shed 1 centimeter from the outermost edge.

Unpublished.

34. Brocade with Hares

Tabby, brocaded
Warp 26 cm (10¼ in.); weft 42.8 cm (16⅞ in.)
North China, Mongol period, 13th–mid-14th century
The Cleveland Museum of Art. Seventy-fifth anniversary gift of
Lisbet Holmes (1991.113)

This textile preserves two staggered rows of five-sided units brocaded in gold against a purple ground. Each unit consists of a hare running under a flowering shrub and has the appearance of having been cut from a larger image. The hares in the upper row are oriented to the left, those in the lower row to the right. Along the right edge is a selvage woven with red warps; the left edge of the textile is damaged.

There is at least one other piece that survives from this textile, and another brocaded with the same design in gold against a purple ground but with a green selvage.[1] The complete width of the present brocade, 66.5 centimeters, incorporates six brocaded units per horizontal row. Although the asymmetry of the brocaded scene belongs to the earlier tradition of Jin brocades, the paired warps reveal the influence of weavers originally from the eastern Iranian world. Like the brocade with lotus flowers (cat. no. 33), these brocades were perhaps produced in a center such as Hongzhou.

1. The present whereabouts of the former are unknown; the latter is published in Spink & Son 1994, no. 12.

TECHNICAL ANALYSIS

Warp: Purple silk, z, and paired (occasionally tripled or quadrupled). Step: irregular. Count: 72 pairs (114 warp ends) per centimeter. *Weft:* Foundation: purple silk, without apparent twist; thick. Supplementary: gold thread composed of flat strips of animal substrate, coated with a yellowish brown substance on both sides, and gilded on one side. Pass: 1 foundation and 1 supplementary weft. Step: 1 pass. Count: 16 passes per centimeter. *Weave:* Tabby, brocaded. Foundation: warp-faced tabby; the thickness of the wefts produces a ribbed effect. There are many mistakes: warps that pass over or under more than one weft and wefts that pass over or under more than one paired warp. Brocade: tabby binding of gold supplementary wefts by every first and second pair of warps within each group of eight pairs of warps (i.e., two consecutive paired warps bind the gold wefts, the next six paired warps do not). On the reverse side of the brocaded areas, the gold wefts float. In this fragment, all are broken, so that it is not certain if they were cut at each shed or if they formed loops (now broken) while turning into the next shed. The selvage, about 6 millimeters wide, is composed of a tabby binding of foundation wefts with coral silk warps, z, and mostly paired (one is single and two are triple). The warps are denser than those in the body of the fabric. At the outer edge, the foundation wefts turn around the

Detail, cat. no. 34

outermost warp, which is triple. The brocaded unit, interrupted by the selvage down its center, ends 5 millimeters from the inner selvage edge.

The textile was woven on a drawloom. The warp ends were threaded individually through the heddles of the shafts. (This is apparent from the occasional passage of one end of a paired warp over more than one foundation weft.) The ends, however, were threaded in pairs through the mails of the figure harness.

Unpublished.

34

4. Luxury-Silk Weaving under the Mongols

The textiles in the exhibition that date from the Mongol period (13th–mid-14th century) can be attributed primarily to Central Asia and the eastern Iranian world.[1] Those that have been in the Cleveland and Metropolitan Museum collections for some years are among the many that were transported through trade or possibly diplomatic missions to Europe, where they were preserved in church treasuries. Within recent years, however, other examples have come to light, greatly expanding our knowledge of luxury-silk weaving under the Mongols.

Central Asian textiles of this period defy any attempt at definition. As armies and merchant caravans, travelers, and missionaries traversed this vast region that linked the eastern Iranian world with China, goods—especially luxury silks—moved from one part of Asia to another, and with them the motifs with which they were woven. Entire colonies of craftsmen, moreover, who had been captured by the Mongols in northern China and the eastern Iranian world and resettled in distant cities of Mongolia and Central Asia brought with them the weaving techniques and decorative repertories of their homelands. Consequently, and not surprisingly, a bewildering variety of designs and structures appear in Central Asian textiles of the Mongol period. Unfortunately, written sources say virtually nothing about the everyday operation of weaving workshops, about the types of textiles produced in one center or region versus another, or about the various qualities of the textiles made and the functions that they served. Despite these and other questions that still remain, our understanding of luxury-silk weaving in Central Asia is far greater today than it was only a decade ago.

One of the most important developments in recent years has been the identification of textiles that were produced in Central Asian cities where craftsmen from conquered territories had been resettled. Two key silks are

in the exhibition, the silk with winged lions and griffins and the silk with displayed falcons (cat. nos. 35 and 36). Both are what was known at the time as *nasij*, or cloth of gold, textiles in which both ground and pattern are gold, with the design merely delineated by the silk foundation weave. Textiles woven with the high technical expertise observed in both these silks were certainly the products of imperial workshops. A comparison of the heads of the falcons with those of the griffins and of the cloudlike background of the silk with displayed falcons with that of the roundels enclosing the lions leaves no question that the two silks were woven in the same workshop (figs. 50 and 51). This is further indicated by the shared technical details of their weaves, which combine Chinese and eastern Iranian elements (fig. 52): the single foundation warps common in silks from China and the binding of gold wefts in pairs seen in eastern Iranian silks. In both textiles, the substrate of the gold thread is a very thin, translucent paper.

The designs of the textiles combine eastern and western elements. In the silk with winged lions and griffins (cat. no. 35), the paired animals enclosed in roundels and the paired animals in the interstices derive from eastern Iranian silk patterns. In the silk with displayed falcons (cat. no. 36), by contrast, the principal motifs are unframed, a convention common in textiles of the Liao (907–1125) and Jin (1115–1234) dynasties. The primary motifs (animals and birds) in the two silks derive from models that were current in the eastern Iranian world, while the secondary motifs (e.g., the cloudlike background ornament and the decorative details) were inspired by Chinese sources. The latter, however, are so far removed from their original context that the result is neither Chinese nor eastern Iranian but essentially Central Asian. One detail that can only be Central Asian is the curious transformation of the curling outer tail feathers of the falcons. In eastern Iranian art these feathers curl, terminate in a dragon's head, and are grasped by the talons of a bird (fig. 53). In the silk with displayed falcons, however, the motif has been misunderstood and reinterpreted as the wrinkled necks and heads of dragons that do not

Figure 50. Detail, cat. no. 35

Figure 51. Detail, cat. no. 36

curl but rather curve upward to threaten the bird itself. Given the combination of Chinese, Persian, and Central Asian elements, it is clear that both the silk with winged lions and griffins and the silk with displayed falcons were woven in a Central Asian city in which artisans from the conquered northern Chinese territories as well as from the eastern Iranian world had been resettled and were working together with local craftsmen for the Mongol court.[2] That both textiles, like the vast majority of luxury silks produced under the Mongols, were woven with silk of one color and gold is significant. According to historical works and eyewitness accounts, "robes of one color," called *zhisun* in China, were given by the Mongol emperors to members of the court to be worn on festivals and important occasions, events that usually included lavish banquets.[3]

Figure 52. Micrographic detail, cat. no. 35

Figure 53. Detail, cat. no. 43

The silk with winged lions and griffins and the silk with displayed falcons probably do not date much before the middle of the thirteenth century, given their preservation in Tibet. For it was in 1240 that a small Mongol army invaded that country, followed seven years later by an agreement signed with the Sakya sect, which resulted in Mongol control over Tibet.[4] Beginning in 1251, members of the Mongol imperial family began to patronize Tibetan sects and to give gifts, including precious textiles, to leading monasteries.[5] While it cannot be proved, the two textiles very likely reached Tibet as imperial gifts.

Two items in the exhibition are woven with floral designs so tiny and so dense that their repeats are difficult to discern. The Cleveland fragment with tiny leaves (cat. no. 38) has a supplementary-weft structure in which the flat gold wefts float on both the face and the reverse as required by the design.[6] Both the widely spaced single warps and the fringe of foundation wefts that form the selvage (preserved in another piece of the same textile in the Kunstgewerbemuseum, Berlin) indicate a Central Asian provenance.[7] Another textile with a tiny pattern

of leaves and flowers woven with the same supplementary-weft structure as the Cleveland textile forms part of a dalmatic now in the Church of San Domenico in Perugia.[8] Also in Perugia is a cope to which the fragments with tiny leaves (cat. no. 37) originally belonged.[9] That textile has a design of tiny flowers and leaves, but it is woven with a lampas structure and closely spaced warps. The only known textile with miniature animals and birds in addition to tiny flowers and/or leaves is in Verona, also woven with a lampas structure (fig. 54). Dissimilarities in the spacing of the warps and in the selvage structures among these textiles indicate that dense, small-scale patterns were produced in different weaving centers.[10]

What distinguishes the designs of these textiles from the small-scale patterns that had long been produced in Central Asia and China is the seemingly haphazard abandon with which the tiny motifs have been strewn across the surface. Notwithstanding obvious differences in style, a similar effect occurs in some of the late eastern Central Asian (Uyghur) *kesi* in which flowers, animals, and birds appear on a dense ground of small, scattered leaves.

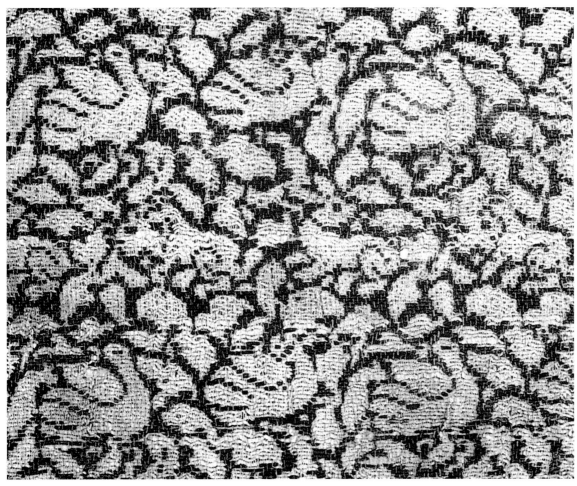

Figure 54. Textile G, from the tomb of Cangrande della Scala, detail of reverse. Central Asia, before 1329. Silk and gold thread, lampas weave. Loom width 97 × 46.5 cm (38¼ × 18¼ in.). Museo di Castelvecchio, Verona

Apart from the general patterning scheme, there are also similarities in small details, such as the tripartite leaves, which occur in both the Cleveland textile and the *kesi* with aquatic birds and recumbent animal (cat. no. 16), while the backward-looking geese and rabbits in the Verona textile also occur in the *kesi*.[11] The stylistic similarity between the designs of the tiny-patterned silks and the *kesi* of the Uyghurs raises the interesting possibility that the tiny-patterned silks were woven in the eastern part of Central Asia and that their designs were drawn from the same decorative repertory used by Uyghur weavers. Unfortunately, it is not possible at present to pursue the implications of this evidence, as records that document weaving among the Uyghurs are scarce and fragmentary. It would be extremely useful to know whether the several varieties of luxury textiles presented to Chinggis Khan in 1209 and 1211 by Barchuq Art Tegin, chief of the Uyghurs, were locally made or trade goods—or a combination of both.[12]

All the tiny-patterned textiles known thus far are preserved in Europe. Both the cope (of which the textiles in cat. no. 37 are fragments) and the dalmatic in Perugia have long been associated with Pope Benedict XI, who died in 1304.[13] The silk with animals and birds was found in the tomb of Cangrande della Scala, who died in 1329.[14] Other tiny-patterned silks are described in the 1311 inventory of Pope Clement V and in the Vatican inventory of 1361.[15]

Few silks better demonstrate the extraordinary imagination and vitality that were indigenous to Central Asia than catalogue number 39, a fragment from a silk-and-gold textile in which rows of phoenixes alternate with rows of bizarre beasts. The phoenixes have outspread wings, curling feathers, and necks curving down and back, while the winged beast, with a humped back lined with a dragonlike spine, has a curling tail, short clawed front feet, and vestigial hind feet that defy description. Sadly, the head of this extraordinary creature is missing. The dynamic interaction between the agitated phoenix reaching with its open bill toward the beast below and the beast itself, whose attention was undoubtedly directed toward the bird, is somewhat lost in the sequence of the preserved repeat. The interaction of the animals in one row with those in the row below is clearer in a silk in Stralsund that has a design that is similarly imaginative and energetic (fig. 55), in which a row of fantastic creatures with lions' heads, wings, long tails, and dragon-like spines and wearing loose collars and bells plunge with open mouths toward dragons in the row below, whose bodies contort as they spin to ward off the attack. Although Chinese fauna served as the point of departure for most of the creatures in these silks, the peculiar

Figure 55. Dalmatic, detail. Central Asia, late 13th–mid-14th century. Silk and gold thread, lampas weave with areas of compound weave. Kulturhistorisches Museum der Hansestadt Stralsund (1862.16)

imagination with which they have been transformed and the almost electric energy that drives them are qualities indigenous to the artistic heritage of Central Asia.

In contrast to the numbers of Mongol textiles that have survived from Central Asia, examples woven in northern China at that time are scarce. Not many tombs of the Mongol period have been found (and reported) in that region, and the documentation on the several tombs that have yielded textiles does not, unfortunately, give a clear idea of their structure.[16] Luxury textiles woven in northern China in the Mongol period can, moreover, be difficult to distinguish from those produced in Central Asia or Mongolia because of the presence of Chinese craftsmen in those regions and the eventual resettlement of craftsmen from Central Asia and Mongolia in northern China. In 1275, Khubilai Khan (r. 1260–94) moved craftsmen from Besh Baliq to Daidu to weave *nasij* for use as collars and cuffs. In the *Yongle dadian* (Grand Compilation of Yongle) is the record: "Besh Baliq Office. In the twelfth year of the Zhiyuan reign [1275], the fields, land, and artisans of Besh Baliq were uprooted after the military actions. [The artisans were] moved to the capital and an office was established for the weaving of *nashishi*

[Chinese for *nasij*] and other textiles for imperial use as collars and cuffs. In the thirteenth year [1276] the Besh Baliq Office of Various Classes of Artisans was established."[17] In the *Yuanshi* (History of the Yuan Dynasty), this passage is condensed into "Besh Baliq Office . . . to weave *nashishi* and other textiles for collars and cuffs for imperial use," giving the impression that the office was established at Besh Baliq. Both texts almost certainly derive from the *Jingshi dadian* (Record of Yuan Institutions), the chief source for information on Yuan administration. Because the *Yongle dadian* is composed of extracts of early texts copied verbatim, whereas the compilers of the *Yuanshi* were free to edit, it is the more detailed *Yongle dadian* that has the greater credibility. Moreover, the *Yongle dadian* version makes much more sense in the historical context. In 1275, Uyghur lands (Khara Khojo, or Huozhou, and Besh Baliq) were under fierce attack from forces of the house of Chaghadai, and from this time on, the control of the government at Daidu over the lands of the Uyghurs was tenuous.[18] In 1275, moving the weavers to the capital was a logical step. We may even assume that the Besh Baliq office was established (in 1276) in Daidu to accommodate the various classes (ethnic groups) of artisans from Besh Baliq who arrived in 1275. Thus, after 1275 Daidu became one of the chief centers for the production of *nasij*. This may explain the similarity of the heads of the griffins in the silk with winged lions and griffins (cat. no. 35) and of the falcons in the silk with displayed falcons (cat. no. 36) to those of the birds, also in *nasij*, that edge the collar in the portrait of Chabi, wife of Khubilai Khan, in the National Palace Museum, Taipei (fig. 56).

In addition to the workshops at Daidu, other textile centers were also at about this time established or reactivated specifically for the production of *nasij*. In 1278, the administrator of the Longxing Circuit (in which Xunmalin was situated), Bie-du-lu-din (Baidu al-Din), was ordered by the crown prince to gather "scattered and vagrant" households, to teach artisans to weave *nasij*, and to establish offices at both Hongzhou and Xunmalin to be administered, respectively, by Hu-san-wu-din (Husain al-Din?) and a superintendent Yang.[19] (This is the earliest record that relates the two workshops specifically to the manufacture of *nasij*.) According to the Persian historian Rashid al-Din (1247–1318), the majority of the craftsmen at Xunmalin were from Samarkand.[20] In 1280, as the number of artisans at Xunmalin was small, this office was combined with the Hongzhou office under Hu-san-wu-din, and in 1282, eight boys from Xi-hu-xin joined the artisans already at Xunmalin. In 1294, as Xunmalin was over six hundred miles from Hongzhou, making it difficult to administer the two offices in rotation,

the two workshops were again put under separate management, though they continued to operate under the overall supervision of Hu-san-wu-din. Finally, in 1307, two independent administrations were set up, each with superintending officers.[21]

We do not know how quickly the artisans who relocated from Central Asia to northern China adopted Chinese motifs and techniques. The silk with winged lions and griffins (cat. no. 35) and the silk with displayed falcons (cat. no. 36) we tend to place in Central Asia on the basis both of their techniques and especially of their designs, which are a characteristically Central Asian synthesis of foreign motifs. Far less clear is the provenance of two other textiles, one with phoenixes among lotus and another with phoenixes and *makaras* (cat. nos. 40 and 41). Technically, both are very similar to the *nasij* with winged lions and griffins and the *nasij* with displayed falcons, including the fringed selvages, which appear to be a Central Asian type. The metal surface of the gold threads, however, is not solely gold (as it is in the winged lions and griffins and the displayed falcons), but has a layer of silver under the layer of gold. Nevertheless, the substrates of the gold threads consist of paper that is

Figure 56. *Chabi, Consort of Khubilai Khan.* Yuan dynasty (1279–1368), 13th century. Album leaf, ink and color on silk, 61.5 × 48 cm (24¼ × 18⅞ in.). National Palace Museum, Taipei

131

exceedingly thin and somewhat transparent in all four textiles. Whether the dissimilarity in the metallic surfaces implies an intentional difference, or whether it has more far-reaching implications (such as different places of production) is not known. From the standpoint of design, the textiles with phoenixes among lotus and phoenixes and *makaras*, unlike the *nasij* with winged lions and griffins and displayed falcons, were woven with entirely Chinese motifs and patterns.

Of all the textiles in the exhibition, only one, a lampas silk-and-gold fragment from Cleveland (cat. no. 42), can be securely assigned to northern China on both technical and stylistic grounds. It is woven with single phoenixes or coiled dragons in lobed roundels that are arranged in rows against a ground of tiny hexagons. Aside from the lobed roundels that derive from eastern Iranian models, the design is Chinese, showing none of the combining of styles and imaginative transformations that occur in some of the Central Asian silks.[22] Moreover, the substrate of the gold thread is paper, and the single blue foundation warps, twisted z, as well as the bundles of warps in the selvage recall the earlier Jin brocades. Another textile, woven with exactly the same design, though in gold on red silk rather than in gold on blue, forms the main portion of a cloud collar in the Palace Museum, Beijing (fig. 57). It, too, is a lampas weave with a structure that corresponds to that of the Cleveland fragment, except for the tabby bindings of the foundation and the supplementary weaves. These textiles are evidence of the repeated use of patterns, a practice also observed among the brocades.[23] Attached to the cloud collar are pendants made, in part, from a purple silk woven with gold phoenixes (fig. 58). The birds are a curious hybrid of the Chinese phoenix and the eastern Iranian eagle (compare, in particular, the detail of the ornamental "feathers" that extend from the birds' eyes with those of the eagles in cat. no. 43). Similarly, gold thread composed of flat strips of gilded paper, so commonly found among Chinese silks, is combined with paired foundation warps characteristic of textiles woven in the eastern Iranian world.[24] Similar combinations of elements very likely characterized many of the luxury silks produced in northern China following the resettlement of artisans from Central Asia by Khubilai Khan.

Richly woven textiles from the eastern Mongol territories were traded in great quantities with the Ilkhanid empire, the Mamluk empire, and Europe.[25] In Italy, the impact of their exotic designs triggered the most imaginative chapter in the history of European silk weaving. An entire class of textiles was woven with tiny floral and animal designs that were inspired by textiles like catalogue numbers 37 and 38 and the silk from the tomb of

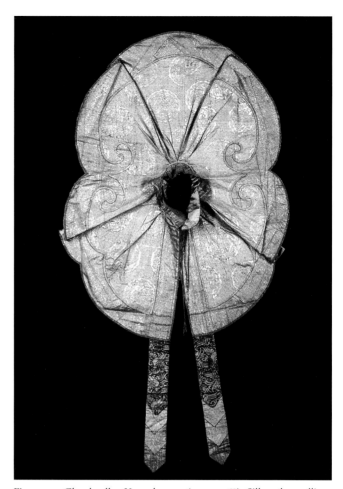

Figure 57. Cloud collar. Yuan dynasty (1279–1368). Silk and metallic thread, lampas weave. Width at shoulder 70 cm (27½ in.), collar to hem 43 cm (16⅞ in.). Palace Museum, Beijing

Cangrande della Scala (fig. 54).[26] In other textiles, exotic patterns or motifs from the Mongol empire were copied outright, causing subsequent confusion about their provenance. The 1311 inventory of Pope Clement V, for example, mentions a tunic of Mongol or Lucchese cloth. More often, foreign motifs were absorbed and used in new and creative ways. In a silk formerly in Berlin (fig. 59), for example, the winged water creature spewing forth a dragon as a dog walks up its back was most likely inspired by a *makara* (see cat. no. 41). Similarly, the provocative stance of the phoenix in catalogue number 39 reappears in several Italian silks.[27] What most inspired Italian designers, and appears in Persian designs as well, was the dramatic interaction of the animals or birds in one row with those in the next.[28]

The eastern Iranian tradition of silk weaving, which had so great an impact on the luxury textiles produced in Central Asia and northern China, is represented by catalogue numbers 43 to 47. Key to their identification is the textile with felines and eagles (cat. no. 43). This panel, which preserves both side selvages, is woven with

Figure 58. Detail of cloud-collar pendants, fig. 57

Figure 59. Textile with water creature and dog. Italy, last third of the 14th century. Silk and silver thread, lampas weave. Formerly Kunstgewerbemuseum, Berlin

a design current in eastern Iran in the twelfth and early thirteenth centuries: aligned roundels enclosing pairs of animals; a symmetrical device, in this case displayed birds, in the interstices; and, across the top, a band of pseudoinscription consisting of the interlaced stems of Kufic letters.[29] Above the inscription is a short segment of the principal design. The textile is woven with a lampas weave having paired foundation warps, wrapped gold threads bound in pairs, and flat gold wefts bound singly and carried from one shed into the next (fig. 60). Both types of gold thread are made with an animal substrate that was silvered and then gilded; the core of the wrapped threads is silk. The two selvages are composed of a fringe of weft loops.

   Particularly important are the felines' tails, which are strikingly similar to those of the griffins in the silk with winged lions and griffins (figs. 61 and 62). Both are exceptionally long and loop around a rosette before terminating in a head (a western Asian dragon's head in the case of the felines and a feline head in the case of the griffins).

Figure 60. Micrographic detail, cat. no. 43

Figure 61. Detail, cat. no. 43

Figure 62. Detail, cat. no. 35

The rosette around which both tails loop, the personal touch of a craftsman or workshop rather than a stock motif, and the looping tail, prevalent in the art of the eastern Iranian world in the twelfth and thirteenth centuries,[30] associate the two textiles with craftsmen from Khurasan and Transoxiana who were resettled in the eastern Mongol territories. It is important to remember that the artisans sent to Mongolia and Central Asia were artisans from the eastern Iranian world, not craftsmen from cities west of Khurasan that were subsequently conquered by Hülegü (d. 1265), beginning in 1253. One of the cities in which they were settled was Besh Baliq, the former Uyghur capital. Considering that one of the generals who distinguished himself in the destruction of Nishapur was Barchuq, chief of the Uyghurs, it is very likely that artisans of Nishapur were among the craftsmen sent to Besh Baliq. Others from Herat—including weavers—were also resettled there, according to the fourteenth-century Herati historian Sayfi.[31] Some of these artisans were allowed to return to Herat, one group in 1236 and another group in 1239, in order to restore the weaving industry there.[32] This is the only record of weavers from the eastern Iranian world being permitted to return to their homeland, and it may offer further

explanation for the occurrence in the two textiles of the motif of the tail looping around a rosette.

Supporting the attribution of the silk with felines and eagles to the eastern Iranian world is the pseudoinscription. Not only had the style of interlaced Kufic originated in that part of the world, but the reduction of the Kufic letters to interlaced stems belongs to the final stage of that style as seen, for example, in the inscription on the *qibla iwan* in the madrasa, dated 1219, at Zuzan in northeastern Iran.[33] The juxtaposition of highly reflective flat gold threads used for the ground of the inscription band with less reflective wrapped gold threads used for the interlaced stems produces a three-dimensional effect. This is alluded to by Rashid al-Din in his descriptions of two magnificent tents composed of "cloth made of gold on gold," which were twice presented to Hülegü, once outside Samarkand in 1255 and again near Balkh in 1256.[34] Although wrapped gold had long been used in the West, the art of weaving with flat gold wefts that are carried from one shed into the next was introduced into the eastern Iranian world in the early Mongol period. Evidence of its having been learned from Chinese craftsmen is provided by a rare Iranian tiraz (fig. 63) in which the flat gold threads are composed of strips of animal substrate gilded on both sides. This particularly rich type of gold thread had been incorporated into imperial textiles woven in both the Jin and the Song dynasties.[35] The technique of weaving with flat gold thread was probably introduced into Transoxiana and Khurasan by the Chinese craftsmen brought to Samarkand from conquered northern China and by weavers returning to Herat from Besh Baliq, where they had learned it from Chinese craftsmen. In addition to the gold threads, the selvages of the textile with felines and eagles also support an attribution to the eastern Iranian world, composed as they are of a fringe of weft loops, a type of selvage that can be traced back at least to eighth-century Transoxiana.

On the basis of the style of the pseudoinscription and the preservation of the textile in Tibet, the silk with felines and eagles probably dates close to but not much later than the middle of the thirteenth century. That was the very time when Hülegü, embarking on his western campaign, received the two tents of "cloth made of gold on gold."

Figure 63. Tiraz of Abu Bakr (r. ca. 1226–60). Eastern Iranian world, ca. 1260. Silk and gold thread, lampas weave. 66.5 × 41 cm (26⅛ × 16⅛ in.). The David Collection, Copenhagen (20/1994)

Similarly, it was in the 1250s until his death in 1265 that Hülegü patronized the Yabzang, Phagmogru, Nyamg, and Brigung sects of Tibet.[36]

The only datable textile that is closely related to the silk with felines and eagles is the tiraz of Abu Bakr (fig. 63), which must have been woven in, or very shortly before, 1260. It is a lampas weave, woven with flat and wrapped gold threads, and with foundation warps that are both paired and single.[37] Toward the top is an inscription written in Persian that reads: *Salghur Sultan Abu Bakr ibn Saud.*[38] In the main body of the tiraz, cloud collars ornamented with flowers and palmettes are arranged in staggered horizontal rows; birds and flowers fill the interstices. A short section of this design appears at the top edge above the inscription band. Abu Bakr ibn Saud, the Salghurid ruler of Fars from 1226 to 1260, had long-standing connections with Transoxiana. Not only had Fars been annexed by the shahs of Khwarazm prior to the Mongol conquest, but Abu Bakr's sister was married to the Khwarazmian shah Jalal al-Din. Abu Bakr himself, following the Mongol conquest of Transoxiana, was a vassal of Ögödei (r. 1229–41) and, after 1256, of Hülegü. Because tiraz were produced for the exclusive use of a ruler and his high officials, this textile must have been woven before Abu Bakr's death in 1260. The exceptional richness and importance of the textile are underscored by the fact that the flat gold wefts are gilded on both sides. Both the ground and the pattern, moreover, are woven with gold thread—wrapped juxtaposed to flat—while the red silk foundation weave is reserved for the delineation of the motifs.[39] Similarities in the design of the tiraz to that of the silk with felines and eagles, the use of flat gold thread gilded on both sides, and particularly the fact that the tiraz was preserved in Tibet strongly suggest that it was made not in Fars but in the eastern Iranian territories, very likely as a gift for Abu Bakr. However, it appears never to have reached Abu Bakr, as it was sent instead to Tibet, presumably as part of an imperial donation from Hülegü. From this, it may be inferred that the textile was woven about the time of Abu Bakr's death, after which it would have been of no use to the court of Fars.[40]

The large panel with griffins in the Metropolitan Museum (cat. no. 44) was woven with an overall design similar to that of the silk with felines and eagles: linked roundels enclosing pairs of addorsed, regardant griffins, four-directional palmettes in the interstices, and a band of interlaced pseudo-Kufic across the top.[41] It is a lampas weave, with foundation warps that are both paired and, more often, single. The wrapped gold thread is composed of an animal substrate that was silvered and gilded and wrapped around a cotton core. There are numerous weaving errors throughout, particularly in the area of the inscription band.

The textile shares stylistic and technical elements with other thirteenth-century silk-and-gold fabrics that appear to have been produced in the eastern Iranian world. Similar griffins with curved bills, "ears," scalloped neckbands, thick tails, and joined wings terminating in a palmette occur, for example, in a textile in the Gemeentemuseum, The Hague, and in another in Copenhagen that is woven with flat gold thread (fig. 64).[42] In a related textile in Bremen Cathedral, the animals are winged lions rather than griffins, but they, too, have thick tails that curve behind their inner, extended hind legs.[43] Similar tails, as well as the unusual stance of the animals, can be found among the stucco carvings that ornament the twelfth-century palace at Termez.[44] The wings of the lions in the Bremen textile and the curls of fur on their necks are nearly identical to those of the griffins, as are the floral motifs between the pairs of animals. As in the panel with griffins, the gold threads of the textiles in The Hague, Copenhagen, and Bremen are made with animal substrates that have been silvered and gilded. The wrapped gold threads of the silks in The Hague and Bremen, moreover, were made with a cotton core. This type of gold thread is coarse and inferior in quality to

Figure 64. Textile from a cope. Eastern Iranian world, 13th century. Silk and gold thread, lampas weave. Warp repeat 17.1 cm (6¾ in.), weft repeat 30.8 cm (12⅛ in.). Nationalmuseet, Copenhagen

Figure 65. Reconstructive drawing of a silk-and-gold textile from the tomb of Bishop Hartmann (d. 1286). Lampas weave. Diözesanmuseum, Augsburg

that made with a silk core and without a layer of silver under the gold. It is not known whether it was used prior to the Mongol conquest, or if its use in these textiles is a consequence of the economic depression that prevailed for the decades following the conquest. Supporting the attribution of the panel with griffins to the eastern Iranian world is the formation of its selvages (a fringe of all wefts). It is not known if the predominance of single foundation warps was the result of the presence of Chinese craftsmen in Samarkand,[45] or if single foundation warps were used for lampas weaves produced in Central Asia prior to the Mongol conquest.

It is interesting to note that, despite the mid-thirteenth-century date of the silk with felines and eagles and of the textile with griffins, their designs rely on Persian patterns and motifs of the late twelfth and early thirteenth centuries. The same phenomenon can be observed not only in the related textiles just discussed but in a number of other silk-and-gold textiles as well. One in the Diözesanmuseum, Augsburg, for example, was woven with the Persian theme of Bahram Gur and his companion, Azade (fig. 65). Like the textile with felines and eagles, this textile has a lampas structure of paired foundation warps, gold wefts bound in pairs, and a selvage composed of a fringe of weft loops.[46] The textile was preserved in the tomb of Bishop Hartmann in Augsburg Cathedral and must date to between 1248, when he became bishop, and 1286, when he died. Several silk-and-gold bands that ornament a coat worn by a military officer who was buried along the shores of Salt Lake, outside Urumqi, also are woven with motifs found in the decorative repertory of Iran prior to the Mongol invasion.[47] One represents a king (fig. 66), while another has a design of paired griffins, addorsed and regardant, whose wings join to form a palmette (fig. 67). The latter is particularly similar in design and style to the textile in Copenhagen (fig. 64). Not only their designs but also their structures correspond to those of textiles attributed to the eastern Iranian world.[48] They may have been woven there and transported to Central Asia as imperial property or through trade, or they may have been produced in Central Asia by craftsmen from Khurasan or Transoxiana.[49]

Another cloth of gold in the exhibition, catalogue number 45, was woven with rabbit wheels, a motif commonly found in the metalwork of Khurasan dating from the middle of the twelfth century until the Mongol conquest.[50] In keeping with Mongol taste, however, the entire textile was woven in gold except for the delineation of the design in red silk. Its lampas structure has paired warps, wrapped gold threads (made with an animal substrate and a silk core) that are bound in pairs, and a selvage

Figure 66. Reconstructive drawing and detail of the band of a coat excavated at Salt Lake. Eastern Iranian world or Central Asia, Mongol period, 13th century. Silk and gold thread, lampas weave. Xinjiang Institute of Archaeology, Urumqi

Figure 67. Reconstructive drawing of the band of a coat excavated at Salt Lake. Eastern Iranian world or Central Asia, Mongol period, 13th century

composed mainly of a fringe of wefts. In the upper part of the selvage, however, there are still preserved fragments of two cotton cords around which the wefts turn. This rare and important detail reveals that selvages consisting of a fringe of weft loops originally had cords of cotton or some other plant fiber around which the wefts turned. These cords disintegrated over time, leaving a fringe of wefts.[51]

Although Iranian designs and motifs predominate in textiles produced in Khurasan and Transoxiana in the mid-thirteenth century, the tiraz of Abu Bakr (fig. 63) is evidence of the inclusion of Central Asian motifs as well. Chinese influence, conversely, appears to have been limited at this time to the occasional occurrence of single foundation warps, the use of flat gold thread, and minor details such as the ruffled feathers of the eagles and an occasional lotus flower as seen in the silk with felines and eagles. Eventually, however, Chinese elements became much more common in Transoxiana and Khurasan. The design of a textile in the Kunstgewerbemuseum, Berlin, for example, is a synthesis of western and eastern motifs (fig. 68). The lobed roundels arranged in staggered horizontal rows, the inscription band toward the top,[52] above which is a quotation from the main design, as well as the paired foundation warps, the binding of wrapped gold wefts in pairs, and the selvage composed of a fringe of wefts typically occur in eastern Islamic textiles. Within the roundels, however, are Chinese coiled dragons, while delicate vines with fungi fill the interstices.[53]

The textile with phoenixes dating from the late thirteenth or fourteenth century (cat. no. 47) reveals even greater Chinese influence. Not only is it woven with a design of phoenixes arranged in horizontal rows among vertically curving floral vines, but its foundation warps are single.[54] Unfortunately, no sequence of dated textiles from the thirteenth century survives to indicate when Chinese flowers, birds, and animals began to be absorbed into the repertory of textile design in the western Mongol territories. In the medium of ceramics, however, there is evidence that this occurred after about 1270.[55]

A Note on Some Luxury Textiles at the Yuan Court

In Yuan China the *zhisun* (from the Mongolian *jisün*) banquet was commonly called the *zhama* banquet. According to Han Rulin, one of the leading historians of the Mongol period in China, *zhama* is a transliteration of the Persian word *jamah*, meaning coat or clothing. Han Rulin also points out that several foreign terms

used in connection with the formal wear at these banquets all appear to be Persian in origin, such as *da'na* for *dana* (pearl) and *yahu* for *yaqut* (precious stone). These jewels came by trade or tribute from the Middle East.[56]

Of the numerous references in Chinese literature to the *zhisun* or *zhama* banquet, the account of greatest interest to textile historians is that of Yu Ji (1272–1348), who served at the imperial court from the time of Temür (r. 1295–1307) to the time of Tugh Temür (r. 1328–32). During the latter's reign he was an academician in the Academy of Scholars of the Kuizhang Pavilion, a special office set up to accommodate the emperor's favorite scholars who, among their other duties, were participants in the compilation of the *Jingshi dadian* (Record of Yuan Institutions). In his composition for the long inscription on the commemorative stele for the family of Alaghan (Prince Caonan; 1233–1281), Yu Ji records that Yesüder, the son of Alaghan, was awarded lavish gifts for his efforts in quelling the opposition to Tugh Temür's accession. The description of the gifts reads, in part: "*Zhisun* banquet robe. *Zhisun* is the robe worn by high officials when they attend an imperial banquet. Nowadays it takes the form of a bright red robe with strings of large pearls sewn on the back and shoulders—the same for the headdress. In addition [he was given] seven outfits of *nashishi*. *Nashishi* is woven with strips of gilded leather."[57] It would thus seem that leather, or some other kind of animal substrate, was used in China for weaving *nasij* well into the fourteenth century.

The *zhisun* robe took many forms, and they are described in some detail in the *Yuanshi* (History of the Yuan Dynasty). For the emperor there were eleven varieties for the winter season and fifteen varieties for the summer. For the nobility and senior officials, there were nine varieties for the winter and fourteen for summer.[58] The great majority were made of *nasij*, but one variety of winter wear was made of *qiemianli*. The annotation in the original text for this term identifies it with *jian-rong*, which may be interpreted as cut velvet—*jian* is the word for cut, and *rong* is a word that variously refers to fine animal fur, new shoots of grass, and silk floss for embroidery. *Sufu* (from the Persian *suf*), a material for summer wear, the annotation adds, is the finest wool cloth of the Muslims. It would seem that the difference between an ordinary *nasij* robe and the more formal *zhisun* wear was the addition of pearls and precious stones. The *zhisun* robe was so highly prized that in the year 1332 an edict was issued which proclaimed that "all officials and members of the imperial guard upon whom the *zhisun* robe has been conferred should wear it when attending imperial banquets. Those who pawn their robes will be punished."[59]

Figure 68. Textile with coiled dragons and inscription, detail. Eastern Iranian world, late 13th–mid-14th century. Silk and gold thread, lampas weave. Kunstgewerbemuseum, Berlin (00.53)

Apart from the cloths of gold, another fabric that was accorded high esteem was *zhusi*. This name has caused much confusion and discussion in the past, the problem arising from the character *zhu*, one of whose meanings is ramie. In the Ming period, however, *zhusi* was a term for a kind of damask, as there are bolts of this material found at Ding Ling, the tomb of Emperor Shenzong (r. 1573–1620), with the original factory wrapping and labeled *zhusi*.[60] However, true to the literal meaning of the term, some of the colored threads in the *zhusi* from Ding Ling appear to have been spun from a combination of fibers of silk and ramie.[61] Perhaps the term serves to distinguish damask woven (at least partially) with combined fibers from ordinary silk damask, known since the Ming period as *duan*—and also found in Ding Ling. Whether this identification can be extrapolated backward in time is another question. The earliest description of *zhusi* we can find is in the writings of Kong Qi, who was active in the late Yuan period and was something of a connoisseur of works of art. He compares *zhusi* with *kesi* of the Song period: "*Gesi* [another name for *kesi*] is like the *zhusi* of today. Within one section of the pattern the color is both light and dark. This is the

cleverness of workmanship. In recent times, the weaving of imperial portraits is in the same manner, but the subtlety of color is not equal [to that of the Song]. There are several varieties of *gesi*. The best includes a complete composition of gold branches and blossoms; those with floral sprays of various kinds are next best. There are both multicolor pieces and pieces with only two colors, as lifelike as paintings. There are shaded patterns [*anhua*] on *zhusi*, but there is nothing special about them, except that they are more dense and complex [than in *gesi*?]; ultimately, they are not equal to the patterns on *gesi*. However, *zhusi* is still worth treasuring."[62] This is hardly an example of clear expository writing, and further confusion may have been caused by corruption of the text. But it is nevertheless possible to make sense out of this passage on the assumption that *zhusi* refers to a damask weave, perhaps with mixed fibers.

The term *zhusi* seems to have first appeared in the beginning of the twelfth century. One of the earliest mentions of the term occurred in the story of a resourceful, if unsavory, character by the name of Guo Yaoshi. A native of Bohai, northeastern China, serving in the Liao military, Guo surrendered to the Song in 1122 at the final stages of the collapse of the Liao dynasty. He gained great favor at the Song court by distributing exotic and precious gifts to all officials, high and low. In 1125, he went over to the Jin and in the following year guided the Jurchen army into the Northern Song capital and directed the looting of the imperial palaces.[63] Among the exotic gifts he gave to officials at the Song court was "*zhusi* woven with wrapped gold [thread]," made by artisans he had brought together from former Liao territories.[64] It would seem that *zhusi* was manufactured in North China by the beginning of the twelfth century. By Yuan times, *zhusi* was in regular production. The *Jingshi dadian* records specifications of "muted blue shaded pattern *zhusi*" for mounting imperial portraits.

Just as they decorated their tents with cloths of gold, the Mongols used precious textiles as wall and ceiling coverings in the interiors of their palace buildings and for furnishings. Xiao Xun, a member of the team of officials charged with the task of clearing out and demolishing the Yuan palaces at Daidu following the eviction of the Mongols, left a description of the layout of the palace structures and some of the courts and rooms.[65] In one room, the ceiling was covered with "plain *zhusi*." Xiao Xun also relates that in the bedchambers mattresses were stacked several deep and covered with *nasij* sheets on which were pasted patches of aromatics decorated with gold flowers. In the large *kesi* mandala with imperial portraits (cat. no. 25), the emperors and empresses are depicted sitting on cushion covers of a gold fabric

Figure 69. Detail, cat. no. 25

whose pattern is delineated by the red silk foundation weave (fig. 69).

Finally, there was apparently a fabric called *sa-da-la-qi*, which was manufactured in one of the numerous textile workshops administered by the Ministry of Works of the Yuan government. The name must be a transliteration of *zandaniji*. According to the *Yuanshi*, in the year 1287 a Jamal al-Din (Zha-ma-la-ding) directed (or arrived with) artisans to weave *sa-da-la-qi* in the same workshops as those for silks. A separate superintendency was subsequently established for the production of *sa-da-la-qi*.[66] However, we have not been able to locate another Yuan text in which *sa-da-la-qi* is mentioned, and there is no means of telling whether it is anything like the Sogdian silks which have been called *zandaniji*.

1. For additional material on this subject, see Wardwell 1988–89, pp. 97–106.
2. Another textile in which Chinese and eastern Iranian elements have been transformed into a design that is essentially Central Asian is a large silk panel excavated in Inner Mongolia (Huang Nengfu, Arts and Crafts, 1985, pl. 11).
3. For Persian and Western accounts of the *zhisun* robe, see Allsen (forthcoming). For accounts from Chinese sources, see Han Rulin 1981.
4. Petech 1983, pp. 181–82.
5. Ibid., pp. 182–83.
6. For an earlier example of a Central Asian textile with a supplementary-weft structure and widely spaced single warps, see catalogue number 12. There, however, the gold wefts float only on the face.
7. For details of the selvage structure, see catalogue number 38, note 1. Regarding widely spaced foundation warps in Central Asian textiles, see Wardwell 1988–89, pp. 97–98.
8. Florence 1983, pp. 170–71.
9. Ibid., pp. 164, 172–76.
10. Selvages on the textile of which the Metropolitan fragments were a part are still preserved on the cope in Perugia. See catalogue number 37, Technical Analysis, note 1, for a description of the structure.
11. Spink & Son 1989, no. 3, p. 13.
12. Allsen (forthcoming).
13. Florence 1983, pp. 164ff.
14. Ibid., pp. 130–44.
15. *Regestum Clementis* 1892, p. 430; Müntz and Frothingham 1883, pp. 36, 37 (references quoted in Wardwell 1988–89, p. 143).
16. For excavation reports of sites producing textiles dating from the Mongol period, see Beijing City Cultural Bureau 1958, CPAM Zouxian 1978, and Gansu Provincial Museum 1982. Textile finds from Inner Mongolia, Gansu, Shandong, and Beijing have been selectively published in Huang Nengfu, Arts and Crafts, 1985. For brief discussions of the finds from the old city of Jining, Inner Mongolia, see Pan Xingrong 1979 and Li Yiyou 1979. For a brief discussion of embroideries from Zouxian, Shandong, see Wang Xuan 1978.
17. *Yongle dadian*, vol. 92, chap. 19781, leaf 17.
18. See Allsen 1983.
19. For the office at Hongzhou, see, in this volume, "Brocades of the Jin and Mongol Periods," note 21. For the original founding of the textile workshop in Xunmalin, see Pelliot 1927.
20. Pelliot 1927.
21. *Yongle dadian*, vol. 92, chap. 19781, leaf 17. Again, the *Yuanshi* is quoted as the source for this long passage on the *nashishi* offices at Hongzhou and Xunmalin, but the detailed information must have been copied from the *Jingshi dadian* (see chap. 2, note 19).
22. Compare this design with the silk panel excavated in Inner Mongolia (see note 2).
23. See the introduction to "Brocades of the Jin and Mongol Periods."
24. The silk is a lampas weave with purple silk, z, foundation warps that are paired. There are 4 foundation warps (two pairs) to each coral silk supplementary warp, and a warp step of 4 foundation warps (two pairs). The thick foundation wefts are purple silk, without apparent twist. The supplementary wefts are gold—flat strips of gilded paper. The pass is 1 foundation and 1 supplementary weft. The binding of both the foundation weave and the supplementary weave is tabby.
25. Many Mongol designs were described in the inventories of European church treasuries; see Wardwell 1988–89, pp. 134–44.
26. See also Wardwell 1976–77, figs. 11–13.
27. See, for example, Wardwell 1976–77, fig. 33; Falke 1913, fig. 407.
28. See, for example, Wardwell 1976–77, figs. 26, 35, 44, 51; Falke 1913, figs. 401–6; and Wardwell 1988–89, fig. 67.
29. Identified by Sheila S. Blair (correspondence to Anne E. Wardwell, May 25, 1989).
30. For a discussion of the looping tail, see Wardwell 1992, p. 363. Although the double-headed displayed eagle is too ancient and widely distributed an image to suggest a particular provenance for the textile, it is interesting to note that the detail of the bird grasping its outer curling tail feathers occurs in the art of the eastern Iranian world as early as the Kushan period (Hackin 1954, fig. 198).
31. See *Ta'rikh nama-i-Harat* 1944, pp. 106–9; for English translations of pertinent passages, see Allsen (forthcoming), pp. 39–40.
32. Allsen (forthcoming).
33. Blair 1985; Blair 1992, pp. 12–13; Blair 1994, p. 5.
34. Rashid 1968, pp. 149, 159.
35. Flat gold thread gilded on both sides occurs, for example, on Jin imperial textiles found near Acheng; in the Southern Song *kesi* with a dragon among flowers (cat. no. 22); and in a Southern Song silk in Japan (Ogasawara 1989, p. 33, and fig. 2).
36. Petech 1983, pp. 182–83.
37. *Warp:* Foundation, red silk, z, irregularly paired and single; 4 foundation warps (6–8 ends, depending if single and/or paired) to each pink silk, z, supplementary warp; the warp step is 2 (2–4 ends, depending if single and/or paired); 44 foundation warps (about 63 ends) and 12 supplementary warps per centimeter. *Weft:* Foundation: pink silk (faded

from red), without apparent twist. Supplementary: 1) wrapped gold thread (gilded strips of animal substrate wrapped z around a white silk core, z). 2) flat gold thread (flat strips of animal substrate, gilded on both sides); the pass is 1 foundation weft, 1 flat gold supplementary weft, and one pair of wrapped gold supplementary wefts, except in the bands flanking the inscription, where there is 1 foundation weft and one pair of wrapped gold supplementary wefts. Weft step: 1 pass; weft count: 19 passes per centimeter. *Weave:* Lampas. Foundation: tabby. Supplementary: tabby (wrapped gold wefts are bound in pairs, flat gold wefts are bound singly). No selvage is preserved.

38. Translated by Sheila S. Blair. The inscription refers to Abu Bakr ibn Saud, but does not give the usual form of his titles. This was probably because of their length, which would have exceeded the weft repeat of the textile.

39. The deterioration of both the wrapped and the flat gold wefts, together with the density of the design, makes the pattern extremely difficult to read.

40. A similar scenario may apply to the Ilkhanid tiraz of Abu Said, from which the burial garment of Rudolf IV of Hapsburg was made (Wardwell 1988–89, p. 108).

41. Identified by Sheila S. Blair (correspondence to Anne E. Wardwell, January 22, 1997).

42. Wilckens 1987, fig. 24. These textiles, originally thought to date to before 1220 (Wardwell 1989), are now believed to date to after the Mongol conquest.

43. Stockholm 1986, no. 12, p. 56.

44. Rempel 1978, fig. 95; Brentjes 1979, fig. 216.

45. Waley 1931, p. 93.

46. The weave is lampas. The foundation warps are dark brown silk, z, and paired. The supplementary warps are tan silk, z. There are two pairs of foundation warps to each supplementary warp, and the warp step consists of two pairs of foundation warps. The foundation wefts are dark brown silk, without apparent twist, and the supplementary wefts are cream and blue silk, without twist, and wrapped gold (gilded animal substrate wrapped z around a brown silk, z, core). The pass is 1 foundation weft, 2 silk supplementary wefts, and one pair of gold supplementary wefts. The foundation weave is tabby, and the supplementary weave a 1/3 s twill with the gold wefts bound in pairs. The selvage is composed of a fringe of all wefts.

47. Wang Binghua 1973.

48. The band with a king was not examined by the authors. According to the archaeological report (Wang Binghua 1973, p. 34), it is a lampas weave with paired foundation warps, and 4 foundation warps (two pairs) to each supplementary warp. The foundation wefts are cotton, and the wrapped-gold supplementary wefts have a silk core (the substrate has disintegrated). The weft pass is 1 foundation weft and one pair of supplementary wefts. The binding of the foundation weave is tabby, and that of the supplementary weave is 1/3 s twill with the gold wefts bound in pairs. The band with griffins (examined by the authors) is also a lampas weave with tan silk, z, paired foundation warps. There are 8 foundation warps (four pairs) to each supplementary warp. The foundation wefts are tan silk, without apparent twist, and quite thick. There are 2 supplementary wefts: 1) gold thread composed of flat strips of gilded animal substrate and 2) silk (the color can no longer be identified). The weft pass is 1 foundation weft and 2 supplementary wefts (one

gold and one silk). As is characteristic of eastern Iranian textiles woven with flat gold thread, the gold wefts are bound singly. Both the foundation weave and the supplementary weave have a tabby binding. Another band, with a floral pattern (examined by the authors), has the same structure as the band with griffins.

49. Another band from the coat in Urumqi (which the authors did not see) was woven with a floral design that, according to the drawing in the archaeological report (Wang Binghua 1973, p. 29), includes a lobed arch (as in fig. 67) and lotuses. The band is a lampas weave with paired silk foundation warps and 2 supplementary wefts: flat gold thread made with an animal substrate and cotton (undoubtedly the core of metal thread, possibly silver, considering the fact that apparently no metallic surface survives). Given the combination of Chinese and eastern Iranian elements, this textile may well have been woven in Central Asia.

50. See, for example, Ettinghausen 1957, figs. L and 21; Darkevich 1976, pl. 34, fig. 6; and Baer 1983, pp. 172–74, 292.

51. This may be due to preservation in acidic conditions (Crowfoot et al. 1992, p. 2).

52. According to H. W. Glidden, the Arabic letter *ha'* is repeated in groups of three repetitions (correspondence to Anne E. Wardwell, April 11, 1983).

53. The substrate of the gold thread in the Berlin textile has been published as paper, based on the supposed examination of a sample at the Rathgen-Forschungslabor in Berlin (Folsach and Bernsted 1993, p. 54 n. 90). However, when a copy of the examination results was requested from the Rathgen-Forschungslabor, there was no report on the gold thread of that textile on file (Christian Goedicke, correspondence to Anne E. Wardwell, April 15, 1994). The piece in Berlin is from the same textile as a smaller fragment in the Deutsches Textilmuseum, Krefeld (acc. no. 06109), of which a sample of gold thread has been examined using a scanning electron microscope and an energy-dispersive X-ray spectrometer. The substrate was identified as leather (Indictor et al. 1988, p. 15).

54. Other textiles from Iran dating from the late thirteenth and fourteenth centuries that combine Chinese with West Asian elements may be found in Wardwell 1988–89, figs. 34–38, 42, 44, 48–51, 53–55, 63, 66, 70.

55. Ceramic tiles from Takht-i Sulayman, the summer palace of the Ilkhanid ruler Abakha in western Iran, dating from 1271–75, are among the earliest datable ceramics decorated with Chinese motifs (O. Watson 1985, p. 136; see also Crowe 1991).

56. Han Rulin 1981.

57. See Yu Ji, "Caonan wang xunde bei," in *Daoyuan xuegu lu,* chap. 24.

58. *Yuanshi,* vol. 7, chap. 78, p. 1938.

59. Ibid., vol. 3, chap. 37, p. 812.

60. *Ding Ling* 1990, vol. 1, p. 346, and vol. 2, pls. 25, 75.

61. Huang Nengfu and Chen Juanjuan 1995, p. 305.

62. Kong Qi, *Zhizheng zhiji,* chap. 1.

63. *Songshi,* vol. 39, chap. 472, pp. 13737–40; *Jinshi,* vol. 6, chap. 82, pp. 1833–34.

64. *Sanchao beimeng huibian,* chap. 17, p. 123. The novelty of the term at this time may be the cause of the clerical errors in various texts. In the edition we cite, the word order for *zhusi* is reversed, while in the 1878 Yuan Zu'an edition the character *si* is missing.

65. See Xiao Xun, *Yuan gugong yilu.*

66. *Yuanshi,* vol. 7, chap. 85, p. 2149.

35. Cloth of Gold with Winged Lions and Griffins

Lampas
Warp 124 cm (48⅞ in.); weft 48.8 cm (19¼ in.)
Central Asia, mid-13th century
Cleveland Museum of Art. Purchase from the J. H. Wade Fund
(1989.50)

Woven in brilliant gold against a dark brown, nearly black ground are aligned, tangent roundels, each enclosing a pair of winged lions standing back to back with heads turned. Their wings, ornamented at the shoulder with cloud decoration, join to form a palmette, and their long tails pass around and under the inner hind legs before terminating in a dragon's head. The ground of each roundel is completely filled with palmettes and scrolling vines, which terminate in curious cloudlike formations. Pairs of griffins between the roundels are also addorsed and regardant. Their wings, too, join to form a palmette, while the tail of each passes between its hind legs, loops around a rosette, and terminates in a feline head. The ground is densely filled with curling leaves and palmettes.

Other, smaller sections of this textile have recently come on the market. One is now in the collection of the Association pour l'Étude et la Documentation des Textiles d'Asie (AEDTA), Paris.[1]

1. Paris, AEDTA, no. 3729.

TECHNICAL ANALYSIS

Warp: Foundation: charcoal gray silk, z, mostly single but sometimes double and occasionally triple. Supplementary: coral silk, z. Proportion: 8 foundation warps to 1 supplementary warp. Step: 2 foundation warps. Count: 66 foundation and 9 supplementary warps per centimeter. *Weft:* Foundation: charcoal gray silk, without apparent twist. Supplementary: gold thread composed of strips of paper (very thin and translucent), gilded on one side[1] and wrapped z around a yellow silk core, z. Pass: 1 foundation weft and 1 pair of supplementary wefts. Step: 1 pass. Count: 19–21 passes per centimeter. *Weave:* Lampas. Foundation: tabby. Supplementary: tabby, gold wefts bound in pairs (fig. 52). Selvage: the inner selvage edge is delineated by a narrow stripe of foundation weave using two foundation warps; this is followed by a fringe, approximately 6 millimeters long, of loops of all wefts. The selvage intersects the design along its vertical axis.

1. Identified by Norman Indictor and Denyse Montegut (correspondence to Anne E. Wardwell, May 10, 1991).

PUBLICATIONS: CMA 1991, no. 47; *CMA Handbook* 1991, p. 45; "Golden Lampas" 1991, p. 125; "Recent Acquisitions" 1991, p. 419; CMA 1992, p. 37; Wardwell 1992, fig. 1, p. 356, fig. 2, p. 357, fig. 3, p. 358; Wardwell 1992–93, fig. 6, p. 249.

36. Cloth of Gold with Displayed Falcons

Lampas
Warp 57.5 cm (22⅝ in.); weft 18.4 cm (7¼ in.)
Central Asia, mid-13th century
The Cleveland Museum of Art. Edward L. Whittemore Fund
(1996.297)

Figure 70. Reconstructive drawing, cat. no. 36

Displayed, double-headed falcons are here arranged in staggered horizontal rows against a dense background of vine scrolls that terminate in clouds and palmettes (fig. 70). The design is based on Islamic and Chinese elements transformed into a genre that is neither Chinese nor Islamic but Central Asian. The falcons, identified by the bells strapped to their legs, derive from Islamic models. Like the eagles in the textile with felines and eagles (cat. no. 43), they have "ears," wattles, and ornamental feathers that extend from the eye to the back of the head. They also have neck ornaments and a floral device in the center of the stomach. What were originally outer curling tail feathers terminating in dragons' heads and grasped by the falcons' talons have been reinterpreted as the wrinkled necks and heads of dragons.

TECHNICAL ANALYSIS

Warp: Foundation: red silk, z, single. Supplementary: red silk, usually without apparent twist (occasionally a slight s or z twist can be detected). Proportion: 4 foundation warps, 1 supplementary warp. Step: 2 foundation warps. Count: 78 foundation and 20 supplementary warps per centimeter. *Weft:* Foundation: red silk, without apparent twist; about twice the density of the foundation warps. Supplementary: gold thread composed of strips of gilded paper (thin and somewhat translucent) wrapped z around a yellow silk core, z. Pass: 1 foundation weft and 1 pair of supplementary wefts. Step: 1 pass. Count: 19 foundation wefts and 19 pairs of supplementary wefts per centimeter. *Weave:* Lampas. Foundation: tabby binding, single weave; supplementary warps usually lie next to foundation warps. Supplementary: 1/2 s twill binding (gold wefts bound in pairs). Selvage: (on left side) 3 guard stripes, each formed by 4 foundation warps, bound in tabby; the remainder of the selvage has been cut off. The selvage intersects the design slightly off-center to the warp axis.

Unpublished.

37. Textiles with Floral Design

Lampas
Top: Warp 12.1 cm (4¾ in.); weft 18.2 cm (7⅛ in.)
Bottom: Warp 5 cm (2 in.); weft approx. 19.3 cm (7⅝ in.)
Central Asia, Mongol period, ca. late 13th–mid-14th century
The Metropolitan Museum of Art, New York. Rogers Fund, 1919
(top: 19.191.3); Fletcher Fund, 1946 (bottom: 46.156.22)

The fragment shown at the top was originally part of a cope now in the Church of San Domenico in Perugia that has long been associated with Pope Benedict XI (r. 1303–4).[1] The fragment shown at the bottom, which has the same design and structure, is in all likelihood also from the same cope. The design, woven with gold thread against a white ground, consists of a profusion of tiny leaves and flowers (fig. 71).

1. Florence 1983, pp. 164, 172–76.

TECHNICAL ANALYSIS

Warp: Foundation: white silk, z, single. Supplementary: tan (faded from coral) silk, z. Proportion: 4 foundation warps to 1 supplementary warp. Step: 2 foundation warps. Count: 72 foundation and 18 supplementary warps per centimeter. *Weft:* Foundation: white silk, without apparent twist (approximately 3 to 4 times the density of the foundation warps). Supplementary: gold thread composed of flat strips of animal substrate, gilded on one side. Pass: 1 foundation and 1 supplementary weft. Step: 1 pass. Count: 18 passes per centimeter *Weave:* Lampas variation. Foundation: 3/1 z twill. Supplementary: 1/2 s twill. No selvages are preserved.[1]

1. A selvage, approximately 6 millimeters wide, is preserved on the cope in Perugia. The inner edge is delineated by a guard stripe of gold wefts followed by a tabby binding of foundation wefts with white silk, z, foundation warps that are paired. At the outer edge are two bundles of warps, each composed of three warps, around which the foundation wefts turn. On the reverse side, the gold supplementary wefts are unbound after the guard stripe and cut (Florence 1983, p. 174).

PUBLICATIONS: Fragment 19.191.3: New York 1931, p. 14; Klein 1934, p. 127, pl. 22; London 1935, no. 1341; Simmons 1948, p. 23, fig. 29; Simmons 1950, p. 93, illus.; Cleveland 1968, no. 301; fragment 46.156.22: Hoeniger 1991, p. 158, fig. 8.

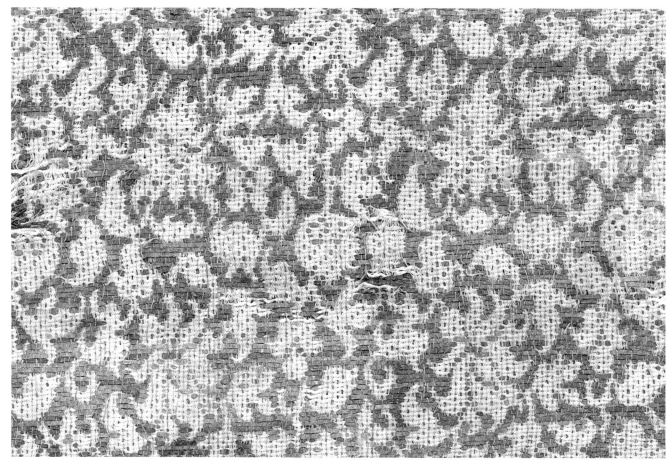

Figure 71. Enlarged detail of reverse, cat. no. 37, top

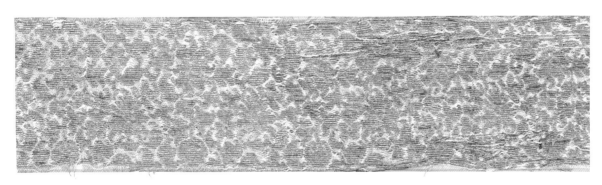

37

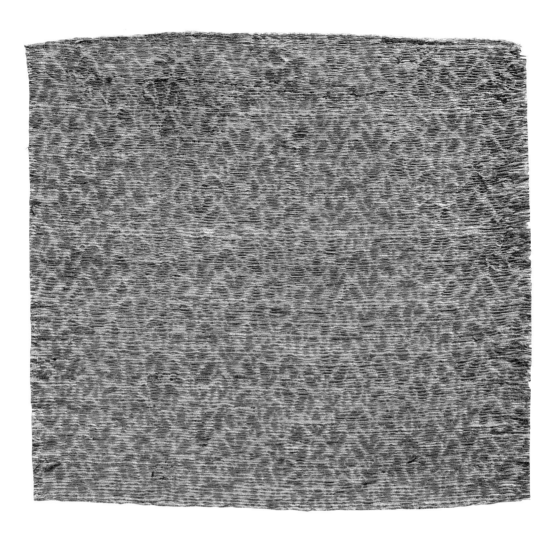

38. Textile with Tiny Leaves

Tabby with supplementary weft
Warp 14.5 cm (5¾ in.); weft 15.5 cm (6⅛ in.)
Central Asia, Mongol period, late 13th–mid-14th century
The Cleveland Museum of Art. The Dudley P. Allen Fund
(1985.33)

This textile is woven with a dense profusion of tiny leaves in gold against a white ground. Another, larger section of the textile, in the Kunstgewerbemuseum, Berlin, preserves a selvage.[1]

1. Kunstgewerbemuseum, acc. no. 79.47. The foundation warps at the inner edge are white silk, z (1 paired, 1 single, and 1 paired), which serve to bind the foundation wefts in tabby. Next is a guard stripe of gold wefts, followed by a triple foundation warp, a bundle of six white silk warps, and finally a fringe of loops, about 1 centimeter wide, of foundation wefts. On the reverse, the gold wefts are cut following the guard stripe.

TECHNICAL ANALYSIS

Warp: Foundation: white silk, z, single. Step: 2 foundation warps. Count: approximately 30 warps per centimeter. *Weft:* Foundation: white silk, without apparent twist, approximately six times the density of the warps. Supplementary: gold thread composed of flat strips of gilded animal substrate. Pass: 1 foundation and 1 supplementary weft. Step: 1 pass. Count: 12 passes per centimeter. *Weave:* Tabby with supplementary weft. Foundation: tabby, single weave; the warps are widely spaced. Supplementary: the gold wefts float on the face or on the reverse. Foundation and supplementary wefts lie side by side.

PUBLICATIONS: Wardwell 1987, p. 9; Wardwell 1988–89, fig. 3, p. 147; Indictor et al. 1989, p. 172.

39. Phoenixes, Monsters, and Flowers

Lampas
Warp 23.7 cm (9⅜ in.); weft 16.5 cm (6½ in.)
Central Asia, Mongol period, 13th–early 14th century
The Metropolitan Museum of Art, New York. Gift of
Mrs. Howard J. Sachs, 1973 (1973.269)

Woven in gold against a white ground are portions of two horizontal rows of mythical creatures with lotus, peonies, and leaves in the interstices. In the lower row are phoenixes oriented to the left, each with wings outstretched and head bent toward the left foot. The upper row preserves parts of two mythological creatures oriented to the right with humped backs, dragonlike spines, wings, long curling tails, and long necks. The short front legs terminate in clawed feet, while the vestigial hind legs are purely fanciful. The heads, unfortunately, are missing.

Where this silk was woven is far from clear.[1] There are no known antecedents for the animals depicted. The forms of the phoenixes and exotic animals are far removed from the Chinese style, making it highly unlikely that the textile was woven in China or in eastern Central Asia. On the other hand, the vitality of the animals and birds, and the lively interaction between them are qualities indigenous to Central Asian art. For this reason, and because of the composition of the gold thread, we have broadly assigned the silk to Central Asia.

This fragment is said to have been found in Iran. Textiles similar to this example appear to have been extensively traded, especially to the West.

1. The textile was first acquired by Arthur Upham Pope in Isfahan (Metropolitan Museum of Art archives).

TECHNICAL ANALYSIS

Warp: Foundation: white silk, z, single. Supplementary: tan silk, z. Proportion: 4 foundation warps to 1 supplementary warp. Step: 4 foundation warps. Count: 72 foundation and 18 supplementary warps. *Weft:* Foundation: white silk, without apparent twist. Supplementary: gold thread composed of flat strips of gilded animal substrate. Pass: 1 foundation and 1 supplementary weft. Step: 1 pass. Count: 18 passes per centimeter. *Weave:* Lampas. Foundation: 3/1 broken twill. Supplementary: 1/2 s twill. No selvage is preserved.

PUBLICATIONS: MMA *Notable Acquisitions* 1965–1975, p. 113, illus.; Cleveland 1968, no. 303; Wardwell 1988–89, p. 100, fig. 8, p. 149.

40. Phoenixes amid Lotuses and Tree Peonies

Lampas
Warp 66.2 cm (26⅛ in.); weft 72.2 cm (28⅜ in.)
Central Asia or Daidu, 13th century
The Metropolitan Museum of Art, New York. Purchase, Anonymous Gift, in honor of James C. Y. Watt, 1989 (1989.19 1)

Figure 72. Floral ornament (*yutian*). Jin dynasty (1115–1234), 13th century. Jade, 3 × 4 cm (1⅛ × 1½ in.). Private collection

Woven in gold against a red ground, phoenixes fly among vertically undulating vines with lotus flowers and tree peonies. Arranged in staggered horizontal rows, they shift their orientation from one row to the next. The left edge of the textile is a complete selvage.

The design of this silk is Chinese, though its structure is strikingly similar to that of the silk with winged lions and griffins (cat. no. 35), woven in Central Asia. As was noted earlier (pp. 131–32), it is not clear if the textile was woven in Central Asia or in Daidu, where craftsmen from Besh Baliq were resettled in 1275.

The form of the peony blossoms closely resembles that of a number of small jade carvings of peonies with perforations to facilitate attachment to garments (fig. 72). The *Jinshi* (History of the Jin Dynasty) describes a form of headgear "for older ladies" called *yuxiaoyao*, which was composed of a kerchief of black gauze on which were sewn several *yutian* (jade floral ornaments).[1] The jade in the figure is very likely a *yutian* used by Jurchen women and dating from about the same period as the silk.

1. *Jinshi*, vol. 3, chap. 43, p. 985.

TECHNICAL ANALYSIS

Warp: Foundation: red silk, z, single. Supplementary: tan silk, z. Proportion: 8 foundation warps to 1 supplementary warp. Step: 2 foundation warps. Count: approximately 72 foundation and 9 supplementary warps per centimeter. *Weft:* Foundation: cream silk, without apparent twist. Supplementary: gold thread composed of strips of silvered and gilded paper (thin and somewhat translucent) wrapped z around a yellow silk core, z.[1] Pass: 1 foundation weft and 1 pair of supplementary wefts. Step: 1 pass. Count: 19 passes per centimeter. *Weave:* Lampas. Foundation: tabby, single weave; the supplementary warps are sometimes next to the foundation warps and sometimes underneath. Supplementary: tabby, with the gold wefts bound in pairs. A selvage is preserved on the left side. Against the gold supplementary weave are three thin stripes of foundation weave, each composed of 4 foundation warps. At the outermost edge is a fringe of loops, approximately 8 millimeters wide, of foundation and supplementary wefts.

1. Identified by Norman Indictor and Denyse Montegut (correspondence to Anne E. Wardwell, May 10, 1991).

PUBLICATION: Wardwell 1992, p. 372, fig. 17.

150

Detail, cat. no. 40

41. Makaras, Phoenixes, and Flowers

Lampas
Warp 51.3 cm (20¼ in.); weft 75.6 cm (29¾ in.)
Central Asia or Daidu, 13th century
The Cleveland Museum of Art. Purchase from the J. H. Wade Fund (1991.5,a,b)

The textile is composed of three pieces mounted together to form three vertical repeats. The degree and pattern of fading indicate that the textile was cut a long time ago. The top and bottom pieces are complete loom widths; in the middle segment, only the left selvage is preserved. A starting edge consisting of a thin gold guard stripe runs along the lower edge of the bottom piece.

The design, woven in gold against a pink ground (faded from red), depicts *makaras* and phoenixes arranged alternately in staggered horizontal rows. In the interstices are lotuses, tree peonies, and leaves. Each *makara* has a horned dragon's head with upturned snout and extended tongue, the wings of a bird, and the body of a fish. The phoenixes, soaring upward with wings outstretched, have crests, neck plumes, and five long, serrated tail feathers.

Two other sections of this textile are in the David Collection, Copenhagen.[1]

1. Folsach and Bernsted 1993, no. 18.

TECHNICAL ANALYSIS

Warp: Foundation: red silk, z, single. (Occasionally a foundation warp is paired, but the ends are threaded individually through the mails of the loom.) Supplementary: coral silk (mostly faded to tan), z (slight twist). Proportion: 8 foundation warps to 1 supplementary warp. Step: 2 foundation warps. Count: 64–66 foundation and 9 supplementary warps per centimeter. *Weft:* Foundation: pale yellow silk, without apparent twist. Supplementary: gold thread composed of silvered and gilded strips of thin, translucent paper wrapped z around a cream silk core, z, and plied z.[1] The metallic surface is very worn. Pass: 1 foundation and 1 supplementary weft. Step: 1 pass. Count: 20 passes per centimeter. *Weave:* Lampas. Foundation: tabby binding, single weave, warp-faced; supplementary warps lie next to foundation warps. Supplementary: tabby binding of single gold wefts. The selvages are composed of a striped border and a fringe of foundation and supplementary weft loops. Each border is woven with the supplementary weave articulated by two thin stripes of foundation weave.

1. Identified by Norman Indictor and Denyse Montegut (correspondence to Anne E. Wardwell, May 10, 1991).

PUBLICATIONS: Wardwell 1992, fig. 18, p. 373; Wardwell 1992–93, fig. 7, p. 250; Cleveland 1994, no. 38, pp. 329–32

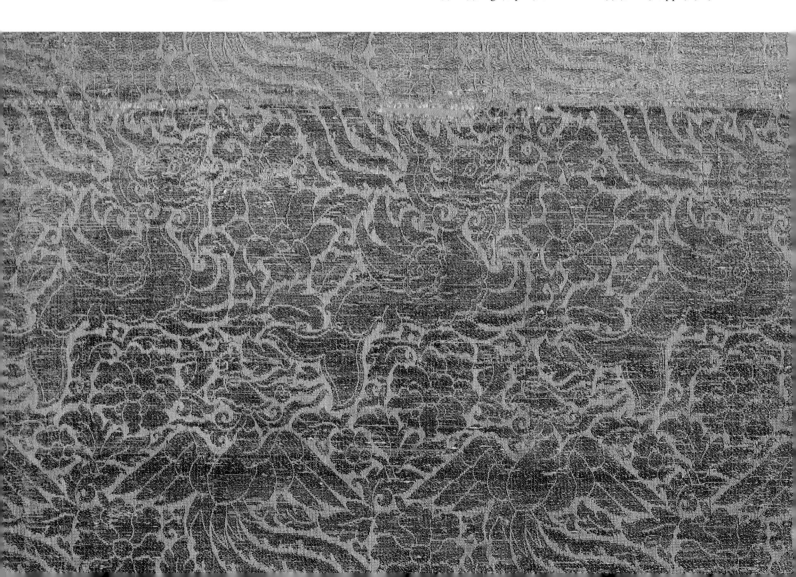

42. Phoenixes and Dragons

Lampas
Warp 20.3 cm (8 in.); weft 20.3 cm (8 in.)
Yuan dynasty (1279–1368)
The Cleveland Museum of Art. Edward L. Whittemore Fund
(1995.73)

This textile preserves one, plus part of a second, lobed roundel enclosing a coiled dragon chasing a flaming pearl amid scattered clouds; partially preserved are two additional lobed roundels, each enclosing a flying phoenix against a ground of clouds and flowers. These are arranged in staggered horizontal rows against a ground of tiny hexagons. The ground is blue and the pattern gold. The left side is a complete selvage; the other three sides are cut.

The key textile forming a cloud collar is in the Palace Museum, Beijing; it is woven with the same design in gold against a red ground (fig. 57).[1] The fortuitous survival of these two textiles is evidence of the repeated use of the same patterns in weaving workshops during the Yuan dynasty, a practice documented also in the earlier Jin brocades.

1. The structure is lampas. The foundation warps are red silk, z, single; the supplementary warps are also red silk, z; there are 4 foundation warps to each supplementary warp, and a step of 4 foundation warps. The foundation wefts are red silk without apparent twist; the supplementary wefts are gold thread (flat strips of paper gilded on one side); the pass is 1 foundation weft and 1 supplementary weft. Both the foundation and the supplementary weaves have a tabby binding.

TECHNICAL ANALYSIS

Warp: Foundation: blue silk, z, single. Supplementary: blue silk, z. Proportion: 1 supplementary warp to 4 foundation warps. Step: 4 foundation warps. Count: approximately 80 foundation and 20 supplementary warps per centimeter. *Weft:* Foundation: blue silk, without apparent twist; thick. Supplementary: gold thread composed of flat strips of paper coated with pale orange bole and gilded on one side. Pass: 1 foundation and 1 supplementary weft. Step: 1 pass. Count: approximately 22 passes per centimeter. *Weave:* Lampas. Foundation: 2/1 s twill, single weave. Supplementary: 1/2 z twill. A selvage is preserved on the left side; on the face, the pattern ends about 1 centimeter from the outer edge; the inner half of the selvage border is woven in the foundation weave, which is then followed by 18 bundles of warps. The foundation wefts turn around the outermost bundle of warps. On the reverse, the supplementary wefts are cut about 5 millimeters from the outermost edge.

Unpublished.

43. Felines and Eagles

Lampas weave
Warp 170.5 cm (67⅛ in.); weft 109 cm (43 in.)
Eastern Iranian world, mid-13th century
The Cleveland Museum of Art. Purchase from the J. H. Wade
Fund (1990.2)

The panel, a complete loom width, preserves nearly three vertical repeats of two lobed medallions, each enclosing a pair of addorsed, regardant, rampant felines. Each animal wears a collar and leash, and has a long tail that loops around a rosette and terminates in a dragon's head. The ground of each medallion is filled with floral vines, and between each pair of felines is a palmette. In the interstices between the medallions are double-headed eagles grasping curled outer tail feathers that terminate in dragons' heads. The eagles have "ears," wattles, and ornamental feathers that extend from the eye to the back of the head; ornamental bands form collars around the necks, delineate the bodies, and serve as a decorative stripe across each wing. The ground is filled with foliate and floral motifs. Toward the top of the panel is a band of pseudoinscription composed of interlaced Kufic shafts; the borders of the band are ornamented with a repeated stylized flower. Above the inscription is a small portion of the main design. The top edge is delineated by a gold guard stripe. The ground is tan (faded from red) and the pattern woven with wrapped gold, except in the inscription band, in which both wrapped and flat gold threads are used, and in the eyes of the felines, which are brocaded with white silk wefts (preserved only in the bottom repeat). The red marks across the textile are areas once covered with pieces of cloth sewn to the panel with black thread.

Another section of this textile, cut from the bottom of the panel, is in the David Collection, Copenhagen.[1]

1. Folsach and Bernsted 1993, no. 14, illus. p. 48.

TECHNICAL ANALYSIS

Warp: Foundation: coral silk (mainly faded to tan), z, paired. Supplementary: coral silk, z. Proportion: 4 foundation warps (2 pairs) to 1 supplementary warp. Step: 4 foundation warps (2 pairs). Count: 88 foundation and 20 supplementary warps per centimeter. *Weft:* Foundation: coral silk, without apparent twist, twice the density of each foundation warp. Supplementary: 1) gold thread composed of silvered and gilded strips of animal substrate wrapped z around an undyed silk core, z;[1] 2) gold thread composed of strips of silvered and gilded animal substrate, woven flat; 3) white silk, z, 3-ply z with slight twists, brocaded. Pass: 1 foundation weft and 1 pair of wrapped gold supplementary wefts; or 1 foundation weft, 1 pair of wrapped gold wefts, and either 1 flat gold weft or 1 silk brocading weft. Step: 1 pass. Count: 18 passes per centimeter. *Weave:* Lampas. Foundation: tabby binding, single weave; supplementary warps lie underneath or next to foundation warps. Supplementary: 1/3 s twill binding; the wrapped gold wefts are bound in pairs, and the flat gold and white silk wefts are bound singly. The brocading wefts turn around the binding warps on the reverse. There are mistakes here and there, especially a supplementary warp binding of 3/1 instead of 1/3, a foundation weft passing over more than one pair of foundation warps, and missing (or broken?) supplementary warps that leave vertical lines in patterned areas. Both selvages are preserved, intersecting the design along its warp axis. At the inner selvage edge is a thin line of four pairs of foundation warps; after 3 millimeters of supplementary weave using wrapped gold wefts is a fringe approximately 7 millimeters wide of continuous wefts. A starting (or finishing) edge is preserved at the top of the panel. Beginning at the cut edge is a short section of foundation weave (8 foundation wefts), a guard stripe of 8 wrapped gold wefts bound in pairs in 1/3 s twill, and a small segment of the pattern repeat. The ground areas are woven in the foundation weave and the patterned areas in the supplementary weave, except for the inscription band and its borders, where the ground is woven also with the supplementary weave using flat gold wefts, while the foundation weave is reserved for outlining motifs.

1. Metal surface identified by Bruce Christman, chief conservator, The Cleveland Museum of Art, December 2, 1992.

PUBLICATIONS: *CMA Handbook* 1991, p. 47; "Golden Lampas" 1991, p. 125 (color illus.); Wardwell 1992, pp. 359–60; Wardwell 1992–93, p. 249; Reynolds, "Silk," 1995, fig. 7.

43

44. Textile with Griffins

Lampas
Warp 177 cm (69¾ in.); weft 98 cm (38⅝ in.)
Eastern Iranian world, mid-13th century
The Metropolitan Museum of Art, New York. The Cloisters Collection, 1984 (1984.344)

The panel preserves nine vertical repeats of linked roundels and part of an inscription band at the top. Each roundel encloses a pair of rampant griffins that are addorsed and regardant. The wings join to terminate in a palmette, and the thick tails curve behind the extended inner hind legs. In the interstices are four large palmettes that radiate from the cardinal points of a roundel; between the palmettes are knots, and in the center of each roundel, four small palmettes. Although the top of the panel is cut, part of a band of pseudoinscription is preserved.[1] Below the inscription is a border of ornamental hearts and a plain stripe.

The design of the panel is woven entirely with gold thread; in the roundels, the motifs are outlined with pink against a blue ground, and in the interstices, with blue against a pink ground. Although the bottom edge is cut, both selvages are preserved.

1. The inscription was identified by Sheila S. Blair (correspondence to Anne E. Wardwell, January 22, 1997).

TECHNICAL ANALYSIS

Warp: Foundation: blue silk, z, usually single but occasionally paired. Supplementary: tan silk, z. Proportion: 4 foundation warps to 1 supplementary warp. Step: 2 foundation warps. Count: 47–48 warps and 12 supplementary warps per centimeter. *Weft:* Foundation: blue silk, without apparent twist; the density varies from slightly thicker than the foundation warps to three times the thickness of the foundation warps. Supplementary: 1) coral silk; occasionally a z twist can be detected, but otherwise the weft appears to be without twist; 2) gold thread: strips of silvered and gilded parchment or membrane wrapped z around a cotton core, z.[1] The substrate is coated with a brown adhesive. Only traces of gold remain and some silver, most of which is now black. The substrate is wrapped so that the core is visible. Pass: 1 foundation weft and 2 supplementary wefts. Step: 1 pass. Count: 18 passes per centimeter. *Weave:* Lampas. The foundation weave has a tabby binding and is single weave; foundation warps are spaced, and the supplementary warps are visible beside them. There are numerous weaving flaws, consisting specifically of short warp and weft floats. The supplementary weave has a 1/2 twill, z binding; the supplementary wefts are bound singly. Both side selvages are preserved. The left selvage intersects the design along the warp axis, whereas the right selvage interrupts the design off-center to the warp axis, leaving the outermost roundels incomplete. At the inner edge of the left selvage, the outermost foundation warps are triple and supplementary warps are single. At the inner selvage edge of the right side, the penultimate foundation warp is paired while the outermost warp is single; supplementary wefts are all single, except for the outermost weft, which is paired. The selvages are composed of a fringe of approximately 7 millimeters in length of foundation and supplementary weft loops.

1. Analysis by Norman Indictor.

PUBLICATIONS: MMA *Notable Acquisitions* 1984–1985, p. 12, illus.; Parker 1985, p. 173, fig. 19; Ginsberg 1987, p. 92, illus.; Wardwell 1988–89, pp. 99, 106, fig. 33, p. 157; *Textiles* 1995–96, p. 36, illus.

Detail, cat. no. 44

44

45. Cloth of Gold with Rabbit Wheels

Lampas
Warp 65.5 cm (25⅞ in.); weft 23.2 cm (9⅛ in.)
Eastern Iranian world, second quarter to mid-13th century
The Cleveland Museum of Art. John L. Severance Fund (1993.140)

The design of this textile displays aligned, tangent ovals, each enclosing an animal wheel of four running rabbits with shared ears in the center. The direction in which the rabbits run, clockwise or counterclockwise, alternates from one horizontal row of ovals to the next. Filling the interstices between the ovals are geometric figures facing in four directions. Both the ground and the pattern are woven with gold thread; the delineation and details of the design are outlined in red silk. One selvage is preserved.

The motif of the animal wheel in Asia is one that dates to antiquity and had a broad geographic distribution.[1] A variety of animals and birds, as well as human figures, appear in such wheels; rabbit wheels with three or four animals having shared ears occur in eastern Central Asia as early as the Sui dynasty (A.D. 581–618).[2] The motif later became popular in the decorative repertory of Khurasan, particularly in metalwork dating from about 1150 to 1225.[3] From the same period in the western Himalayas, rabbit wheels occur in the design of the dhoti worn by Maitreya in the Sumtsek Temple and in the ceiling paintings of the Great Stupa at Alchi (Ladakh).[4]

In later Chinese art, the animal wheel evolved into a design of four boys sharing two heads and two pairs of legs (fig. 73). A number of Ming and Qing bronzes and carvings in various media (particularly wood and ivory) used as toggles are in this form and acquired a characteristically Chinese interpretation. The configuration, known as "two boys make four images," occurs as a rebus for one of the best-known lines from the commentary on the *Yijing* (Book of Changes): "The two *yi* [opposites, i.e, heaven and earth] beget the four *xiang* [elements, i.e., metal, wood, water, and fire]." The word *yi*, interpreted as opposites, is a homonym for the word *boy* in earlier pronunciation and in some contemporary dialects, and the word *xiang*, normally meaning image, is interpreted as element.[5]

The selvage is of particular importance because portions of the original cotton cords are still preserved. In virtually every other textile with this selvage structure, the cords are completely disintegrated, leaving a fringe of foundation and supplementary wefts.[6]

---

1. For the history of this motif, see Roes 1936–37, pp. 85–105.
2. See, for example, the ceiling paintings at Dunhuang: *Dunhuang bihua* 1985, vol. 1, p. 190, and Dunhuang wenwu yanjiusuo 1980–82, ser. 1, vol. 2, pl. 95.
3. Ettinghausen 1957, text fig. L, fig. 21; Darkevich 1976, pl. 34, fig. 6; Baer 1983, pp. 172–74, 292.

Figure 73. Toggle. Ming dynasty (1368–1644), 16th–17th century. Bronze, 6.4 × 6 cm (2½ × 2⅜ in.). Shanghai Museum

4. Goepper 1982, pl. 7; Goepper 1993, p. 116 (for the date of Sumtsek and the Great Stupa), fig. 9.
5. The full passage from which this quotation is taken reads: "The primal 'one' [*taiji*] begets the two opposites [*yi*], the two opposites beget the four elements [*xiang*], and the four elements beget the eight trigrams [*gua*]." This interpretation of the passage was made by the Tang scholars Kong Yingda et al. in *Zhou yi zhengyi*, in *Shisan jing zhushu*, p. 82.
6. This may be due to preservation in acidic conditions (Crowfoot et al. 1992, p. 2).

TECHNICAL ANALYSIS

Warp: Foundation: red silk, z (unevenly twisted); usually paired, occasionally single or multiple. Supplementary: pale yellow silk, z. Proportion: 8 (four pairs) foundation warps to 1 supplementary warp. Step: 4 (two pairs) foundation warps. Count: 96 (48 pairs) foundation and 12 supplementary warps per centimeter. *Weft:* Foundation: red silk, without apparent twist; approximately 2–3 times the density of the foundation warps. Supplementary: gold thread composed of gilded strips of animal substrate wrapped z around a pale yellow silk core, z, 2-ply z. The substrate is coated with a reddish brown substance. Pass: 1 foundation weft and 1 pair of supplementary wefts. Step: 1 pass. Count: 19 passes per centimeter. *Weave:* Lampas. Foundation: tabby binding, single weave. The supplementary warps appear next to, or very occasionally under, the pairs of foundation warps. The foundation weave is replete with flaws, and broken warps occur here and there. Supplementary: tabby binding; the gold wefts are bound in pairs. The one preserved selvage intersects the design along the warp axis. At the outermost edge, all wefts turn around two cotton cords (each consisting of two cotton threads, plied z; each thread is composed of 5 strands of cotton, z, and plied s). Only small portions of the cords remain; where they are missing, the foundation and supplementary wefts form a fringe of loops.

Unpublished.

Opposite: Detail, cat. no. 45, including cords in selvage

46. Textile with Palmettes

Tabby with supplementary weft
Warp 88.5 cm (34⅞ in.); weft 35 cm (13¾ in.)
Central Asia(?), Mongol period, 13th–14th century
The Cleveland Museum of Art. John L. Severance Fund (1993.253)

Floral palmettes enclosed by ogival frames with outer borders of flames are in this textile arranged in staggered horizontal rows in a design woven with gold thread against an off-white (originally red) ground.

From a technical point of view, the textile is unique; and geographically it cannot be placed. Both the pairing of the foundation warps and the binding of the gold supplementary wefts in pairs are characteristic of silk weaving in the eastern Iranian world, while parallels for binding the supplementary wefts on the face and floating them on the reverse can be found among brocades woven in the former Jin territories. Neither the weft pass nor the binding of the supplementary wefts by the right warp of every third pair of warps, however, has been seen in other extant examples.

TECHNICAL ANALYSIS

Warp: Foundation: coral (faded to off-white on face), z, paired. Step: 4 warps (2 pairs). Count: 84–86 warps per centimeter. *Weft:* Foundation: coral silk (faded to off-white on face), without apparent twist; of the same density as the warps. Supplementary: gold thread composed of strips of gilded animal substrate, wrapped z around a coral silk core, z; the adhesive is a translucent golden tan. Pass: alternately 1 foundation weft and 1 foundation weft plus 1 pair of supplementary wefts. Step: 1 pass. Count: 24 passes per centimeter. *Weave:* Tabby with supplementary weft. Foundation: tabby binding. Supplementary: 1/3 s twill binding of gold wefts in pairs by the right warp of every third pair of warps (this warp passes over 3 foundation wefts and 1 pair of supplementary wefts); on the reverse side, the gold supplementary wefts are not bound. No selvage is preserved.[1]

1. Another section of the textile (present whereabouts unknown) preserves one selvage composed of a fringe of all wefts that intersects the design off-center to the warp axis.

Unpublished.

Detail, cat. no. 46

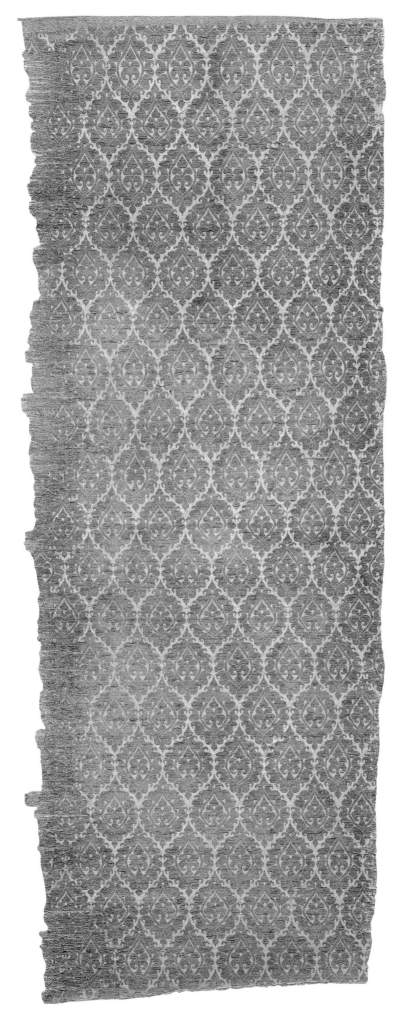

47. Textile with Phoenixes

Lampas
Warp 43.4 cm (17⅛ in.); weft 39.5 cm (15⅝ in.)
Eastern Iranian world, Transoxiana, late 13th–14th century
The Cleveland Museum of Art. Purchase from the J. H. Wade Fund (1985.4)

The design of this textile consists of parallel undulating floral vines between which are arranged rows of standing phoenixes facing left and looking back that alternate with rows of diving phoenixes. Both the standing and the diving phoenixes appear to be transformations of the type of phoenix seen on the embroidered canopy (cat. no. 60), a popular motif in Yuan China. A selvage is preserved along the right edge.

The textile belongs to a small group characterized by single, widely spaced silk foundation warps, thick cotton foundation wefts, gold thread composed of strips of silvered and gilded animal substrate wrapped around a cotton core, and a common selvage structure.[1] Because of the coarseness of both the foundation and the gold supplementary wefts, the dense patterns of these textiles are often difficult to read. The textiles in this group were preserved in European church treasuries.

1. Wardwell 1988–89, pp. 105–6.

TECHNICAL ANALYSIS

Warp: Foundation: yellow-green silk, z, single. Supplementary: tan silk, z (with a slight twist). Proportion: 3 foundation warps to 1 supplementary warp. Step: 3 foundation warps. Count: 54 foundation and 18 supplementary warps per centimeter. *Weft:* Foundation: blue-green cotton, z, thick. Supplementary: gold thread composed of strips of silvered and gilded membrane wrapped z around a white cotton core, z, 3(?)-ply z. Pass: 1 foundation and 1 supplementary weft. Step: 1 pass. Count: 16 passes per centimeter. *Weave:* Lampas. Foundation: 2/1 s twill, single weave. Supplementary: tabby. On the right side is a selvage approximately 8 millimeters wide; in the selvage border, the foundation warps are paired; the supplementary weave on the face is articulated by three thin stripes formed by the foundation weave; at the outermost edge, the foundation and supplementary wefts turn around two bundles of silk warps.

PUBLICATIONS: Neils 1985, no. 70, p. 359; Wardwell 1987, pp. 10–11, illus. p. 10; Indictor et al. 1988, pp. 5, 10, 13, 15, 22; Wardwell 1988–89, fig. 30, p. 156, and fig. 74, p. 173; Wardwell 1989, fig. 10, p. 182; *CMA Handbook* 1991, p. 47.

47

5. Embroideries

The embroideries in the Metropolitan and Cleveland collections span the entire chronological and geographical range of *When Silk Was Gold*. Yet they represent only a little over one quarter of the textiles in the exhibition. While some of them are singular examples of their type (discussions of these pieces are confined to individual entries), others can be broadly grouped, and a few comments on these groups are offered here by way of an introduction to this chapter.

The first three textiles (cat. nos. 48–50) are related to the eclectic or international style that developed during those periods in which the Chinese political and commercial presence in Central Asia was particularly strong, the Han (206 B.C.–A.D. 220) and the Tang (618–907) dynasties. The embroidery with birds and the embroidery with confronted birds (cat. nos. 48 and 49) are both in the High Tang style, and there are many examples of such textiles extant, mostly preserved in Japan and also excavated from eastern Xinjiang. The embroidered square (cat. no. 50) is of particular interest because although it dates from long after the Tang dynasty, it preserves stylistic conventions going back both to the Han and to the Tang, testifying to a cultural tradition that continued in eastern Central Asia before the political and military upheavals in the region associated with the coming of the Mongols.

Liao embroideries, represented by the robe (cat. no. 51) and by the pair of headpieces (cat. no. 52), have been found in considerable numbers in recent archaeological work. Much of this material, however, remains to be conserved and studied by Chinese scholars.

A type of embroidery that has drawn a great deal of attention in recent years is needleloop embroidery (cat. nos. 54–57). Ever since the acquisition in 1987 by the Cooper-Hewitt Museum of a temple hanging incorporating a needleloop embroidery of a Buddhist image, and the subsequent publication of a technical study by

Milton Sonday and Lucy Maitland,[1] there have been many questions raised about the origin and history of this embroidery technique, as well as some attempts to answer them.[2] The Cooper-Hewitt piece is not the first known example of needleloop embroidery, but it was the first to have been acquired by a museum since the appearance on the market of a number of such works— at one time thought to be extremely rare. The Nelson-Atkins Museum of Art in Kansas City has a small example of this type of embroidery in its collection, and there is a Daoist robe in the Metropolitan Museum that incorporates embroideries of various dates and techniques, including a section of a border that is a needleloop embroidery with a motif of animals and clouds. However, the best-known examples of early needleloop embroideries, which are those associated with historical personages of known dates, are in Japanese temples. The most important are in the Nanzen-ji, Kyoto, and in the Engaku-ji, Kamakura.[3] A *kesa* (Buddhist robe) with needleloop embroidery in the Nanzen-ji is associated with Daimin Kokushi (Mukan Fumon; 1212–1291), the founder of the temple.[4] The two examples of needlelooping in the Engaku-ji, a *kesa* and an altar cover, are said to have been brought to Japan by the founder of the temple, Bukkō Kokushi (Chinese name: Wuxue Zuyuan; Japanese name: Mugaku Sōgan; 1226–1286), in 1279, the year that marked the end of the Song dynasty.[5] The Engaku-ji examples are of special significance because they predate the end of the Song dynasty and because Bukkō Kokushi is known to have stayed in various monasteries in Hangzhou and Wenzhou (both in Zhejiang Province). The dating of the needleloop embroidery is supported by several pieces of lacquer that Bukkō Kokushi brought with him, in addition to textiles; Japanese scholars have confirmed the lacquerware as Southern Song (1127–1279) in date and most likely the product of Hangzhou or another site in Zhejiang.[6] Given that Hangzhou was a great center of the silk industry (among many others), it is perfectly possible that needleloop work was also a product of Hangzhou.

There are historical and art-historical considerations that would support this proposition as well. For one, the motifs on needleloop embroidery are either purely Chinese or Buddhist. If the technique had been introduced into Song China from the northern or western states, it is highly unlikely that it would have been without trace of a motif or stylistic marker from outside the Song empire. Furthermore, the technique's pre-Yuan beginning also makes it improbable that any Central or North Asian element played a role in its evolution.

In Tibet, the large number of needleloop embroideries preserved is not unexpected, given the large number of powerful Tibetan monks who operated in Hangzhou after its conquest by the Mongols and given that Hangzhou in the Yuan period became a service center for the printing of Buddhist sutras and for the weaving of religious icons;[7] indeed, the needleloop pieces with Buddhist images may well have been special commissions.[8]

The idea of using reflective surfaces behind openwork structures in textile or other materials seems to have been a Southern Song innovation. There are a number of sutra wrappers, originally from the Jingo-ji, a temple near Kyoto, dating from about 1150, which consist of thin bamboo splints bound together by polychrome silks that make up a decorative pattern; the structure can be described as a weaving of warp threads of silk and weft of bamboo splints. Underneath the bamboo splints is a sheet of mica, which reflects light through the narrow gaps between the bamboo splints. The borders are of woven silks typical of the Southern Song period.[9] The basic construction of these sutra covers goes back to at least the eighth century;[10] what is different in the Jingo-ji sutra covers is the use of reflective mica as backing rather than the paper seen in the earlier versions.

The total absence of examples of needleloop embroidery in Chinese collections or archaeological finds can be at least partially explained by the plundering and destruction of temples in Hangzhou and by the sanction of ransacking and desecration of tombs and palaces of Song emperors by the Buddhist monk-official Yang Lian-zhen-jia, who was for more than ten years supervisor of Buddhist teachings in Jiangnan at the beginning of the Yuan period.[11]

There are to date no finds of major burials of the Southern Song period apart from the tomb of Huang Sheng in Fujian, which produced mainly light clothing suitable for a semitropical climate.[12] On the other hand, a number of imperial tombs of the Liao and Jin periods in North China, while they have produced a considerable quantity of luxury textiles, have yielded no needle-loop embroidery. In any case, the present evidence would indicate that the history of needlelooping is inextricably connected with the history of textile production and

with Buddhist activities in Hangzhou, though study of these areas is only just beginning. We should like to point out, however, that the known examples of this technique vary greatly in quality and that the use in a few cases of gilt animal substrates may indicate the later spread of this technique farther north.

A number of embroideries of the Yuan (1279–1368) to the early Ming period with Buddhist motifs were made for religious use, and they testify to the extravagant largess bestowed on Buddhist monks and monasteries by emperors of the Yuan and Ming dynasties. The enormous expenditures associated with imperial patronage of Buddhism by Mongol rulers can be gauged from memoranda submitted to the throne by Chinese officials in the early fourteenth century, which claim that one-half to two-thirds of the wealth of the state was in the hands of the Buddhist establishment.[13] These may be overestimations. But whatever the actual figures, they must have been very large.

One can also assume that the lion's share of imperial donations went to Tibetan monasteries and monks, particularly those of the Sakya order. The Yongle emperor, Chengzu (r. 1403–24), of the early Ming dynasty, nearly outdid his Mongol predecessors in his personal devotion and in the employment of state resources to procure religious offerings. Repeatedly he sent envoys to Tibetan monasteries with offerings of lavish gifts. Furthermore, he invited every major lama in Tibet to the capital. He himself wrote biographies of Buddhist monks with supernatural powers. He composed a large volume of Buddhist chants based on the names of various buddhas, and had them performed by court musicians.[14] And he commissioned the printing of 108 volumes of the bKa'-gyur (Kanjur), the Tibetan Buddhist canon, each volume fitted with lacquered wood covers with *qiangjin* (etched gold) decoration.[15]

An astonishing number of religious artifacts preserved in Tibet and abroad to this day bear the reign mark of Yongle. Three embroideries in the exhibition (cat. nos. 62–64) are believed to be products of this period, and they represent the highest level of skill and artistry in the kind of embroidery work that was developed beginning in the Song dynasty; catalogue number 59 is an example from the Yuan dynasty. In the history of Chinese art, these works of the early fifteenth century also represent the last great moment of imperial patronage of the arts in China before its revival under the early Qing emperors centuries later. After the Xuande reign (1426–35) there was a deterioration in the quality, if not the quantity, of products in all media made in the official workshops; this trend was even more marked from the beginning of the sixteenth century. The reasons for this have yet to be fully explored.[16] The several embroideries from the early Ming period thus make a fitting conclusion to this exhibition, which documents, if only in an incomplete way, a glorious period in the history of Asian textiles.

1. Sonday and Maitland 1989.
2. Berger 1989. The textile in figure 2 in this article is not a needleloop embroidery (verbal communication from Zhao Feng).
3. Ogasawara 1989, p. 34. A third piece, now in the Zenkō-ji, Nagano, was taken to Japan from Korea in the late sixteenth century. See *Jūyō Bunkazai* 1976, vol. 25, p. 142.
4. Kyoto 1983, pl. 30.
5. The altar cover is illustrated in Ogasawara 1989, p. 34. See also Kyoto 1981, p. 77.
6. Okada Jō 1978; also Nishioka Yasuhiro 1984.
7. Su Bai 1990.
8. Tibetan commissions of woven Buddhist images at Hangzhou continued into the twentieth century. A woven image of Sakya Pandita (1182–1251) in the Tashilhunpo Temple, Shigatse, Tibet, bears an inscription in Chinese stating that it was woven in Hangzhou in the Republic of China. Illustrated in Huang Ti 1985, pl. 60. See also Su Bai 1990, p. 63.
9. For an example from Jingo-ji, see Nara 1982, no. 171. There are other examples from the same set in various collections outside Japan, one in the Burke collection in New York. See Pal and Meech-Pekarik 1988, p. 279, pl. 83.
10. For a discussion of early bamboo and silk sutra wrappers found in Dunhuang and those preserved in the Shōsō-in, Nara, see Whitfield 1985, pp. 287–88, pl. 7.
11. Rossabi 1988, pp. 196–97.
12. Fujian Provincial Museum 1982.
13. Han Rulin 1986, vol. 2, p. 35.
14. Deng Ruiling 1989, pp. 51–56, 70. A copy of Chengzu's Buddhist chants is in the Rare Book Section of Hong Kong University Library. See also Karmay 1975, pp. 72–103.
15. See New York 1991, no. 49. In this catalogue entry for the Yongle lacquer sutra covers it is stated, following previous authors, that they were produced in Beijing. But this is by no means certain. There seems to be no clear evidence that the printing of the Kanjur or the production of the lacquered wood covers occurred in Beijing. As the Yongle emperor did not himself move with the craftsmen to the northern capital, Beijing, until 1420, it is far more likely that both the printing and the production of the covers were done in the south.
16. The demise of court painting in the sixteenth century is discussed in Dallas 1993. For a brief account of the changes in the production of porcelain for the Ming court in the sixteenth century, see Fong and Watt 1996, pp. 441–51.

48. Embroidery with Birds

Embroidery
25.7 × 157.5 cm (10⅛ × 62 in.)
Tang dynasty (618–907), 8th–9th century
The Cleveland Museum of Art. Andrew R. and Martha Holden
Jennings Fund (1994.96)

Paired and single birds are here embroidered on a patterned tan silk ground. The birds have crested heads, small beaks, curving wing feathers, long tail feathers, and large clawed feet. A row of widely spaced, single birds alternates with a row of similarly spaced, paired birds, both facing the same direction. In the center of the textile, a pair of birds stand on a stylized hill at either side of a central tuliplike flower (see detail). With the exception of one fragmentary bird in the top register, all the birds face away from the central pair. Although the birds appear to be virtually identical, slight differences reveal that they were, in fact, hand drawn and not stamped prior to being embroidered. Traces of the blue-green ink outlines can be observed under magnification. The tan silk ground fabric is woven with rosettes within a lozenge grid. Because the birds were embroidered at right angles to the warp, the bottom edge of the textile is a selvage.

A dating to the eighth to the ninth century is indicated by the naturalistic, spontaneous style of both the birds and the flower, and their arrangement in the central motif is one of the many combinations of birds and flowers that occur in Tang art.[1] In both the embroidered motifs and the design of the ground fabric, Sasanian and Sogdian influence is apparent. These include the style of the rosettes on the ground, the birds and particularly the treatment of their upper wing feathers, the tuliplike flower, and the tripartite form of the hill.[2] Such motifs were absorbed into the decorative repertory of Central Asian and Chinese art as a result of active trading in precious objects during the Tang period. Similar birds can be found in Tang metalwork, while a similar tripartite hill supporting a flowering plant

occurs on an eighth-century felt rug preserved in Nara, Japan.[3]

The juxtaposition of embroidered and woven patterns is an aesthetic that occurs in many embroideries dating from the Tang period. Also characteristic is the predominance of satin stitches and discrete color areas with no attempt at shading. The *liseré* technique of the ground fabric is known in a number of variations among Tang textiles excavated in eastern Central Asia.[4]

Although the original function of this embroidery is not known, the light weight of the fabric, in particular, and the choice of birds for the decoration suggest that it may have been part of a garment. In any case, a long horizontal panel was clearly required, given the orientation of the embroidery at right angles to the warp.

1. Laing 1992.
2. New York 1978, pp. 57, 66, 95, and fig. κ on p. 121; Ann Arbor 1967, no. 24, p. 111; Smirnov 1909, pls. LII, CXXIII, no. 307, LVII, CXXII; Marshak 1986, figs. 23, 55.
3. Lu Jiugao and Han Wei 1985, p. 120, fig. 239; Royal Ontario Museum 1972, no. 142. For closely related birds, see Laing 1992, figs. 32, 33; Matsumoto 1984, pl. 113.
4. See note 1, Technical Analysis, below.

TECHNICAL ANALYSIS

GROUND: *Warp:* Tan silk, without apparent twist (a very slight s or z twist can occasionally be detected); the warp step is 4 warps; 54 warps per centimeter. *Weft:* Tan silk, without apparent twist (a very slight s or z twist can occasionally be detected); 32 wefts per centimeter. *Weave:* Twill, *liseré.* The ground weave has a 3 / 1 z twill binding. The decorative motifs are composed of a checkerboard grid based on units of four warps and four wefts. A group

of four wefts floating over four warps (which, of necessity, float on the reverse) alternates with the adjacent group of four warps and wefts bound in 3 / 1 z twill.[1] Several types of weaving faults occur: a mistake in the warp repeat results in two incomplete repeats that are juxtaposed; sometimes the pattern unit is limited to 1 or 2 passes instead of 4; long, arbitrary floats of wefts occur, especially in the pattern areas but also in the ground (this is particularly frequent in the area of the repeat error). One selvage is preserved. The pattern ends 1.3–1.5 centimeters from the outermost edge. The selvage border is woven in the same weave as the ground, but the warps are more closely spaced. At one point, the direction of the twill changes briefly from z to s because of a treadling fault.

EMBROIDERY: Polychrome silk floss. Colors: pale, medium, and dark plum, mustard yellow, deep blue, light green, and cream. *Stitches:* Satin, split. The embroidery is oriented at right angles to the warp of the ground fabric. Traces of blue-green drawing appear along the contours of the birds. That the outlines were drawn by hand and not stamped is evident from slight differences in the sizes and details of the birds. Some of the birds (the central pair flanking a flower, the paired birds to the right of the central motif, and the single birds to the left of the central motif) are embroidered over two layers of silk, the ground fabric and a second layer in the form of a patch on the reverse side.

PATCHES: 1) Under the single bird closest to the left edge. *Warp:* Tan silk, without apparent twist; unevenly twisted; 60–68 per centimeter. *Weft:* Tan silk, without apparent twist; unevenly twisted; 40 per centimeter. *Weave:* Tabby binding. There are variations in the tightness of the weave, and weaving mistakes (in the warp and weft floats). Selvage: the wefts turn around the outer warp. 2) Under the single bird just to the left of the central pair. *Warp:* Tan silk, without apparent twist; 60 per centimeter. *Weft:* Tan silk, without apparent twist; slightly thicker than the warps; 46 per centimeter. *Weave:* Tabby. 3) Under the

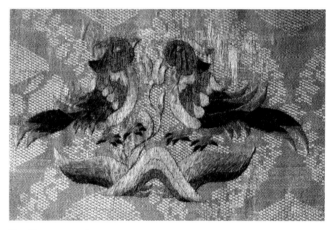

Detail, cat. no. 48

central pair of birds on the hill. *Warp:* Tan silk, without apparent twist; unevenly twisted; 48 per centimeter. *Weft:* Tan silk, without apparent twist; unevenly twisted; 36 per centimeter. *Weave:* Tabby. 4) Under the paired birds to the right of the central pair. *Warp:* Tan silk, without apparent twist; slightly unevenly twisted; 64 per centimeter. *Weft:* Tan silk, without apparent twist; slightly unevenly twisted; 34 per centimeter. *Weave:* Tabby. 5) Under the rightmost pair of birds. *Warp:* Tan silk, without apparent twist; slightly unevenly twisted; 52 per centimeter. *Weft:* Tan silk, without apparent twist; slightly thicker than the warp; 50 per centimeter. *Weave:* Tabby; occasional flaws (in the warp and weft floats); the weave varies in tightness. Selvage: the wefts turn around the outermost warp.

1. For a similar weave and variations, see Riboud and Vial 1970, EO 3660 (pp. 63–68), BN 2849 (pp. 409–16), MG 22798,C (pp. 356–57, 359–60, 362), and BN 2876 (pp. 417–24).

Unpublished.

49. Confronted Birds

Embroidery
31.1 × 30.8 cm (12¼ × 12⅛ in.)
Tang dynasty (618–907), 8th century
The Metropolitan Museum of Art, New York. Purchase, Joseph Pulitzer Bequest, 1996 (1996.103.2)

In this embroidery, confronted birds (ducks or geese) standing on open lotuses flank a large, leafy flowering stem. The design is executed in long satin stitches in graduated layers of different colors, becoming lighter toward the outer edges, and in a chain stitch that delineates the thinner stems, the veins of the leaves, and the outline of the birds. The technique is very similar to that seen on fragments of embroidery found at Dunhuang by Sir Aurel Stein and Paul Pelliot, usually dated to the eighth century.[1] A length of resist-dyed silk with a similar pattern is in the Shōsō-in, Nara, dated also to the eighth century.[2]

The motif of confronted animals or birds came to China ultimately from West Asia, but was transmitted through Sogdiana (see cat. no. 3). Initially, the Chinese patterns followed West Asian models more closely and the animals or birds were enclosed in circular frames. Beginning in the High Tang (roughly the first half of the eighth century), paired birds came to predominate, both with and without a plant between them, but always unconfined by a border. Another Chinese modification was for the ducks to stand on open lotuses, as in the present example, a development perhaps indirectly influenced by contemporary Buddhist narrative paintings, in which most of the figures stand or sit on lotuses.[3] On some Tang mirrors larger animals, such as the horse, are also represented standing on open lotuses that issue from either side of a central stem.[4]

This square, although of relatively small size, is one of the very few surviving examples of Tang embroidery that are complete works. On the back, at the corners, are traces of stitching, and part of a cord is still attached to the bottom corner. The silk lining on the reverse, woven with small rosettes, is original. Portions of the floss silk threads were unraveled from woven fabrics,[5] an occurrence commonly observed in early embroideries found in Xinjiang.[6]

1. For an example of the Stein finds, see Whitfield 1985, pl. 4; for the Pelliot finds, see Riboud and Vial 1970, pl. 52, EO. 1191/F.
2. Matsumoto 1984, no. 51.
3. See, for example, the painting on the north wall (upper section) in Cave 148 at Dunhuang, illustrated in Su Bai 1989, vol. 16, pl. 88. See also figure 6.
4. Chen Peifen 1987, pl. 76.
5. Conservation report by Nobuko Kajitani, conservator in charge, Textile Conservation, The Metropolitan Museum of Art.
6. According to Wu Min of the Xinjiang Uyghur Autonomous Regional Museum, Urumqi (verbal communication).

TECHNICAL ANALYSIS

GROUND: Silk. *Warp and weft:* Tan silk, without apparent twist; warp 34 per centimeter; weft 38 per centimeter. *Weave:* Tabby. The selvage is composed of wefts turning around the outermost warp.

EMBROIDERY: Polychrome silk floss. Colors: light to deep green, shades of tan, shades of yellow, light to dark blue, dark brown, cream, and pale and medium plum. *Stitches:* Satin, encroaching satin, and split. The ink drawing of the motifs is visible in places.

LINING: *Warp and weft:* Tan silk, without apparent twist; 50 warps per centimeter; and 34 wefts per centimeter. *Weave:* Tabby, *liseré* (the wefts float over 3 warps); the selvage consists of wefts turning around the outermost warp.

CONSTRUCTION: The square is finished on all four sides (the silk ground of the embroidery is turned under). Remnants of tassels remain on three corners; part of a cord is preserved on the back of the bottom corner. The square is backed with a silk lining woven with small rosettes.

PUBLICATION: MMA *Recent Acquisitions* 1995–1996, p. 76, illus.

49

50. *Animals, Birds, and Flowers*

Embroidery
37.1 × 37.8 cm (14 ⅝ × 14 ⅞ in.)
Eastern Central Asia, late 11th–early 13th century
The Metropolitan Museum of Art, New York. Rogers Fund, 1988
(1988.296)

This square is embroidered with a rich assortment of animals and birds amid flowers. Clockwise from top left are a wild goose, a parrot, a phoenix, and a pheasant. At the four sides are a standing deer, a reclining spotted deer, a rabbit, and a spotted horse. In the center are a lotus and a trefoil aquatic plant. Strewn over the remaining space are flowers, including camellia, poppy, tree and herbaceous peonies, hibiscus, and rose of Sharon.

The basic technique is not very different from that of the earlier Tang example (cat. no. 49), except that the long and short stitches allow for a more gradual change of colors, creating the effect of shading.

One can hardly find a better example than this textile to illustrate the eclectic art of eastern Central Asia. First, the combination of animals, birds, and flowers in a general pattern is a distinct artistic tradition in eastern Central Asia. Second, the disposition of the four animals on the sides of the square suggests the continuation of a compositional device that goes back to the Han period, the time of the first major Chinese expansion into Central Asia. This schema is best illustrated by the decoration on the back of Han mirrors, particularly those of the type known as the four spirits mirror, which was prevalent in the late Western Han to early Eastern Han (1st century B.C.– A.D. 1st century). In these mirrors (fig. 74) the four spirits, in the form of animals that symbolize the four quarters, are represented as the dragon (east), the tiger (west), the vermilion bird or phoenix (south), and the composite animal *xuanwu* (tortoise and snake; north). This symbolic arrangement, seen on many objects of the Han period, must have been introduced into Central Asia together with the four-leaf pattern that is seen at the base of the central knob handle.[1] The significance of the animals of the four quarters was later forgotten or ignored, but the compositional device persisted, not only in Central Asia but also in interior China, where mirrors of the late Han and post-Han were often decorated with animals other than the symbolic four or with just two of the animals repeated on either side.

On this embroidery, the animals are disposed according to Han convention, but the animals themselves are all of Central Asian origin, and their stance, with heads turned back, is characteristic of the so-called animal style in Central Asia. The reclining deer with the small, mushroom-shaped antler to which a crescent shape is added is a cross between

the deer and the *djeiran*—both seen on Sogdian art, which came into eastern Central Asia with early trade along the Silk Roads, particularly during the sixth century. The spotted horse is native to northern Asia and first came to the attention of the Chinese in the early Tang. In the *Xin Tangshu* (New History of the Tang), it is recorded that in the time of Emperor Taizong (r. 626–49) contacts were for the first time established with a country to the north of the Turks (the Tujue, who at that time occupied the area later overtaken by the Uyghurs; see the map on page 8) by the name of Jiaoma—which means piebald horse—so called because all the horses in that country had "mixed colors."[2] The spotted horse was by this time known also in Central Asia. Clay mortuary figures of horses from seventh-century sites at Astana (in the Turfan area) often are painted with spots of color (fig. 75). Indeed, spotted or mottled hide was such a popular artistic idiom that the fantastic guardian beasts at the same Astana sites are nearly all decorated with round dots or splashes of color.[3] Thereafter, the spotted horse seems to have remained in the artistic tradition of eastern Central Asia—if not as a physical presence— to resurface again on embroidery. (In interior China

Figure 74. Four spirits mirror. Late Western Han–early Eastern Han dynasty. Bronze, diameter 11.8 cm (4⅝ in.). National Palace Museum, Taipei

50

after the Tang dynasty, the spotted horse is rarely seen in any artistic medium—except in paintings of tribute horses ascribed to such artists as the Northern Song painter Li Gonglin—though it became a constant motif in the Yuan and later dynasties.)

The four embroidered birds occupy the same relative positions as the circles at the corners of the square frame on the mirror. (On most mirrors of this period, the line relief circles are replaced by hemispherical knobs, which

are much more prominent.) Again, while the placement of the birds may follow a Han scheme, their individual forms owe much to the art of the Tang, especially that of the High Tang period. Their general form, with wings outstretched and long tail feathers, is in accordance with that of birds seen in Tang decorative arts in all media. This feature, however, persisted in Chinese art generally until the Yuan period. A more characteristic feature of Tang style is seen in the treatment of the parrot, which is often

Figure 75. Horse and rider. Central Asia, 7th century. Painted baked clay, height 39 cm (15⅜ in.). Xinjiang Uyghur Autonomous Regional Museum, Urumqi

Figure 76. Mirror with parrots and flowers. Tang dynasty (618–907) Bronze, diameter 23.8 cm (9⅜ in.). The Metropolitan Museum of Art, New York. Rogers Fund, 1917 (17.118.96)

represented in a perched position, with or without support (fig. 76). It is similarly depicted on the embroidery (see bottom detail on facing page).

The only element in the design of the embroidery that is likely to have been a recent or contemporary innovation, and not inherited from tradition, is the floral pattern. Of particular interest is the center motif of lotus blossoms, a lotus leaf seen from the side, and a trefoil water plant (top detail). The same assemblage is seen in a floral arrangement in a wall painting in a Liao tomb dated 1116 (fig. 77).[4] A more complex arrangement, combining the same elements, is illustrated in the *Yingzao fashi*, a manual for construction work and architectural decoration by Li Jie (d. 1110), first published in 1103 toward the end of the Northern Song dynasty.[5] However, this motif became universally popular only in the Yuan dynasty, while the earliest-known examples of this particular representation of the lotus plant are to be found in northern and western China (see also cat. no. 13).

These considerations lead us to conclude that the embroidery was done in eastern Xinjiang, perhaps in the Turfan area, sometime between the late eleventh and the early thirteenth century. Several aspects of the design can be explained only in terms of the formation of the eastern Central Asian style (the results of two periods of strong Chinese influence in Central Asia), as outlined above; the dating can be established by the floral pattern alone.

1. For a discussion of the four-leaf pattern and its evolution in Central Asia, see Cammann 1951.
2. *Xin Tangshu*, vol. 19, chap. 217, p. 6146.
3. *Xinjiang Museum* 1987, pls. 125, 126.
4. *Xuanhua Liao bihua mu* 1975.
5. In modern editions of the *Yingzao fashi*, supposedly based on exact reproductions of the Southern Song edition of 1145, the illustrations may have been modified in their details during the copying process in later reprints.

TECHNICAL ANALYSIS

GROUND: *Warp and weft:* White silk, one z and the other without twist; 32 × 36 per centimeter. *Weave:* Tabby.

EMBROIDERY: Polychrome silk, s and z. Colors: brown, very dark brown, light, medium, and dark blue, light, medium, and dark green, yellow, mustard yellow, mauve, white, coral, rose, pink, and light coral. *Stitches:* Satin, long and short, and split.

COMMENTARY: Only the design is embroidered; the background is ground fabric. None of the contours is finished; the embroidery over tears seems to be more or less intact.

PUBLICATIONS: Krahl 1989, p. 70, fig. 21, p. 72; *Textiles* 1995–96, p. 73, illus.

174

Detail, cat. no. 50

Figure 77. Tomb mural, detail. Liao dynasty (907–1125), 1116

Detail, cat. no. 50

51, front

51. Robe

Outer fabric: Embroidery
Length (collar to hem): 130 cm (51⅛ in.); width (across sleeves):
177 cm (69¾ in.)
Liao dynasty (907–1125)
The Cleveland Museum of Art. Purchase from the J. H. Wade
Fund (1995.20)

This full-length robe with long, ample sleeves has been reconstructed from fragments based on sel-vages, hems, and the embroidered decoration. The robe is made of several layers: an outer silk gauze with a lozenge pattern, a silk tabby, a layer of silk batting, and a silk tabby lining; the embroidery was worked through the two outer layers (gauze and silk tabby). The front open-ing, which overlaps to the right as opposed to the left, accords with Chinese custom. From the rather cryptic records in the *Liaoshi* (History of the Liao Dynasty), we may surmise that the rules for wearing Khitan-style dress, even at court, were increasingly relaxed toward the end of the dynasty.[1]

The robe is embroidered with an overall design of gold vines with wide stems and foliate terminals. Such vines occur in a number of variations in Khitan art, sometimes with terminals that resemble clouds, at other times with terminals that are more foliate, as on this robe.[2] The couched gold thread composed of flat strips of gilded ani-mal substrate has almost entirely disintegrated. What therefore remains of the embroidery are the couching stitches and the gold leaf that has adhered to the gauze ground.

At the center of the back is a large silk-and-gold em-broidery of two confronted phoenixes with wings out-stretched among clouds (see detail on page 179). Their heads are crowned with crests and long feathers, and their plumed tails arch majestically over their heads. The clouds, in characteristic Liao style, are in the shape of a *ruyi* fungus, with opposed scrolls and a "tail." Although there is no frame to enclose the birds, their bodies and the clouds form a roundel. At the top of each shoulder, a single phoenix—also with crest, head feathers, and plumed tail feathers arching over the head—and a single cloud are embroidered with silk and gold thread. On the

176

51, back

front of the robe is preserved part of the embroidered tail
feathers and plumes of a phoenix, the scale of which suggests that the complete embroidery would have corre-
sponded to the embroidery with paired phoenixes on the
back. Technically, the embroidery is very similar to other
Liao examples.[3]

Judging by the preserved selvages and hems, the robe
was made in much the same way as were later embroidered
Chinese dragon robes.[4] The left and right sides (each comprising the front, back, and upper portion of the sleeve)
were cut from lengths of fabric that were complete loom
widths (see fig. 78). The outer portions of the sleeves and
front overlap were cut from additional lengths of fabric.
The two back portions were joined along their selvage edges
to form the center back seam. The overlapping front panel
was sewn to the left front along the selvage edges, forming
the center front seam. The outer portions of the sleeves
were joined along the selvage edges to the sleeve portions
of the right and left sides of the robe. The robe was then
folded in half across the shoulders and joined along the sides
and bottom edges of the sleeves. The neck opening was

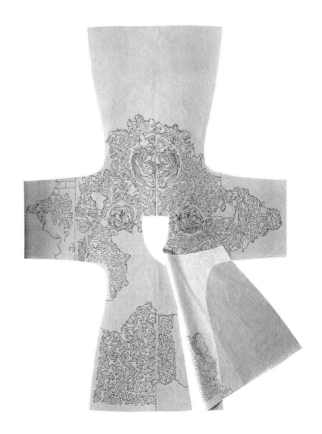

Figure 78. Reconstructed robe showing the placement of the fragments and their designs. Drawing by Karen A. Klingbiel

177

finished with a collar, and the bottom edge of the robe was hemmed.

Close examination reveals that the design was hand drawn and then embroidered on the lengths of fabric before they were cut and assembled into the robe. The overall design of gold-embroidered vines not only varies subtly in the direction and form of the vines from one part of the robe to another but is completed well before the bottom hem and some of the seams. Moreover, the pair of large phoenixes and clouds on the back of the robe are neither identical nor perfectly aligned, suggesting that the later Chinese technique of sewing the back center seam before embroidering the design on the uncut lengths of fabric was not yet in practice.[5]

Sets of garments found in the tombs of two aristocratic women, one at Yemaotai in present-day Liaoning Province and the other at Wanzishan in Inner Mongolia, give an idea of the costume to which this robe once belonged.[6] Khitan women dressed in many layers. They wore full-length outer robes over short jackets, skirts, and sometimes vests, and long pants, short or high silk boots, and undergarments. Hats and gloves completed the outfit. The styles of the outer robes worn by the two women are different. The robe at Yemaotai has wide sleeves and a front opening that overlaps to the left, while the robe from the tomb at Wanzishan has a round collar, narrow sleeves, and a flared, pleated skirt. Both robes, however, were made to be worn with belts. The single long outer robe worn by the woman buried at Yemaotai is embroidered at the collar, shoulders, and center front. The woman buried at Wanzishan, by contrast, wore three long robes, each made of gauze and lined with silk tabby with a layer of silk batting between. Only the outermost robe, however, was embroidered, with an over-all design of floral vines.

Where the Cleveland robe would have fit into the sequence of layers comprising the original costume is not known. Despite the numbers of textiles that have been found in recent decades, only a few have been published in archaeological reports, and no comprehensive study of the material has yet been undertaken.

1. Wittfogel and Feng Chia-sheng 1949, pp. 227–28.
2. Inner Mongolia 1993, p. 38; Tamura and Kobayashi 1953, fig. 214:2.
3. For two published examples, see Gao Hanyu 1992, pl. 59, and Liaoning Provincial Museum 1975, pl. III, 2.
4. V. Wilson 1986, pp. 18–20.
5. Ibid., p. 20.
6. Liaoning Provincial Museum 1975, pp. 28–30; Inner Mongolia 1985, pp. 72–88.

TECHNICAL ANALYSIS

GAUZE: *Warp:* Brown silk, without apparent twist; approximately 80 warps per centimeter. *Weft:* Brown silk, without apparent twist; approximately 11 per centimeter. *Weave:* Complex gauze.[1] Selvage: the border, about 1 centimeter wide, is a tightly woven gauze (unit of 4 warps); at the outer edge, the wefts turn around the outermost single warp.

SILK TABBY:[2] *Warp:* Brown silk, without apparent twist; 48–54 per centimeter. *Weft:* Brown silk, without apparent twist; 31 per centimeter. *Weave:* Tabby. Selvage: for 2 millimeters the warps are more closely spaced; the wefts turn around the outermost warp.

SILK TABBY (lining):[3] *Warp:* Tan silk, without apparent twist. *Weft:* Tan silk, without apparent twist; the wefts are denser than the warps; 37–38 per centimeter. *Weave:* Tabby. Selvage: toward the outer edge the warps are more closely spaced; at the outer edge the wefts turn around the outermost warp.

EMBROIDERY: 1) Polychrome silk floss. 2) Gold thread (flat strips of animal substrate; nearly all the substrate has disintegrated, leaving traces of gold leaf lying on the gauze ground). *Stitches:* Couching, satin, and split. The embroidery is worked through two layers, gauze over silk tabby. The overall pattern of vines is executed in couched gold thread. The phoenixes are embroidered with satin stitches; split stitches are used to outline the eyes; couching stitches and traces of gold leaf remain from the couched gold threads that originally delineated the contours and details of the birds.

RECONSTRUCTION (fig. 78: right and left are oriented from the point of view of the wearer).[4] There are three fragments from the original robe. The largest fragment includes the upper back, shoulders, collar, parts of the sleeves, and the upper sections of the front. The seam joining the two sections of the right sleeve (along the selvages) is almost entirely intact, and part of the corresponding seam of the left sleeve is preserved. Because the outer edges of both sleeves are missing, the length of the sleeves is only an estimate. The seams joining the robe at the sides and under the sleeves are sufficiently preserved to provide the circumference of the sleeves and the cut of the upper sides.

The second fragment, from the lower right front section of the robe, consists of two pieces seamed along their selvage edges. Its placement is indicated by the presence of a hem in the weft direction, by stitching holes of what was a side seam on the right, by the seam joining the two pieces along their selvages (which would have formed part of the center front seam of the robe), and by the left edge which has been finished by being turned under.

The third fragment is believed to be the lower left front section because it preserves the bottom hem in the weft direction and the remains of a seam about one centimeter from the cut left edge. Part of an embroidered phoenix, comparable in size to each of the phoenixes on the back of the robe, is preserved to the left of the center seam. Because there is no trace of the companion to this phoenix on the second fragment (the lower front section), the robe is believed to have had an additional panel forming an overlap to the right. The panel would have been attached to the inner selvage edge of the left front section to form a center front seam. The companion to the fragmentary phoenix preserved on the left front section would have been embroidered on the overlap.

The placement of the embroidered phoenixes on the robe accords with the description in the archaeological report of the outer robe worn by the woman in the tomb at Yemaotai: it was embroidered on the top of each shoulder and on the front with a figure riding a phoenix, along with floral motifs, birds, and butterflies.[5]

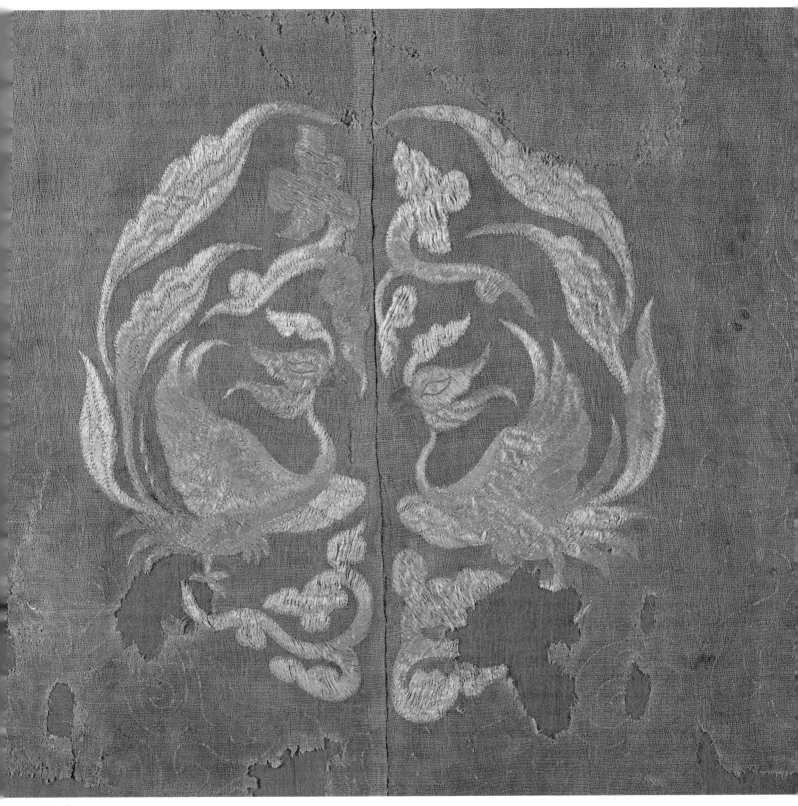

Detail, cat. no. 51

1. A similar complex gauze was published with schematic drawings by G. Vial: Riboud and Vial 1970, EO. 1203/F, esp. pp. 375–76, 378–79.
2. Based on Karen A. Klingbiel, "Conservation Report: A Burial Robe from a Liao Tomb in Northeastern China" (copyright 1996, unpublished). The conservation was performed at the Abegg-Stiftung, Riggisberg, under the guidance of Mechthild Flury-Lemberg and Gisela Illek.
3. Ibid.

4. Ibid.
5. There was most likely a corresponding embroidery on the back, but it is not mentioned in the archaeological report (Liaoning Provincial Museum 1975, pp. 28–30). Given that an embroidered dragon on the back of the collar is damaged, the embroidery of the center back may have been destroyed in burial.

PUBLICATION: Wardwell 1995, p. 7.

52. Pair of Headpieces

Embroidery
A: 21.8 × 34.9 cm (8⅝ × 13¾ in.)
B: 22.3 × 31.7 cm; width with tie, 53.8 cm (8¾ × 12½ in.; 21⅛ in.)
Liao dynasty (907–1125)
The Cleveland Museum of Art. Gift of Lisbet Holmes
(A: 1995.109,b; B: 1995.109,a)

Divided into four sections, these two headpieces are embroidered with butterflies, leaves, and flowers, including lotus, prunus, and chrysanthemum, and delicate vine scrolls. Pairs of waterbirds resembling geese are seen in the upper right section of A and in the upper right and left sections of B, while a pair of animals is seen in the upper left section of A. The design seems, overall, to be related to the theme of the lotus pond. The motif of waterbirds looking forward and back appears to have been particularly popular in northern China and occurs in Liao tomb painting (see cat. no. 16). Obvious counterparts for the particular form of some of the flowers and for the delicate curling tendrils are, however, difficult to find. Technically, the embroidery corresponds to Liao examples in the Liaoning Provincial Museum in Shenyang and in the Museum of Inner Mongolian Autonomous Region, Hohhot.[1]

Similar headgear has been found in Liao excavations, and a replica in gold was found in a tomb dating to as early as the Northern Wei dynasty (the first half of the sixth century).[2] Clearly, such head coverings had a very long history in the northern regions.

1. Unpublished.
2. Uldry et al. 1994, no. 121, p. 141.

TECHNICAL ANALYSIS

GROUND: *Warp:* Green silk, s, single; approximately 80 per centimeter. *Weft:* Green silk, without apparent twist; approximately 50 per centimeter. *Weave:* Satin damask.

EMBROIDERY: Polychrome silk, z, slight twist, 2-ply s (best seen in areas of satin stitches; the manipulation of the threads for split stitches distorts the twists). Colors: tan, pale green. *Stitches:* Split, satin, and long and short. Embroidery: Only the motifs are embroidered. The flowers, birds, butterflies, and animals are worked in satin and in long and short stitches, while the delicate vine scrolls are worked in a split stitch. The stitches appear to have been worked over a now disintegrated cord that originally defined the contours of the motifs.

HORIZONTAL BANDS: *Warp and weft:* Tan silk, without apparent twist; approximately 50 warps × approximately 30 wefts per centimeter. *Weave:* Tabby. Selvage: the warps are more closely spaced toward the edge, where the wefts turn around the outermost single warp.

VERTICAL BANDS: *Warp:* Tan silk, z, single; approximately 50 per centimeter. *Weft:* Tan silk, z; approximately 28 per centimeter. *Weave:* $\frac{3}{1}\frac{1}{1}$ z twill. Sewing thread: tan silk, z, 2-ply s.

LINING: *Warp and weft:* Tan silk, without apparent twist; approximately 48 × 34 per centimeter. *Weave:* Tabby.

CONSTRUCTION: Each headpiece is composed of the embroidered ground fabric, a layer of silk batting, and the lining. The band dividing each headpiece horizontally originally formed ties (all are missing except the left tie of B). Intersecting each headpiece vertically are two bands, each with rolled edges, placed side by side and sewn into place.

Unpublished.

52A

52B

53. Pillow Cover

Embroidery and weaving
57.28.5: 16 × 16 cm (6¼ × 6¼ in.)
57.28.6: 64 × 4.1 cm (26¾ × 1⅝ in.)
Eastern Central Asia or China, Mongol period, 13th century
The Metropolitan Museum of Art, New York. Gift of Mrs. Willis Wood, 1957 (57.28.5,6)

This square pillow cover consists of a patchwork of woven and embroidered fragments cut into diamonds or tri-angles. The sections numbered 1 and 2 (fig. 79) are embroidered with floral sprays; the others are fragments of woven fabrics. Although the pillow cover was clearly made from leftovers, it was very carefully pieced together and then finished with an embroidered border of pendants. A silk strip, part of which originally had a gold leaf floral design, was found with the pillow.

The thirteenth-century date is indicated by the eastern Iranian elements in the techniques of some of the frag-ments—paired warps (section 3) and supplementary wefts

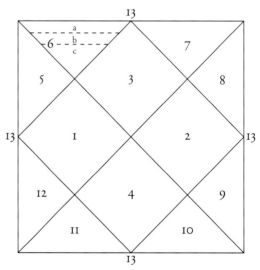

Figure 79. Diagram showing placement of 13 sections, cat. no. 53

bound in pairs (sections 5, 6a, and 8). Section 12 is a rare damask brocaded in the Jin tradition.

TECHNICAL ANALYSIS

SECTION 1: Square embroidered with flowers. Ground: Silk. *Warp:* Golden brown silk, z, single; approximately 60 per

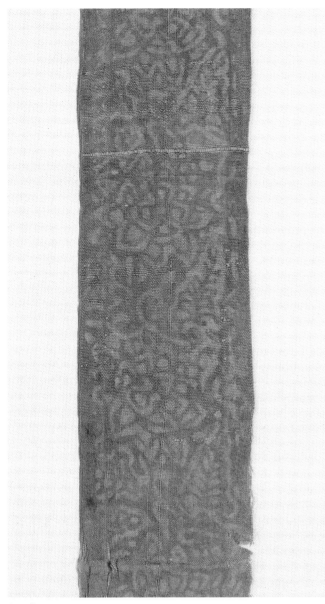

Detail, cat. no. 53

centimeter. *Weft:* Golden brown silk, z, about the same diameter as the warp; 30 per centimeter. *Weave:* Damask: 1/2 z twill, and reverse. Embroidery: Golden tan silk, without twist, 2-ply s. *Stitches:* Encroaching satin, split, long and short, knot.

SECTION 2: Square embroidered with flowers. Ground: Silk. *Warp:* Golden tan silk, s, slight twist, single; 52 per centimeter. *Weft:* Golden tan silk, s, slight twist; 40 per centimeter, approximately the same diameter as the warp. *Weave:* 2/1 z twill. Embroidery: Golden tan silk, without apparent twist, 2-ply s. *Stitches:* Interlocking satin, split, long and short, and knot.

SECTION 3: Silk, originally brocaded. *Warp:* Golden tan silk, z, single; approximately 60 per centimeter. *Weft:* Foundation: tan silk, z, paired; approximately 24 pairs per centimeter. The brocading wefts are now entirely gone. *Weave:* Twill, originally brocaded. The foundation has an irregular twill binding, and the brocade a regular 2/1 s twill binding. In certain areas, after every 5 to 6 wefts, the successive 3 pairs of wefts are floated across the reverse.

SECTION 4: Lampas weave. *Warp:* Foundation: golden tan silk, z, single. Supplementary: golden tan silk, z, single. Proportion:

3 foundation warps to 1 supplementary warp. Step: 3 foundation warps; approximately 60 foundation and 20 supplementary warps per centimeter. *Weft:* Foundation: golden tan silk, without apparent twist. Supplementary: gold or silver thread (now missing except for traces of the silk core on the reverse). Pass: 1 foundation and 1 supplementary weft; approximately 26 passes per centimeter. *Weave:* Lampas. The foundation weave has a 2/1 s twill binding and the supplementary weave a tabby binding.

SECTIONS 5 AND 8: Fragment of a lampas weave. *Warp:* Foundation: golden tan silk, z, single. Supplementary: golden tan silk, without apparent twist, thin. Proportion: 6 foundation warps to 1 supplementary warp. Step: 2 foundation warps; approximately 72 foundation and 13 supplementary warps per centimeter. *Weft:* Foundation: golden tan silk, without apparent twist. Supplementary: golden tan silk, z, paired (clearly the core of gold or silver thread). Pass: 1 foundation weft and 2 supplementary wefts. Step: 1 pass; 22 passes per centimeter. *Weave:* Lampas; the foundation and supplementary weave are bound in tabby (gold/silver wefts are bound in pairs).

SECTION 6a: Fragment of a lampas weave. *Warp:* Foundation: golden tan silk, z, single. Supplementary: golden tan silk, without apparent twist. Proportion: 4 foundation warps to 1 supplementary warp. Step: 2 foundation warps; approximately 84 foundation and 20 supplementary warps per centimeter. *Weft:* Foundation: golden tan silk, without apparent twist. Supplementary: golden tan silk, z (the core of gold or silver thread). Pass: 1 foundation weft and 2 supplementary wefts. Step: 1 pass; 20 passes per centimeter. *Weave:* Lampas; the foundation weave is bound in tabby, the supplementary in 1/2 s twill (the wefts are bound in pairs).

SECTION 6b: Fragment of a lampas weave. *Warp:* Foundation: tan silk, s, single. Supplementary: tan silk without apparent twist. Proportion: 3 foundation warps to 1 supplementary warp. Step: unknown; approximately 60 foundation and 20 supplementary warps per centimeter. *Weft:* Foundation: appears to be a composite weft, each weft consisting of 3 threads, tan silk, s. Pass: 1 foundation weft and 1 supplementary weft. Step: 1 pass; approximately 20 passes per centimeter. *Weave:* Lampas; the binding of the foundation weave is a 2/1 z twill; the binding of the supplementary weave is tabby.

SECTION 6c: Fragment of a patterned twill weave (very damaged). *Warp or weft:* Tan silk, without apparent twist; approximately 52 × 32 per centimeter. *Weave:* 2/1 twill and irregular twill.

SECTION 7: Fragment of a twill weave. *Warp or weft:* Tan silk, z, single; approximately 52 per centimeter. *Warp or weft:* Tan silk, z, 2-ply s; approximately 48 per centimeter. *Weave:* 1/3 s twill.

SECTION 8: Same as section 5.

SECTION 9: Fragment of a tabby weave. *Warp or weft:* Tan silk, without apparent twist; 22 per centimeter. *Warp or weft:* Tan silk, with an occasional slight s twist; approximately 26 per centimeter. *Weave:* Tabby.

SECTION 10: Fragment of a damask. *Warp:* Golden tan silk, without apparent twist; approximately 100 per centimeter. *Weft:* Golden tan silk, without apparent twist; approximately 3 times the thickness of the warp; 42 per centimeter. *Weave:* Satin damask (4/1 satin, and reverse).

SECTION 11: Fragment of a twill weave (mounted upside down).

Warp: Golden tan silk, z, paired; 80 per centimeter. *Weft:* Golden tan silk, z; approximately 90 per centimeter. *Weave:* 4/1 z twill.

SECTION 12: Fragment of a damask, originally brocaded. *Warp:* Golden tan silk, s, single; approximately 60 per centimeter. *Weft:* Golden tan silk, z, 2-ply s; approximately 24 per centimeter; the brocading wefts are now entirely gone. *Weave:* Damask, sometimes 2/1 z twill, other times 3/1 z twill; and reverse of both twills. On the reverse, groups of 3 paired wefts float after every 7–8 wefts, indicating that the damask was once brocaded with gold or silver thread.

SECTION 13: Embroidered border. Ground: *Warp:* Golden tan silk, s, single; 60 per centimeter. *Weft:* Golden tan silk, s, without apparent twist; 42 per centimeter. *Weave:* Fancy twill: indicated as $\frac{3}{1}\frac{1}{1}$, z. Embroidery: Tan silk, z, 2-ply s. *Stitches:* Detached looping.

FABRIC AT SIDES: *Warp:* Tan silk, without apparent twist; 60 per centimeter. *Weft:* Tan silk, without apparent twist; 30 or 50 per centimeter. *Weave:* Tabby. At intervals, the wefts are loosely beaten in (approximately 30 per centimeter), creating a striated effect. Selvage: The wefts turn around the outermost warp; toward the outer edge, the warps are closely spaced.

DETACHED STRIP: Painted end. *Warp:* Reddish brown silk, without apparent twist (densities vary); approximately 34 per centimeter. *Weft:* Reddish brown silk, without apparent twist; 32 per centimeter. *Weave:* Tabby. Selvage: the wefts turn around the outermost warp. The faint floral design of the strip, originally in gold leaf, is indicated by the adhesive; occasional tiny flecks of gold remain. Slight variations in the repeat of the design indicate that it was painted and not printed. Plain end. *Warp:* Tan silk, without apparent twist; approximately 40–42 per centimeter. *Weft:* Tan silk, without apparent twist; considerable variation in the densities of the threads; approximately 24–40 per centimeter. *Weave:* Tabby; the uneven beating in of the wefts plus variations in their densities result in the wide range of thread counts. Selvage: the wefts turn around the outermost warp; the warps are more closely spaced toward the outer edge.

Unpublished.

54. *Peonies and Butterfly*

Needleloop embroidery, 21.6 × 26 cm (8½ × 10¼ in.)
Yuan dynasty (1279–1368)
The Metropolitan Museum of Art, New York. Purchase, Joseph E. Hotung Gift, 1987 (1987.277)

Against a dark green silk damask, woven with a cloud pattern, are embroidered tree peonies and, at the top, a butterfly. The embroidery is worked in the needlelooping technique over pieces of gilded paper. Superimposed on the motifs are a variety of diaper patterns, created by tiny holes from skipped stitches, through which the gilded paper shimmers. The embroidered motifs are enclosed within a gold border formed by strips of gilded paper held in place by open chain stitching.

A Yuan date has been assigned to this piece. The butterfly is a popular motif in Song decorative arts, but is not unknown in the Yuan period. The geometrized form of the blossoms, with three-lobed petals, is seen also on one of the embroideries on the Cleveland pendant (cat. no. 57). The same geometric treatment is accorded the lotus blossoms of the early Mongol *kesi* with aquatic birds and recumbent animal (cat. no. 16).

TECHNICAL ANALYSIS

GROUND: 1) Silk. *Warp:* Green silk, s, single; approximately 90 per centimeter. *Weft:* Green silk, s; paired; 32 per centimeter. *Weave:* Satin damask (5-end satin and reverse). 2) Paper.

EMBROIDERY: 1) Polychrome silk, z, 2-ply s. Colors: deep coral, medium coral, pink, brown, reddish brown, tan, light green, medium green, chartreuse, white, and pale, medium, and dark blue. 2) Gilded paper (coral bole is present under the metallic surface). 3) Gold thread composed of strips of gilded paper wrapped z around a white or yellow silk core, z; coral bole under the metallic surface. *Stitches:* Detached looping, s slant of closure, buttonhole, open chain, knot, and running (connecting the knots on the body of the butterfly).

COMMENTARY: The needleloop embroidery is composed of rows of detached buttonhole stitches worked over gilded paper. The tiny holes that form the diaper patterns were created by skipping stitches. Along the contours and details of the design, open chain stitches are worked over strips of gilded paper. The first row of detached loops along one side of the open chain stitches incorporates gold thread. Rows of loops overlap where one portion of the design borders another.

PUBLICATIONS: MMA *Recent Acquisitions* 1987–1988, p. 84, illus.; Berger 1989, p. 49, fig. 4; Milhaupt 1992, p. 75, fig. 3, p. 73; *Textiles* 1995–96, p. 84, illus.

54

55. Ocean, Rocks, and Peonies

Needleloop embroidery, 63.2 × 59.9 cm (24⅞ × 23⅝ in.)
Yuan–early Ming dynasty, 14th century
The Cleveland Museum of Art. Purchase from the J. H. Wade
Fund (1993.10)

Against a deep blue satin ground, a tree peony with symmetrically arranged flowers grows behind or out from three rocks that emerge from the sea. On either side of the tree peony, fungi grow along the shore. Buddhist and Daoist symbols fill the spaces between the leaves and peony flowers: a drum, a book, a *mala* (noose), musical stones, a swastika, cash, coral, a pair of rhinoceros-horn cups, and a pearl. Preserved in the lower portion is a segment of a bracketed border. The embroidery is executed in the needlelooping technique using silver thread and polychrome silk thread over silvered paper. The exceptionally high quality of the embroidery is apparent in the intricacy and variety of the diaper patterns that embellish the embroidered motifs.

Two themes have been combined in the embroidered design. The tree peony and rocks belong to the Chinese genre of plants growing among rocks.[1] Associated with gardens, these scenes often include ponds. In the case of the embroidery, however, the rocks emerge directly out of the sea, recalling the Daoist Islands of the Immortals in the Eastern Ocean. On an embroidery dating to the Yuan dynasty, the same combination of themes occurs (fig. 80). That embroidery, a complete cloud collar, has been combined with other embroideries to form a canopy. Repeated within each of the four lobes of the cloud collar is the image of ocean, rocks, and flowers. The bracketed border of the Cleveland embroidery delineates the lobe of a similar cloud collar, revealing the original context of the embroidery.

The embroidery with ocean, rocks, and peonies belongs to a small group of needleloop embroideries that are distinguished by the exceptional refinement of the technique and by the intricacy and variety of the diaper patterns (see also cat. no. 56).[2] The style of the water, rocks, and flowers, together with such motifs as the Buddhist and Daoist symbols and the floral imagery within a cloud collar which commonly occur in Chinese blue-and-white ceramics, points to a fourteenth-century date.

    1. For the earlier development of this theme, see Laing 1994.
    2. See also Spink & Son 1994, no. 23, p. 27.

TECHNICAL ANALYSIS

GROUND: 1) Satin. *Warp:* Blue silk, z, single; approximately 140 per centimeter. *Weft:* Dark brown silk, without apparent twist (three times the density of the warp ends); 45 per centimeter. *Weave:* 5-end satin. With the exception of a few small areas, the

Figure 80. Canopy made from the cloud collar of a robe. Yuan dynasty (1279–1368). Embroidery. Private collection

wefts have disintegrated, leaving the warps loose. 2) Paper under the satin ground fabric.

EMBROIDERY: 1) Polychrome silk, s, 2-ply z. Colors: red, coral, light coral, light pink, yellow, pale yellow, mustard yellow, white, light and dark brown, light, medium, and dark blue, blue green, and light green. 2) Silvered paper; bole (medium coral color) under silver. 3) Silver thread composed of strips of silvered paper wrapped z around a yellow silk core, z; bole (medium coral color) under silver. 4) Strips of silvered paper; bole (medium coral color) under silver. *Stitches:* Detached looping, s slant of closure, open chain, and knot.

COMMENTARY: The motifs are embroidered in the usual needle-looping technique, in which rows of detached loops are worked over silvered paper, attaching to the ground only along the contours of the design. The diaper patterns are created by tiny holes left by skipped stitches. The contours and details of the design are delineated by open chain stitches worked over strips of silvered paper. In many of the contours, the first row of detached loops formed on one side of the open chain stitches incorporates silver thread; in the delineation of details, the first row of detached loops on both sides of the open chain stitches incorporates silver thread.

Unpublished.

56. Phoenix and Tree Peony

Needleloop embroidery, 24.4 × 17.6 cm (9⅝ × 6⅞ in.)
China, 14th century
The Cleveland Museum of Art. Gift of David Tremayne (1992.95)

This fragment preserves most of the image of a phoenix in flight holding what is perhaps a pearl in its bill. Above the phoenix is a tree peony with two leaves, and to the right of the pearl are scrolling clouds. The ground along the right edge of the clouds is turned under and glued.

Despite the fragmentary condition of the embroidery, it is distinguished by an exceptional fineness of execution. Few other needleloop embroideries incorporate the variety of intricate diaper patterns that here ornament the components of each motif.

TECHNICAL ANALYSIS

GROUND: 1) Satin. *Warp:* Red silk, s; approximately 110 per centimeter. *Weft:* Red silk, s; approximately 40 per centimeter. *Weave:* 5-end satin. 2) Paper.

EMBROIDERY: 1) Polychrome silk, s, 2-ply z. Colors: yellow, green (unevenly faded), coral, pale pink, pale blue, deep blue, white, and cream. 2) Silvered paper with pink bole under (very tarnished) silver.[1] 3) Silver thread composed of strips of silvered paper (pink bole beneath silver) wrapped z around an ecru silk core, z. *Stitches:* Detached looping, s slant of closure, buttonhole, open chain, and knot.

COMMENTARY: The motifs are filled by row upon row of detached loops worked over silvered paper that once glittered through intricate diaper patterns of tiny holes formed by skipped loops. The edges and details of the design are delineated by open chain stitches worked over strips of silvered paper. These are executed through the silk satin ground fabric backed by paper. The first row of detached loops on one or both sides of the open chain stitches incorporates silver thread. Often the last row of loops in one part of the design overlaps the first row of stitches in the adjacent part of the design.

1. Examination in 1996 by Bruce Christman, chief conservator, The Cleveland Museum of Art, with an X-ray fluorescence spectrometer revealed the metallic surface to contain iron, zinc, copper, and a trace of silver.

Unpublished.

57. Pendant

Needleloop embroidery and knotting, 84.7 × 21.7 cm (33⅜ × 8½ in.)
China, 14th century
The Cleveland Museum of Art. Edward L. Whittemore Fund
(1994.20)

The pendant consists of a heading and six overlapping five-sided tiers. The tiers are embroidered with flowers (lotus, peony, morning glory[?], and others) in shades of coral, pink, green, blue, yellow, and white on different ground fabrics: blue gauze, coral satin, yellow damask, and blue damask. Embroidered in the needle-looping technique, the flowers are ornamented with diaper patterns formed by tiny holes through which the gilded paper sparkles. Gold bands frame the floral decoration of the tiers, while a narrow edging of plaited embroidery finishes both the four visible edges of each tier and the edges of the heading. The pendant is bordered with decoratively knotted green and coral cords. Three long tassels of coral, blue, and yellow silk are secured to the bottom tier, and a yellow cord for hanging is attached at the top. Tied to the yellow cord is a torn strip of what is most likely cotton with a resin seal. A small fragment of gilded paper (with bole) is glued to the heading. The pendant is lined with blue-green silk.

Pendants were used extensively in Buddhist settings, where they were attached to almost anything that called for decoration—ritual objects, canopies, valances, and pillars and other architectural elements. Although pendants were variously made, the construction in tiers of this example is known as early as the Tang dynasty (618–907).[1] The floral designs on the pendant are Chinese in style and in the choice of flowers, and the presence of the animal substrate in the sixth tier would tend to support production more specifically in northern China. A date within the fourteenth century is indicated by the style of the flowers.[2]

57

1. The altar valance found by Sir Aurel Stein at Dunhuang is ornamented with tiered pendants (Whitfield 1985, pl. 8). For pendants made without tiers, see Spink & Son 1989, nos. 7, 40.

2. See, for example, Krahl 1986, illus. on p. 237, and no. 178, p. 281; Misugi 1981, pl. 44; Addis 1978, pl. 35A.

TECHNICAL ANALYSIS

HEADING: *Warp:* Orange silk, z, single; thin. Step: 5 warps; 120 per centimeter. *Weft:* Foundation: orange silk, slightly z; thick (approximately 4 times the density of the warp). Supplementary: flat strips of silvery paper (the metallic content is unknown) with a coral bole between the metal and the paper. Pass: 2 foundation wefts and 1 supplementary weft. Step: 1 pass; 25 passes per centimeter. *Weave:* Satin with supplementary weft. Foundation: 5-end satin. Supplementary: twill (too few silver wefts remain to determine the binding).

NEEDLELOOP EMBROIDERED TIERS: Ground. *Tier 1:* 1) Gauze: *Warp:* blue silk, z; 76 per centimeter. *Weave:* Blue silk, z (slight twist), about twice the thickness of the warp; 20 per centimeter. *Weave:* Complex gauze based on unit of 4 warps. 2) Paper. *Tier 2:* 1) Satin. *Warp:* coral silk, z, single, approximately 114 warps per centimeter. *Weft:* Coral, without apparent twist, approximately twice the density of the warp; 36 per centimeter. *Weave:* 5-end satin. 2) Paper. *Tier 3:* 1) Damask. *Warp:* Yellow silk, z, single, approximately 94 per centimeter. *Weft:* Yellow silk, z, paired; 44 (pairs) per centimter. *Weave:* Damask, 5-end satin and reverse. 2) Paper. *Tier 4:* 1) Satin. *Warp:* Coral silk, z, single, approximately 120 per centimeter. *Weft:* Coral silk, without apparent twist, about twice the density of the warp; 36 per centimeter. *Weave:* 5-end satin. 2) Paper. *Tier 5:* 1) Damask. *Warp:* Blue silk, z, single; approximately 120 per centimeter. *Weft:* Blue silk, slightly z, about twice the density of the warp; 60 per centimeter. *Weave:* Damask, 5-end satin and reverse. 2) Paper. *Tier 6:* 1) Satin. *Warp:* Coral silk, z, single; approximately 120 per centimeter. *Weft:* Coral silk, without apparent twist, about twice the density of the warp; 38 per centimeter. *Weave:* 5-end satin. 2) Paper.

EMBROIDERY: Polychrome silk, s, 2-ply z; gilded paper, with silver-colored metal and bole under the gold layer;[1] flat strips of animal substrate, with black metallic surface and yellowish brown adhesive (tier 6 only); gold thread composed of strips of gilded paper, without bole, wrapped z around a white silk core, z (tiers 1 and 6 only); horsehair (tiers 2–6). *Stitches:* Buttonhole, detached looping, s slant of closure, open chain, and double chain (tiers 1–5).

COMMENTARY: The embroidery is worked over silk backed by paper. The fillings of flowers, leaves, and buds consist of rows of detached loops worked over pieces of gilded paper laid on top of the ground fabric. Stitches are skipped, leaving holes through which the gold paper sparkles. Open chain stitches over strips of gilded paper form the narrow framing borders of all the tiers; open chain stitches over strips of silvered animal substrate form the tendrils in tier 6. The flowers, buds, and leaves are delineated with buttonhole stitches in which are incorporated gold thread (tiers 1 and 6), horsehair (tiers 2–6), or silk threads, s, 2-ply z (tier 5). In tier 3, there is one area in which nothing is incorporated in the buttonhole stitches. Buttonhole stitches overlap the previously worked detached loops. The four visible edges of each tier are finished with a narrow edging of embroidered plaiting, using silk s, 2-ply z. Colors (from tiers 1–6): coral, blue, light coral (faded to tan), light gray green, pink, and blue.

LINING: *Warp:* Blue-green silk, z, single, very thin. *Weft:* Blue-green silk, z, thick. *Weave:* 5-end satin (loose weave with occasional treadling flaws resulting in warps passing over fewer than 4 wefts).

KNOTTED BORDER, HANGING CORD, AND TASSELS: The border is formed by green and coral silk cords decoratively knotted at intervals; each cord consists of plaited threads (silk, s, 2-ply z). The hanging cord is composed of plaited threads, each yellow silk, s, 2-ply z. The tassels are composed of bundles of coral, yellow, and blue silk (s, 2-ply z) threads.

CONSTRUCTION: The tiers are embroidered separately. The edges of the ground fabric of each tier are turned under on the reverse and sewn with running stitches using silk (s, 2-ply z) matching the color of the ground fabric. The tiers are arranged so that the bottom of each tier overlaps the top of the next; they are secured with coral silk thread (s, 2-ply z). The same thread is used to attach the heading to the top tier and to sew the lining to the back of the pendant.

1. X-ray fluorescence analyses suggest that the silver metal is lead that has been gilded (Bruce Christman, chief conservator, The Cleveland Museum of Art, June 3, 1994).

PUBLICATIONS: Barnett 1995, p. 142; *TSA Newsletter* 1995, p. 4.

58. *Thangka with Garuda*

Embroidery and painting, 114.6 × 44.5 cm (45⅛ × 17½ in.)
Embroidery: Yuan dynasty (1279–1368); painting: Tibet, 17th century
The Cleveland Museum of Art. Purchase from the J. H. Wade Fund (1989.11)

This composite *thangka* is composed of embroideries, damask, and a painting. The top and bottom panels are embroidered with the mythical bird Garuda hovering amid clouds over the Daoist Eastern Ocean, from which rise the three Islands of the Immortals. Part bird and part human, Garuda is crowned, wears a jeweled necklace and earrings, and holds a noose in his left hand and perhaps a mace in his right. His lower garment is secured around his waist by a sash, which flutters to either side. Superimposed over the embroidered motifs in the two panels are a variety of geometric designs finely worked in the damask darning technique. Both panels are complete, with finished edges.

In the middle of the *thangka* is a painting on silk of the Dhyanibodhisattva, Vajrapani, in his ferocious aspect.[1] Kneeling, he is surrounded by golden flames; below are Buddhist symbols, and above five *garuda* birds grasping snakes in their talons. The painting is bordered on either side by bands of green damask, with a design of flowers and butterflies. Applied to the damask are four fragments of needleloop embroidery, two embroidered with a tree peony and two with a rosette and part of a scroll border.

The *thangka* is backed by a plain, loosely woven green silk in fragmentary condition. Also preserved is a greenish yellow curtain that covers the central painting. The top edge of the upper panel is secured to a wooden dowel that was originally wrapped with silk and, at the ends, with leather. Although the original dowel at the bottom edge of the lowest panel has been replaced, the silk in which it was wrapped remains.[2] Two rawhide thongs are attached to the upper dowel for hanging.

The most important elements of the *thangka* are the two panels embroidered with Garuda, who appears frontally in a dramatic moment of arrested motion. This mythical bird, which originated in Hinduism as the vanquisher of *nagas* (serpents) and the vehicle of Vishnu, became in Buddhism the vehicle of Vajrapani.[3] He has the same Himalayan form—half human, half bird—as the Garuda on the arch of the Juyong Guan, the gateway built in 1342–45 northwest of Beijing in what is known as the Sino-Tibetan style, which developed during Mongol rule in China (see fig. 89). The Garuda panels are among the very few Sino-Tibetan embroideries that can be solidly attributed to the Yuan dynasty (1279–1368). Not only does the style correspond to that of the carving on the arch of the Juyong Guan, but actual and pseudo-Phagspa characters have been incorporated into the designs that ornament the body of Garuda in the top panel (see detail below).[4] Phagspa characters have not otherwise been observed in the designs of Yuan textiles, but they do occur on blue-and-white porcelain of the period.[5]

The two panels are the only examples of damask darning currently known from the Yuan dynasty. Despite their

Detail, cat. no. 58

58

191

uniqueness, however, they do share certain technical features with needleloop embroidery: the threads are polychrome silk, s, 2-ply z; the embroidery is worked over silvered paper; the metallic surface of the paper contains lead as well as silver; and the embroidery threads attach to the ground fabric only along the contours of the design. Superimposed on the different elements of the design, moreover, are a variety of geometric diaper patterns. The silvered paper here, however, unlike that in needleloop embroidery, is concealed by the embroidery. Why paper with a metallic surface was used remains a question.

The painting of Vajrapani in his terrible aspect in the central section is later in date. Heather Stoddard believes that it was painted by the Tenth Black Hat Karmapa, Choying Dorje (1604–1674), who is known to have been the painter of another *thangka* rendered in the same archaistic style.[6] The date and circumstances under which the painting was combined with the embroidered panels of Garuda to form the *thangka* are not known. Nevertheless, in the context of Lamaism, they are an appropriate combination. Not only is Garuda the vehicle of Vajrapani, but Vajrapani at times assumes the form of Garuda.[7]

1. Silk ground of painting. *Warp:* Dark blue silk, z, single; approximately 90 per centimeter. *Weft:* Dark blue silk (without apparent twist), 2–3 times the density of the warps; approximately 36 per centimeter. *Weave:* 4 / 1 satin.
2. The fabrics that covered the dowels were removed during conservation and are separately preserved.
3. Liebert 1976, p. 92.
4. The authors are grateful to Robert Tevis for bringing the characters to their attention, and to Morris Rossabi for confirming that they are Phagspa and pseudo-Phagspa.
5. Krahl 1986, p. 237 and no. 137; *Zhongguo taoci shi* 1982, p. 337.
6. Correspondence to Anne E. Wardwell, May 24, 1996. Although the painting by Choying Dorje is unpublished, an article about Choying by Dr. Stoddard is in preparation.
7. Liebert 1976, p. 92.

TECHNICAL ANALYSIS

GARUDA PANELS: Ground: *Warp:* Orange silk, z, single; approximately 120 per centimeter. *Weft:* Orange silk, without apparent twist, twice the density of the warp; approximately 50 per centimeter. *Weave:* 5-end satin. A selvage is preserved on both the top and bottom panels; at the inner selvage edge are three guard stripes formed by dark blue, coral, and pale coral silk (z, single) warps in the top panel and by navy blue, coral, and white silk (z, single) warps in the bottom panel; the selvage border, 5 millimeters wide, is composed of pale blue silk warps, z, paired or tripled, woven in a 3 / 1 z twill binding; the wefts turn around the outermost warp.

EMBROIDERY: 1) Polychrome silk, spun s, 2-ply z. Colors: coral, dark blue, medium blue, light blue, blue green, light green, medium green, pink, ecru, brown, white, cream, and yellow. 2) Cords: polychrome silk floss wrapped s around an ecru silk core, z. 3) Silvered paper: paper with metallic surface composed of lead, iron, and silver.[1] *Stitches:* Damask darning, couching, and open chain.

COMMENTARY: The embroidery is composed of damask darning worked over silvered paper that is completely concealed. The embroidery threads catch the ground fabric only along the contours of the design. Contours and details are delineated by couched silk cords. The outer edges of the panels are finished by open chain stitches worked over narrow strips of silvered paper.

NEEDLELOOP EMBROIDERIES: Rosettes. Ground: 1) Silk damask. *Warp:* Yellow silk, z; approximately 80 per centimeter. *Weft:* Yellow silk, z; approximately 65 per centimeter. *Weave:* Damask with 5-end satin ground and 1 / 2 z twill pattern. 2) Paper (only traces remain).

EMBROIDERY: 1) Polychrome silk, spun s, 2-ply z. Colors: coral, pink, yellow, blue, and white silk, s. 2) Silvered paper with coral bole under silver surface. 3) Silver thread composed of strips of silvered paper wrapped z around a white silk core, z; coral bole under metallic layer. *Stitches:* Detached looping, s slant of closure, and open chain.

COMMENTARY: The embroidery is worked over silk damask (reverse side up) backed with paper. The motifs are filled with rows of detached loops worked over pieces of silvered paper that originally sparkled through diaper patterns of tiny holes formed by skipped stitches. Delineating the motifs is an open chain stitch worked over strips of silvered paper. In the rosettes and the white leaf, the row of loops attached to the chain stitch incorporates silver thread; in the yellow leaf, yellow silk (s, 2-ply z) is used in place of the silver thread.

Sewn with running stitches to the top edges of the needleloop embroideries with rosettes are two narrow borders, one of gray silk (4 / 1 z twill with single gray silk warps, z, and gray silk wefts, without apparent twist), and the other of green silk (2 / 1 s twill with single green silk warps, z, and green silk wefts, z). The sewing thread is cream silk, s, 2-ply z, or z, 2-ply s.

NEEDLELOOP EMBROIDERIES: Tree peonies. Ground: 1) Silk damask. *Warp:* Deep blue silk, z, single; approximately 120 per centimeter. *Weft:* Deep blue silk, without apparent twist; approximately 50 per centimeter. *Weave:* Damask with 4 / 1 satin and reverse. 2) Satin: *Warp:* Navy blue silk, z, single; approximately 120 per centimeter. *Weft:* Navy blue silk, without apparent twist; approximately 70 per centimeter. *Weave:* 5-end satin. 3) Paper.

EMBROIDERY: 1) Polychrome silk, s, 2-ply z. Colors: coral, white, yellow, pink, ecru, and light green. 2) Silver thread formed by strips of silvered paper (coral bole under silver) wrapped z around a core of ecru silk, z. 3) Silvered paper, with coral bole under a metallic surface. *Stitches:* Detached looping, s slant of closure, open chain, knot, straight, and couching.

COMMENTARY: The needleloop embroidery is worked through a single layer of silk ground backed with paper. The motifs are filled with rows of detached loops worked over silvered paper. The diaper pattern of tiny holes is formed by skipped loops. The contours of the motifs and detailing are formed by open chain stitches over strips of silvered paper. The inner row of loops that attach to the chain stitches incorporates a silver thread. Sometimes there is an outer row of loops attached to the open chain stitches that also incorporates a silver thread. The tendrils of the peony are embroidered with open chain stitches worked over silver thread. The fan-shaped details are embroidered using straight stitches.

The fragmentary embroideries are bordered on three sides by a guard stripe formed by open chain stitches over strips of silvered

Detail, cat. no. 58

paper. The navy blue silk ground is sewn to the blue ground using running stitches just below the top guard stripe. It is embroidered with "fans" formed by straight stitches that alternate with triangles composed of loose, detached loops worked over silvered paper. The triangles terminate in crosses formed by straight stitches and couching, and the loops attach to the open chain stitches of the guard stripe.

DAMASK BORDERS OF CENTRAL SECTION: *Warp:* Green silk, s, single; approximately 96 per centimeter. *Weft:* Green silk, without apparent twist, twice the density of the warp; 40 per centimeter. *Weave:* Damask with 3/1 z twill for the ground and 1/7 z twill for the pattern.

CURTAIN: *Warp:* Greenish tan silk, without apparent twist; approximately 44 warps per centimter. *Weft:* Greenish tan silk, without apparent twist, twice the density of the warp; 24 per centimeter. *Weave:* Tabby; two complete selvages are preserved (loom width 56 centimeters);[2] the inner selvage edge is delineated by a

thick warp; the warps of the selvage border are closely spaced (approximately 52 per centimeter); the wefts turn around the outermost single warp.

SILK LINING: *Warp:* Blue-green silk, without apparent twist, single; approximately 20–30 per centimeter. *Weft:* Blue-green silk, without apparent twist, about twice the thickness of the warp; 14–21 per centimeter. *Weave:* Tabby; the warps are very unevenly spaced, and the wefts unevenly beaten in. The selvage is composed of a border in which the warps are closely spaced; the wefts turn around the outermost single warp.

1. Determined in 1988 by X-ray fluorescence spectrometry by Bruce Miller, formerly chief conservator, The Cleveland Museum of Art.
2. The side edges have been folded to accommodate the narrower width of the *thangka*.

PUBLICATIONS: Berger 1989, fig. 3, p. 48; Lee 1993, fig. 6, p. 226.

Detail, cat. no. 59

59. Welcoming Spring

Embroidery, 213.3 × 63.5 cm (84 × 25 in.)
Yuan dynasty (1279–1368)
The Metropolitan Museum of Art, New York. Purchase,
The Dillon Fund Gift, 1981 (1981.410)

This embroidery is remarkable for its size, complex imagery, and painstaking workmanship. The entire composition is worked in silk on a fine silk gauze. The major motifs—the boys, sheep and goats, and rocks—are worked in satin stitches with details and texture indicated by couched cords and directional satin stitches, while the background of earth, water, and sky, together with most of the flora, is in counted stitch. In the National Palace Museum, Taipei, there is an embroidered panel of virtually identical size, workmanship, and subject matter (fig. 81). This piece entered the Palace collection in the eighteenth century at the latest, as it is recorded in the *Shiqu baoji xubian*, part of the catalogue of the paintings collection (embroideries and tapestries based on paintings are traditionally included in the paintings collection) in

the Qing palace at the time of the Qianlong emperor (r. 1736–95). In the catalogue, the Palace embroidery is assigned a date in the Song dynasty (960–1279). In view of the Mongol attire of the boys and, further, because one of the goats is caparisoned for riding (an ancient custom of nomadic peoples for training children to ride), a date in the Yuan period (1279–1368) is proposed for the Metropolitan piece.

The title of this embroidery, as well as that of the one in the National Palace Museum, derives from the symbolism of the sheep and goats—*yang*, a homonym for *yang* (the spirit or breath of light and life), which returns at the end of winter and the beginning of spring.

TECHNICAL ANALYSIS

GROUND: Gauze. *Warp:* Faded coral silk, z; 28 per centimeter. *Weft:* Faded coral silk, without apparent twist; thick (3 times the diameter of the warps); 20 per centimeter. *Weave:* Gauze, unit of 2 warps.

Figure 81. *Kaitai tu* (Goats, symbol of spring). Yuan dynasty (1279–1368). Hanging scroll, embroidered gauze, 217.1 × 64.1 cm (85½ × 25¼ in.). National Palace Museum, Taipei

EMBROIDERY: 1) Polychrome silk, without twist. Colors: dark, medium, and light blue, orange, teal blue, cream, tan, pale green, brown, dark brown, white, yellow, and coral. 2) White silk, z, used for the details of the blue ram's hair. 3) Silk cords formed by silk floss wrapped around: a) a core of silk, s, 2-ply z (used singly or in pairs); b) horsehair; c) silk, z, 2-ply s (used singly or in pairs). *Stitches:* Encroaching satin, satin, outline, couching, fancy couching over satin stitches or over laid stitches, knot, and counted stitch.

COMMENTARY: The embroidery is primarily a combination of counted stitch and satin stitch. Details in satin-stitched areas are delineated by couched cords. To create clean edges for satin-stitched areas, the outermost stitches were either worked over a strand of horsehair that had been couched into place or the edges around the satin-stitched areas were finished with a couched cord.

PUBLICATIONS: Levinson 1983, pp. 496–97; MMA *Notable Acquisitions* 1981–1982, p. 75, illus.; *Textiles* 1995–96, pp. 74–75, illus.

60. Canopy

Embroidery, 143 × 135 cm (56¼ × 53⅛ in.)
Yuan dynasty (1279–1368)
The Metropolitan Museum of Art, New York. Purchase, Amalia Lacroze de Fortabat Gift, Louis V. Bell and Rogers Funds, and Lita Annenberg Hazen Charitable Trust Gift, in honor of Ambassador Walter H. Annenberg, 1988 (1988.82)

This embroidery can be dated with certainty to the middle Yuan period by reference to a relief carving on a stone slab found at the site of a Daoist temple in Beijing, the Fushouxingyuan Guan, founded in 1316 (fig. 82).[1] The combination of the two types of phoenixes seen both on the carving and on the embroidery was a popular motif in the Yuan period (1279–1368) and was most likely a Yuan innovation. During the Song dynasty (960–1279) both types belonged to two distinct "species," the *fenghuang* (fig. 83, upper register) and the *luan* (lower register), as illustrated in the *Yingzao fashi*, a manual for con-struction work and architectural decoration in use during the Song period.[2]

On the embroidery the vases in the four corners, from which issue floral scrolls, are an adaptation of a Sino-Tibetan motif (see cat. no. 26), but are here further sinicized. Not only is the form of the floral scrolls distinctly Chinese but the vases have been given Chinese bases with feet in the form of *ruyi* (fungus) heads (see detail on page 198).

The extravagant use of gold threads is, of course, typical of the Yuan period. Considering the refinement and delicacy of the polychrome silk embroidery, the unusually thick paper substrate for the gold threads is probably a deliberate measure to raise the gold patterning and to achieve the effect of relief (fig. 84). The use of silk cord under the satin stitches for the delineation of details is likely to be another means toward this end. Indeed, relief work is one

Figure 82. Relief carving. Yuan dynasty (1279–1368). Stone, 121 × 105 cm (47⅝ × 41⅜ in.)

Figure 83. Illustrations from *Yingzao fashi*, chap. 33, leaf 10 (1989 reprint of the Song edition)

60

Detail, cat. no. 60

of the hallmarks of Yuan decorative arts. The type of complex gauze used for the ground, which is based on a unit of four warps, is often found in textiles of the Liao to the Yuan dynasty, though it became less common in later periods.

1. Institute of Archaeology 1972, p. 25. See also "Short Introduction" 1972, no. 1, p. 85, and illustration on back cover.
2. *Yingzao fashi*, chap. 33, leaf 10.

TECHNICAL ANALYSIS

EMBROIDERY: Ground: Gauze. *Warp:* Purple silk, without apparent twist; single; approximately 52 per centimeter. *Weft:* Purple silk, without apparent twist (2–3 times the density of the warp); 17 per centimeter. *Weave:* Complex gauze based on a unit of 4 warps. 1) Polychrome silk floss, without apparent twist. Colors: pale and medium green, light and medium chartreuse, pale and medium pink, light coral, mustard yellow, lemon yellow, blue, teal blue, deep blue green, and white. 2) Gold thread (fig. 84) composed of thick strips of paper gilded on one side; an orange-red bole is visible under the layer of gold. 3) Silk cord: used under the satin stitches to delineate motifs (and therefore invisible). *Stitches:* Long and short, satin, couching, split (in single and double rows), and knot. The flowers, leaves, and clouds are filled with long and short and satin stitches; split stitches are used to delineate motifs and to

Figure 84. Micrographic details, cat. no. 60

define the stems of flowers and leaves; couching is used for the gold thread; knots occur on some of the flowers; details are sometimes delineated by working satin stitches over a silk cord or thread.

LINING: *Warp:* Blue-green silk, z, 2-ply s; 62 per centimeter. *Weft:* Blue-green silk, slight s twist; the same thickness as the warp; 30 per centimeter. *Weave:* Tabby.

CONSTRUCTION: The gauze ground consists of three panels (approximately 48, 50, and 47 centimeters wide) embroidered separately and joined with purple thread. The canopy is lined with blue-green silk.

PUBLICATIONS: MMA *Recent Acquisitions* 1987–1988, p. 85, illus.; Simcox, "Tracing the Dragon," 1994, p. 40, fig. 4, p. 37.

61. Celestial Musician

Embroidery, 66.5 × 45 cm (26⅛ × 17¾ in.)
Central Asia, 14th century
The Cleveland Museum of Art. John L. Severance Fund
(1987.145)

On this fragmentary embroidery is preserved a Buddhist goddess standing on a lotus support and playing a bowed lute. Dark blue in color, she is surrounded by a rainbow mandorla articulated by alternately wavy and curving rays. Wearing a skirt and a long scarf that drapes about her shoulders, loops at the left hip, drapes across her skirt, and flutters to the right, she is crowned with an elaborate headdress and adorned with festive jewelry.

Another goddess, holding a bowl of curds, survives from the embroidery to which the Cleveland fragment originally belonged (fig. 85). That figure, similarly clad, is yellow in color. The objects held by the embroidered figures suggest that they are Mahasahasrapramardani (hearing) and Mahamantrausarini (taste), two of the Buddhist protective goddesses known as Pancharakshas and associated with the five senses.[1]

A number of stylistic details in the two embroideries—the extension of the eye beyond the outline of the face, the hairstyle and the form of the crown, the nervously

ruffled hem, the fluttering, scrolling scarves, the rainbow halo, and the halo articulated with rays—indicate an attribution to Central Asia, where such conventions were established as early as the Tang dynasty (618–907).[2] This attribution is further supported by the upper ground fabric, which is cotton, a fiber long used for the ground fabrics of embroideries produced in Central Asia.[3]

The two embroidered figures closely resemble, in anatomical drawing, costume, hairstyle, crown, and jewelry, a goddess depicted in a painting in the Metropolitan Museum, *Shadakshari Lokeshvara with Deities and Monks* (fig. 86). The painting can be assigned to the fourteenth or, at the very latest, the early fifteenth century on the basis of stylistic elements and, particularly, by the representation of two lamas identified by inscriptions and known to have lived in the fourteenth century.[4] The painting is believed to have been executed in Tibet. Given its similarities to the embroideries, a Tibetan attribution for the latter cannot be entirely ruled out. Nevertheless, it seems much

Figure 85. Offering figure. Central Asia, 14th century. Embroidery, 66 × 45 cm (26 × 17¾ in.). Chris Hall Collection Trust, Jobrenco Limited Trustee

Figure 86. *Shadakshari Lokeshvara with Deities and Monks*, detail. Tibet, late 14th–early 15th century. Gold, ink, and colors on cloth, 102.5 × 79.4 cm (40⅜ × 31¼ in.). The Metropolitan Museum of Art, New York. Gift of Margery and Harry Kahn, 1985 (1985.390.3)

more likely that the painting and the embroideries were based on similar Central Asian prototypes, and that the embroideries were, indeed, executed in Central Asia.

1. Foucher 1905, p. 99; Hong Kong 1995, p. 134; Dayton 1990, p. 264.
2. See, for example, New York 1982, no. 117; Sirén 1956, fig. 1; Whitfield 1982–83, vol. 1, pls. 8-6, 9-10, 11-13, 15, and fig. 71; vol. 2, pl. 39.
3. For example, the embroideries in the Museum für indische Kunst, Berlin, that were excavated in the Turfan region: III 6169a-d, III 7042, and III 6184.
4. Kossak 1994, p. 112.

TECHNICAL ANALYSIS

GROUND: Fabric 1: Cotton. *Warp and weft:* Ecru cotton, z; 30 × 26 per centimeter. *Weave:* Tabby. Fabric 2: Silk and cotton cloth that appears to have been composed of stripes of cotton warps(?) and silk wefts(?), the cotton warps and silk wefts bound in tabby, and the silk warps and wefts forming an extended tabby. *Warp* (?): Cotton, z, 30 per centimeter; ecru silk, s, 70 or 120 per centimeter. *Weft* (?): Ecru silk, s; 32 per centimeter. *Weave:* Cotton warps(?) alternating with silk warps(?) to form a striped fabric. The cotton warps(?) and silk wefts(?) are bound in tabby; the silk warps(?) and silk wefts(?) are bound either in tabby (70 warps per centimeter) or in a warp(?)-faced (120 warps per centimeter) extended tabby, each warp(?) passing over and under two wefts(?). Fabric 3: Cotton. *Warps and wefts:* Cotton, z, very unevenly twisted; 21 × 19 per centimeter. *Weave:* Tabby.

EMBROIDERY: 1) Polychrome silk, z. Colors: ecru, pale green, white, pale blue, mustard yellow; polychrome silk, s; deep blue, dark blue, coral, yellow, dark brown, very pale pink, pale yellow, pinkish tan (faded from red), and green. 2) Metal thread composed of paper substrate coated with a coral bole and wrapped z around a heavy coral or ecru silk core, plied z (no gold or silver remains). *Stitches:* Outline, couching, satin, and long and short.

CONSTRUCTION: The embroidery was worked over two layers. The top layer is cotton fabric 1. The bottom layer is composed of fabrics 2 and 3, which have been pieced together. Much of fabric 2 has been stained red. The gold (or silver?) threads are couched in pairs or singly, and edged with outline stitches. Outline stitches are used for all contours and long and short stitches or satin stitches for the filling.

PUBLICATIONS: *CMA Handbook* 1991, p. 65; Wardwell 1992–93, p. 250.

62. Thangka with Yamantaka

Embroidery and weaving
146 × 76 cm (57½ × 29⅞ in.)
Ming dynasty (1368–1644), early 15th century
The Metropolitan Museum of Art, New York. Purchase,
Lila Acheson Wallace Gift, 1993 (1993.15)

This hanging vertical scroll is made up of a large embroidered *thangka* in silk and gilt thread on a dark blue satin ground. It is framed on the sides by various woven fabrics, and at the bottom is a trapezoidal panel embroidered in the same technique as the *thangka*. These component pieces are stitched together, and most of the original stitching has survived intact.

The central image of the *thangka* is Yamantaka, also known as Vajrabhairava in this representation (see page 100). He stands on a double-lotus base on top of an elaborate pedestal. In front of the pedestal Mahakala, at left, holds in his raised hands a broad-blade sword of wisdom and a trident-shaped *khatvanga* staff and in his front hands (like Yamantaka) a *vajra* chopper and a *kapala* (skull bowl); Kubera, in armor, holds a tasseled staff in one hand and a mongoose in the other; and Yama (or Dharmaraja), at right, holds a skull-headed club and a lasso. Above Yamantaka is a *garuda* flanked by *nagarajas* in the form of youths with serpent bodies. On either side of Yamantaka are two columns partially obscured by lotus plants that emerge from vases in front of the columns. The tops of the columns support two *makaras* spewing flowers and jewels, whose foliate tails rise up to meet the *nagarajas*. At the top left is the bodhisattva Manjushri, the benign form of Yamantaka, and at the top right is a lama wearing a five-leaved black crown surmounted by a large red jewel. Next to these figures are two celestial beings borne on clouds and holding initiation vessels. In the trapezoidal panel below are eight dancing *dakinis* on open lotuses connected to scrolling stems issuing from a vase in the center. The four on the right bear sacrificial gifts: (from right) a shell, a lamp, a mountain, and a flower. The second figure from the left plays a *pipa* (lute); to the right a dancer holds a string of

flowers; and the light blue figure farther to the right holds a *vajra* and a bell. Tibetan inscriptions appear above the scroll and on the reverse. A preliminary reading has revealed neither dates nor names.

This work is one of the supreme achievements of the embroiderer's art in China. It is unsurpassed in the fineness of the silk floss used, the high density of the stitches, the brilliant and subtle coloration, and the ingenious use of a variety of embroidery techniques to achieve chiaroscuro and textural effects. It is what may be called needle painting. The complex composition is worked mostly in long and short and satin stitches using brightly tinted untwisted silk floss that has a soft glossy sheen. Shading and modeling are achieved by varying the direction of the stitches so that, when viewed from different angles, some sections of the surface are highlighted while other sections appear duller. Shading is also achieved by the use of the long and short stitch, while the interlocking satin stitch is used for both shading and color gradation. The split stitch is used to indicate details on the faces of Yamantaka. Raised outlines of individual pattern elements are worked over silk cords or horsehair, or are indicated by couched gilt thread or by outline stitches. Gilt threads are couched for the golden crowns of Yamantaka. Where elements of the same color overlap, as in the legs of Yamantaka, the boundary is raised by means of an underlying horsehair. Horsehair is used also for the rippled surface of large stretches of the background. The satin stitch is raised in certain areas, such as the eyes and jewels, by working it over an underpadding of paper or cloth. Fine jewelry is indicated by the use of knots and fancy couching of gold thread. Brocading patterns are simulated by fancy couching over laid floss, as in the trousers of the *nagarajas* and the dancing goddesses in

Detail, cat. no. 62

Figure 87. *Thangka* with Yamantaka. Ming dynasty (1368–1644), Yongle reign (1403–24). Embroidery, 79 × 63 cm (31⅛ × 24¾ in.). Potala Palace, Lhasa

Figure 88. Portrait of Sakya Ye-shes. Ming dynasty (1368–1644), Xuande period (1426–35). Silk tapestry (*kesi*). Sera Monastery, Lhasa

the lower panel. Flat gold strips are used to represent ornaments such as bracelets. In short, the finely drawn and elaborate design is brilliantly realized by the embroiderer. Although a number of embroidered *thangkas* of the same subject are known, including another of Ming date preserved in the Potala Palace in Lhasa (fig. 87), none of them approaches the Metropolitan piece in sheer artistic and technical quality.

The dating of this embroidery is based on reference to *thangkas* in similar style and technique, including one that carries a donation mark of the Yongle reign (1403–24).[1] There are other reasons for assigning a date in the Yongle reign, which involve the identification of the lama at the top right corner. The representation of this lama finds close parallels in a *kesi* portrait of Sakya Ye-shes (1352–1435), a disciple of Tsong-kha-pa (1357–1419), the founder of the Gelugs-pa order of Tibetan Buddhism (fig. 88). In 1413, Sakya Ye-shes visited the Yongle emperor and stayed at the Chinese capital (presumably Nanjing) until 1416.[2] In 1418, he founded the Sera Monastery, situated at the foot of a mountain north of Lhasa.[3] It was in the Sera Monastery that the *kesi* portrait of Sakya Ye-shes was kept until recently.[4] Even in a poor reproduction, it can readily be seen that the *kesi* portrait shares many of the essential features of the portrait on the embroidery, including the hand gestures, the hat, and the robe. Also woven on the *kesi* is Sakya Ye-shes's seal and full title, conferred on him by the Xuande emperor in 1434 on his last visit to the Ming capital—then in Beijing. Both the portrait on the *kesi* and that on the embroidery must have been based on an official portrait of Sakya Ye-shes—in which he was depicted wearing the hat, or crown, and the robe, which the Yongle emperor conferred on him when he left for Tibet in 1416.[5] It is not surprising to find the portrait of Sakya Ye-shes on a Yamantaka *thangka*, as his teacher, Tsong-kha-pa, was supposed to have been an incarnation of Manjushri, and Manjushri/Yamantaka is central to the art and teaching of the Gelugs-pa order.

It may be mentioned as a matter of incidental interest that the iconography of Yamantaka's setting is very much in the Sino-Tibetan style—exemplified by the ornamentation on the Juyong Guan, northwest of Beijing, which was built at that time—which was fully developed by the middle of the fourteenth century (fig. 89).[6] This style owes much to the art of the Sakya order, which played an important role in the art, politics, and religion of the Yuan dynasty. It is characterized by elaborate shrines with ornate columns from which emerge foliate arches with swirling scrolls and volutes bearing mythical creatures, and is certainly applicable both to the Juyong Guan and to the embroidered *thangka* in the Metropolitan Museum.

1. Pal 1994, pp. 62–63.

Detail, cat. no. 62

Figure 89. Juyong Guan, stone gate northwest of Beijing. Yuan dynasty (1279–1368), ca. 1350

Detail, cat. no. 62

2. *Mingshi*, Biography of Daci Fawang, vol. 28, chap. 331, p. 8577. See also Karmay 1975, pp. 80–82.

3. Wang Furen 1982, p. 198.

4. Wang Yi 1960, illus. The portrait is reported to have been removed to the Bureau for the Preservation of Relics of the Tibet Autonomous Region (Ou Chaogui 1985).

5. *Mingshi*, vol. 28, chap. 331, p. 8577.

6. The Juyong Guan, a gateway situated northwest of Beijing, occupied an important strategic position along the Great Wall in the defense of the Beijing area in early historic times. In the Yuan period, when the areas north and south of the gate were in the same empire, the gate was a ceremonial arch on the imperial highway between Shangdu, the Upper Capital, and Daidu, the Great Capital. For a detailed study of the Juyong Guan, see Murata 1957.

TECHNICAL ANALYSIS

EMBROIDERY (center): Ground: Dark blue silk. *Warp:* Dark blue silk, z, single; approximately 100 per centimeter. *Weft:* Composite weft composed of 4 wefts, each dark blue silk, z (not plied together); 32 per centimeter. *Weave:* 5-end satin. 1) Polychrome silk, lightly twisted s. Colors: red, deep rose, pink, light and dark blue, teal blue, light, medium, and dark green, mustard yellow, yellow, black (very dark brown?), brown, and gray. 2) Wrapped gold thread composed of strips of gilded paper wrapped z around a white silk core, spun z. No coral bole apparent. 3) Flat gold thread composed of strips of gilded paper; a pink bole is used under the metal surface. 4) Cords: a) white, cream, or green silk yarn, s, 2-ply z. b) horsehair wrapped with silk. 5) White thread, silk, s, 2-ply z (couched for delineation of details of Yamantaka). *Stitches:* Long and short, encroaching satin, satin, outline, couching, split, knot, fancy couching over satin stitch, split and knot stitches over satin stitch, and split and outline stitches over encroaching satin stitch.

COMMENTARY: The embroidery is oriented in the warp direction of the ground fabric. Only the motifs of the design are embroidered; otherwise, the deep blue ground shows. Contours of motifs and details are delineated by horsehair over which are worked interlocked satin stitches, gold thread, outline stitches using silk, couched silk thread, or knots.

EMBROIDERY (bottom): Ground: Satin. *Warp:* Tan (faded from red) silk, z, single; approximately 90–100 per centimeter. *Weft:* Composite weft composed of 4 wefts of tan silk (faded from red), z (the yarns are not plied); 36 per centimeter. *Weave:* 5-end satin. 1) Polychrome silk, slight s twist. Colors: pale, medium, and dark blue, teal blue, pale, medium, and dark green, bright coral red, pink, yellow, white, and brown. 2) Wrapped gold thread composed of strips of gilded paper wrapped z around a white silk core, z. No bole apparent. 3) Flat gold thread composed of flat strips of gilded paper; pink bole visible under layer of gold. 4) Silk cord: silk, spun s, 2-ply z. *Stitches:* Long and short, encroaching satin, outline, couching, fancy couching over satin stitch or laid floss, split, split stitch over laid floss, and knot.

COMMENTARY: The design is embroidered at right angles to the warp of the ground fabric. The figures and motifs are outlined with gold thread or silk, or finished by a strand of horsehair under the outer edges of encroaching satin stitches. Details are indicated by couched gold thread, fancy couching, and knot.

MOUNTING FABRIC (above and below *thangka*): Against a light blue ground is a gold pattern of parallel undulating vines with peonies and leaves. In the interstices between the vines are auspicious symbols. There are six vines across the loom width. *Warp:* The single foundation warps are light blue silk, z. The supplementary warps are light blue silk, z. There are 4 foundation warps to every supplementary warp. The step is 4 foundation warps, and the count is approximately 100 foundation and 20 supplementary warps per centimeter. *Weft:* The foundation wefts are composite, each consisting of 4 blue silk z wefts. The supplementary wefts are gold thread composed of flat strips of gilded paper with coral bole under the gold leaf. The pass consists of one composite foundation and one supplementary weft. The step is one pass, and there are 16 passes per centimeter. *Weave:*

Lampas. The foundation weave is 1/2 z twill; the supplementary warps lie by the side of the foundation warps. The supplementary weave is tabby. Two selvages, each one centimeter wide, are preserved with a loom width of 61 centimeters: the inner 4 millimeters consist of paired warps (blue silk, z); the outer 6 millimeters consist of paired warps, each plied s; the binding is 1/2 z twill; the foundation wefts turn around the outermost warp; on the reverse, the gold supplementary wefts are cut 6 millimeters from the outermost edge.

MOUNTING FABRIC (on either side of *thangka*): Against a deep blue ground are gold clouds and auspicious symbols. *Warp:* The single foundation warps are dark blue silk, z; the supplementary warps are dark blue silk, z. There are 5 foundation warps to each supplementary warp, the step is 5 foundation warps, and the count is approximately 105 foundation warps and 22 supplementary warps per centimeter. *Weft:* The foundation wefts are dark blue silk without apparent twist; the supplementary wefts are gold thread composed of flat strips of gilded paper with coral bole under the gold leaf. Pass: 1 foundation weft to 1 supplementary weft. Step: 1 pass; 22 passes per centimeter. *Weave:* Lampas. The foundation weave is a 2/1 z twill, the supplementary weave is 1/2 s twill.

RED SILK BORDERS: The warps are coral red silk, z, single. The wefts are coral red silk without apparent twist. There are approximately 88 warps and 44 wefts per centimeter. The weave is a 5-end satin.

LINING (tie-dyed): The warps and wefts are silk without apparent twist; approximately 23 warps and 21 wefts per centimeter. The weave is tabby. The selvage is also a tabby weave, but with more warps per centimeter; the wefts turn around the outermost warp.

LINING (plain): The single warps and wefts are yellow silk without apparent twist. There are 24 warps and 18 wefts per centimeter. The weave is tabby. There is a simple selvage: the wefts turn around the outermost warp.

PUBLICATION: MMA *Recent Acquisitions* 1992–1993, pp. 86–87.

63. *Thangka with the Seventh Bodhisattva*

Embroidery
43.8 × 19.7 cm (17¼ × 7¾ in.)
Early Ming dynasty, 1368–1424
The Cleveland Museum of Art. Purchase from the J. H. Wade Fund (1991.2)

In this embroidered *thangka*, divided by bands of classic scroll design into three registers, the principal figure, a bodhisattva wearing the five-petaled crown and jeweled ornaments and garments of his rank and with hands held in a *mudra*, is shown seated on a lotus throne. His red color and the jar supported by a lotus next to his right arm suggest that he is Amitaprabha, Infinite Light.[1] On either side is a jar of immortality (or abundance) that bears a column surmounted by a *makara* spewing flowers and jewels. The floral tails of these fanciful water creatures support an arch of wish-fulfilling creepers (*kalpa lata* or *kalpa vriksha*) over the bodhisattva. This setting derives from the Nepali-Tibetan tradition of *thangka* painting, and often occurs in a much more complex form, as, for example, in the *thangka* with Yamantaka (cat. no. 62).

63

Figure 90. Drawing of Buddhist temple interior, showing placement of painted consecration *thangkas*

In the top register is a sacred parasol, flanked by clouds and offering protection from the heat of evil desires. The lower, and largest, register shows a vase that contains three vertically arranged lotuses, symbols of Amitaprabha's divine origin and purity. From the lower lotus spring four delicate scrolling vines terminating in lotus flowers that support Buddhist symbols: Mount Meru (center of the Buddhist universe), a conch (symbolizing the blessedness of turning to the right), a ritual bowl of curds, and a stupa. The workmanship and high quality of the embroidery are comparable to that of the *thangka* with Yamantaka and the *kashaya* with the Thousand Buddhas (cat. nos. 62 and 64). A resist-dyed silk curtain, intended to protect the *thangka*, is attached to the top edge.

Penned on the reverse is a Tibetan inscription that translates as "the Seventh Bodhisattva." Like most *thangkas*, this one was made as part of a set. Another *thangka* from that set, now in the Indianapolis Museum of Art, is inscribed on the reverse, "the Tenth Bodhisattva." That figure's white color, *mudra*, and sword identify him as Manjushri.[2] In other respects the two *thangkas* are identical. Because Tantric Buddhist texts classify bodhisattvas into groups of six, eight, and sixteen, the original set must have included fourteen additional *thangkas* with bodhisattvas.

In addition to the Cleveland and Indianapolis *thangkas*, at least ten other small *thangkas*, apparently from five different sets, are known.[3] All are embroidered with polychrome silk floss and gold thread on a deep blue silk ground and have the same tripartite divisions delineated by classic scroll borders. Moreover, all have a sacred umbrella in the upper register, a figure within an arch in the middle register, and lotuses in the bottom register. They vary, however, in the figures depicted in the middle registers (buddhas, gods, and *lokapalas*) and in the composition of the arches over the figures, in the details of the upper registers, in

the choice of the symbols or Sanskrit letters supported by the lotuses in the lower register, and in the use of a vase or a mountain to contain the lotus vines. In addition, there are differences in technical and artistic quality within the group.

The *thangkas* are similar in both size and subject matter to seven painted *thangkas* that have survived from a late-fourteenth- to early-fifteenth-century set of at least twenty-four consecration *thangkas*.[4] This suggests that the embroidered *thangkas* may also have served as consecration materials for a Tibetan Buddhist temple, in which case they would probably have hung along the interior beams and side walls of a temple (fig. 90). Their nearly perfect state of preservation indicates that, with one exception, they were hung only briefly and otherwise kept in storage, where they were protected from light, smoke, and abrasion.

1. Mallmann 1975, pp. 96–97.
2. Simcox, "Tracing the Dragon," 1994, fig. 11.
3. Cleveland 1994, p. 344; Reynolds, "Silk," 1995, figs. 2–8. (The *thangka* illustrated in figure 7 does not belong to the same set as those in figures 2–6 and 8.)
4. Dayton 1990, pp. 346–48, no. 119.

TECHNICAL ANALYSIS

EMBROIDERY: Ground: Satin. *Warp:* Navy blue silk, s, single; approximately 80 per centimeter. *Weft:* Dark navy blue silk, without apparent twist; approximately 28 per centimeter. *Weave:* 5-end satin. 1) Polychrome silk, without apparent twist. Colors: coral, pink, pale pink, deep, medium, and light green, white, deep blue, light blue, mustard yellow, tan, pinkish tan, deep teal blue, chartreuse, gray green, and dark forest green. 2) Cable: red silk, z, 2-ply s, and s, 2-ply z. 3) Cord: silk floss wrapped around a single strand of horsehair.[1] 4) Couching thread: red silk, s, 2-ply z. 5) Gold thread composed of strips of gilded paper[2] wrapped z around a yellow or an ecru silk core, z, with translucent yellowish tan adhesive. *Stitches:* Long and short, encroaching satin, outline, split, knot, couching, fancy couching over satin stitch, and running. Only the motifs are embroidered through the dark blue satin ground.

LINING: Tabby weave. *Warp*(?): Red silk, s (slight twist); 30 per centimeter. *Weft*(?): Red silk composed of multiple untwisted strands, unevenly twisted s (slight twist); 17–19 per centimeter.

CURTAIN: Tabby weave. *Warp*(?): Silk without apparent twist; the densities of the yarns vary greatly; 24 per centimeter. *Weft*(?): Silk, slight s twist, thicker than most warps; 15 per centimeter. Colors: yellow, pale orange, dark blue green, and green. The floral pattern of the silk is resist-dyed, probably using a clamp resist. The fabric was folded before dyeing.

1. Identified by Bruce Christman, chief conservator, The Cleveland Museum of Art, January 10, 1991.
2. Ibid.

PUBLICATIONS: Wardwell 1992–93, fig. 9, p. 251; Cleveland 1994, no. 43, pp. 342–45; Reynolds, "Silk," 1995, no. 11, p. 93.

64. Kashaya

Embroidery, 118.8 × 302 cm (46¾ × 118⅞ in.)
Ming dynasty (1368–1644), early 15th century
The Cleveland Museum of Art. Leonard C. Hanna, Jr. Fund
(1987.57)

A *kashaya*, or Buddhist priest's robe, made with twenty-five columns was reserved for special ceremonial occasions and worn by the highest official of a monastery. The iconographic program of this sumptuously embroidered robe is based on the doctrines of Mahayana Buddhism. The twenty-five vertical columns ornamented with swastikas and lotuses are separated and subdivided by small buddhas seated on lotuses amid clouds. The theme of the Thousand Buddhas expresses the idea that the cosmic consciousness of the Buddha can be attained by every individual and, hence, is limitless. In the corners of the *kashaya* are the Four Heavenly Kings, believed to reside on the slopes of Mount Meru, the center of the universe. Bestowers of wealth, success, and victory, they are also the guardians of the four quarters (clockwise, beginning in the upper right): Vaishravana (north), Dhrtarashtra (east), Virudhaka (south), and Virupaksha (west). Centered at the top of the *kashaya* are the Three Jewels, symbols of the teacher, the teaching, and the community of Buddhism, which provide refuge from the endless suffering of repeated births and deaths. Similarly situated at the bottom is the Wheel of the Law, whose three revolutions signify the teachings given to the early disciples and the two principal philosophical schools of Mahayana Buddhism. Finally, repeated along the outer borders of the *kashaya* are the Five Transcendent Buddhas, who symbolize the purity of the five elements, the five directions, the five colors, the five addictions, and the five wisdoms.

The twenty-five vertical columns are embroidered directly onto the gauze ground. The remainder of the embroidery is worked separately and applied. Being pieced together is an important feature of *kashaya* that signifies the vow of poverty taken in the sixth century B.C. by Shakyamuni, the founder of Buddhism, and thereafter by Buddhist priests. The ties and buttons required to secure the robe when worn draped about the body have been preserved. The buddhas and the king in the upper left corner, oriented upside down when the garment is viewed flat, would appear right-side up when the garment is worn.

This *kashaya* is one of several that were preserved until recently in Tibet and that range in date from the Ming (1368–1644) through the Qing (1644–1911) dynasty.[1] The appearance of the theme of the Thousand Buddhas as a decorative program on a garment long predates these, however. It first occurs in the fifth-century carving of Vairochana at Yungang, a Buddhist site in northern Shanxi Province.[2] The only surviving embroidery with the theme that spans the long centuries between the date of this carving and that of the robes preserved in Tibet is a Tang fragment found by Sir Aurel Stein at Dunhuang, which may have been a hanging rather than a garment.[3] An early-fifteenth-century date for the Cleveland robe is indicated by the costumes of the Four Heavenly Kings and by similarities in style and technique with those of the *thangkas* with Yamantaka and with the Seventh Bodhisattva (cat. nos. 62 and 63). The technical expertise and artistic refinement of the *kashaya* leave little doubt that it was made in an imperial embroidery workshop in China. That some of the gold embroidery thread was made with an animal substrate and some with a paper substrate suggests that the

workshop was in the north, in Beijing, where gold thread made with an animal substrate had long been in use (see page 108 and note 18 on page 110).

In all likelihood, the *kashaya* was either commissioned by a major Tibetan monastery or sent by the Chinese court to an important Tibetan lama as an imperial gift. The condition of the Cleveland robe suggests that it was used only rarely, if ever, and was otherwise stored, folded, over a long period of time. Not only does it show no signs of wear, but at some point in time, the reverse (and hence the ties and buttons) was covered by a lining.

Kashaya were not always used as garments. One embroidered *kashaya*, for example, is known to have been given in the eleventh century by two Chinese monks to Mahabodhi Temple in Bodh Gaya, to be spread over the throne of the Buddha.[4]

1. Reynolds 1990, and Reynolds, "'Thousand Buddhas,'" 1995; Wentworth 1987.
2. Huntington 1986, figs. 2, 4.
3. Stein 1921, vol. 4, pl. cv; for color illustrations, see Reynolds 1990, fig. 11, and Paris 1995, no. 154.
4. Liu Xinru 1995, p. 34.

TECHNICAL ANALYSIS

GROUND: Counted stitch (twenty-five columns): Plain gauze, with a unit of two warps. *Warp:* Light coral silk, without twist (the apparent s and z twists were caused by the manipulation of the warps on the loom), thin; 32 per centimeter. *Weft:* Deep coral silk, without apparent twist, thick; 19 per centimeter. *Applied embroidery:* Tabby silk: warps and wefts are yellow silk, without apparent twist (no count possible).

EMBROIDERY: 1) Silk floss. Colors: shades of blue, green, yellow, red, tan, orange, black, gray, and white; occasionally white and black floss are twisted together. 2) Cords: silk floss wrapped around a z-twisted white silk thread. 3) Cables: two silk threads,

each s and plied z, or z and plied s. 4) White thread, z. 5) Wrapped gold thread composed of strips of animal substrate coated with translucent brown adhesive and gilded;[1] wrapped z around a yellow silk core. 6) Flat gold thread composed of strips of paper of varying widths, coated with bole and gilded. *Stitches:* Counted stitch (the twenty-five columns), encroaching satin, knot, couching, fancy couching, split, and chain (the applied embroidery).

CONSTRUCTION: The *kashaya* is composed of a single layer of red gauze, parts of which are embroidered with swastikas and lotuses to form the twenty-five columns. The Thousand Buddhas, clouds, Four Heavenly Kings, Wheel of the Law, Three Jewels, and Transcendent Buddhas were embroidered separately and then sewn to bands of red gauze that were, in turn, sewn to the gauze ground. Buttons and ties were attached to the back side to secure the robe when worn. At some point, a lining was added.

The applied motifs were embroidered on a yellow silk tabby ground. To create defined edges, white silk thread was laid along contours and embroidered over with satin stitches; cords were couched to the surface of the embroidery to delineate details of the figures and other motifs. Wrapped and flat gold threads were reserved for details of the Four Heavenly Kings. After embroidery, the motifs were cut from the silk tabby, the narrow edges were turned under, and the back sides were covered with paste and backed with paper. Occasional details were embroidered after the paper backing had been applied. The vertical bands with the Thousand Buddhas were sewn to the gauze ground along the edge closest to the center of the *kashaya*, while the short bands of buddhas were sewn along the top edges. The edges of the applied bands were finished with cabled yarns.

1. The animal substrate was identified by the McCrone Research Institute (correspondence to Anne E. Wardwell, March 4, 1996).

PUBLICATIONS: Simcox 1989, pp. 27–31, fig. 11 and cover; Reynolds 1990, figs. 10, 10a, p. 48; *CMA Handbook* 1991, p. 59; Wardwell 1992–93, fig. 10, p. 251; Reynolds, "'Thousand Buddhas,'" 1995, fig. 6.

Glossary of Weaving Terms

The following terms have been defined according to the specific contexts in which they occur in the textiles in this exhibition. Most of the definitions are derived entirely or in part from the Centre International d'Étude des Textiles Anciens, *Vocabulary of Technical Terms: Fabrics* (Lyons, 1964), and Dorothy K. Burnham, *Warp and Weft: A Textile Terminology*, Royal Ontario Museum (Toronto, 1980). The authors would like to thank Milton Sonday for his help with this terminology.

Binding point
The point at which a warp is fixed by a weft, or a weft by a warp.

Binding warp
A secondary warp that binds weft floats (used here in the context of weft-faced compound weaves).

Brocade
1. A textile woven with discontinuous supplementary wefts.
2. To weave with an additional (supplementary) weft introduced into a ground weave. The movement of this weft is limited to the width of the area where it is required and does not extend from selvage to selvage.

Broken twill
Any form of twill in which the diagonal alignment of floats or binding points has been deliberately broken.

Compound weave
A weave with more than one warp and/or weft, as opposed to a simple weave. In this catalogue, the term refers specifically to a weft-faced compound weave.

Damask
A simple weave with one warp and one weft, in which the pattern is formed by a contrast of binding systems.

Dovetail joins
The turning of the weft threads in groups of two or more alternately around a common warp in tapestry weave where colors areas meet.

Drawloom
A hand loom for weaving figured textiles, equipped with a special type of figure harness that controls some or all of the warp thread and permits the automatic repeat of a pattern both vertically and horizontally.

Eccentric weave
Areas of tapestry weave where the wefts are not at right angles to the warp, but follow the contours of the design.

Float
The segment of a warp or weft that crosses at least two threads between binding points.

Flying shuttle
A decorative technique used in tapestry weaving in which a weft is carried freely from one area to another.

Foundation warp
The principal warp in a textile.

Foundation or ground weft
The principle weft in a textile.

Gauze
A simple weave in which one or more warps are displaced to cross over one or more other warps. The resulting crossings and recrossings of warps are held in place by wefts. In a complex gauze, a combination of crossings produces a pattern.

Kesi
The Chinese term for slit tapestry woven of silk, or of silk and metal threads.

Lampas weave
A compound weave in which a supplementary weave with its own warps and wefts that is weft dominant is combined with a foundation weave with its own warps and wefts that is warp dominant. Lampas variation: a variation of lampas that has areas in which the foundation and supplementary weaves form separate layers.

Liseré
A simple weave in which the pattern is formed by floats of warps and/or wefts.

Metal thread
Gold or silver threads made by the application of gold or silver to a paper or animal substrate that is cut into strips. These are used flat, or wrapped around a core thread of silk or cotton.

Pass
One complete cycle of weft threads carried through the shed that produces, by varied interlacements with the warp, the weave and pattern in the full width of the textile.

Pattern weft
A supplementary weft that is either continuous or discontinuous (brocaded).

Ply
The twisting together of two or more threads that are either spun or previously twisted filaments.

Satin
A broken twill based on a unit of five warps and five wefts.

Satin binding
A binding system of five or more warps and wefts in which none of the floats or binding points are aligned on the diagonal.

Selvage
The longitudinal finished edge of a textile formed by the turns of wefts as they pass back and forth through the sheds, thereby interlacing with the warp.

Shed
The space made by the separation of the warps into two layers, thus permitting the passage of the shuttle, which carries the weft.

Simple weave
A weave formed by one set of warps and one set of wefts.

Slit join
In a tapestry weave where color areas meet, the slit in the weave formed when weft threads turn back around adjacent warps.

Step
The smallest gradations of a design: the smallest number of warps or of weft passes that forms one step in the outline of a design.

Soumak
A weft-wrap weave with a weft that is carried manually over a group of warps, and then passed under and back around part of the group.

Substrate
Leather, membrane, parchment, or paper to which is applied gold and/or silver.

Supplementary weft
A nonstructural weft added to create a pattern; called a brocading weft if discontinuous.

Tabby
A simple weave based on a unit of two warps and two wefts in which each warp passes over one weft and under the next; warp A passes over weft A and under weft B, warp B passes under warp A and over weft B, and so on. Extended tabby designates a tabby in which warps or wefts, or both, move in groups of two or more.

Tapestry
A weave with one warp and wefts of two or more colors that are discontinuous. The bindings of the tapestries in this exhibition are tabby.

Throw
To twist silk filament yarns.

Toothed join
In tapestry weave where color areas meet, the closure of a slit by weft threads that turn alternately around a common warp. (Also called a single dovetail join.)

Twill
A simple weave based on a unit of three or more warps and three or more wefts, in which each warp passes over two or more adjacent wefts and under the next, or under two or more adjacent wefts and over the next. The diagonal alignment of binding points is indicated by the slant of the letters z or s. The twill binding is described in diagrammatic form. For example, 3/1 z twill indicates that the warps pass over three wefts and under one weft and that the diagonal alignment of binding points is to the right.

Twist
The action of spinning or plying threads, the direction of which is indicated by the diagonals of the letters s (left) and z (right).

Warp
The longitudinal threads of a textile that are stretched on the loom.

Weft
The transverse threads of a textile that interlace with the warp.

Weft-faced compound weave
A weave employing a main warp, a binding warp, and a weft composed of two or more series of threads, usually of different colors. By the action of the main warps, only one weft thread appears on the face, while the others remain on the reverse. The binding warps bind the wefts in passes, and the ground and pattern are formed simultaneously. The entire surface is covered by weft floats, which hide the main warps. The bindings of the textiles in this exhibition are twill or satin.

Glossary of Embroidery Stitches

Fifteen of the seventeen stitch diagrams are from Mary Thomas, *Mary Thomas's Dictionary of Embroidery Stitches* (New York, 1935). The diagram for the counted stitch and damask darning were drawn by Ellen Levine, The Cleveland Museum of Art.

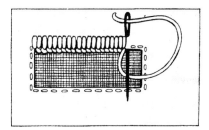

1. Buttonhole stitch

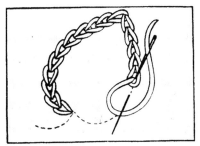

2. Chain stitch

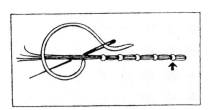

3. Couching

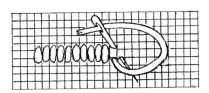

4. Counted stitch (also known as the straight Gobelin stitch)

5. Damask darning

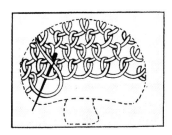

6. Detached looping stitch (also known as open buttonhole filling). See also Sonday and Maitland 1989 on needlelooping.

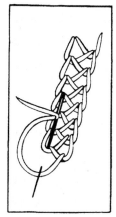

7. Double chain stitch

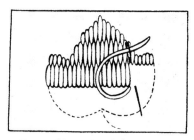

8. Encroaching satin stitch

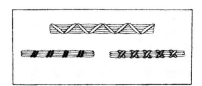

9. Fancy couching

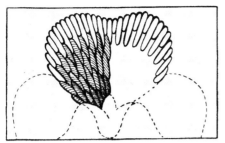

10. Long and short stitch

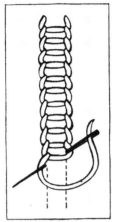

11. Open chain stitch

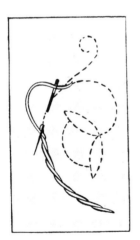

12. Outline stitch

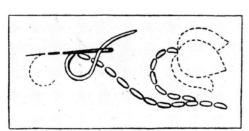

13. Running stitch

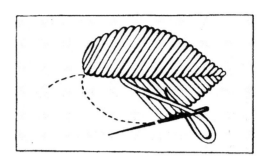

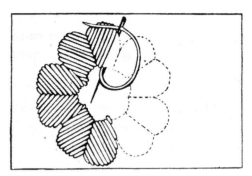

14, 15. Satin stitch
Two diagrams are provided for the satin stitch as both produce the same effect on the surface. The reverse sides of most of the embroidered textiles in the exhibition were not accessible.

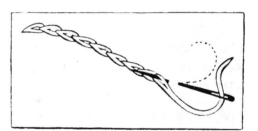

16. Split stitch

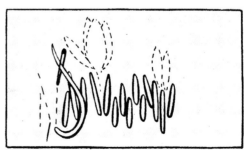

17. Straight stitch

Glossary of Chinese and Japanese Names and Terms

Acheng　阿城

Aguda　阿骨打

Akira Fujieda　藤枝晃

An Lushan　安禄山

anhua　暗花

Anige　阿尼哥

Anxi　安西

Astana　阿斯塔那

Babusha　八不沙

Baibu congshu jicheng　百部叢書集成

Baocheng Temple　寶成寺

Baoding　保定

Barchukh Art Tegin　巴而朮阿而忒的斤

Beijing　北京

Beishi　北史

Bianjing　汴京

Bie-du-lu-din　別都魯丁

Bohai　渤海

Bukkō Kokushi　佛光国師

Caonan wang xunde bei　曹南王勳德碑

Caonan　曹南

Chabi　徹伯爾

Chan (Zen)　禪

Chang Kwang-chih (Zhang Guangzhi)　張光直

Chang'an　長安

Changsha　長沙

Chen　陳

Chen Cheng (Ch'en Ch'eng)　陳誠

Chen Guo'an　陳國安

Chen Juanjuan　陳娟娟

Chen Peifen　陳佩芬

Chen Qingying　陳慶英

Chen Xiangwei　陳相偉

Chen Xiasheng　陳夏生

Chen Yinke　陳寅恪

Cheng Suluo　程溯洛

Chenguo　陳國

Chengzong　成宗

Chengzu　成祖

Chin (*see* Jin)

Chinggis Khan　成吉思汗

Ch'ing-ling (*see* Qingling)

Chinkhai (*see* Zhen Hai)

Chü-Yung-Kuan (*see* Juyong Guan)

Chūgoku Sekkutsu, Tonkō Bakkōkutsu
　中國石窟：敦煌莫高窟

chunshui　春水

Chuogeng lu　輟耕錄

Congshu jicheng jianbian　叢書集成簡編

Cui Wenyin　崔文印

Da Jin guo zhi　大金國志

Da Jin guo zhi jiaozheng　大金國志校正

Daci Fawang　大慈法王

Daidu　大都

Daimin Kokushi　大明国師

da'na　答納

Daoyuan xuegu lu　道園學古錄

Datong　大同

Dazhi Chanshi　大智禪師

Deng Ruiling　鄧銳齡

Ding　定

Ding Ling　定陵

Dingzhou　定州

Donggong　東宮

Dou Kang　竇抗

Dou Shilun　竇師綸

Du Huan　杜環

duan　緞

Duan Wenjie　段文傑

Duanwu festival　端午節

Dulan　都蘭

Dun Lichen　敦禮臣

Dunhuang　敦煌

Dunhuang bihua　敦煌壁畫

Dunhuang yanjiu wenji　敦煌研究文集

Duosang Menggu shi　多桑蒙古史

Engaku-ji　円覺寺

Faku　法庫

Fanxiang Tijusi　梵像提舉司

Feng Chengjun　馮承鈞

Feng Chia-sheng (Feng Jiasheng)　馮家昇

Feng Xianming　馮先銘

217

fenghuang 鳳凰

Fong, Wen C. 方聞

fotan 佛壇

Foxiang Tijusi 佛像提舉司

Fozu lidai tongzai 佛祖歷代通載

Fu Lehuan 傅樂煥

Fujian 福建

Fushouxingyuan Guan 福壽興元觀

Fuzhou 福州

Fuzhou Nansong Huang Sheng mu 福州南宋黃昇墓

Gansu 甘肅

Gao Hanyu 高漢玉

Gaochang 高昌

Gaozong 高宗

ge 葛

gesi 緙絲

gua 卦

Guangcang xuequn congshu 廣倉學䆫叢書

Guangzhou 廣州

Gugong bowuyuan yuankan 故宮博物院院刊

Guo Xi 郭熙

Guo Yaoshi 郭藥師

guoshi 國師

Guoxue jiben congshu 國學基本叢書

Ha-san-na 哈散納

haidongqing 海東青

Haiyun 海雲

Halahezhuo 哈喇（拉）和卓

Hami 哈密

Han 漢

Han Rulin 韓儒林

Han Rulin wenji 韓儒林文集

Han Wei 韓偉

Hanaike 花生

Hangzhou 杭州

Haoqianying 豪欠營

Harbin 哈爾濱

he 褐

He Chou 何稠

He Tuo 何妥

Hebei 河北

Heilongjiang 黑龍江

Hejiazao 何家皂

Hengyang 衡陽

Ho Wai-kam (He Huijian) 何惠鑑

Hong Hao 洪皓

Hongwu 洪武

Hongzheng xian 弘政縣

Hongzhou 弘州

Hōryū-ji 法隆寺

Hsi Hsia (see Xixia)

Hsi-yü fan-kuo chih (see Xiyu fanguo zhi)

Huai River 淮河

Huang Ch'ao (Huang Chao) 黃巢

Huang Nengfu 黃能馥

Huang Sheng 黃昇

Huang Ti 黃迷

Huashi Congshu 畫史叢書

Huhehaote 呼和浩特

Huigu or Huihu 回鶻

Huiqing Pavilion 徽清亭

Hunan 湖南

Huozhou 火州

Hu-san-wu-din 忽三烏丁

Isiha (or Ishiha) 亦失哈

jian 繭

Jiang Zuyi 蔣祖怡

Jiangling 江陵

Jiangzuo Yuan 將作院

jianrong 繭茸

Jianwen 建文

Jiaoma 駮馬

Jile bian 雞肋編

jin 錦

jin 金

Jin 金

Jin Fengyi 靳楓毅

Jin Qicong 金啟孮

Jing Anning 景安寧

Jingo-ji 神護寺

Jingshi dadian 經世大典

Jingzong 景宗

Jining 冀寧

Ji-ning Sha-luo-ba-guan-zhao 積寧沙囉巴觀照

Jininglu 集寧路

jinjin 金錦

Jinshi 金史

Jiuquan 酒泉

ju 局

Jurchen 女真

Jūyō Bunkazai 重要文化財

Juyong Guan 居庸關

Juyuan 巨源

Kaifeng 開封

Kaitai tu 開泰圖

Kajitani Nobuko 梶谷宣子

Kaogu 考古

Ke'an 可庵

Tiansheng 天聖
Tianshi 天師
Tianshui 天水
Tianshun 天順
Tokugawa 德川
Tokyo Kokuritsu Hakubutsukan kiyō 東京国立博物館紀要
Tonkō Bakkōkutsu 敦煌莫高窟
Torii Ryūzō 鳥居龍藏
T'oung Pao 通報
Tōyō shitsugei-shi no kenkyū 東洋漆芸史の研究
Tsien Tsuen-Hsuin (Qian Cunxun) 錢存訓
Tsong-kha-pa 宗喀巴
Tu Ji 屠寄
Tujue 突厥
Tulufan xue yanjiu zhuanji 吐魯番學研究專集
Tuoba 拓跋，拓拔，托跋
Uragami Sōkyū-dō 浦上蒼穹堂
Urumqi 烏魯木齊
Uyghur (Uygur or Uighur) 維吾爾
Wang Binghua 王炳華
Wang Furen 王輔仁
Wang Guowei 王國維
Wang Jianqun 王健羣
Wang Shixian 汪世顯
Wang Xizhi 王羲之
Wang Xuan 王軒
Wang Yi 王毅
Wang Yong 王梀
Wang Zhenpeng 王振鵬
Wanzishan 灣子山
Watt, James C. Y. 屈志仁
Wei 魏
Wenjin Ju 紋錦局
Wenqi Ju 紋綺局
Wenwu 文物
Wenzhou 溫州
Wenzong 文宗
Wu 吳
Wu, Han emperor 武帝
Wu Chengluo 吳承洛
Wu Min 武敏
Wu Zhefu 吳哲夫
Wudang, Mount 武當山
Wuxue Zuyuan 無學祖元
Wuying Dian 武英殿
Wuzong 武宗
Xia 夏
Xiamen 廈門
Xi'an 西安

xiang 象
Xiang Da 向達
Xiao Xun 蕭洵
Xici 繫辭
Xi-hu-xin 西忽辛
Xijin 析津
Xijin zhi 析津志
Xijin zhi jiyi 析津志輯迭
Xin Tangshu 新唐書
Xingzong 興宗
xiniu 犀牛
Xinjiang 新疆
Xiong Mengxiang 熊夢祥
Xiupu 繡譜
Xixia (or Xi Xia) 西夏
Xixia wenwu 西夏文物
Xiyu fanguo zhi 西域番國志
Xizang fojiao shilue 西藏佛教史略
Xizang tangka 西藏唐卡
Xizang yanjiu 西藏研究
Xu Handu 許涵度
Xu Mengxin 徐夢莘
Xu Xinguo 許新國
Xu Zizhi tongjian changbian 續資治通鑑長編
Xuande 宣德
Xuanhua 宣化
Xuanhui Yuan 宣徽院
xuanwu 玄武
Xunmalin 蕁麻林
yahu 牙忽
yan 雁
Yan 燕
Yan Hui 顏輝
yang 羊
yang 陽
Yang 楊
Yang Boda 楊伯達
Yang Kuan 楊寬
Yang Lien-chen-chia 楊璉真加
Yang Lien-sheng (Yang Liansheng) 楊聯陞
Yang Renkai 楊仁愷
Yangyuan xian zhi 陽原縣志
Yanhu 鹽湖
Yanjing 燕京
Yanjing suishi ji 燕京歲時記
Yanjing xuebao 燕京學報
Yanyi yimou lu 燕翼貽謀錄
Yao Yuehua 姚月華
Ye Longli 葉隆禮

Bibliography of Works Cited

EDITED BY ALARIK W. SKARSTROM

The following abbreviations have been used in the notes and in the short-reference list:

AEDTA   Association pour l'Étude et la Documentation des Textiles d'Asie
CASS   Chinese Academy of Social Science
CIETA   Centre International d'Étude des Textiles Anciens
CMA   The Cleveland Museum of Art
CPAM   Committee for Preservation of Ancient Monuments
MMA   The Metropolitan Museum of Art
TSA   Textile Society of America

Addis 1978   John M. Addis. *Chinese Ceramics from Datable Tombs and Some Other Dated Material: A Handbook.* New York, 1978.

Al'baum 1975   Lazar' Izrailevich Al'baum. *Zhivopis' Afrasiaba* (Paintings of Afrosiab). Tashkent, 1975.

Allsen 1983   Thomas T. Allsen. "The Yüan Dynasty and the Uighurs of Turfan in the 13th Century." In Rossabi, *China,* 1983, pp. 243–80.

Allsen 1989   Thomas T. Allsen. "Mongolian Princes and Their Merchant Partners, 1200–1260." *Asia Major,* 3d ser., 2, no. 2 (1989), pp. 83–126.

Allsen (forthcoming)   Thomas T. Allsen. *Commodity and Exchange in the Mongol Empire: A Cultural History of Islamic Textiles.* Cambridge, forthcoming.

Alsop 1984   Ian Alsop. "Five Dated Nepalese Metal Sculptures." *Artibus Asiae* 45 (1984), pp. 207–21.

"American Museum News" 1996   "American Museum News." *Ghereh: International Carpet & Textile Review,* no. 9 (August 1996), pp. 51–52.

Ames et al. 1997   Kenneth L. Ames et al. "Top 100 Treasures." *Art & Antiques* 20, no. 3 (March 1997), pp. 54–113.

Ang 1983   Melvin T. L. Ang. "Sung–Liao Diplomacy in Eleventh- and Twelfth-Century China." Ph.D. diss., University of Pennsylvania. Philadelphia, 1983.

Ann Arbor 1967   Oleg Grabar, ed. *Sasanian Silver: Late Antique and Early Medieval Arts of Luxury from Iran.* Exh. cat., Museum of Art, University of Michigan. Ann Arbor, 1967.

Baer 1983   Eva Baer. *Metalwork in Medieval Islamic Art.* Albany, 1983.

***Baibu congshu jicheng* 1970**   *Baibu congshu jicheng* (One hundred collections of reprinted texts). Yiwen Yinshuguan edition. Taipei, 1970.

Barnett 1995   Cherry Barnett. "Chinese Textiles: Technique, Design and Patterns of Use." *Arts of Asia* 25, no. 6 (November–December 1995), pp. 137–43.

Barthold 1968   V. V. Barthold. *Turkestan Down to the Mongol Invasion.* Trans. T. Minorsky. 3d ed. London, 1968.

Beckwith 1987   Christopher I. Beckwith. *The Tibetan Empire in Central Asia: A History of the Struggle for Great Power among Tibetans, Turks, Arabs, and Chinese during the Early Middle Ages.* Princeton, 1987.

Beckwith 1991   Christopher I. Beckwith. "The Impact of the Horse and Silk Trade on the Economies of T'ang China and the Uighur Empire." *Journal of the Economic and Social History of the Orient* 34, no. 2 (June 1991), pp. 183–98.

Beijing City Cultural Bureau 1958   Beijing City Cultural Bureau, Cultural Relics Investigation and Study Group. "Beijingshi Shuangta Qingshousi chutu de simian zhipin ji xiuhua" (Silk and cotton textiles and embroidery excavated from the Double Pagoda at Qingshou Temple, Beijing City). *Wenwu,* no. 9 (1958), p. 29.

***Beishi* **   *Beishi* (History of the Northern dynasties). Zhonghua Shuju edition. Beijing, 1974.

Belenitskii and Bentovich 1961   A. M. Belenitskii and I. B. Bentovich. "Iz istorii sredneaziatskogo shelkotkachestva: K identifikatsii tkani 'zandanechi'" (From the history of Central Asian silk weaving: On the identification of the Zandaniji textiles). *Sovetskaia arkheologiia,* no. 2 (1961), pp. 66–78.

Berger 1989   Patricia Berger. "A Stitch in Time: Speculations on the Origins of Needlelooping." *Orientations* 20, no. 8 (August 1989), pp. 45–53.

Berger 1994   Patricia Berger. "Preserving the Nation: The Political Uses of Tantric Art in China." In Lawrence 1994, pp. 89–122.

Blair 1985   Sheila S. Blair. "The Madrasa at Zuzan: Islamic Architecture in Eastern Iran on the Eve of the Mongol Invasions." In *Muqarnas: An Annual on Islamic Art and Architecture,* ed. Oleg Grabar, vol. 3, pp. 75–91. Leiden, 1985.

Blair 1992   Sheila S. Blair. *The Monumental Inscriptions from Early Islamic Iran and Transoxiana.* Leiden, 1992.

Blair 1994   Sheila S. Blair. "An Inscription from Barūjrd: New Data on Domed Pavilions in Saljūq Mosques." In *The Art of the Saljūqs in Iran and Anatolia: Proceedings of a Symposium Held in Edinburgh in 1982,* ed. Robert Hillenbrand, pp. 4–11. Costa Mesa, Cal., 1994.

Bosworth 1995   C. E. Bosworth. "Salghurids." In *Encyclopaedia of Islam,* vol. 6, pp. 978–79. 2d ed. Leiden, 1995.

Boyle 1968   John Andrew Boyle. "Dynastic and Political History of the Īl-Khāns." In *The Saljuq and Mongol Periods,* pp. 303ff. Vol. 5 of *The Cambridge History of Iran.* Cambridge, 1968.

Boyle 1971   John Andrew Boyle. *The Successors of Genghis Khan.* New York, 1971.

Brentjes 1979   Burchard Brentjes and Karin Ruhrdanz. *Mittelasien Kunst des Islam.* Leipzig, 1979.

Bretschneider 1967   Emil Bretschneider. *Mediaeval Researches from Eastern Asiatic Sources.* 2 vols. Reprint, New York, 1967.

Burnham 1980   Dorothy Burnham. *Warp and Weft: A Textile Terminology.* Toronto, 1980.

Bush 1995   Susan Bush. "Five Paintings of Animal Subjects or Narrative Themes and Their Relevance to Chin Culture." In *China under Jurchen Rule,* ed. Hoyt Cleveland Tillman and Stephen H. West, pp. 183–215. Albany, 1995.

Cammann 1948   Schuyler Cammann. "Notes on the Origin of Chinese *K'ossu* Tapestry." *Artibus Asiae* 11 (1948), pp. 90–110.

Cammann 1951   Schuyler Cammann. "The Symbolism of the Cloud Collar Motif." *The Art Bulletin* 33 (1951), pp. 3–10.

Cammann 1953   Schuyler Cammann. "Chinese Mandarin Squares." *University of Pennsylvania Museum Bulletin* 17 (June 1953), pp. 5–42.

Cammann 1962   Schuyler Cammann. "Embroidery Techniques in Old China." *Archives of the Chinese Art Society of America* 16 (1962), pp. 16–39.

Chang Kwang-chih 1986   Chang Kwang-chih. *The Archaeology of Ancient China.* 4th ed. New Haven, 1986.

Ch'en 1964   Kenneth Ch'en. *Buddhism in China: A Historical Survey.* Princeton, 1964.

Cheng Suluo 1994   Cheng Suluo. *Tang Song Huihu shi lunji* (Collected essays on Uyghur history during the Tang and Song dynasties). Beijing, 1994.

Chen Guo'an 1984   Chen Guo'an. "Qiantan Hengyangxian Hejiazao Beisong mu fangzhi pin" (Discussion on the textiles from the Northern Song tomb at Hejiazao, Hengyang County). *Wenwu,* no. 12 (1984), pp. 77–81.

Chen Peifen 1987   Chen Peifen. *Shanghai bowuguan cang qingtong jing* (Bronze mirrors in the collection of the Shanghai Museum). Shanghai, 1987.

Chen Qingying 1992   Chen Qingying. *Yuanchao dishi Basiba* (Phagspa: Imperial preceptor of the Yuan dynasty). Beijing, 1992.

Chen Yinke 1944   Chen Yinke. *Sui Tang zhidu yuanyuan luelun gao* (Preliminary study on the origins of governmental systems of the Sui and Tang dynasties). Chongqing and Taipei, 1944.

CIETA 1964   CIETA. *Vocabulary of Technical Terms: Fabrics.* Lyons, 1964.

Clabburn 1976   Pamela Clabburn and Helene Von Rosenstiel. *The Needleworker's Dictionary.* New York, 1976.

Cleveland 1968   Sherman Lee and Wai-kam Ho. *Chinese Art under the Mongols: The Yuan Dynasty (1279–1368).* Exh. cat., Cleveland Museum of Art. 1968.

Cleveland 1994   J. Keith Wilson and Anne E. Wardwell, eds. "New Objects/New Insights: Cleveland's Recent Chinese Acquisitions." Exh. cat., Cleveland Museum of Art. Published in *CMA Bulletin* 81, no. 8 (October 1994), pp. 325–32 and 342–45.

CMA Handbook 1991   Cleveland Museum of Art. *Handbook of The Cleveland Museum of Art.* Cleveland, 1991.

CMA 1991   Cleveland Museum of Art. *Interpretations: Sixty-Five Works from The Cleveland Museum of Art.* Cleveland, 1991.

CMA 1992   Cleveland Museum of Art. *Masterpieces from East and West.* New York, 1992.

Congshu jicheng jianbian   *Congshu jicheng jianbian* (A selected compendium of collections of writing). Taipei, 1965–66.

CPAM Zouxian 1978   CPAM Zouxian, Shandong Province. "Zouxian Yuandai Li Yu'an mu qingli jianbao" (Excavation of the Yuan dynasty tomb of Li Yu'an at Zouxian in Shandong Province). *Wenwu,* no. 4 (1978), pp. 14–20.

Crowe 1991   Yolande Crowe. "Late Thirteenth-Century Persian Tilework and Chinese Textiles." *Bulletin of the Asia Institute* (Bloomfield Hills) 5 (1991), pp. 153–61.

Crowfoot et al. 1992   Elisabeth Crowfoot, Frances Pritchard, and Kay Staniland. *Textiles and Clothing, c. 1150–1450.* Medieval Finds from Excavations in London, 4. London, 1992.

Da Jin guo zhi jiaozheng   Yuwen Mouzhao. *Da Jin guo zhi jiaozheng* (History of the great Jin kingdom). Annotated by Cui Wenyin. Zhonghua Shuju edition. Beijing, 1986.

Dallas 1993   Richard M. Barnhart et al. *Painters of the Great Ming: The Imperial Court and the Zhe School.* Exh. cat., Dallas Museum of Art. 1993.

Daoyuan xuegu lu   *See* Yu Ji

Darkevich 1976   Vladislav T. Darkevich. *Khudozhestvennyi metall Vostoka, VII–XIII vv.* Moscow, 1976.

Datong Municipal Museum 1972   Datong Municipal Museum, Shanxi Province, and Committee on Cultural Relics, Shanxi Province. "Shanxi Datong Shijiazhai Beiwei Sima Jinlong mu" (The tomb of Sima Jinlong of the Northern Wei dynasty at Shijiazhai, Datong, Shanxi Province). *Wenwu,* no. 3 (1972), pp. 20–33.

Dayton 1990   Susan L. Huntington and John C. Huntington, eds. *Leaves from the Bodhi Tree: The Art of Pala India (8th–12th Centuries) and Its International Legacy.* Exh. cat., Dayton Art Institute. Seattle, 1990.

Deng Ruiling 1989   Deng Ruiling. *Yuan Ming liangdai zhongyang yu Xizang difang de guanxi* (The relationship between the central government and Tibet region during the Yuan and Ming periods). Beijing, 1989.

Ding Ling 1990   The Institute of Archaeology, CASS; Museum of Ding Ling; and The Archaeological Team of the City of Beijing. *Ding Ling* (The imperial tomb of the Ming dynasty Ding Ling). 2 vols. Beijing, 1990. [In Chinese with English summary.]

Dunhuang bihua 1985   Duan Wenjie et al., eds. *Dunhuang bihua (shang)* (Wall paintings of Dunhuang, part 1). In *Zhongguo meishu quanji: Huihua bian 14* (The great treasury of Chinese fine arts: Painting, 14). Shanghai, 1985.

Dunhuang wenwu yanjiusuo 1980–82   Dunhuang wenwu yanjiusuo. *Tonkō Bakkōkutsu* (Mo-kao-k'u caves of Tun-huang). Chūgoku Sekkutsu, 5. Tokyo, 1980–82.

Dun Lichen 1936   Dun Lichen. *Yanjing suishi ji.* Trans. Derk Bodde as *Annual Customs and Festivals in Peking as Recorded in the Yen-ching Sui-Shih-chi by Tun Li-ch'en.* Beijing, 1936.

Dunnell 1983   Ruth Dunnell. "Tanguts and the Tangut State of Ta Hsia." Ph.D. diss., Princeton University, 1983.

Dunnell 1992   Ruth Dunnell. "The Hsi Hsia." In *Alien Regimes and Border States, 907–1368,* ed. Herbert Franke and Denis Twitchett, pp. 154–214. Vol. 6 of *The Cambridge History of China.* Cambridge, 1992.

Dunnell 1994   Ruth Dunnell. "The Hsia Origins of the Yüan Institution of Imperial Preceptor." *Asia Major* 7 (1994), pp. 85–111.

Dunnell 1996   Ruth Dunnell. *The Great State of White and High: Buddhism and State Formation in 11th-Century Xia.* Honolulu, 1996.

Duosang Menggu shi   *See* Feng Chengjun 1962

Endicott-West 1989   Elizabeth Endicott-West. "Merchant Associations in Yuan China: The Ortogh." *Asia Major,* 3d ser., vol. 2, no. 2 (1989), pp. 127–54.

Erdmann 1942   Kurt Erdmann. "Eberdarstellung und Ebersymbolik in Iran." *Bonner Jahrbücher* 147 (1942), pp. 345–82.

Esin 1973–74   Emel Esin. "The Turk al'Agam of Sammarra and the Paintings Attributable to Them in the Gawaq al'Haqani." *Kunst des Orients* 9 (1973–74), pp. 47–88.

Ettinghausen 1957   Richard Ettinghausen. "The 'Wade Cup' in The Cleveland Museum of Art, Its Origin and Decorations." *Ars Orientalis* 2 (1957), pp. 327–66.

Ettinghausen 1984   Richard Ettinghausen. "Kufesque in Byzantine Greece, the Latin West and the Muslim World." In Richard Ettinghausen, *Islamic Art and Archaeology: Collected Papers,* ed. Myriam Rosen-Ayalon, pp. 752–71. Berlin, 1984.

Falke 1913   Otto von Falke. *Kunstgeschichte der Seidenweberei.* Berlin, 1913.

Falke 1922   Otto von Falke. *Decorative Silks.* New York, 1922.

Farquhar 1990   David Farquhar. *The Government of China under Mongolian Rule: A Reference Guide.* Münchener Ostasiatische Studien, 53. Stuttgart, 1990.

Feng Chengjun 1962   Feng Chengjun. *Duosang Menggu shi.* 2 vols. Beijing, 1962. A translation of Baron Constantin d'Ohsson's

Histoire des Mongols, depuis Tchinguiz-Khan jusqu'à Timour Bey, ou Tamerlan (1824).

"Fit for an Empress" 1994–95 "Fit for an Empress." *Hali* 16, no. 6 (December 1994–January 1995), p. 99.

Flemming 1927 Ernst Flemming. *An Encyclopedia of Textiles.* New York, 1927.

Florence 1983 Licisco Magagnato, ed. *Le Stoffe di Cangrande: Ritrovamenti e ricerche sul 300 veronese.* Florence, 1983.

Flury-Lemberg 1988 Mechthild Flury-Lemberg. *Textile Conservation and Research: A Documentation of the Textile Department on the Occasion of the Twentieth Anniversary of the Abegg Foundation.* Bern, 1988.

Folsach 1996 Kjeld von Folsach. "Pax Mongolica: An Ilkhanid Tapestry-Woven Roundel." *Hali*, no. 85 (March–April 1996), pp. 81–87, 117.

Folsach and Bernsted 1993 Kjeld von Folsach and Anne-Marie Keblow Bernsted. *Woven Treasures: Textiles from the World of Islam.* Copenhagen, 1993.

Fong 1992 Wen C. Fong. *Beyond Representation: Chinese Painting and Calligraphy, 8th–14th Century.* Princeton Monographs in Art and Archaeology, 48. New York and New Haven, 1992.

Fong and Watt 1996 Wen C. Fong and James C. Y. Watt. *Possessing the Past: Treasures from the National Palace Museum, Taipei.* New York and Taipei, 1996.

Foucher 1905 Alfred Foucher. *Étude sur l'iconographie bouddhique de l'Inde d'après des documents nouveaux.* Bibliothèque de l'École des hautes études: Sciences religieuses, 13. Paris, 1905.

Fozu lidai tongzai *Fozu lidai tongzai* (Accounts of Buddhist patriarchs of successive generations). Taishō Shinshū Daizōkyō edition. Reprint, Taipei, 1994.

Franke 1981 Herbert Franke. "Tibetans in Yuan China." In *China under Mongol Rule*, ed. John Langlois, pp. 296–328. Princeton, 1981.

Frye 1954 Richard Frye. *The History of Bukhara of Narshakhi Muhammad ibn Ja Far.* Cambridge, Mass., 1954.

Fujian Provincial Museum 1982 Fujian Provincial Museum. *Fuzhou Nansong Huang Sheng mu* (The Southern Song tomb of Huang Sheng in Fuzhou). Beijing, 1982.

Fu Lehuan 1984 Fu Lehuan. "Liaodai sishi nabo kao" (Study on the Liao custom of *nabo* through the four seasons). In Fu Lehuan, *Liaoshi congkao* (Studies on the history of the Liao dynasty), pp. 36–172. Beijing, 1984.

Gabain 1973 Annemarie von Gabain. *Das Leben im uigurischen Königreich von Qoco 850–1250.* 2 vols. Wiesbaden, 1973.

Gansu Provincial Museum 1982 Gansu Provincial Museum and Culture Centre of Zhangxian. "Gansu Zhangxian Yuandai Wang Shixian jiazu musang" (Excavations of the Yuan dynasty tombs of the Wang Shixian family at Zhangxian County in Gansu Province). *Wenwu*, no. 2 (1982), pp. 1–21.

Gao Hanyu 1987 Gao Hanyu. *Soieries de Chine.* Paris, 1987.

Gao Hanyu 1992 Gao Hanyu. *Chinese Textile Designs.* Trans. Rosemary Scott and Susan Whitfield. London, 1992.

Ginsberg 1987 Henry Ginsberg. "New Hong Kong Gallery." *Hali*, no. 34 (April–June 1987), pp. 92–93.

Gluckman 1995 Dale Gluckman. "Chinese Textiles and the Tibetan Connection." In Hong Kong 1995, pp. 24–25.

Goepper 1982 Roger Goepper. *Alchi, Buddhas, Göttinnen, Mandalas, Wandmalerei in einem Himalaya-kloster.* Cologne, 1982.

Goepper 1993 Roger Goepper. "The 'Great Stupa' at Alchi." *Artibus Asiae* 53 (1993), pp. 111–43.

"Golden Lampas" 1991 "Golden Lampas: Notable Acquisitions." *Hali* 13, no. 59 (October 1991), p. 125.

Goodrich and Fang 1976 L. C. Goodrich and C. Y. Fang, eds. *A Dictionary of Ming Biography.* 2 vols. New York, 1976.

Gordon 1959 Antoinette K. Gordon. *The Iconography of Tibetan Lamaism.* Rutland, Vt., and Tokyo, 1959.

Granger-Taylor 1983 Hero Granger-Taylor. "The Two Dalmatics of Saint Ambrose?" *Bulletin du CIETA*, nos. 57–58 (1983), pp. 130–32.

Granger-Taylor 1989 Hero Granger-Taylor. "Weft-patterned Silks and Their Braid: The Remains of an Anglo-Saxon Dalmatic of c. 800?" In *St. Cuthbert, His Cult and His Community to A.D. 1200*, ed. Gerald Bonner, pp. 303–27. Woodbridge, Eng., 1989.

Gropp 1974 Gerd Gropp. *Archäologische Khotan, chinesische-Ostturkestan.* Monographien der Wittheit zu Bremen, 11. Bremen, 1974.

Grünwedel 1920 Albert Grünwedel. *Alt-Kutscha: Archäologische und religionsgeschichtliche Forschungen an Tempera-Gemalden aus buddhistischen Hohlen der erstenacht Jahrhunderte nach Christi geburt.* Berlin, 1920.

Guangcang xuequn congshu *Guangcang xuequn congshu* (The Guangcang xuequn collection of reprinted texts). Second Collection. Compiled by Wang Guowei. 32 vols. Shanghai, 1916–. [Vol. 26 contains the text, copied from the *Yongle dadian*, of the chapter on painting and sculpture from the now-lost *Jingshi dadian* under the title *Yuandai huasu ji* (Painting and sculpture of the Yuan period).]

Gyllensvard 1957 Bo Gyllensvard. "T'ang Gold and Silver." *The Museum of Far Eastern Antiquities Bulletin* (Stockholm) 29 (1957), pp. 1–230.

Hackin 1954 J. Hackin. *Nouvelles recherches archéologiques à Begram: Ancienne Kâpicî, 1939–1940, rencontre des trois civilisations, Inde, Grèce, Chine.* Mémoires de la Délégation archéologique française en Afghanistan, 11. Paris, 1954.

Haig 1934 T. W. Haig. "Salghurids." *Encyclopaedia of Islam*, vol. 4, pp. 105–6. Leiden, 1934.

Hamilton 1986 J. Hamilton. *Manuscrits ouïgours du IXe–Xe siècle de Touen-Houang.* Paris, 1986.

Hanaike 1982 *Hanaike* (*Hanaike*: Flower vases in the vogue of *zashiki* display). The Tokugawa Art Museum, Nagoya, and the Nezu Art Museum, Tokyo. Nagoya and Tokyo, 1982.

Han Rulin 1981 Han Rulin. "Yuandai zhama yan xin tan" (New studies on the *zhama* feast of the Yuan period). *Lishi yanjiu* (Historical research), no. 1 (1981), pp. 294–301.

Han Rulin 1986 Han Rulin, ed. *Yuanchao shi* (History of the Yuan dynasty). 2 vols. Beijing, 1986.

Hartford 1951 Wadsworth Atheneum. *2000 Years of Tapestry Weaving: A Loan Exhibition.* Exh. cat., Hartford, 1951.

Heilongjiang 1989 Heilongjiang Provincial Institute of Cultural Relics. "Heilongjiang Acheng Juyuan Jindai Qiguo wangmu fajue jianbao" (Excavation of the tomb of Prince Qi of the Jin dynasty at Juyuan in Acheng, Heilongjiang). *Wenwu*, no. 10 (1989), pp. 1–10, 45.

Hoeniger 1991 Cathleen S. Hoeniger. "Cloth of Gold and Silver: Simone Martini's Techniques for Representing Luxury Textiles." *Gesta*, 30, no. 2 (1991), pp. 154–62.

Hoffman 1994 Helmut Hoffman. "Early and Medieval Tibet." In *The Cambridge History of Early Inner Asia*, ed. Denis Sinor, pp. 371–99. Reprint, Newcastle upon Tyne, 1994.

Hong Kong 1995 Hong Kong Museum of Art. *Jinxiu luoyi qiao tiangong/Heaven's Embroidered Cloths: One Thousand Years of Chinese Textiles Jointly Presented by the Urban Council, Hong Kong, and the Oriental Ceramic Society of Hong Kong, in Association with the Liaoning Provincial Museum.* Exh. cat., Hong Kong Museum of Art, 1995. [In Chinese and English.]

Huang Nengfu, Arts and Crafts, 1985 Huang Nengfu, ed. *Yin ran zhi xiu (shang)* (Printing, dyeing, weaving, and embroidery, part 1). In *Zhongguo meishu quanji: Gongyi meishu bian, 6* (The great treasury of Chinese fine arts: Arts and crafts, 6). Beijing, 1985–87.

Huang Nengfu, Arts and Crafts, 1987 Huang Nengfu, ed. *Yin ran zhi xiu (xia)* (Printing, dyeing, weaving, and embroidery, part 2). In *Zhongguo meishu quanji: Gongyi meishu bian, 7* (The great treasury of Chinese fine arts: Arts and crafts, 7). Beijing, 1985–87.

Huang Nengfu, Arts and Crafts, 1991 Huang Nengfu, ed. *Yin ran zhi xiu (shang)* (Printing, dyeing, weaving, and embroidery, part 1). In *Zhongguo meishu quanji: Gongyi meishu bian, 6* (The great treasury of Chinese fine arts: Arts and crafts, 6). English edition, trans. He Fei, 1991.

Huang Nengfu and Chen Juanjuan 1995 Huang Nengfu and Chen Juanjuan. *Zhongguo fuzhuang shi* (A history of Chinese costumes). Beijing, 1995.

Huang Ti 1985 Huang Ti et al. *Xizang tangka* (Tibetan *thangkas*). Beijing, 1985. 2d printing, 1987.

***Huashi congshu* 1974** *Huashi congshu* (Collection of texts on the history of painting). Compiled by Yu Anlan. 5 vols. Taipei, 1974.

Hulsewé 1974 A. F. P. Hulsewé. "Quelques considerations sur le commerce de la soie au temps de la dynastie des Han." In *Mélanges de sinologie offerts à Monsieur Paul Demieville II*, pp. 117–35. Paris, 1974.

Huntington 1986 John C. Huntington. "The Iconography and Iconology of the 'Tan Yao' Caves at Yungang." *Oriental Art*, n.s., 32, no. 2 (Summer 1986), pp. 142–60.

Ierusalimskaia 1963 Anna A. Ierusalimskaia. "K voprosu o torgovykh sviaziakh Severnogo Kavkaza v rannem srednevekov'e: Neskol'ko shelkovykh tkanei iz Moshchevoi Balki" (On the question of the trade connections of the Northern Caucasus in the early medieval period: A few silk textiles from Moshchevaia Balka). In *Soobshcheniia Gosudarstvennogo Ermitazha*, vol. 24. Leningrad, 1963.

Ierusalimskaia 1967 Anna A. Ierusalimskaia. "O severokavkazskom 'shelkovom puti' v rannem srednevekov'e" (The 'silk road' of the Northern Caucasus in the early Middle Ages). *Sovietskaia arkheologiia*, no. 2 (1967), pp. 55–78.

Ierusalimskaia 1972 Anna A. Ierusalimskaia. "K slozheniyu shkoly khudozhestvennogo shelkotkachestva v Sogde" (Formation of the Sogdian school of artistic silk weaving). In *Sredniaia Aziia i Iran (sbornik statei)*, pp. 5–46. Gosudarstvennyi Ordena Lenina Ermitazh. Leningrad, 1972.

Ierusalimskaia 1996 Anna A. Ierusalimskaia. *Die Gräber der Moščevaja Balka: Frühmittelalterliche Funde an der nordkaukasischen Seidenstrasse*. Munich, 1996.

Indictor et al. 1988 Norman Indictor, Robert J. Koestler, C. Blair, and Anne E. Wardwell. "The Evaluation of Metal Wrappings from Medieval Textiles Using Scanning Electron Microscopy–Energy Dispersive X-Ray Spectrometry." *Textile History* 19, no. 1 (1988), pp. 3–22.

Indictor et al. 1989 Norman Indictor. "Metal Threads Made of Proteinaceous Substrates Examined by Scanning Electron Microscopy–Energy Dispersive X-Ray Spectrometry." *Studies in Conservation* 34 (1989), pp. 171–82.

Inner Mongolia 1985 Inner Mongolia Archaeological Work Team and Archaeological Work Unit at Wumeng. *Qidan nüshi: Haoqianying Liaomu qingli yu yanjiu* (A Khitan female corpse: Examination and research on a Liao tomb at Haoqianying). Hohhot, 1985.

Inner Mongolia 1987 Inner Mongolia Institute of Cultural Relics and Archaeology. "Liao Chenguo gongzhu fuma hezang mu fajue jianbao" (Excavation of the tomb of the princess and her husband of the Liao state of Chen). *Wenwu*, no. 11 (1987), pp. 4–28.

Inner Mongolia 1993 Inner Mongolia Institute of Cultural Relics and Archaeology and Zhelimu League Museum. *Liao Chenguo gongzhu mu* (Tomb of the princess of the state of Chen). Beijing, 1993. [In Chinese with English summary.]

Institute of Archaeology 1972 Institute of Archaeology, Academy of Sciences, and CPAM, Beijing City. "Yuan Daidu de kancha he fajue" (The investigation and excavation of Yuan Daidu). *Kaogu* 1 (1972), pp. 19–28.

Jenyns 1981 R. Soame Jenyns. *Chinese Art*. Vol. 3. Rev. ed. Oxford, 1981.

Jiang Zuyi and Zhang Diyun 1992 Jiang Zuyi and Zhang Diyun, eds. *Quan Liao shihua* (Poems of the Liao dynasty). Changsha, 1992.

Jin Fengyi 1980 Jin Fengyi. "Liaoning Zhaoyang Qianchuanghu cun Liao mu" (The Liao dynasty tomb at Qianchuanghu village in Zhaoyang County, Liaoning Province). *Wenwu*, no. 12 (1980), pp. 17–29.

Jing 1994 Anning Jing. "The Portraits of Kubilai Khan and Chabi by Anige (1245–1306), a Nepali Artist at the Yuan Court." *Artibus Asiae* 54, nos. 1–2 (1994), pp. 40–86.

Jin Qicong 1995 Jin Qicong. "Jurchen Literature under the Chin." In *Chin under Jurchen Rule*, ed. Hoyt Cleveland Tillman and Stephen H. West, pp. 216–37. Albany, 1995.

Jinshi *Jinshi* (History of the Jin dynasty). Zhonghua Shuju edition. Beijing, 1975.

Juvaini 1958 Juvaini [Juvayni]. *The History of the World-Conqueror, by Ala-ad-Din Ata-Malik Juvaini*. Trans. John Andrew Boyle. Cambridge, Mass., 1958.

***Jūyō Bunkazai* 1976** *Jūyō Bunkazai* (Important cultural properties). Vol. 25, *Kōgeihin II: Shikko, tōji, senshoku* (Handicrafts II: Lacquer, ceramics, and textiles). Tokyo, 1976.

Karmay 1975 Heather Karmay. *Early Sino-Tibetan Art*. Warminster, Eng., 1975.

Karmay 1977 Heather Karmay. "Tibetan Costume, Seventh to Eleventh Centuries." In *Essais sur l'art du Tibet*, ed. A. Macdonald and Y. Imaeda, pp. 64–81. Paris, 1977.

Kennedy 1983 Alan Kennedy. "Kesa: Its Sacred and Secular Aspects." *The Textile Museum Journal* 22 (1983), pp. 67–80.

Kerr 1990 Rose Kerr. *Later Chinese Bronzes*. London, 1990.

Klein 1934 Dorothee Klein. "Die Dalmatika Benedikt XI. zu Perugia ein Kinran der Yuan-Zeit." In *Ostasiatische Zeitschrift*, pp. 127–31. Berlin and Leipzig, 1934.

Klesse 1967 Brigitte Klesse. *Seidenstoffe in der italienischen Malerei des 14. Jahrhunderts*. Bern, 1967.

Kong Qi Kong Qi. *Zhizheng zhiji* (Notes from the Zhizheng era, 1341–67), collected in the *Yueya tang congshu* (The Yueya Tang collection of reprinted texts) and reprinted in the *Baibu congshu jicheng* (q.v.).

***Koryo* 1989** *Koryo Celadon Masterpieces*. Exh. cat., National Museum of Korea. Seoul, 1989.

Kossak 1994 Steven M. Kossak. "Aspects of South Asian Art in the New Galleries at The Metropolitan Museum of Art: Nepalese and Tibetan Art." *Arts of Asia* 24, no. 2 (March–April 1994), pp. 105–12.

Krahl 1986 Regina Krahl, with Nurdan Erbahar. *Chinese Ceramics in the Topkapi Saray Museum, Istanbul: A Complete Catalogue*. Ed. John Ayers. Istanbul and London, 1986.

Krahl 1989 Regina Krahl. "Designs on Early Chinese Textiles." *Orientations* 20, no. 8 (August 1989), pp. 62–73.

Krahl 1997 Regina Krahl. "Medieval Silks Woven in Gold: Khitan, Jürchen, Tangut, Chinese or Mongol?" *Orientations* 28, no. 4 (April 1997), pp. 45–51.

Kunsthistorisches Museum 1987 Rotraud Bauer and the Kunsthistorisches Museum Wien. *Weltliche und geistliche Schatzkammer: Bildführer*. Salzburg, 1987.

Kychanov 1989 E. I. Kychanov, ed. and trans. "Izmenennyi i zanovo utverzhdennyi kodeks deviza tsarstvovaniya nebesnoe protsvetanie (1149–1169)" (Changed and newly approved codex of the period of Heavenly Prosperity [1149–1169]). *Pamiatniki pis'mennosti Vostoka* (Writings of the East) 81, bk. 4. Moscow, 1989.

Kyoto 1981   *Art of Zen Buddhism.* Exh. cat., Kyoto National Museum. Kyoto, 1981.

Kyoto 1983   *Nanzenji no meihō / Art Treasures of Nanzen-ji Temple.* Exh. cat., Kyoto National Museum. Kyoto, 1983. [In Japanese and English.]

Laing 1992   Ellen Johnston Laing. "The Development of Flower Depiction and the Origin of the Bird-and-Flower Genre in Chinese Art." *Museum of Far Eastern Antiquities Bulletin* (Stockholm) 64 (1992), pp. 179–223.

Laing 1994   Ellen Johnston Laing. "A Survey of Liao Dynasty Bird-and-Flower Painting." *Bulletin of Sung-Yuan Studies* 24 (1994), pp. 57–99.

Lauf 1976   Detlef Ingo Lauf. *Tibetan Sacred Art: The Heritage of Tantra.* Trans. Ewald Osers. Berkeley, New York, and London, 1976.

Lawrence 1994   Marsha Weidner, ed. *Latter Days of the Law: Images of Chinese Buddhism, 850–1850.* Exh. cat., Spencer Museum of Art, University of Kansas. Lawrence, 1994.

Le Coq 1913   Albert von Le Coq. *Chotscho: Facsimile-wiedergaben der wichtigeren Funde der ersten königlich preussischen Expedition nach Tufan in Ost-Turkistan.* Berlin, 1913.

Lee 1993   Sherman E. Lee. "Yan Hui, Zhong Kui, Demons and the New Year." *Artibus Asiae* 53, nos. 1–2 (1993), pp. 211–27.

Lessing 1913   Julius Lessing. *Die Gewebe-Sammlung des königlichen Kunstgewerbe-Museums.* 11 vols. Berlin, 1913.

Levinson 1983   Susan B. Levinson. "Discovering an Important Mongol Silk Textile." *Hali* 5, no. 4 (1983), pp. 496–97.

Levy 1955   Howard Levy. *Biography of Huang Ch'ao.* Berkeley, 1955.

Liaohai congshu   *Liaohai congshu* (Liaohai collection of reprinted texts). Liaoshen Shushe edition. 5 vols. Shenyang, 1985.

Liaoning Provincial Museum 1975   Archaeological Team of the Liaoning Provincial Museum. "Faku Yemaotai Liaomu jilue" (Excavation of the Liao dynasty tomb at Yemaotai in Faku County, Liaoning Province). *Wenwu,* no. 12 (1975), pp. 26–36.

Liaoshi   *Liaoshi* (History of the Liao dynasty). Zhonghua Shuju edition. Beijing, 1974.

Liebert 1976   Gosta Liebert. *Iconographic Dictionary of the Indian Religions: Hinduism, Buddhism, Jainism.* Leiden, 1976.

Li Jingwei 1990   Li Jingwei. "Dunhuang Huigu wen yishu sizhong" (Four documents in Uyghur script from Dunhuang). In *Tulufan xue yanjiu zhuanji* (Special volume on the study of Turfan), pp. 333–58. Urumqi, 1990.

Linrothe 1995   Rob Linrothe. "Renzong and the Patronage of Tangut Buddhist Art: The Stupa and Ushnishavijaya Cult." Paper delivered at the College Art Association annual conference at San Antonio, Texas, January 26, 1995.

Li Shuhua 1960   Li Shuhua. *Lishi wenwu congkan diyiji* (Collected papers on the history and art of China: First collection). Vol. 3, *Zaozhi de chuanbo ji guzhi de faxian* (The spread of the art of papermaking and the discoveries of old paper). Taipei, 1960. [In Chinese and English.]

Liu Xinru 1995   Liu Xinru. "Silks and Religions in Eurasia c. A.D. 600–1200." *Journal of World History* 6, no. 1 (1995), pp. 25–48.

Liu Yuquan 1982   Liu Yuquan. "Dunhuang Mogao ku, Anxi Yulin ku Xixia dongku fenqi" (On the dating of the Xixia or Mogao, Dunhuang, and Yulin caves, Anxi). In *Dunhuang yanjiu wenji* (Essays in Dunhuang studies), pp. 273–318. Dunhuang Research Institute. Lanzhou, 1982.

Li Yiyou 1979   Li Yiyou. "Tan Yuan Jininglu yizhi chutu de sizhiwu" (On the silk textiles excavated at the Yuan-period Jininglu site). *Wenwu,* no. 8 (1979), pp. 37–39.

London 1935   International Exhibition of Chinese Art. *The Chinese Exhibition: A Commemorative Catalogue of the International Exhibition of Chinese Art.* Exh. cat., Royal Academy of Arts. London, 1935.

London 1982   Asadullah Souren Melikian-Chirvani. *Islamic Metalwork from the Iranian World, 8th–18th Centuries.* Exh. cat., Victoria and Albert Museum. London, 1982.

London, Caves, 1990   Roderick Whitfield and Anne Farrer, eds. *Caves of the Thousand Buddhas: Chinese Art from the Silk Route.* Exh. cat., British Museum. London, 1990.

London, Imperial Gold, 1990   Christian Deydier. *Imperial Gold from Ancient China.* Exh. cat., Oriental Bronzes, Ltd. London, 1990.

Los Angeles 1959   *Woven Treasures of Persian Art: Persian Textiles from the 6th to the 9th Century.* Exh. cat., Los Angeles County Museum of Art, 1959.

Los Angeles 1993   Adam T. Kessler. *Empires beyond the Great Wall: The Heritage of Genghis Khan.* Exh. cat., Los Angeles County Museum of Art, 1993.

Lubo-Lesnitchenko and Sakamoto Kazuko 1987   E. I. Lubo-Lesnitchenko and Sakamoto Kazuko. "Sōryū renjuenmon aya ni tsuite" (Silk bearing the design of two dragons diametrically opposed within the medallions). *Kodai Oriento Hakubutsukan Kiyō/Bulletin of the Ancient Orient Museum* 9 (1987), pp. 93–117. [In Japanese with English summary.]

Lu Jiugao and Han Wei 1985   Lu Jiugao and Han Wei. *Tangdai jinyin qi* (Gold and silver of the Tang dynasty). Beijing, 1985. [In Chinese with English summary.]

Mackerras 1968   Colin Mackerras. *The Uighur Empire (744–840) according to the T'ang Dynastic Histories.* Canberra, 1968.

Mackerras 1994   Colin Mackerras. "The Uighurs." In *The Cambridge History of Early Inner Asia,* ed. Denis Sinor, pp. 317–42. Reprint, Newcastle upon Tyne, 1994.

Mallmann 1955   Marie-Thérèse de Mallmann. "Notes d'iconographie tântrique, II: De Vighnântaka à Mahākāla." *Arts Asiatiques* 2, fasc. 1 (1955), pp. 41–46.

Mallmann 1975   Marie-Thérèse de Mallmann. *Introduction à l'iconographie du tântrisme bouddhique.* Bibliothèque du Centre de recherches sur l'Asie centrale et la haute Asie, 1. Paris, 1975.

Marshak 1971   Boris Il'ich Marshak. *Sogdiiskoe serebro* (Sogdian silver). Kultura narodov Vostoka: Materialy i issledovaniia (Culture of the peoples of the East: Materials and research). Moscow, 1971. [In Russian and English.]

Marshak 1986   Boris Il'ich Marshak. *Silberschatze des Orients, Metallkunst des 3.–13. Jahrhunderts und ihre Kontinuität.* Leipzig, 1986.

Marshak and Raspopova 1990   Boris Il'ich Marshak and V. I. Raspopova. "Wall Paintings from a House with a Granary: Panjikent, 1st Quarter of the Eighth Century A.D." In *Silk Road Art and Archaeology 1,* pp. 124–76. Kamakura, Japan, 1990.

Matsumoto 1984   Matsumoto Kaneo. *Shōsōin gire to Asuka tempyō no senshoku* (Jōdai-Gire: Seventh- and eighth-century textiles in Japan in the Shōsō-in and Hōryū-ji). Kyoto, 1984. [In Japanese and English.]

Miao Liangyun 1988   Miao Liangyun. *Zhongguo lidai sichou wenyang* (China's silk patterns through the ages). Beijing, 1988.

Mikami Tsugio 1969   Mikami Tsugio. *Tōji no Michi* (The ceramics route). Tokyo, 1969.

Milan 1993   Mikhail Piotrovsky. *Lost Empire of the Silk Road: Buddhist Art from Khara Khoto (X–XIIth Century).* Exh. cat., Villa Favorita, Fondazione Thyssen-Bornemisza. Milan, 1993.

Milan 1994   *Tesori del Tibet: Oggetti d'arte dai monasteri di Lhaso.* Exh. cat., Galleria Ottavo Piano. Milan, 1994.

Milhaupt 1992   Terry Milhaupt. "The Chinese Textile and

Costume Collection at The Metropolitan Museum of Art."
Orientations 23, no. 4 (April 1992), pp. 72–78.

Mills 1970   J.V.G. Mills, ed. *Ma Huan: Ying-yai sheng-lan,
The Overall Survey of the Ocean's Shores.* Feng Cheng-chun, trans.
Hakluyt Society, extra ser., 42. Cambridge, 1970.

Mingshi   *Mingshi* (History of the Ming dynasty). Zhonghua
Shuju edition. Beijing, 1974.

Misugi 1981   Misugi Takatoshi. *Sekai no sometsuke* (Blue-and-white
ceramics of the world). Vol. 1, *Gen* (Yuan blue and white). Kyoto, 1981.

MMA *Notable Acquisitions* 1965–1975   Metropolitan Museum
of Art. *Notable Acquisitions, 1965–1975.* New York, 1975.

MMA *Notable Acquisitions* 1981–1982   Metropolitan Museum
of Art. *Notable Acquisitions, 1981–1982: Selected by Philippe de
Montebello, Director.* New York, 1982.

MMA *Notable Acquisitions* 1984–1985   Metropolitan Museum
of Art. *Notable Acquisitions, 1984–1985.* New York, 1985.

MMA *Recent Acquisitions* 1987–1988   Metropolitan Museum of
Art. *Recent Acquisitions: A Selection 1987–1988. MMA Bulletin* 46,
no. 2 (Fall 1988).

MMA *Recent Acquisitions* 1989–1990   Metropolitan Museum
of Art. *Recent Acquisitions: A Selection 1989–1990. MMA Bulletin* 48,
no. 2 (Fall 1990).

MMA *Recent Acquisitions* 1991–1992   Metropolitan Museum
of Art. *Recent Acquisitions: A Selection 1991–1992. MMA Bulletin* 50,
no. 2 (Fall 1992).

MMA *Recent Acquisitions* 1992–1993   Metropolitan Museum
of Art. *Recent Acquisitions: A Selection 1992–1993. MMA Bulletin* 51,
No. 2 (Fall 1993).

MMA *Recent Acquisitions* 1995–1996   Metropolitan Museum
of Art. *Recent Acquisitions: A Selection 1995–1996. MMA Bulletin* 56,
no. 2 (Fall 1996).

Mode 1991–92   Markus Mode. "Sogdian Gods in Exile: Some
Iconographic Evidence from Khotan in Light of Recently Excavated Material from Sogdiana." *Silk Road Art and Archaeology* 2,
pp. 179–214. Kamakura, Japan, 1991–92.

Molinier 1888   Émile Molinier. *Inventaire du trésor du Saint Siège
sous Boniface VIII (Extrait de la bibliothèque de l'École des Chartes,
1882–1888).* Paris, 1888.

Moule and Pelliot 1938   A. C. Moule and Paul Pelliot. *Marco
Polo: The Description of the World.* 2 vols. London, 1938.

Müller-Christensen 1973   Sigrid Müller-Christensen. "Textile
Funde aus dem Grab des Bischofs Hartmann (gest. 1286) im dom
von Augsburg." In *"Suevia Sacra": Frühe Kunst in Schwaben,*
"Textilien" sect. Exh. cat., Augsburger Rathaus. 1973.

Müller-Christensen et al. 1972   Sigrid Müller-Christensen,
H. E. Kubach, and G. Stein. "Die Gräber im Königschor." In *Der
Dom zu Speyer,* ed. Hans Erich Kubach and Walter Haas. Die
Kunstdenkmaler von Rheinland-Pfalz, 5. Munich, 1972.

Müntz and Frothingham 1883   E. Müntz and A. L. Frothingham.
Il tesoro della Basilica di S. Pietro in Vaticano dal XIII al XV secolo.
Rome, 1883.

Murata 1957   Murata Jirō, ed. *Kyoyōkan/Chü–Yung-kuan: The
Buddhist Arch of the Fourteenth Century* A.D. *at the Pass of the Great
Wall Northwest of Peking.* Vol. 2, ed. Murata Jirō and Fujieda Akira.
Kyoto University. Kyoto, 1957. [In Japanese, with plate descrip-
tions and summary in English.]

Mu Shunying 1978   Mu Shunying and the Xinjiang Uyghur
Autonomous Regional Museum (Urumqi). "Tulufan Halahezhuo
gumuqun fajue jianbao" (A brief report on the excavation of the
ancient cemetery at Halahezhuo, Xinjiang). *Wenwu,* no. 6 (1978),
pp. 1–9.

Nara 1982   *Bukkyō kōgei no bi* (Flowers of applied arts). Exh. cat.,
Nara National Museum. 1982. [Checklist in English.]

Narain 1990   A. K. Narain. "Indo-Europeans in Inner Asia." In
The Cambridge History of Early Inner Asia, ed. Denis Sinor,
pp. 151–76. Cambridge, 1990.

al-Narshakhi 1954   Muhammad ibn-Ja'far al-Narshakhi. *The
History of Bukhara.* Trans. Richard N. Frye. Medieval Academy of
America, 61. Cambridge, Mass., 1954.

National Palace Museum 1970   *Tapestry and Embroidery in the
Collection of the National Palace Museum.* Tokyo, 1970. [In
Chinese, Japanese, and English.]

Naymark 1992   Aleksandr Naymark. "Of the Sogdians" (part 4
of "Clothing"). In *Encyclopaedia Iranica,* ed. Ehsan Yar-shater,
vol. 5, pp. 754–57. London, 1992.

Neils 1985   Jennifer Neils. "The Twain Shall Meet." *CMA
Bulletin* 72, no. 6 (October 1985), pp. 326–59.

New York 1931   Alan Priest and Pauline Simmons. *Chinese
Textiles: An Introduction to the Study of Their History, Sources,
Technique, Symbolism, and Use, Occasioned by the Exhibition of
Chinese Court Robes and Accessories.* Exh. cat., The Metropolitan
Museum of Art. New York, 1931.

New York 1971   Jean Mailey. *Chinese Silk Tapestry: K'o-ssu from
Private and Museum Collections.* Exh. cat., China Institute in
America, China House Gallery. New York, 1971.

New York 1978   Prudence Oliver Harper, ed. *The Royal Hunter:
Art of the Sasanian Empire.* Exh. cat., The Metropolitan Museum
of Art. New York, 1978.

New York 1982   *Along the Ancient Silk Routes, Central Asian Art
from the West Berlin State Museums: An Exhibition Lent by the
Museum für Indische Kunst Staatliche Museen Preussischer
Kulturbesitz, Berlin, Federal Republic of Germany.* Exh. cat., The
Metropolitan Museum of Art. New York, 1982.

New York 1991   James C. Y. Watt and Barbara Brennan Ford.
East Asian Lacquer: The Florence and Herbert Irving Collection. Exh.
cat., The Metropolitan Museum of Art. New York, 1991.

New York 1993   *A Decade of Collecting, 1984–1993: Friends of Asian
Art Gifts.* Exh. cat., The Metropolitan Museum of Art. New York, 1993.

Nickel 1991   Helmut Nickel. "The Dragon and the Pearl."
Metropolitan Museum Journal 26 (1991), pp. 139–46.

Nishioka Yasuhiro 1984   Nishioka Yasuhiro. "Nansō Yōshiki no
Chōshitsu: Suiōtei-zu, Sekihekifu-zu bon nado megutte" (Southern
Song–style carved lacquer: A lacquer tray with a scene of the
Zuiweng Pavilion, a lacquer tray with a scene of the Red Cliff,
and others). *Tokyo Kokuritsu Hakubutsukan kiyō,* no. 19 (1984),
pp. 237–60.

Nunome 1992   Nunome Junrō. *Me de miru sen'i no kōkogaku:
Sen'i ibutsu shiryō shūsei* (The archaeology of fiber before your eyes:
A compilation of photographs of fiber artifacts). Kyoto, 1992.

Ogasawara 1989   Sae Ogasawara. "Chinese Fabrics of the Song
and Yuan Dynasties Preserved in Japan." *Orientations* 20, no. 8
(August 1989), pp. 32–44.

Okada Jō 1978   Okada Jō. "Bukkō Kokushi shōrai no chōshitsu"
(Carved lacquer brought by Bukkō Kokushi). In Okada Jō, *Tōyō
shitsugei-shi no kenkyū* (A study of the history of Far Eastern lacquer art), pp. 288–95, xiv (summary in English). Tokyo, 1978. [In
Japanese and English.]

Oriental Lacquer 1977   *Oriental Lacquer Arts: Commemorative
Catalogue of the Special Exhibition.* Exh. cat., Tokyo National
Museum. 1977.

Ou Chaogui 1985   Ou Chaogui. "Daci Fawang Shijiayeshi gesi
xiang" (The *kesi* portrait of Sakya Ye-shes, Great Dharma King of
Compassion). *Xizang yanjiu* (Tibetan studies) 3 (1985), pp. 126–35.

Pal 1975   Pratapaditya Pal. *Bronzes of Kashmir.* Graz, 1975.

Pal 1984   Pratapaditya Pal. *Tibetan Paintings: A Study of Tibetan
Thankas, Eleventh to Nineteenth Centuries.* London, 1984.

Pal 1994   Pratapaditya Pal. "An Early Ming Embroidered Masterpiece." *Christie's Magazine* (May 1994), pp. 62–63.

Pal and Meech-Pekarik 1988   Pratapaditya Pal and Julia Meech-Pekarik. *Buddhist Book Illuminations.* New York and Hunt-Pierpoint, Eng., 1988.

Pan Xingrong 1979   Pan Xingrong. "Yuan Jininglu gucheng chutu de jiaocang sizhiwu ji qita" (Silk cloth and other objects found at the site of the ancient city of Jininglu of the Yuan dynasty). *Wenwu,* no. 8 (1979), pp. 32–35.

Paris 1977   Jean-Paul Roux et al., eds. *Islam dans les collections nationales.* Réunion des Musées nationaux and Musée du Louvre. Paris, 1977.

Paris 1995   *Sèrinde, terre de Bouddha: Dix siècles d'art sur la route de la soie.* Exh. cat., Galeries nationales du Grand Palais. Paris, 1995.

Parker 1985   Elizabeth C. Parker, ed. "Recent Major Acquisitions of Medieval Art by American Museums." *Gesta* 24, no. 2 (1985), pp. 169–74.

Pelliot 1927   Paul Pelliot. "Une Ville musulmane dans la Chine du nord sous les mongols." *Journal asiatique* 211 (1927), pp. 261–79.

Petech 1962   Luciano Petech. "Les Marchands italiens dans l'empire mongol." *Journal asiatique* 250 (1962), pp. 549–74.

Petech 1983   Luciano Petech. "Tibetan Relations with Sung China and the Mongols." In Rossabi, *China,* 1983, pp. 173–203.

Petech 1990   Luciano Petech. *Central Tibet and the Mongols.* Istituto italiano per il medio ed estremo Oriente. Rome, 1990.

Pinks 1968   Elisabeth Pinks. *Die Uighuren von Kan-chou in der frühen Sung-Zeit (960–1028).* Wiesbaden, 1968.

Plum Blossoms 1988   Plum Blossoms, Ltd. *Sō, Gen, Min shokushū meihin ten* (Chinese textile masterpieces: Song, Yuan, and Ming dynasties). Dealer's cat. Hong Kong, 1988. [In English and Japanese.]

Pulleyblank 1952   E. G. Pulleyblank. "A Sogdian Colony in Inner Mongolia." *T'oung Pao* 41, nos. 4–5 (1952), pp. 317–56.

Qidan guo zhi   *Qidan guo zhi* (History of the Qidan [Khitan]). Preface dated 1180 by Ye Longli, but the work probably was completed ca. 1271. *Siku quanshu* edition. Taipei, 1983.

Rashid 1968   Rashid al-Din Tabib. *Histoire des Mongols de la Perse.* Ed. and trans. Étienne Quatremère. Bibliothèque nationale, Collection orientale, 1. Paris, 1836. Amsterdam, 1968.

Ratchnevsky 1991   Paul Ratchnevsky. *Genghis Khan: His Life and Legacy.* Trans. Thomas Nivison Haining. Oxford, 1991.

Rawson 1984   Jessica Rawson. *Chinese Ornament: The Lotus and the Dragon.* London, 1984.

"Recent Acquisitions" 1991   "Recent Acquisitions at The Cleveland Museum of Art, II: Department of Asian Art." *Burlington Magazine* 133, no. 1059 (June 1991), pp. 417–24.

Regestum Clementis 1892   "Inventarium thesauri Ecclesiae Romanae . . . Clementis Papae V, 1311." *Regestum Clementis Papae . . . ex vaticanis archetypis sanctissimi domini nostri Leonis XIII pontificis maximi iussu et munificentia. . . .* Vol. 1, appendices. Rome, 1892.

Rempel 1978   L. I. Rempel. *Iskusstvo Srednego Vostoka* (Art of Central Asia). Moscow, 1978.

Reynolds 1990   Valrae Reynolds. "Myriad Buddhas: A Group of Mysterious Textiles from Tibet." *Orientations* 21, no. 4 (April 1990), pp. 39–50.

Reynolds, "Silk," 1995   Valrae Reynolds. "Silk in Tibet: Luxury Textiles in Secular Life and Sacred Art." *Asian Art: The Second Hali Annual,* ed. Jil Tilden, pp. 86–97. London, 1995.

Reynolds, "Silk Road," 1995   Valrae Reynolds. "The Silk Road: From China to Tibet—and Back." *Orientations* 26, no. 5 (May 1995), pp. 50–57.

Reynolds, " 'Thousand Buddhas,' " 1995   Valrae Reynolds. " 'Thousand Buddhas' Capes and Their Mysterious Role in Sino-Tibetan Trade and Liturgy." In Hong Kong 1995, pp. 32–37.

Rhie et al. 1991   Marilyn Rhie, Robert A. F. Thurman, and John Bigelow. *Wisdom and Compassion: The Sacred Art of Tibet.* New York, 1991.

Riboud 1995   Krishna Riboud. "A Cultural Continuum: A New Group of Liao and Jin Dynasty Silks." *Hali* 17, no. 4 (August–September 1995), pp. 92–105, 119–20.

Riboud and Vial 1970   Krishna Riboud and Gabriel Vial. *Tissus de Touen-Houang conservés au Musée Guimet et à la Bibliothèque nationale.* Mission Paul Pelliot: Documents archéologiques, 13. Paris, 1970.

Richardson 1975   Hugh Richardson. "More of Ancient Tibetan Costumes." *Tibetan Review* (May–June 1975), pp. 15, 24.

Riegl 1992   Alois Riegl. *Problems of Style: Foundations for a History of Ornament.* Princeton, 1992.

Roes 1936–37   Anna Roes. "Tierwirbel." *IPEK: Jahrbuch für prähistorische und ethnographische Kunst,* pp. 85–105. Leipzig, 1936–37.

Rossabi 1970   Morris Rossabi. "Ming China's Relations with Hami and Central Asia, 1404–1513: A Reexamination of Traditional Chinese Foreign Policy." Ph.D. diss., Columbia University. New York, 1970.

Rossabi 1976   Morris Rossabi. "Two Ming Envoys to Inner Asia." *T'oung Pao* 62, no. 3 (1976), pp. 1–34.

Rossabi, China, 1983   Morris Rossabi, ed. *China among Equals: The Middle Kingdom and Its Neighbors, 10th–14th Centuries.* Berkeley, 1983.

Rossabi, "Translation," 1983   Morris Rossabi. "A Translation of Ch'en Ch'eng's Hsi-yu fan-kuo chih." *Ming Studies* 17 (Fall 1983), pp. 49–59.

Rossabi 1988   Morris Rossabi. *Khubilai Khan: His Life and Times.* Berkeley, 1988.

Rowland 1956   Benjamin Rowland, Jr. "The Vine-scroll in Gandhara." *Artibus Asiae* 19 (1956), pp. 353–61.

Royal Ontario Museum 1972   The Royal Ontario Museum. *Chinese Art in the Royal Ontario Museum.* Toronto, 1972.

Sanchao beimeng huibian   Xu Mengxin (1126–1207). *Sanchao beimeng huibian* (Compilation of documents on the treaties with the North during three reigns). Shanghai Guji Chubanshe edition. Shanghai, 1987.

San Francisco 1995   Patricia Berger and Terese Tse Bartholomew, eds. *Mongolia: The Legacy of Chinggis Khan.* Exh. cat., Asian Art Museum of San Francisco. 1995.

Santoro 1994   Arcangela Santoro. "La Seta e le sue testimonianze in Asia Centrale." In *La Seta e le sua vita,* ed. Maria Teresa Lucidi, pp. 43–48. Rome, 1994.

Schafer 1963   Edward Schafer. *The Golden Peaches of Samarkand.* Berkeley, 1963.

Schurmann 1956   Herbert Franz Schurmann. *Economic Structure of the Yuan Dynasty.* Cambridge, 1956.

Serjeant 1972   R. B. Serjeant. *Islamic Textiles: Material for a History up to the Mongol Conquest.* Beirut, 1972.

Sha Biti 1973   Sha Biti. "Cong kaogu fajue ziliao kan Xinjiang gudai de mianhua zhongzhi he fangzhi" (Cotton planting and weaving in ancient Xinjiang in the light of archaeological data). *Wenwu,* no. 10 (1973), pp. 48–51.

Shaffer 1989   Daniel Shaffer. "Marketplace: On the Crest of a Wave." *Hali,* no. 43 (February 1989), pp. 85–108.

Shepherd 1974   Dorothy G. Shepherd. "Medieval Persian Silks in Fact and Fancy: A Refutation of the Riggisberg Report." *Bulletin du CIETA,* nos. 39–40 (1974), pp. 1–239.

Shepherd 1981   Dorothy G. Shepherd. "Zandanījī Revisited." In *Documenta Textilia: Festschrift für Sigrid Müller-Christensen,* ed. Mechthild Flury-Lemberg and Karen Stolleis, pp. 105–22. Munich, 1981.

Shepherd and Henning 1959   Dorothy G. Shepherd and W. B. Henning. "Zandanījī Identified?" In *Aus der islamischen Kunst: Festschrift für Ernst Kühnel zum 75. Geburtstag,* ed. Richard Ettinghausen, pp. 15–40. Berlin, 1959.

Shiba 1970   Yoshinobu Shiba. *Commerce and Society in Sung China.* Trans. Mark Elvin. Center for Chinese Studies, University of Michigan. Ann Arbor, 1970.

Shiba 1983   Yoshinobu Shiba. "Sung Foreign Trade: Its Scope and Organization." In *China among Equals,* ed. Morris Rossabi, pp. 89–115. Berkeley, 1983.

Shi Jinbo et al. 1988   Shi Jinbo et al. *Xi Xia wenwu* (Cultural artifacts of Xi Xia). Beijing, 1988. [In Chinese with English summary.]

Shisan jing zhushu   *Shisan jing zhushu* (Commentaries on the thirteen classics). Zhonghua Shuju edition. Beijing, 1980. Reprint, 1987.

"Short Introduction" 1972   "Wuchan jieji Wenhua Dageming qijian chutu wenwu zhanlan jianjie" (Short introduction to the exhibition of the cultural relics excavated during the proletariat's Cultural Revolution). *Wenwu,* no. 1 (1972), pp. 70–92.

Simcox 1989   Jacqueline Simcox. "Early Chinese Textiles: Silks from the Middle Kingdom." *Hali* 11, no. 1 (February 1989), pp. 16–42.

Simcox, "Tracing the Dragon," 1994   Jacqueline Simcox. "Tracing the Dragon: The Stylistic Development of Designs in Early Chinese Textiles." *Carpet and Textile Art: The First Hali Annual,* ed. Alan Marcuson, pp. 34–47. London, 1994.

Simmons 1948   Pauline Simmons. *Chinese Patterned Silks.* New York, 1948.

Simmons 1950   Pauline Simmons. "Crosscurrents in Chinese Silk History." *MMA Bulletin,* n.s., 9 (November 1950), pp. 87–96.

Sirén 1956   Oswald Sirén. *Chinese Painting: Leading Masters and Principles.* 7 vols. New York, 1956.

Smirnov 1909   Iakov I. Smirnov. *Vostochnoe serebro: Atlas drevnei serebrianoi i zolotoi posudy vostochnago proiskhozhdeniia, naidennoi preimushchestvenno v predielakh Rossiiskoi imperii.* Saint Petersburg, 1909.

Smith 1983   Paul Smith. "Taxing Heaven's Storehouse: The Szechwan Tea Monopoly and the Tsinghai Horse Trade, 1074–1224." Ph.D. diss., University of Pennsylvania, 1983.

Smithsonian 1984   The Smithsonian Institution, National Museum of Design, Cooper-Hewitt Museum. *Stitch Guide: A Study of the Stitches on the Embroidered Samplers in the Collection of the Cooper-Hewitt Museum.* New York, 1984.

Snellgrove and Richardson 1968   David Snellgrove and Hugh Richardson. *A Cultural History of Tibet.* Boston and London, 1968.

Sonday and Maitland 1989   Milton Sonday and Lucy Maitland. "Technique, Detached Looping." *Orientations* 20, no. 8 (August 1989), pp. 54–61.

Songren Huace **1957**   Zheng Zhenduo et al. *Songren Huace* (Song painting albums). 2 vols. Beijing, 1957. Reprint, 1985.

Songshi   *Songshi* (History of the Song dynasty). Compiled by Tuotuo et al. in 1345. Zhonghua Shuju edition. Beijing, 1977.

Soustiel 1985   Jean Soustiel. *La Céramique islamique.* Paris, 1985.

Sperling 1987   Elliot Sperling. "Lama to the King of Hsia." *Journal of the Tibet Society* 7 (1987), pp. 31–50.

Spink & Son 1989   Spink & Son, Ltd. *The Art of Textiles.* Ed. Francesca Galloway and Jacqueline Simcox. Dealer's cat. London, 1989.

Spink & Son 1994   Spink & Son, Ltd. *Chinese Textiles.* Ed. Jacqueline Simcox. Dealer's cat. London, 1994.

Stein 1907   Sir Aurel Stein. *Ancient Khotan: Detailed Report of Archaeological Explorations in Chinese Turkestan, Carried out and Described under the Orders of H. M. Indian Government.* 2 vols. Oxford, 1907.

Stein 1921   Sir Aurel Stein. *Serindia: Detailed Report of Explorations in Central Asia and Westernmost China, Carried out and Described under the Orders of H. M. Indian Government.* 5 vols. Oxford, 1921.

Stein 1928   Sir Aurel Stein. *Innermost Asia: Detailed Report of Explorations in Central Asia, Kan-su and Eastern Iran, Carried out and Described under the Orders of H. M. Indian Government.* 4 vols. Oxford, 1928.

Stockholm 1986   Margareta Nockert and Eva Lundvall. *Ärkebiskoparna från Bremen.* Exh. cat., Statens historiska Museet. Stockholm, 1986.

Stoddard 1995   Heather Stoddard. "The Tibetan Pantheon: Its Mongolian Form." In San Francisco 1995, pp. 206–13.

Su Bai 1989   Su Bai, ed. *Zhongguo meishu quanji: Huihua bian* (The great treasury of Chinese fine arts: Paintings). Vol. 12, *Mushi bihua* (Wall paintings in tombs). Vol. 16, *Xinjiang shiku bihua* (Wall paintings of the caves in Xinjiang). Beijing, 1989.

Su Bai 1990   Su Bai. "Yuandai Hangzhou de Zangchuan mijiao ji qi youguan yiji" (The Yuan dynasty Tibeto-esoteric religion and related sites in Hangzhou). *Wenwu,* no. 10 (1990), pp. 55–71.

Suishu   *Suishu* (History of the Sui dynasty). Zhonghua Shuju edition. Beijing, 1973. Reprint, 1982.

Tamura and Kobayashi 1953   Jitsuzō Tamura and Yukio Kobayashi. *Keiryō/Tombs and Mural Paintings of Ch'ing-ling Liao Imperial Mausoleums of Eleventh Century* A.D. *in Eastern Mongolia: Detailed Report of Archaeological Survey Carried out in 1935 and 1939.* 2 vols. Kyoto, 1953. [In Japanese with English summary by Shinobu Iwamura and Wilma Fairbank.]

Tang huiyao   *Tang huiyao* (Records of Tang institutions). Taiwan Commerical Press, after the Wuying Dian edition. Taipei, 1968.

Tao Jing-shen 1976   Tao Jing-shen. *The Jurchen in Twelfth-Century China.* Seattle, 1976.

Ta'rikh nama-i-Harat **1944**   Sayf ibn Muhammad ibn Ya'qub al'Harawi. *The Ta'rikh nama-i-Harat* (The history of Harat). Ed. Muhammad Zubayr as-Siddiqi. Calcutta, 1944.

Tatsumura 1963   Ken Tatsumura. "Ancient Brocade Brought Back by Ōtani Mission." In *Monographs on Ancient Brocades, Pictures, Buddhist Texts and Chinese and Uigur Documents from Turfan, Tun-huang, and Tibet,* pp. 1–4. Kyoto, 1963.

Taylor 1991   George Taylor. "Official Colours, Dyes on Chinese Textiles of the Northern Song Dynasty." *Hali,* no. 58 (October 1991), pp. 81–83.

Textiles **1995–96**   *Textiles in The Metropolitan Museum of Art.* Published as *MMA Bulletin,* n.s, 53, no. 3 (Winter 1995–96).

Thomas 1935   Mary Thomas. *Mary Thomas's Dictionary of Embroidery Stitches.* New York, 1935.

Tikhonov 1966   D. I. Tikhonov. *Khoziaistvo i obshchestvennyi stroi uigurskogo gosudarstva* (Economy and social system of the Uyghur state). Moscow, 1966.

Torii 1936   Ryūzō Torii. *Culture of the Liao Dynasty from the Viewpoint of Archaeology.* 2 vols. Tokyo, 1936. [In English and Japanese.]

Toronto 1983   John Vollmer, ed. *Silk Roads, China Ships.* Exh. cat., Royal Ontario Museum. Toronto, 1983.

TSA Newsletter **1995**   "Recent Acquisitions at Cleveland and Indianapolis." *Textile Society of America Newsletter* 7, no. 180 (Winter 1995), p. 4.

Tserangja 1995   Tserangja, ed. *Sera Thekchen Ling* (Sera Thekchen Ling monastery). Beijing, 1995. [In Tibetan, Chinese, and English.]

Tsien Tsuen-hsuin 1985   Tsien Tsuen-hsuin. "Paper and Printing." In *Chemical and Chemistry Technology,* part 1. Vol. 5 of *Science and Civilisation in China,* ed. Joseph Needham. Cambridge, 1954–.

Tsui Museum 1993 The Tsui Museum of Art/ *Xushi yishu guan.* Vol. 1, *Neolithic to Liao* [Chinese ceramics]. Hong Kong, 1993. [In English and Chinese.]

Tu Ji Tu Ji. *Mengwuer shiji* (Historical record of the Mongols). Shijie Shuju edition. Reprint, Taipei, 1962.

Twitchett 1979 Denis Twitchett and John K. Fairbank, eds. *The Cambridge History of China.* Vol. 3, part 1, *Sui and Tang China, 589–906.* Cambridge, 1979.

Uldry et al. 1994 Pierre Uldry et al. *Chinesisches Gold und Silber: Die Sammlung Pierre Uldry.* Zurich, 1994.

Vainker 1996 Shelagh Vainker. "Silk of the Northern Song: Reconstructing the Evidence." In *Silk and Stone: The Third Hali Annual,* ed. Jill Tilden, pp. 160–75, 196–97. London, 1996.

Waley 1931 Arthur Waley, trans. *Travels of an Alchemist: The Journey of the Taoist Ch'ang-Ch'un, from China to the Hindukush at the Summons of Chingiz Khan, Recorded by his Disciple, Li Chih-chang.* The Broadway Travellers. London, 1931.

Wang Binghua 1973 Wang Binghua. "Yanhu gumu" (Excavation of the ancient tombs at Salt Lake, Xinjiang). *Wenwu,* no. 10 (1973), pp. 28–36.

Wang Furen 1982 Wang Furen. *Xizang fojiao shilue* (A short history of Tibetan Buddhism). Xining, 1982.

Wang Jianqun and Chen Xiangwei 1989 Wang Jianqun and Chen Xiangwei. *Kulun Liaodai bihua mu* (The tomb at Kulun with wall paintings from the Liao period). Beijing, 1989.

Wang Xuan 1978 Wang Xuan. "Tan Li Yu'an mu zhong de jijian cixiu yiwu" (On several embroidered dresses in the tomb of Li Yu'an). *Wenwu,* no. 4 (1978), pp. 21, 22, 89.

Wang Yi 1960 Wang Yi. "Xizang wenwu jianwen ji" (Notes on Tibetan cultural relics). *Wenwu,* no. 6 (1960), pp. 41, 42, 43–48, 51.

Wang Yong Wang Yong. *Yanyi yimou lu* (Secret writings on the politics of monarchs). Zhonghua Shuju, 1981.

Wardwell 1976–77 Anne E. Wardwell. "The Stylistic Development of 14th- and 15th-Century Italian Silk Design." *Aachener Kunstblätter* 47 (1976–77), pp. 177–226.

Wardwell 1984 Anne E. Wardwell. *Material Matters: Fifty Years of Gifts from The Textile Arts Club, 1934–1984.* Cleveland, 1984.

Wardwell 1987 Anne E. Wardwell. "Flight of the Phoenix: Crosscurrents in Late Thirteenth- to Fourteenth-Century Silk Patterns and Motifs." *CMA Bulletin* 74, no. 1 (January 1987), pp. 2–35.

Wardwell 1988–89 Anne E. Wardwell. "*Panni Tartarici:* Eastern Islamic Silks Woven with Gold and Silver (13th and 14th Centuries)." *Islamic Art* 3 (1988–89), pp. 95–173.

Wardwell 1989 Anne E. Wardwell. "Recently Discovered Textiles Woven in the Western Part of Central Asia before A.D. 1220." In *Ancient and Medieval Textiles: Studies in Honour of Donald King,* ed. Lisa Monnas and Hero Granger-Taylor, pp. 175–84. Published as special issue of *Textile History* 20, no. 2 (1989).

Wardwell 1992 Anne E. Wardwell. "Two Silk and Gold Textiles of the Early Mongol Period." *CMA Bulletin* 79, no. 10 (December 1992), pp. 354–78.

Wardwell 1992–93 Anne E. Wardwell. "Important Asian Textiles Recently Acquired by The Cleveland Museum of Art." *Oriental Art* 38, no. 4 (Winter 1992–93), pp. 244–51.

Wardwell 1993 Anne E. Wardwell. "The *Kesi* Thangka of Vighnāntaka." *CMA Bulletin* 80, no. 4 (April 1993), pp. 136–39.

Wardwell 1994 Anne E. Wardwell. "Gilded *Kesi* Boots of the Liao Dynasty (A.D. 907–1125)." *Bulletin du CIETA* 2 (1994), pp. 6–12.

Wardwell 1995 Anne E. Wardwell. "Royal Regalia." *CMA Members Magazine* 35, no. 8 (October 1995), p. 7.

Wardwell, "Clothes," 1996 Anne E. Wardwell. "Clothes for a Prince." *CMA Members Magazine* 36, no. 8 (October 1996), pp. 4–5.

Wardwell, "For Lust of Knowing," 1996 Anne E. Wardwell. "For Lust of Knowing What Should Not be Known." *Hali,* no. 89 (November 1996), p. 73.

Washington, D.C. 1985 Esin Atil, W. T. Chase, and Paul Jett. *Islamic Metalwork in the Freer Gallery of Art.* Exh. cat., Freer Gallery of Art. Washington, D.C., 1985.

B. Watson 1961 Burton Watson, trans. *Records of the Grand Historian of China.* 2 vols. New York, 1961.

O. Watson 1985 Oliver Watson. *Persian Lustre Ware.* London, 1985.

Wentworth 1987 Judy Wentworth. "From East and West." *Hali* 9, no. 34 (April–June 1987), p. 96.

Whitfield 1982–83 Roderick Whitfield and Bin Takahashi. *The Art of Central Asia: The Stein Collection in the British Museum.* Vol. 2, *Paintings from Dunhuang.* Tokyo, 1982–85.

Whitfield 1985 Roderick Whitfield and Bin Takahashi. *The Art of Central Asia: The Stein Collection in the British Museum.* Vol. 3, *Textiles, Sculpture and Other Arts.* Tokyo, 1985.

Wilckens 1987 Leonie von Wilckens. "Zur kunstgeschichtlichen Einordnung der Bamberger Textilfund." *Textile Grabfunde aus der Sepultur des Bamberger Domkapitels: Internationales Kolloquium, Schloss Seehof, 22.–23. April, 1985.* Bayerisches Landesamt für Denkmalpflege, 33. Munich, 1987.

Wilkinson 1973 Charles K. Wilkinson. *Nishapur: Pottery of the Early Islamic Period.* New York and Greenwich, Conn., 1973.

Willetts 1965 William Willetts. *Foundations of Chinese Art from Neolithic Pottery to Modern Architecture.* London, 1965.

J. Wilson 1990 J. Keith Wilson. "Powerful Form and Potent Symbol: The Dragon in Asia." *CMA Bulletin* 77, no. 8 (October 1990), pp. 286–323.

V. Wilson 1986 Verity Wilson and Ian Thomas. *Chinese Dress.* London, 1986.

Wirgin 1960 Jan Wirgin. "Some Notes on Liao Ceramics." *The Museum of Far Eastern Antiquities Bulletin* (Stockholm), no. 32 (1960), p. 32.

Wirgin 1979 Jan Wirgin. *Sung Ceramic Designs.* London, 1979.

Wittfogel and Feng Chia-sheng 1949 Karl A. Wittfogel and Feng Chia-sheng. *History of Chinese Society: Liao (907–1125).* Transactions of the American Philosophical Society, n.s., 36 (1949). Philadelphia and New York, 1949.

Wu Chengluo 1984 Wu Chengluo. *Zhongguo duliangheng shi* (A history of weights and measures in China). Reprint, Shanghai, 1984.

Wu Zhefu and Chen Xiasheng 1986 Wu Zhefu and Chen Xiasheng, eds. *Zhonghua wuqian nian wenwu jikan* (Five thousand years of Chinese art). Vol. 1, *Fushi pian (shang)* (Chinese costumes). Taipei, 1986.

Xiang Da 1933 and 1957 Xiang Da. *Tangdai Chang'an yu xiyu wenming* (Central Asian civilizations and Chang'an in Tang times). In *Yanjing xuebao,* special no. 2 (1933); reprinted in *Yanjing xuebao,* pp. 1–116. Beijing, 1957.

Xiao Xun Xiao Xun. *Yuan gugong yilu* (Surviving notes on the former palace of the Yuan). A readily available edition is published by Shijie Shuju, Taipei, 1979.

***Xijin zhi jiyi* 1983** The *Xijin zhi,* a gazetteer of Xijin (early name for Beijing), was compiled by Xiong Mengxiang toward the end of the Yuan period (1279–1368). The original is lost. A reconstituted edition, culled from various sources quoting the *Xijin zhi,* has been issued by the Rare Book Section of the Beijing Library under the title *Xijin zhi jiyi* (Collection of lost passages from the *Xijin zhi*), Beijing, 1983. Page references in this catalogue refer to this edition.

Xinjiang Museum 1975   Xinjiang Weiwuer Zizhiqu Bowuguan, Xibei Daxue Lishixi Kaogu Zhuanye (Xinjiang Uyghur Autonomous Regional Museum and the Program of Archaeology, Department of History, Northwest University). "1973-nian Tulufan Asitana gumuqun fajue jianbao" (A brief report on the 1973 excavation of the cluster of ancient graves at Astana, Turfan). *Wenwu*, no. 7 (1975), pp. 8–18.

Xinjiang Museum 1987   *Shinkyō Uyghur Jichiku Hakubutsukan* (Museum of the Xinjiang Uyghur Autonomous Region). Tokyo, 1987.

Xinjiang Museum, *Sichou*, 1973   Xinjiang Weiwuer Zizhiqu Bowuguan, Chutu Wenwu Zhanlan Gongzuo Zu (Xinjiang Uyghur Autonomous Regional Museum and the Department of Exhibition of Excavated Relics). *Sichou zhi lu: Han Tang zhiwu* (The Silk Roads: Textiles of the Han and Tang dynasties). Beijing, 1973.

Xinjiang Museum, "Tulufan," 1973   Xinjiang Weiwuer Zizhiqu Bowuguan (Xinjiang Uyghur Autonomous Regional Museum). "Tulufan xian Asitana–Halahezhuo gumuqun fajue jianbao (1963–1965)" (Excavation of ancient tombs at Astana and Khara Khojo in Turfan, Xinjiang, 1963–1965). *Wenwu*, no. 10 (1973), pp. 7–27.

Xin Tangshu   *Xin Tangshu* (New history of the Tang dynasty). Zhonghua Shuju edition. Beijing, 1975. Reprint, 1986.

Xuanhua Liao bihua mu **1975**   CPAM, Hebei Province, and the Hebei Provincial Museum. "Hebei Xuanhua Liao bihua mu fajue jianbao" (Excavation of the wall-painting tomb of the Liao dynasty in Xuanhua, Hebei Province). *Wenwu*, no. 8 (1975), pp. 31–39.

Xu Xinguo and Zhao Feng 1991   Xu Xinguo and Zhao Feng. "Dulan chutu sizhipin chutan" (Preliminary investigations on the silks excavated at Dulan). *Zhongguo lishi bowuguan guankan* (Bulletin of the National Museum of Chinese History) 15–16 (1991), pp. 63–81.

Xu Zizhi tongjian changbian   Li Tao. *Xu Zizhi tongjian changbian* (Collected data for a continuation of the *Comprehensive Mirror for Aid in Government*). National Public Library facsimile of Song edition. Beijing, 1995.

Yang Boda 1983   Yang Boda. "Nüzhen zu *chunshui qiushan* yu kao" (A study of two kinds of jades carved with different designs of the Nuzhen nationality). *Gugong bowuyuan yuankan* (Palace Museum journal), no. 2 (1983), pp. 9–16.

Yang Boda 1988   Yang Boda, ed. *Zhongguo meishu quanji: Diaosu bian* (The great treasury of Chinese fine arts: Sculpture). Vol. 6, *Yuan Ming Qing diaosu* (Sculpture of the Yuan, Ming, and Qing dynasties). Beijing, 1988.

Yang Kuan 1957   Yang Kuan. *Zhongguo lidai chidu kao* (Research on the Chinese measuring system through the dynasties). Rev. ed. Shanghai, 1957.

Yang Lien-sheng 1952   Yang Lien-sheng [Yang Liansheng]. *Money and Credit in China: A Short History.* Cambridge, Mass., 1952.

Yang Renkai et al. 1983   Yang Renkai et al. *Ryōneishō hakubutsukan zō kakushi shishū/Tapestry and Embroidery in the Collection of the Museum of Liaoning Province.* Ser. 1, vol. 3. Tokyo, 1983. [In Chinese, Japanese, and English.]

Yangyuan xian zhi   *Yangyuan xian zhi* (Gazetteer of Yangyuan xian). Reprint, 1935.

Yingzao fashi   Li Jie. *Yingzao fashi* (Manual on architecture). Zhongguo Shudian reprint of 1145 edition, Beijing, 1989.

Yishu congbian **1962**   *Yishu congbian* (Collection of reprinted texts on art). Shijie Shuju edition. Taipei, 1962.

Yongle dadian   *Yongle dadian* (The grand compilation of Yongle). Shijie Shuju edition. Taipei, 1962.

Yuanshi   *Yuanshi* (History of the Yuan dynasty). Zhonghua Shuju edition. Beijing, 1976.

Yuan wenlei   *Yuan wenlei* (Collection of Yuan writings). Compiled by Su Tianjue (late Yuan period). *Guoxue jiben congshu* edition. Taipei, 1968.

Yu Ji   Yu Ji. "Caonan wang xunde bei" (Commemorative stele for Prince Caonan). In *Daoyuan xuegu lu* (Following the ancient in the garden of Dao), chap. 24. Zhonghua Shuju (after *Sibu beiyao* edition). Shanghai, n.d.[1936].

Yuwen Mouzhao   *See Da Jin guo zhi jiaozheng*

Zangmo 1975   Dejin Zangmo. "Tibetan Royal Dun-huang Wall-Paintings." *Tibetan Review* (February–March 1975), pp. 18–19.

Zhang Yanyuan   Zhang Yanyuan. *Lidai minghua ji* (Records of famous paintings throughout the ages). In *Huashi congshu*, vol. 1. Taipei, 1974.

Zhao Feng, *Sichou*, 1992   Zhao Feng. *Sichou yishu shi* (A history of silk art). Hangzhou, 1992.

Zhao Feng, *Tangdai*, 1992   Zhao Feng. *Tangdai sichou yu sichou zhi lu* (The silks of the Tang period and the silk routes). Sui Tang lishi wenhua congshu (Series: On the history and culture of the Sui and Tang dynasties). Xian, 1992.

Zhongguo taoci shi **1982**   *Zhongguo taoci shi* (History of Chinese ceramics). Ed. Feng Xianming et al. Beijing, 1982.

Zhou Xibao 1984   Zhou Xibao. *Zhongguo gudai fushi shi* (History of ancient Chinese costumes and accessories). Beijing, 1984.

Zhuang Chuo   Zhuang Chuo. *Jile bian* ("Chicken ribs"). In *Congshu jicheng jianbian* (A selected compendium of collections of writing), vol. 727. Taipei, 1965–66.

Zhu Qiqian 1962   Zhu Qiqian. *Sixiu biji* (Notes on silks and embroidery), in *Xiupu* (Manuals of embroideries). In *Yishu congbian* 1962, vol. 1, no. 32.

Zhu Qixin 1990   Zhu Qixin. "Royal Costumes of the Jin Dynasty." *Orientations* 21, no. 12 (December 1990), pp. 59–64.

Index

BY ROBERT J. PALMER

Photograph Credits

Abegg-Stiftung, Riggisberg (Chr. von Viràg): Fig. 78. Christman, Bruce, The Cleveland Museum of Art: Figs. 1, 2, 7, 52, 60. Dayton 1990, p. 346: Fig. 90. Flemming 1927, pl. 59: Fig. 68. Huang Nengfu, Arts and Crafts, 1987, pp. 2, 88: Figs. 57, 87. Huang Ti 1985, pl. 102: Fig. 33. Lessing 1918, vol. VI, pl. 173: Fig. 59. Marshak 1986, fig. 40: Fig. 47. Miao Liangyun 1988, pl. 152: Fig. 58. Milan 1994, p. 135: Fig. 35. Müller-Christensen 1973, p. 209: Fig. 65. Murata and Fujieda 1955, pl. 3: Fig. 89. Shi Jinbo et al. 1988, pl. 60: Fig. 48. Jacqueline Simcox, Ltd.: Fig. 22. Su Bai 1989, vol. 12, nos. 143, 144: Figs. 24, 25.

Sara Tremayne, Ltd.: Fig. 27. Department of Textile Conservation, The Metropolitan Museum of Art: Figs. 49, 84. Tserangja 1995, p. 1: Fig. 88. Wang Binghua 1973, pp. 29, 35: Fig. 66. *Wenwu* 1972, no. 1, back cover: Fig. 82. Ole Woldbye, Copenhagen: Fig. 63. Wu Zhefu and Chen Xiasheng 1986, p. 107: Fig. 8. Xinjiang Museum 1973, pl. 1, fig. 18: Figs. 4, 5. Xinjiang Museum 1987, pl. 127: Fig. 75. Xuanhua Liao bihuya mu 1975, 1975.8, p. 38, fig. 18: Fig. 77. Yang Renkai et al. 1983, pl. 2: Fig. 13. *Yingzau fashi*, chap. 33, leaf 10: Fig. 83.